Kamisama Kiss

VOLMEOW 8!

THIS IS VOLMEOW 8!

Story & Art by
Julietta Suzuki

CHARACTERS

Mamoru

Nanami's shikigami.

Nanami Momozono

A high school student who was turned into a kamisama by the tochigami Mikage.

Tomoe

The shinshi who serves Nanami now that she's the new tochigami. Originally a wild fox ayakashi.

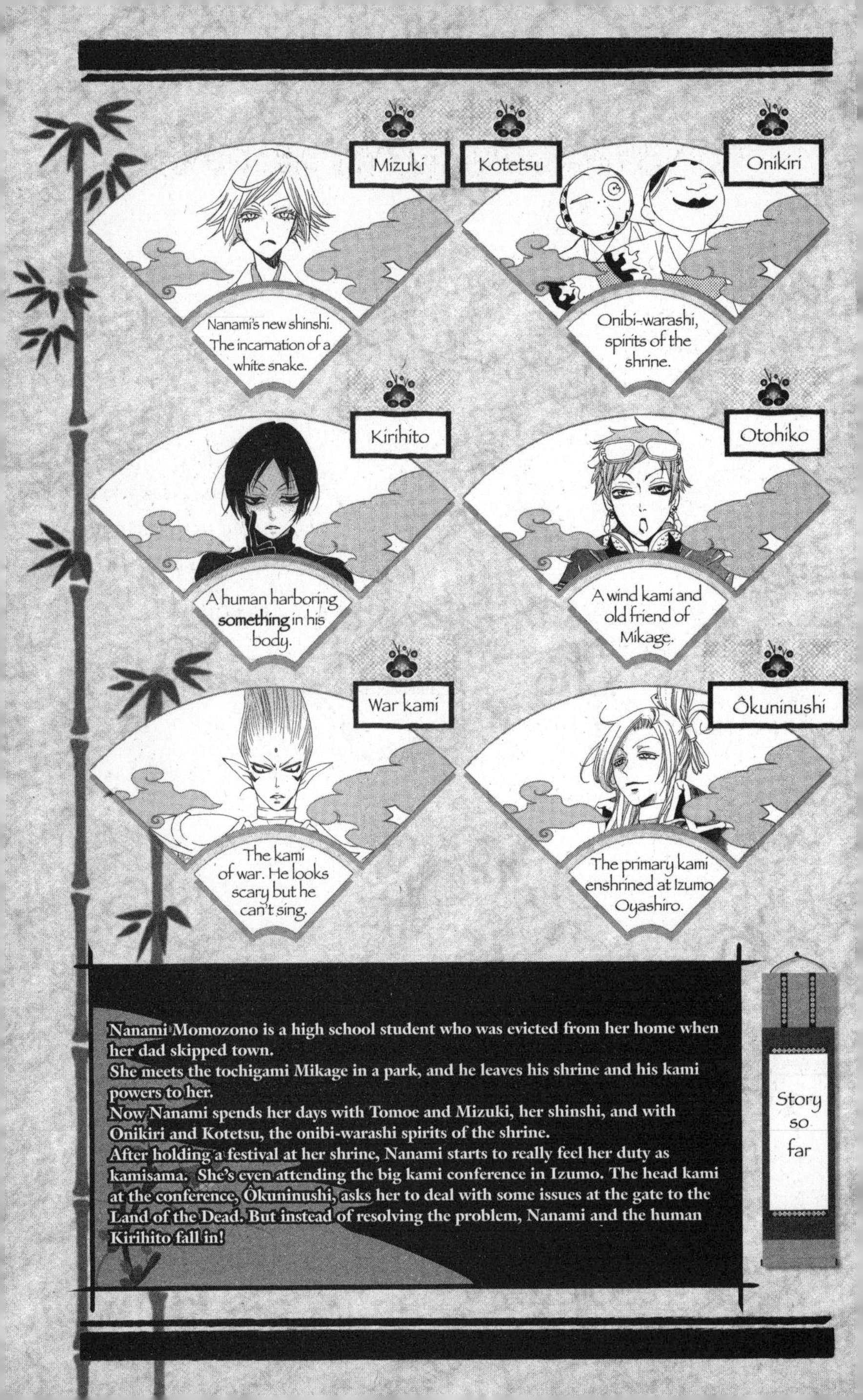
Mizuki
Nanami's new shinshi. The incarnation of a white snake.
Kotetsu
Onikiri
Onibi-warashi, spirits of the shrine.
Kirihito
A human harboring **something** in his body.
Otohiko
A wind kami and old friend of Mikage.
War kami
The kami of war. He looks scary but he can't sing.
Ôkuninushi
The primary kami enshrined at Izumo Oyashiro.

Story so far

Nanami Momozono is a high school student who was evicted from her home when her dad skipped town.
She meets the tochigami Mikage in a park, and he leaves his shrine and his kami powers to her.
Now Nanami spends her days with Tomoe and Mizuki, her shinshi, and with Onikiri and Kotetsu, the onibi-warashi spirits of the shrine.
After holding a festival at her shrine, Nanami starts to really feel her duty as kamisama. She's even attending the big kami conference in Izumo. The head kami at the conference, Ôkuninushi, asks her to deal with some issues at the gate to the Land of the Dead. But instead of resolving the problem, Nanami and the human Kirihito fall in!

Kamisama Kiss

Volume 8
CONTENTS

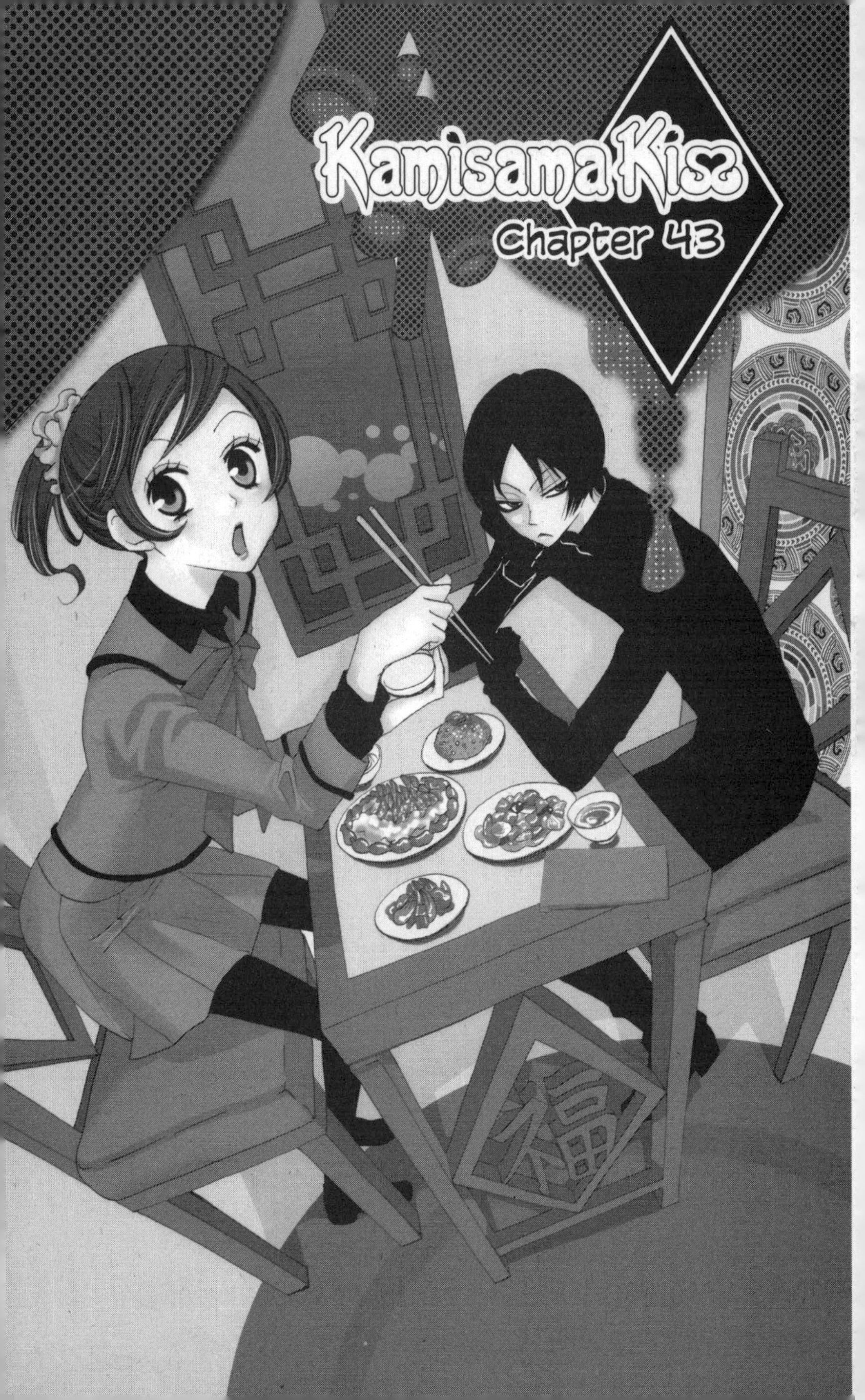
Kamisama Kiss
Chapter 43

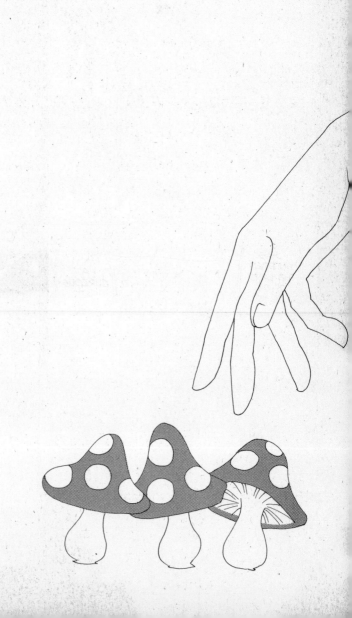

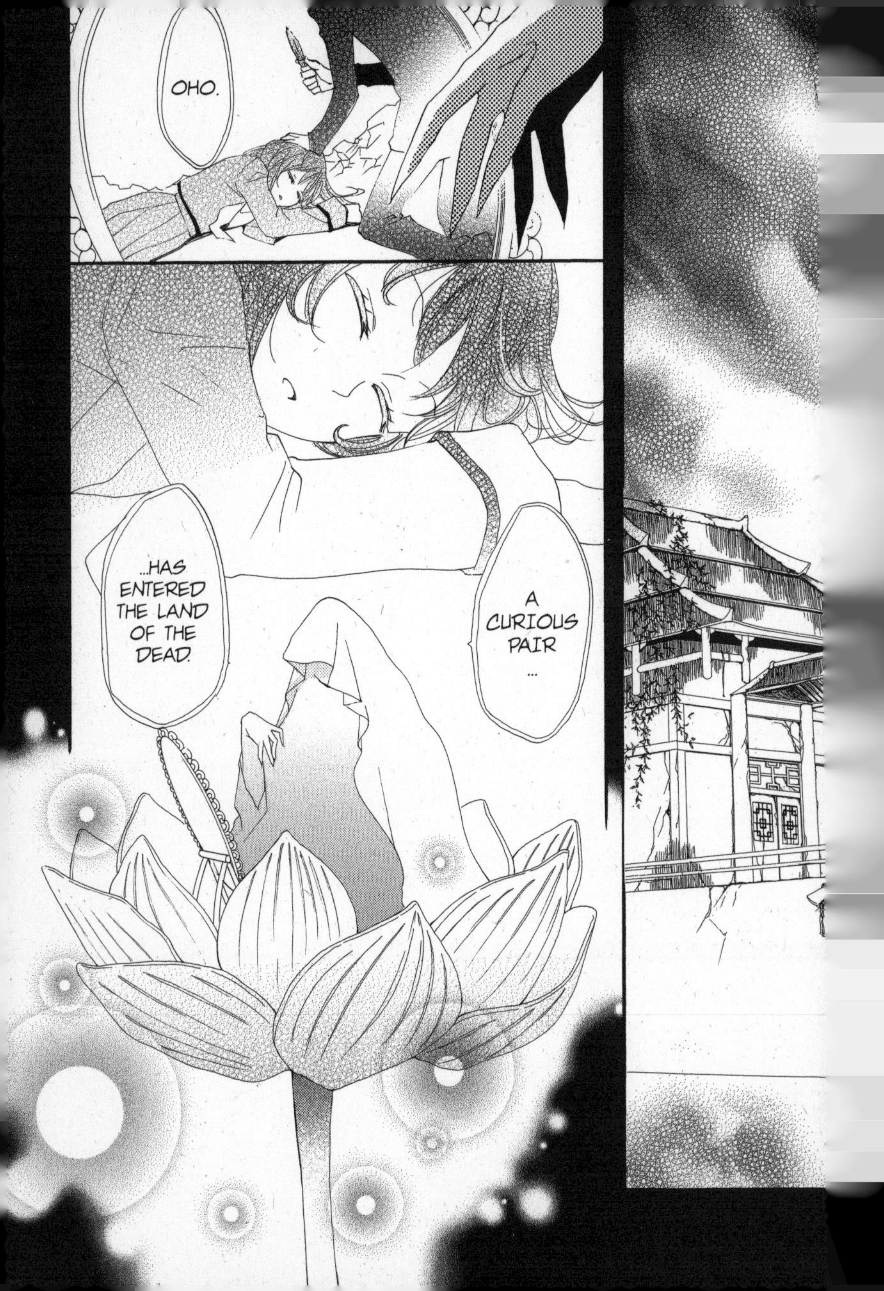
OHO.
A CURIOUS PAIR ...
...HAS ENTERED THE LAND OF THE DEAD.

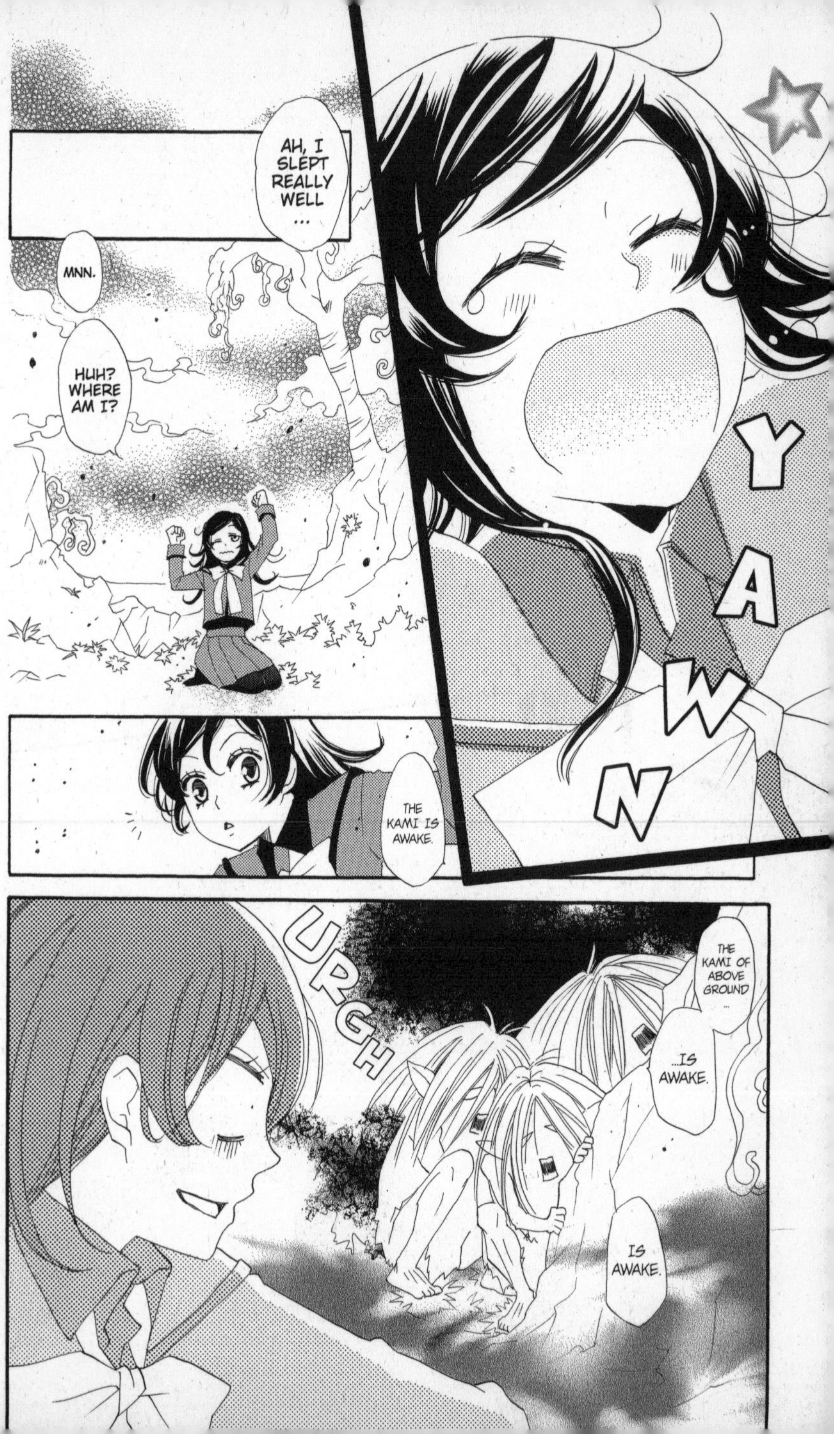
YAWN
AH, I SLEPT REALLY WELL ...
MNN.
HUH? WHERE AM I?
THE KAMI IS AWAKE.
THE KAMI OF ABOVE GROUND ...
...IS AWAKE.
URGH
IS AWAKE.

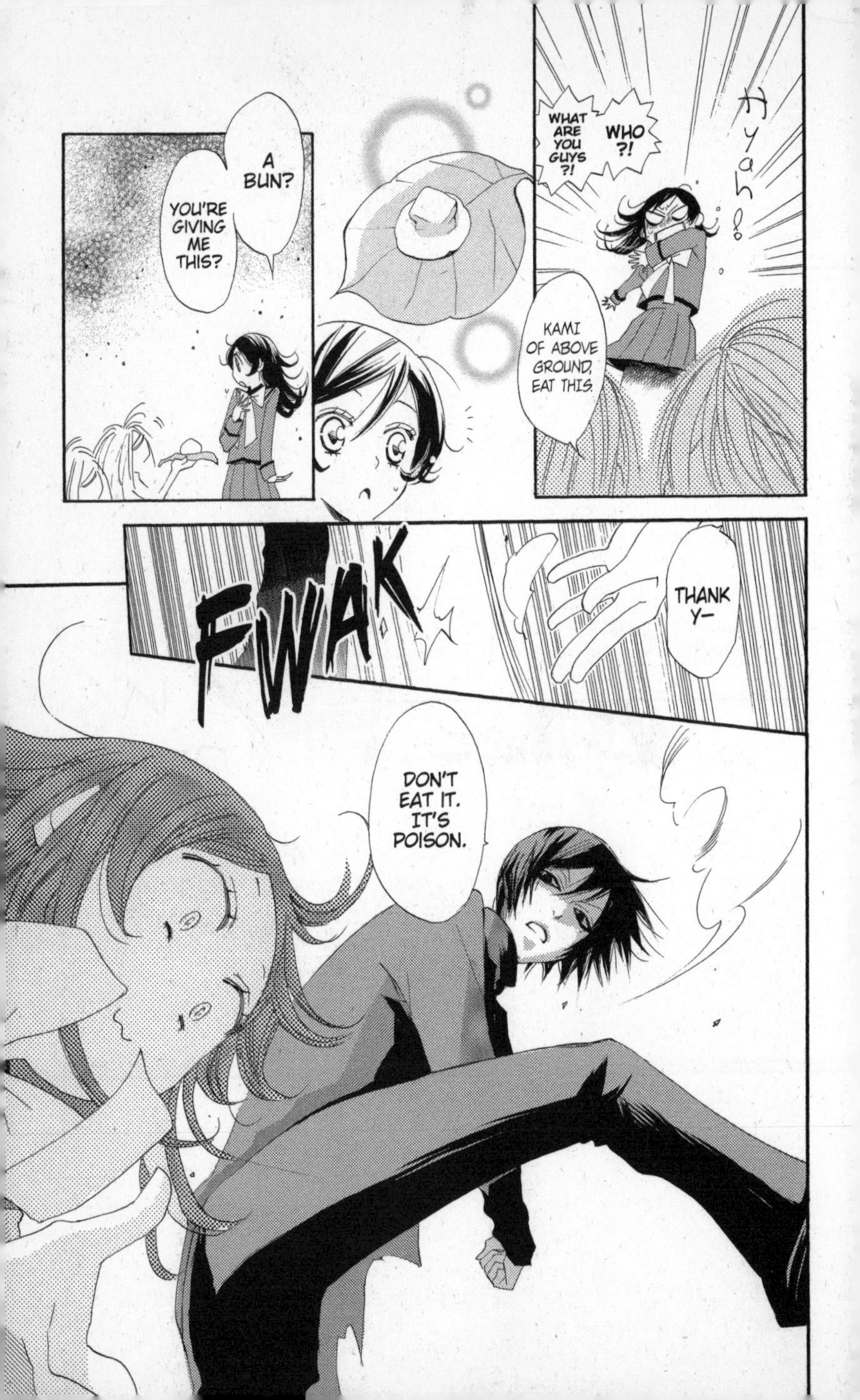
WHO?!
WHAT ARE YOU GUYS?!
KAMI OF ABOVE GROUND, EAT THIS.
A BUN?
YOU'RE GIVING ME THIS?
THANK Y—
FWAK
DON'T EAT IT. IT'S POISON.

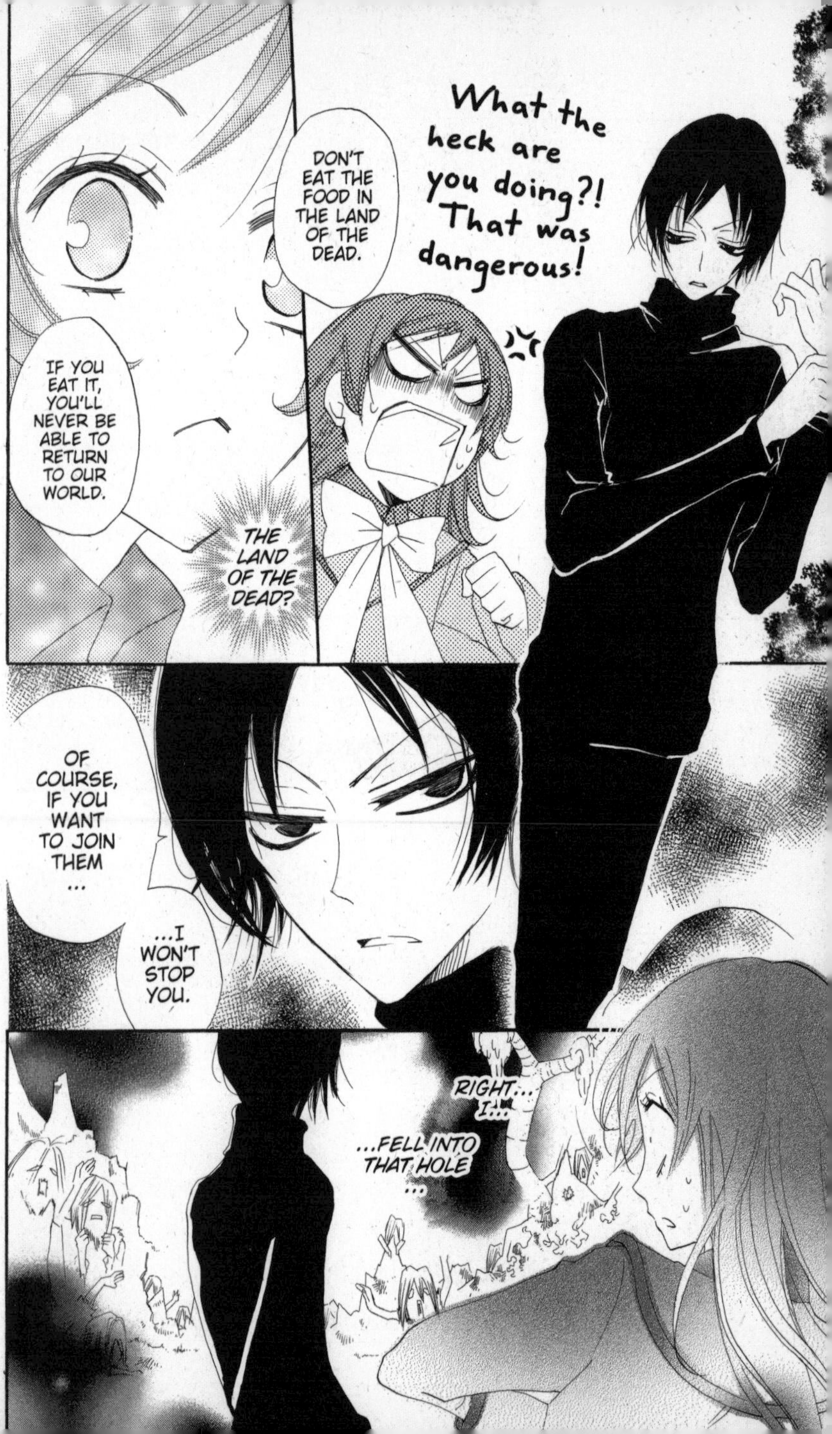
What the heck are you doing?! That was dangerous!
DON'T EAT THE FOOD IN THE LAND OF THE DEAD.
IF YOU EAT IT, YOU'LL NEVER BE ABLE TO RETURN TO OUR WORLD.
THE LAND OF THE DEAD?
OF COURSE, IF YOU WANT TO JOIN THEM...
...I WON'T STOP YOU.
RIGHT... I...
...FELL INTO THAT HOLE...

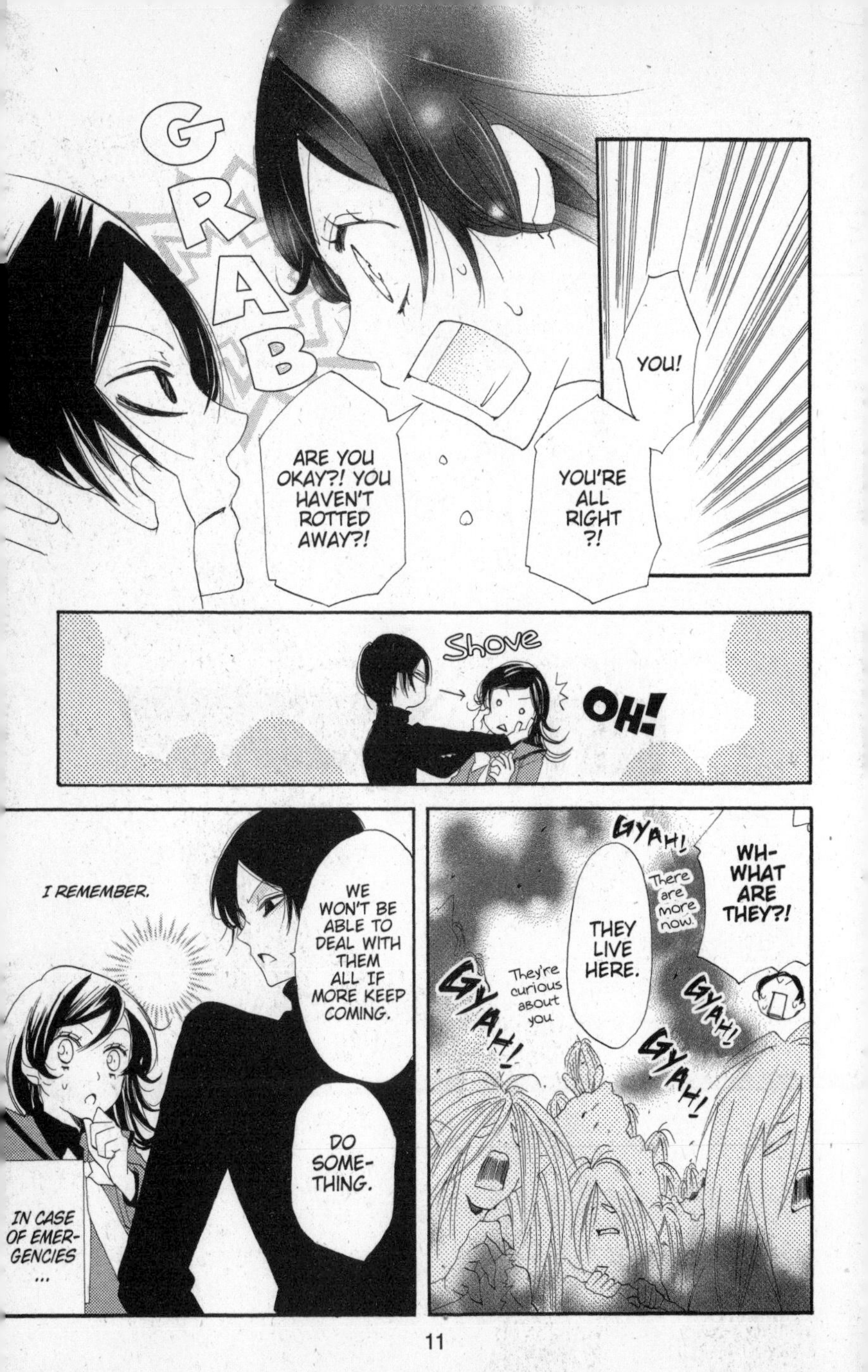
YOU!
YOU'RE ALL RIGHT ?!
GRAB
ARE YOU OKAY?! YOU HAVEN'T ROTTED AWAY?!
Shove
OH!
WH- WHAT ARE THEY?!
GYAH!
There are more now.
THEY LIVE HERE.
They're curious about you.
GYAH!
GYAH!
GYAH!
WE WON'T BE ABLE TO DEAL WITH THEM ALL IF MORE KEEP COMING.
DO SOMETHING.
I REMEMBER.
IN CASE OF EMERGENCIES ...

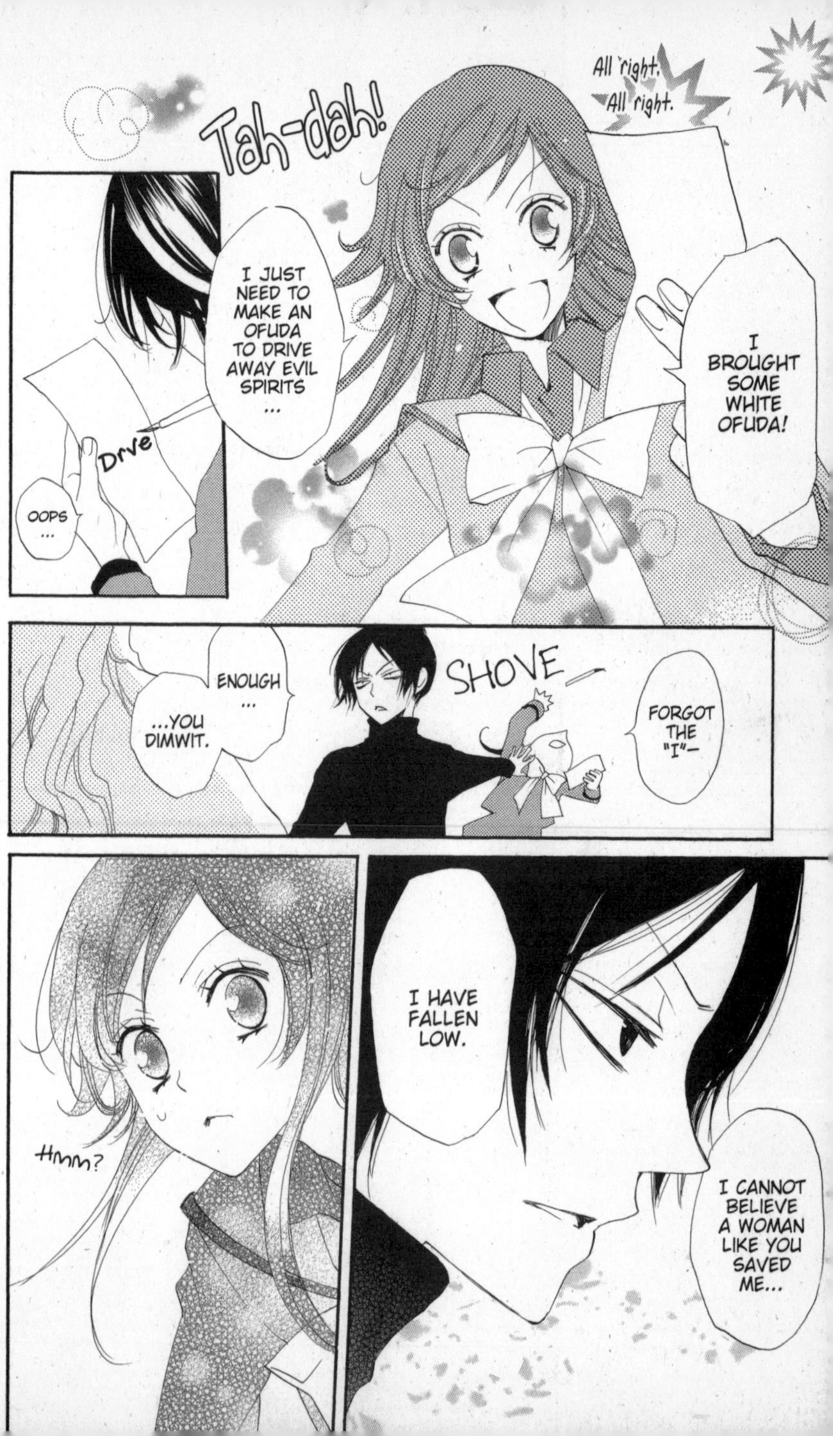
All right. All right.
Tah-dah!
I BROUGHT SOME WHITE OFUDA!
I JUST NEED TO MAKE AN OFUDA TO DRIVE AWAY EVIL SPIRITS...
Drve
OOPS...
FORGOT THE "I"—
SHOVE
ENOUGH...
...YOU DIMWIT.
I HAVE FALLEN LOW.
I CANNOT BELIEVE A WOMAN LIKE YOU SAVED ME...
Hmm?

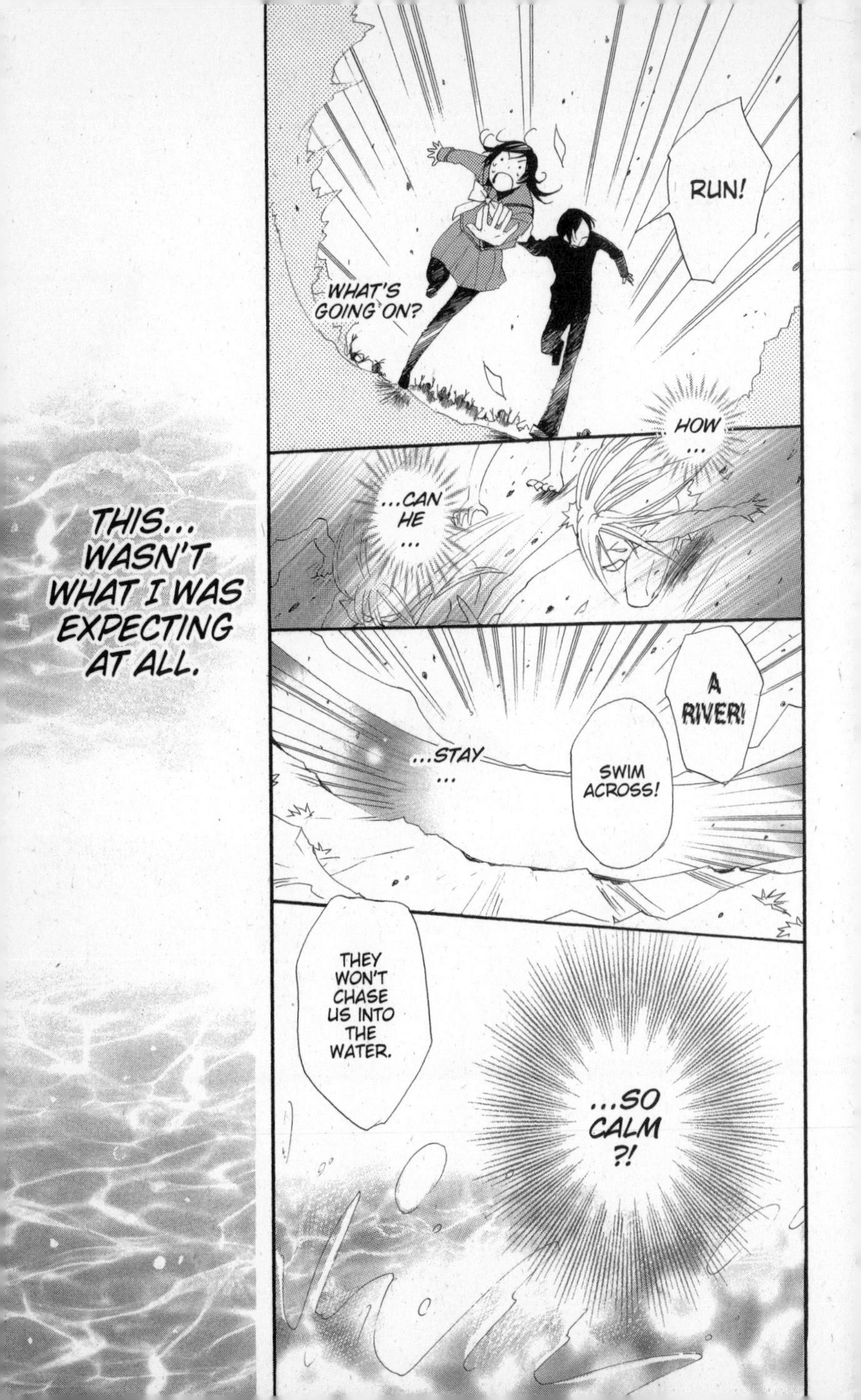
RUN!
WHAT'S GOING ON?
HOW...
...CAN HE...
A RIVER!
SWIM ACROSS!
...STAY...
THEY WON'T CHASE US INTO THE WATER.
...SO CALM?!
THIS... WASN'T WHAT I WAS EXPECTING AT ALL.

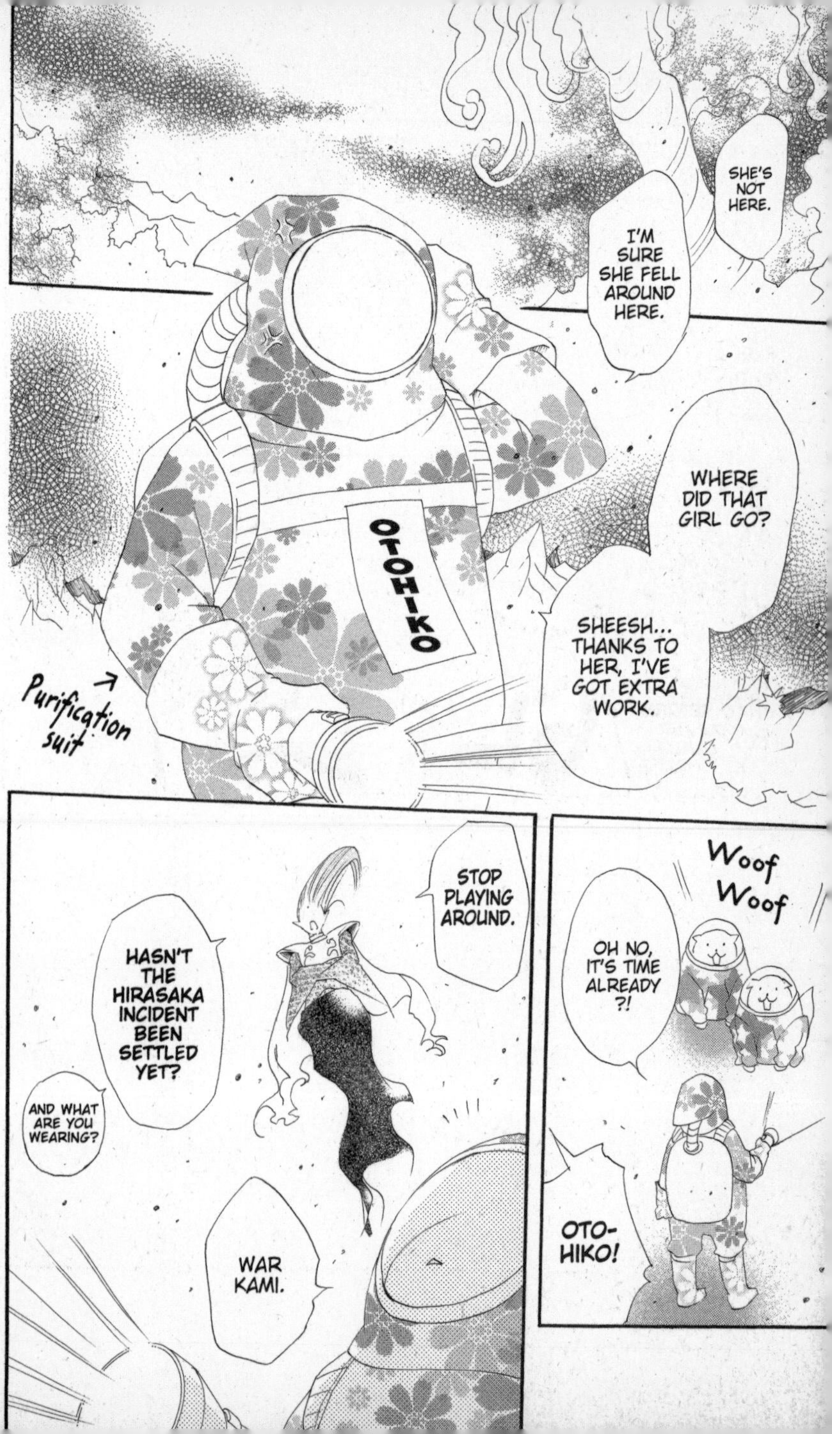
SHE'S NOT HERE.
I'M SURE SHE FELL AROUND HERE.
WHERE DID THAT GIRL GO?
OTOHIKO
SHEESH... THANKS TO HER, I'VE GOT EXTRA WORK.
Purification suit
Woof Woof
OH NO, IT'S TIME ALREADY?!
OTO-HIKO!
STOP PLAYING AROUND.
HASN'T THE HIRASAKA INCIDENT BEEN SETTLED YET?
AND WHAT ARE YOU WEARING?
WAR KAMI.

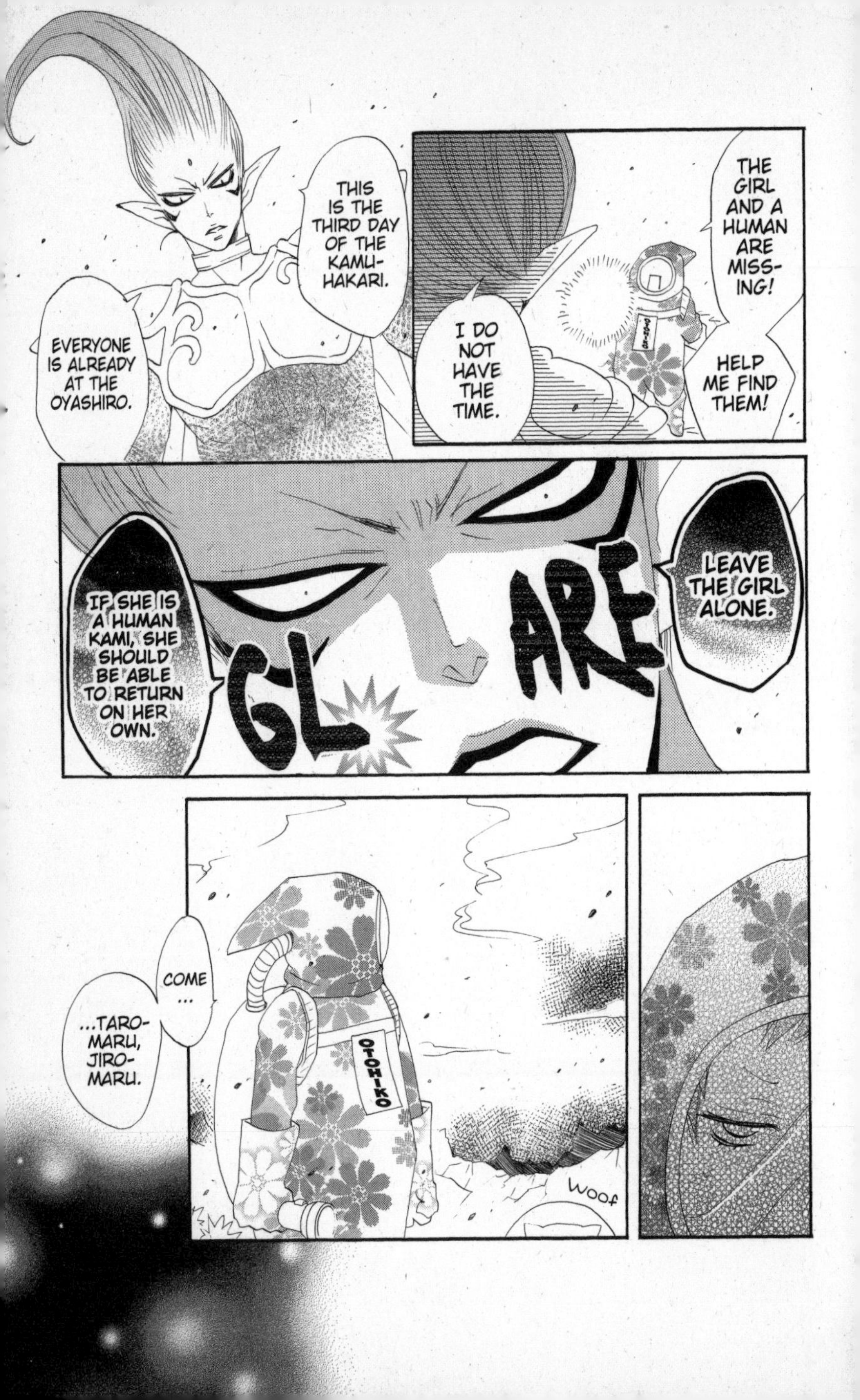
THE GIRL AND A HUMAN ARE MISSING!
HELP ME FIND THEM!
OTOHIKO
I DO NOT HAVE THE TIME.
THIS IS THE THIRD DAY OF THE KAMU-HAKARI.
EVERYONE IS ALREADY AT THE OYASHIRO.
LEAVE THE GIRL ALONE.
GLARE
IF SHE IS A HUMAN KAMI, SHE SHOULD BE ABLE TO RETURN ON HER OWN.
WOOF
OTOHIKO
COME ...
...TARO-MARU, JIRO-MARU.

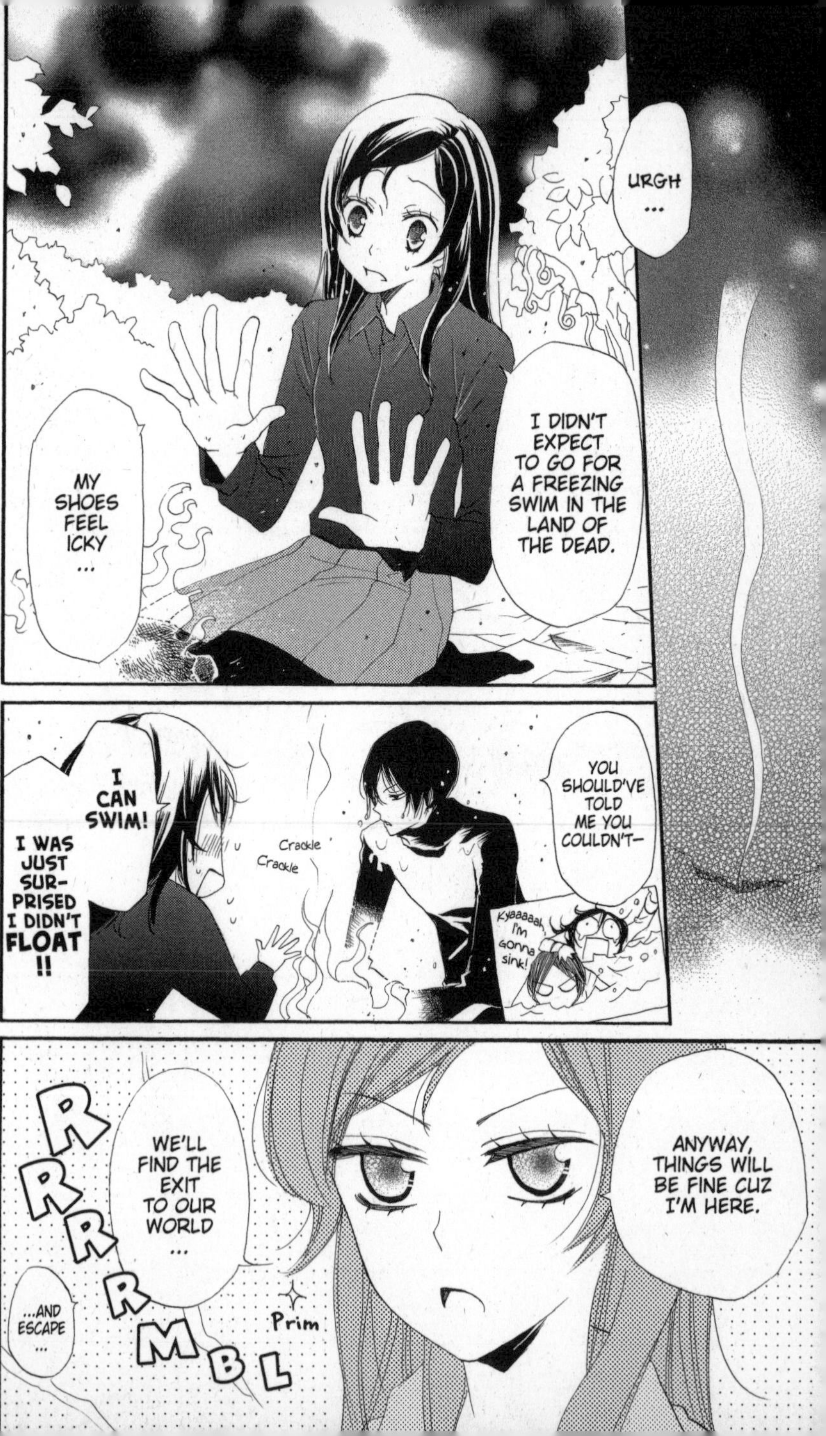
URGH ...
I DIDN'T EXPECT TO GO FOR A FREEZING SWIM IN THE LAND OF THE DEAD.
MY SHOES FEEL ICKY ...
YOU SHOULD'VE TOLD ME YOU COULDN'T—
Kyaaaaa! I'm gonna sink!
Crackle
Crackle
I CAN SWIM!
I WAS JUST SURPRISED I DIDN'T FLOAT!!
ANYWAY, THINGS WILL BE FINE CUZ I'M HERE.
Prim
WE'LL FIND THE EXIT TO OUR WORLD ...
...AND ESCAPE ...
RRRRMBL

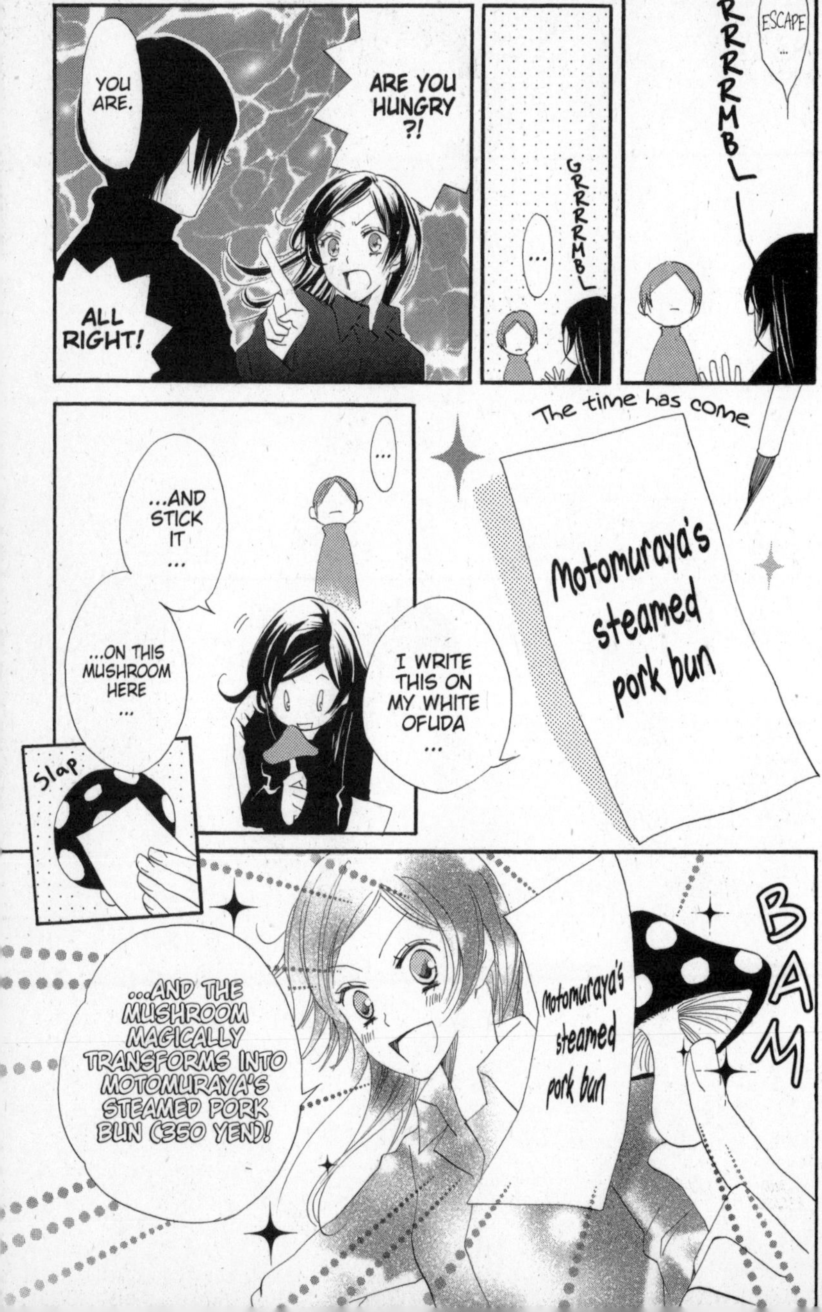
ESCAPE ...
GRRRRMBL
GRRRRMBL
...
ARE YOU HUNGRY ?!
YOU ARE.
ALL RIGHT!
The time has come.
Motomuraya's steamed pork bun
...
I WRITE THIS ON MY WHITE OFUDA ...
...AND STICK IT ...
...ON THIS MUSHROOM HERE ...
Slap
BAM
Motomuraya's steamed pork bun
...AND THE MUSHROOM MAGICALLY TRANSFORMS INTO MOTOMURAYA'S STEAMED PORK BUN (350 YEN)!

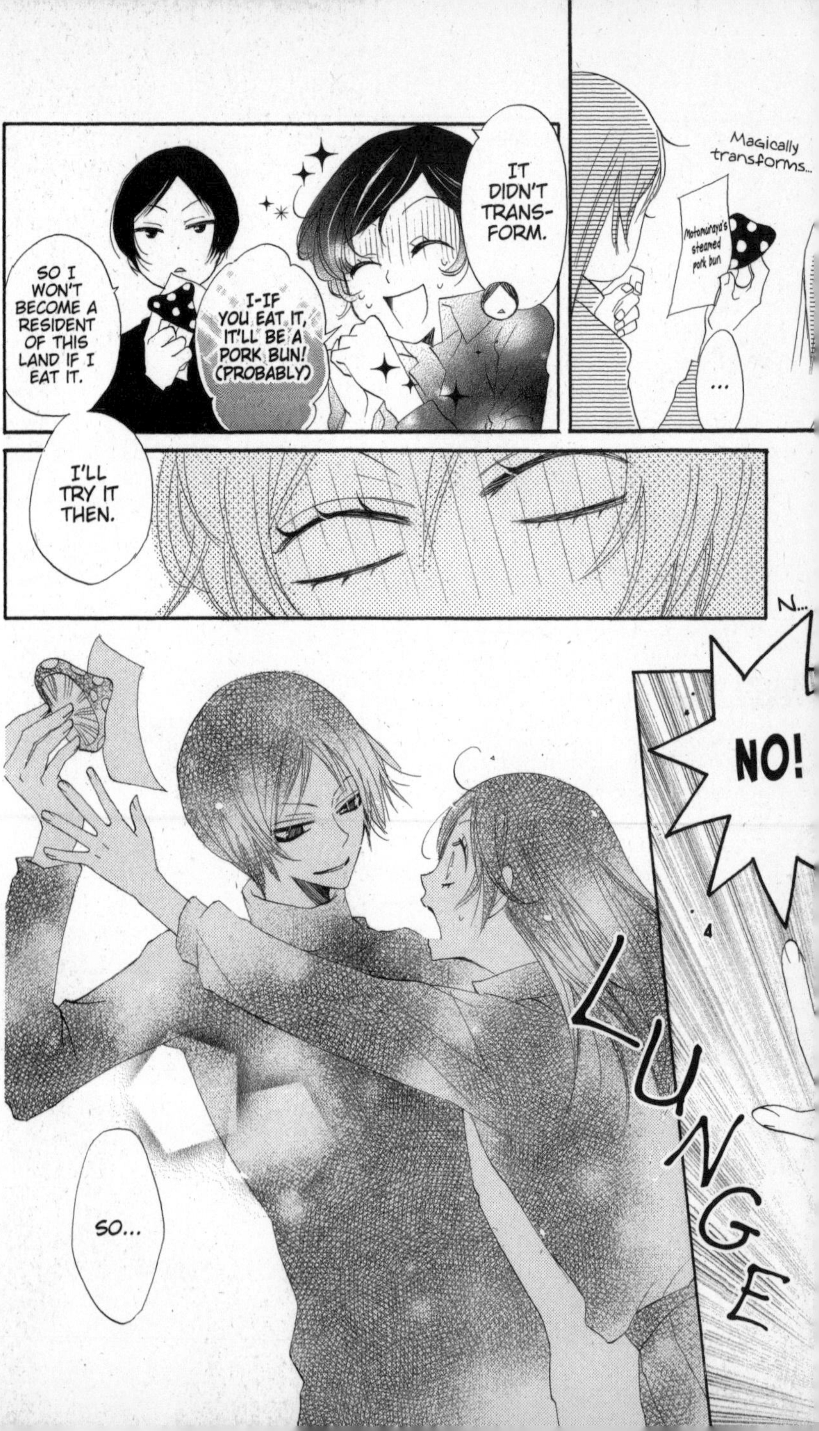

Magically transforms...
Motomuraya's steamed pork bun
...
IT DIDN'T TRANS-FORM.
I-IF YOU EAT IT, IT'LL BE A PORK BUN! (PROBABLY)
SO I WON'T BECOME A RESIDENT OF THIS LAND IF I EAT IT.
I'LL TRY IT THEN.
N...
NO!
LUNGE
SO...

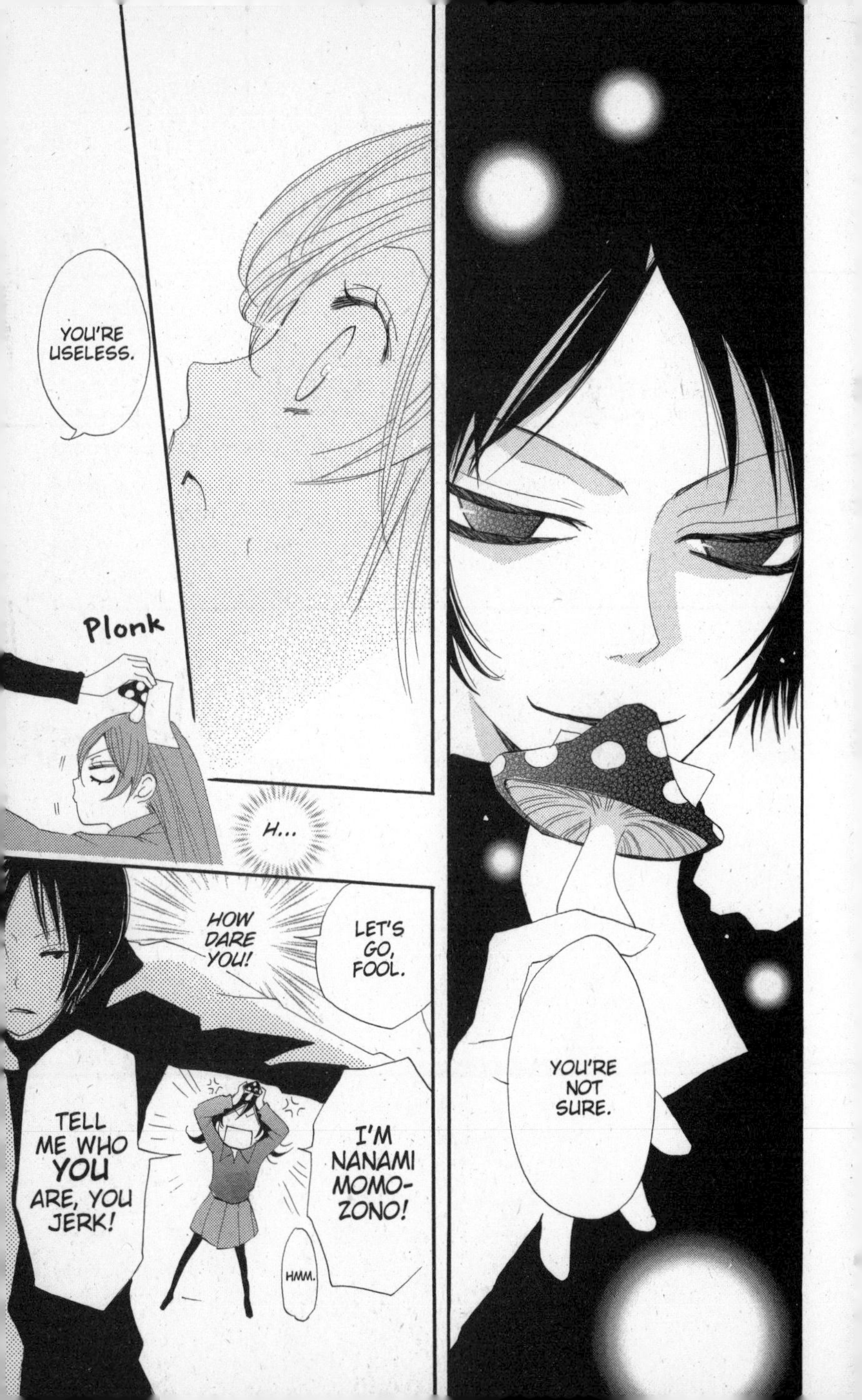
YOU'RE NOT SURE.
YOU'RE USELESS.
Plonk
H...
LET'S GO, FOOL.
HOW DARE YOU!
I'M NANAMI MOMOZONO!
TELL ME WHO YOU ARE, YOU JERK!
HMM.

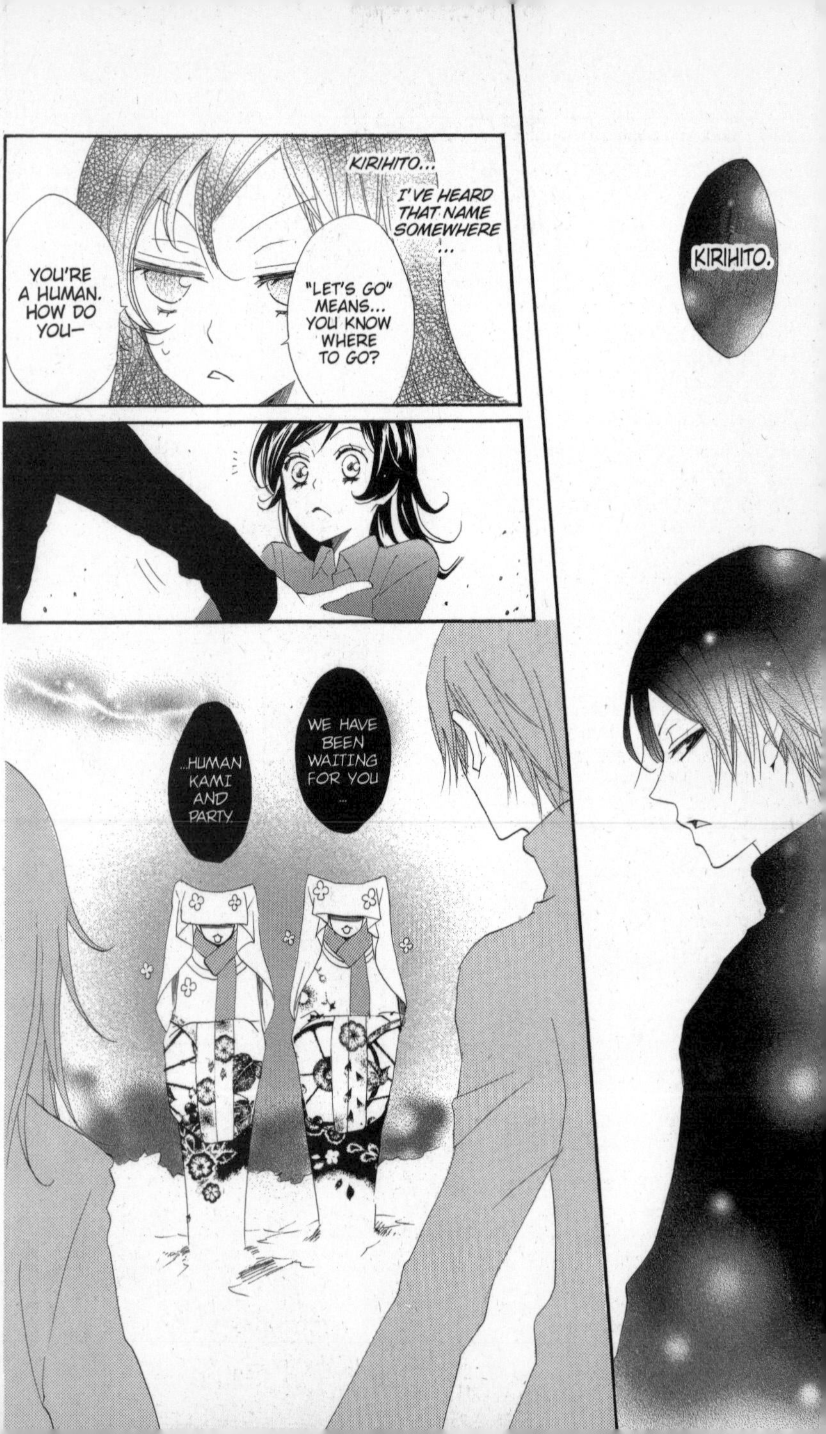
KIRIHITO.
KIRIHITO...
I'VE HEARD THAT NAME SOMEWHERE...
"LET'S GO" MEANS... YOU KNOW WHERE TO GO?
YOU'RE A HUMAN. HOW DO YOU—
WE HAVE BEEN WAITING FOR YOU...
...HUMAN KAMI AND PARTY.

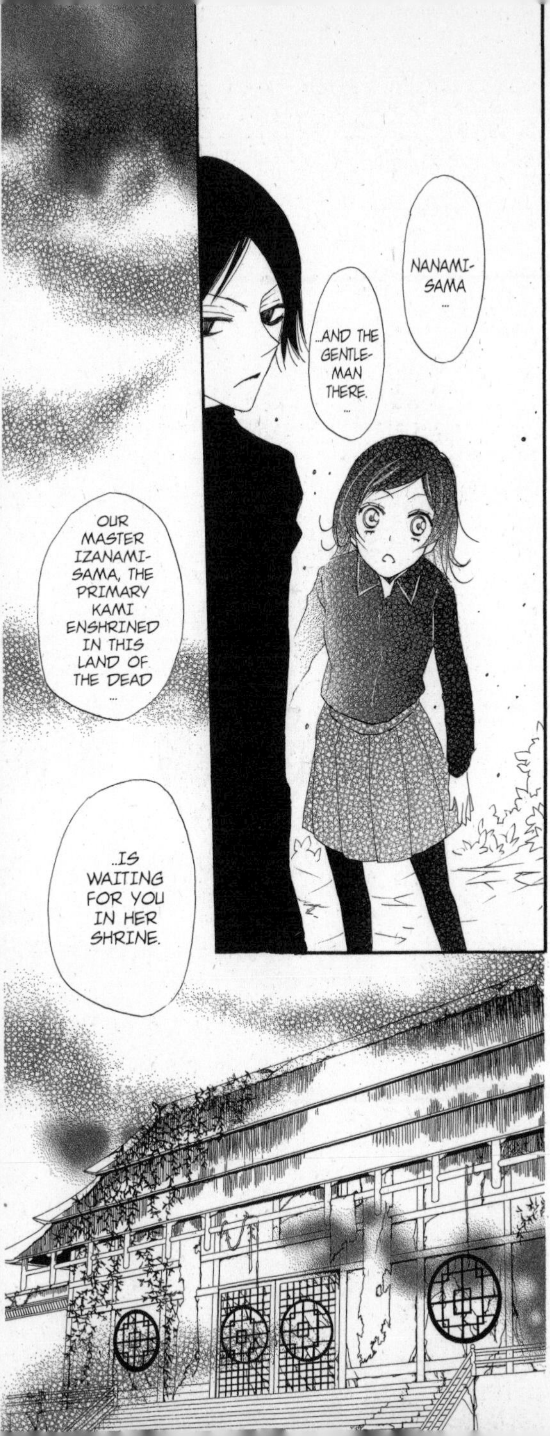
NANAMI-SAMA ...
...AND THE GENTLEMAN THERE. ...
OUR MASTER IZANAMI-SAMA, THE PRIMARY KAMI ENSHRINED IN THIS LAND OF THE DEAD ...
...IS WAITING FOR YOU IN HER SHRINE.

Hello.

I'm Julietta Suzuki.

Thank you for picking up Volume 8 of Kamisama Kiss!

It's winter while I'm writing this. I like winter. Nabe, hot tea, and baths are great, the futon is nice, and I can wear boots! I have a kotatsu as well, and I'm happy. I'm really happy that Volume 8 comes out in such a happy season. Thank you so much.

I'll be even happier if you enjoy reading this volume!

😊

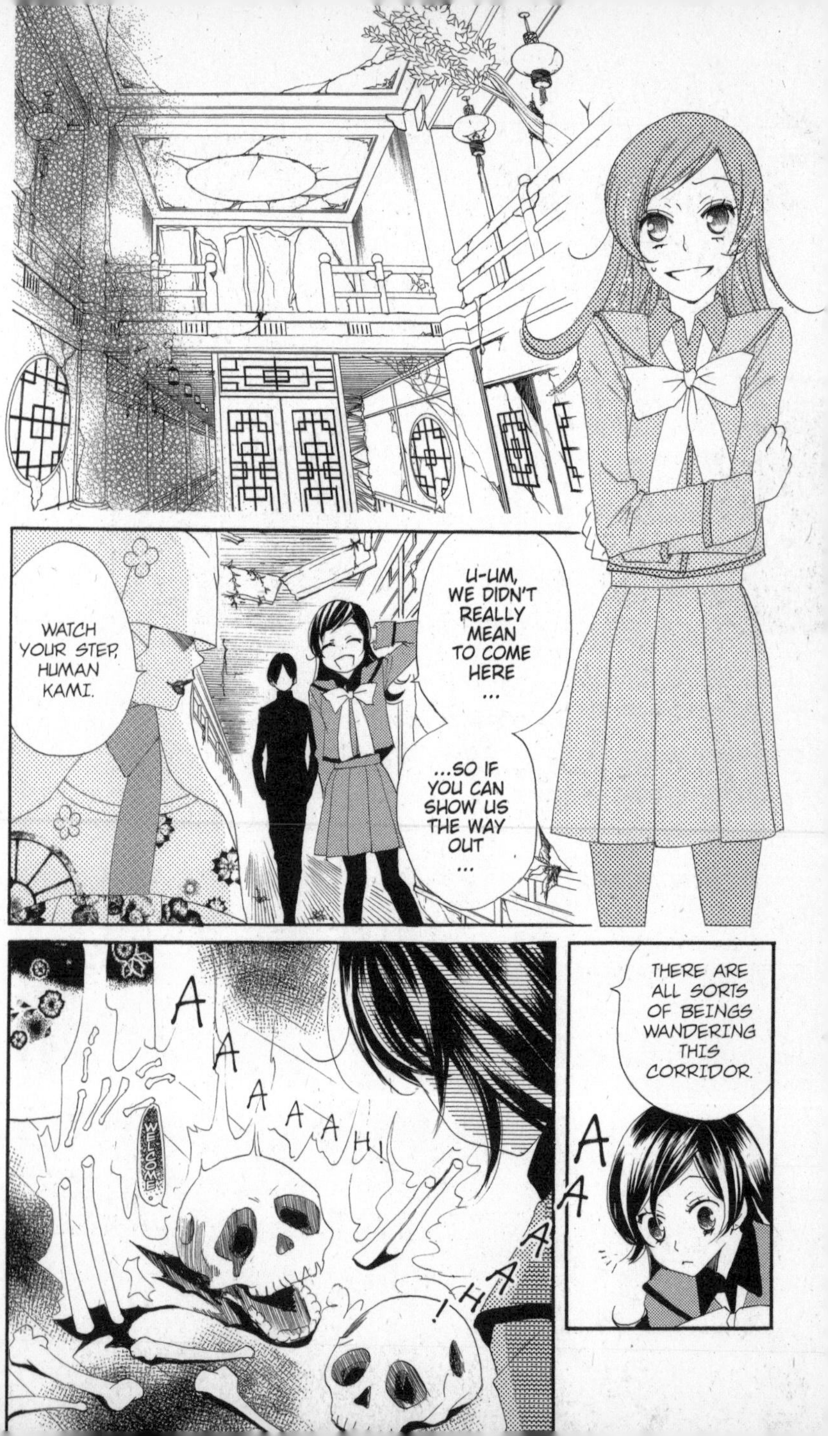
U-UM, WE DIDN'T REALLY MEAN TO COME HERE ...
...SO IF YOU CAN SHOW US THE WAY OUT ...
WATCH YOUR STEP, HUMAN KAMI.
THERE ARE ALL SORTS OF BEINGS WANDERING THIS CORRIDOR.
AAAAH!
AAAAAH!
WELCOME

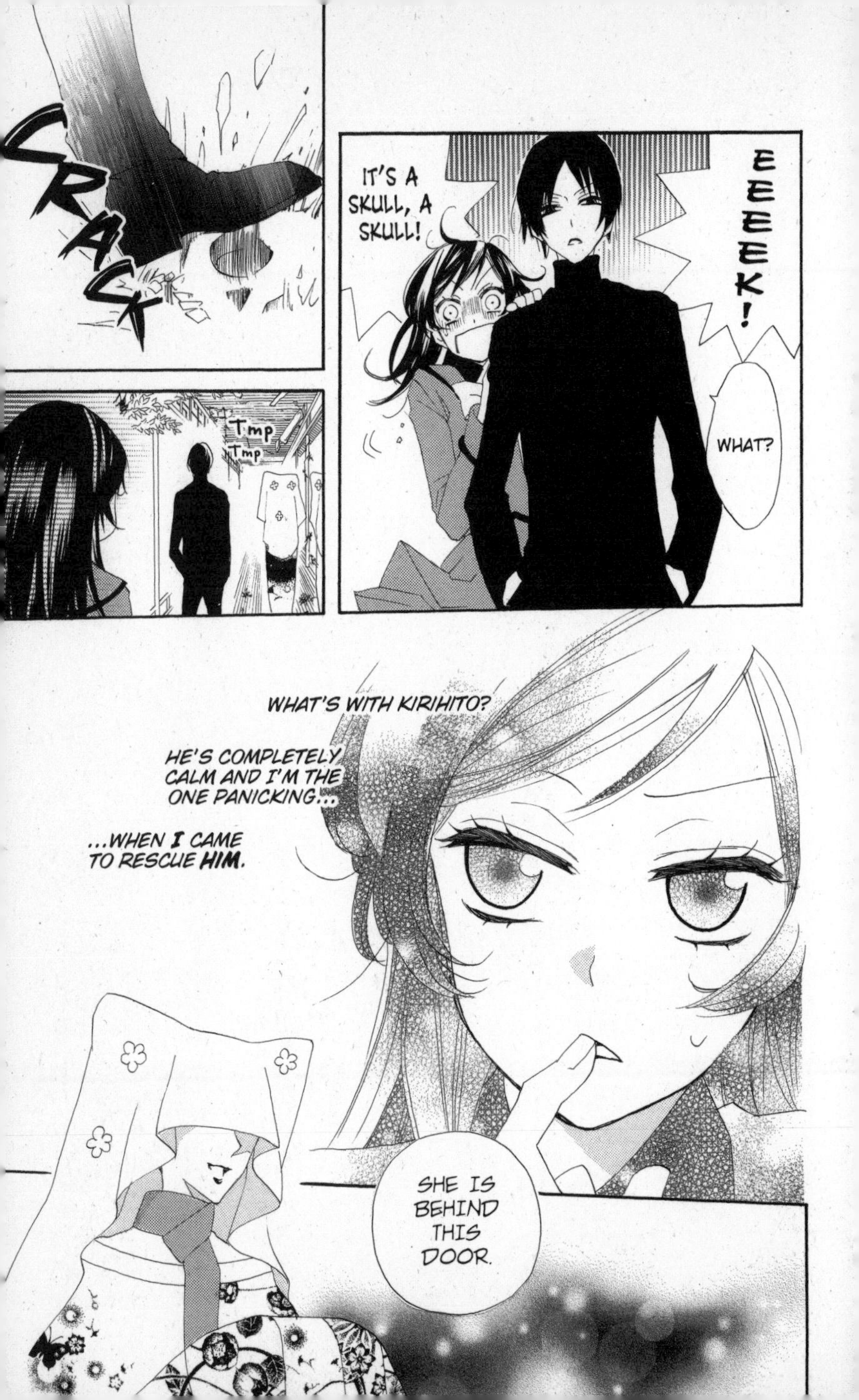
EEEEEK!
IT'S A SKULL, A SKULL!
WHAT?
CRACK
Tmp Tmp
WHAT'S WITH KIRIHITO?
HE'S COMPLETELY CALM AND I'M THE ONE PANICKING...
...WHEN I CAME TO RESCUE HIM.
SHE IS BEHIND THIS DOOR.

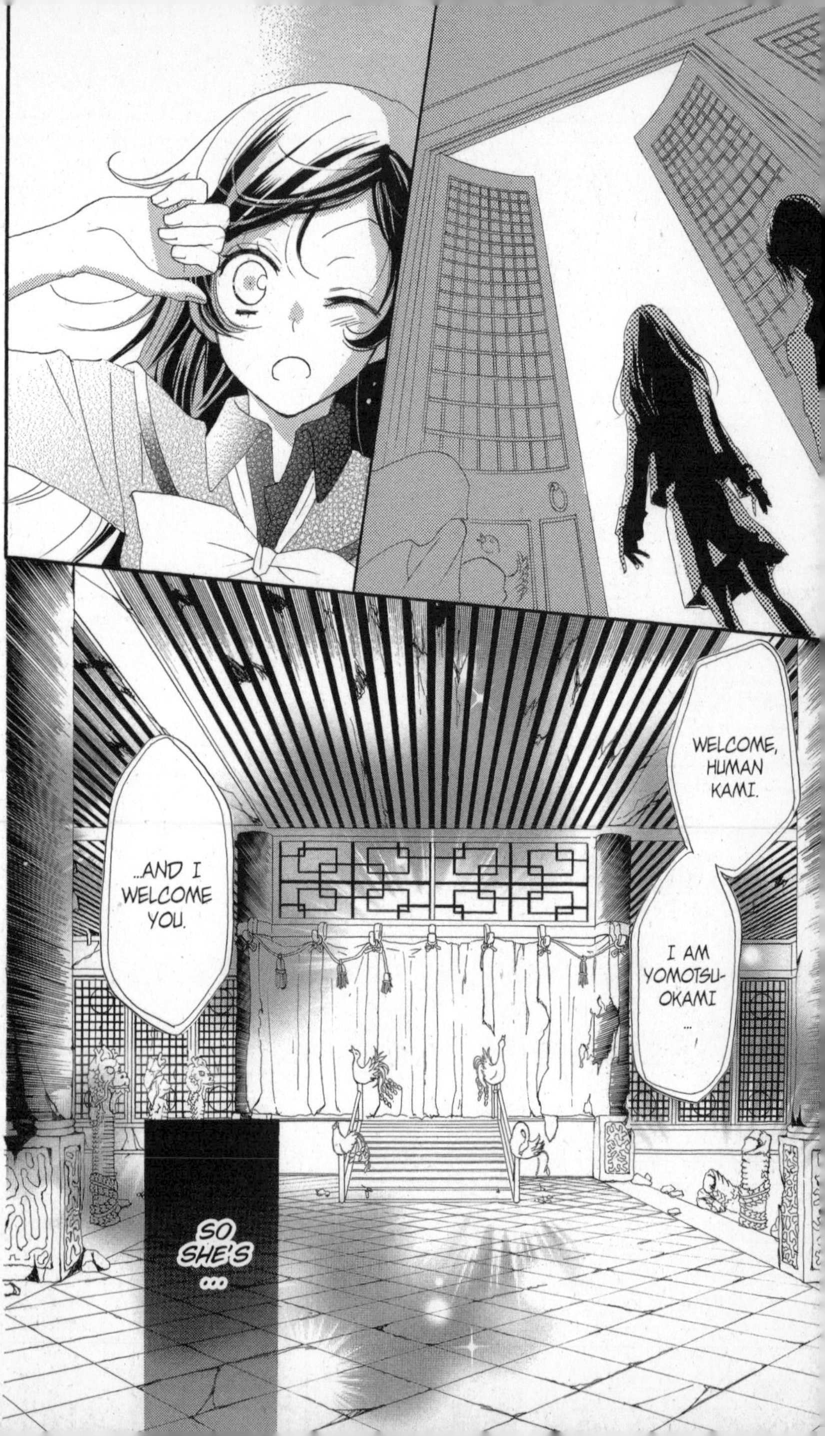
WELCOME, HUMAN KAMI.
I AM YOMOTSU-OKAMI...
...AND I WELCOME YOU.
SO SHE'S...

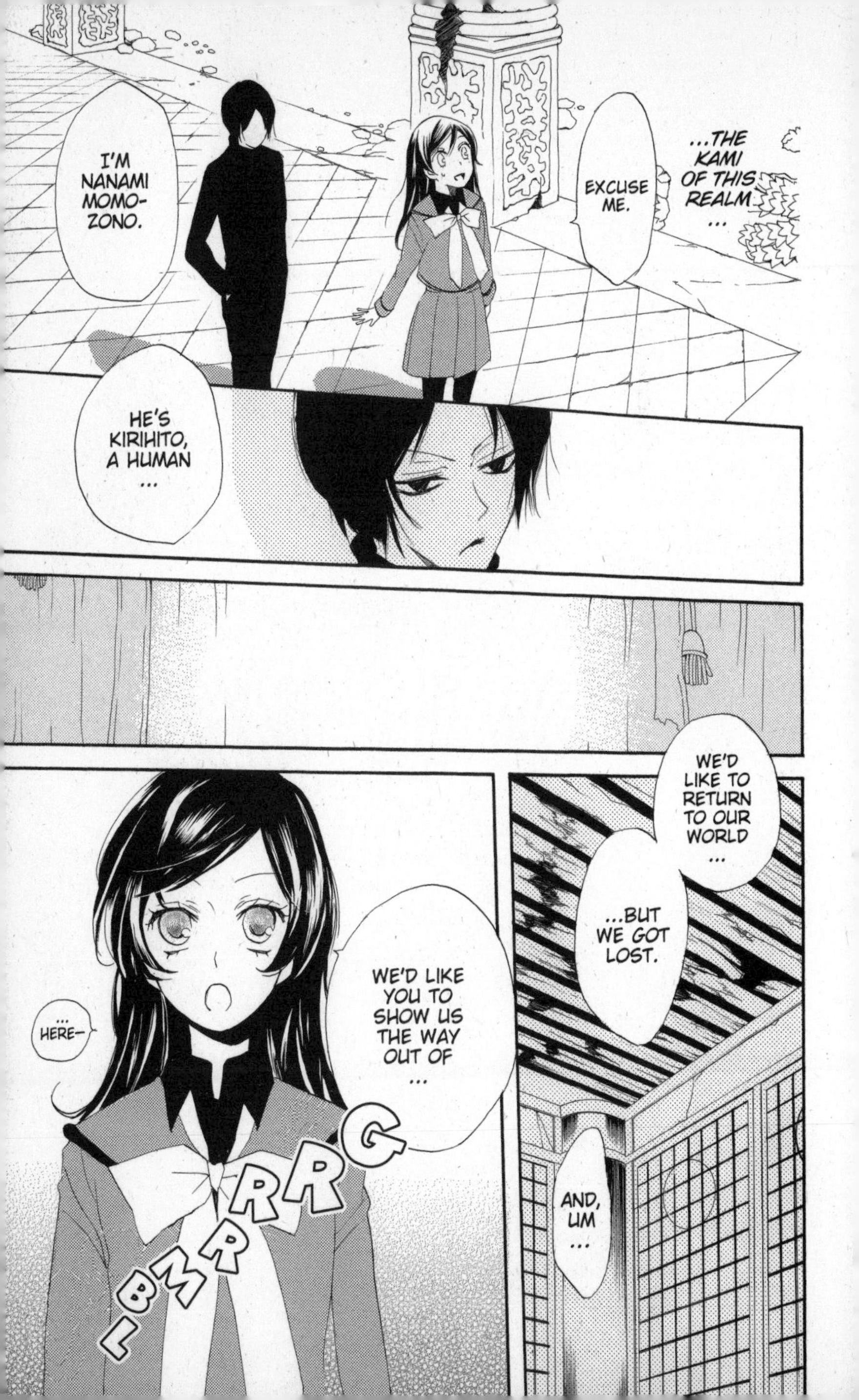
...THE KAMI OF THIS REALM ...
EXCUSE ME.
I'M NANAMI MOMO-ZONO.
HE'S KIRIHITO, A HUMAN ...
WE'D LIKE TO RETURN TO OUR WORLD ...
...BUT WE GOT LOST.
AND, UM ...
WE'D LIKE YOU TO SHOW US THE WAY OUT OF ...
... HERE-
BLMRRRG

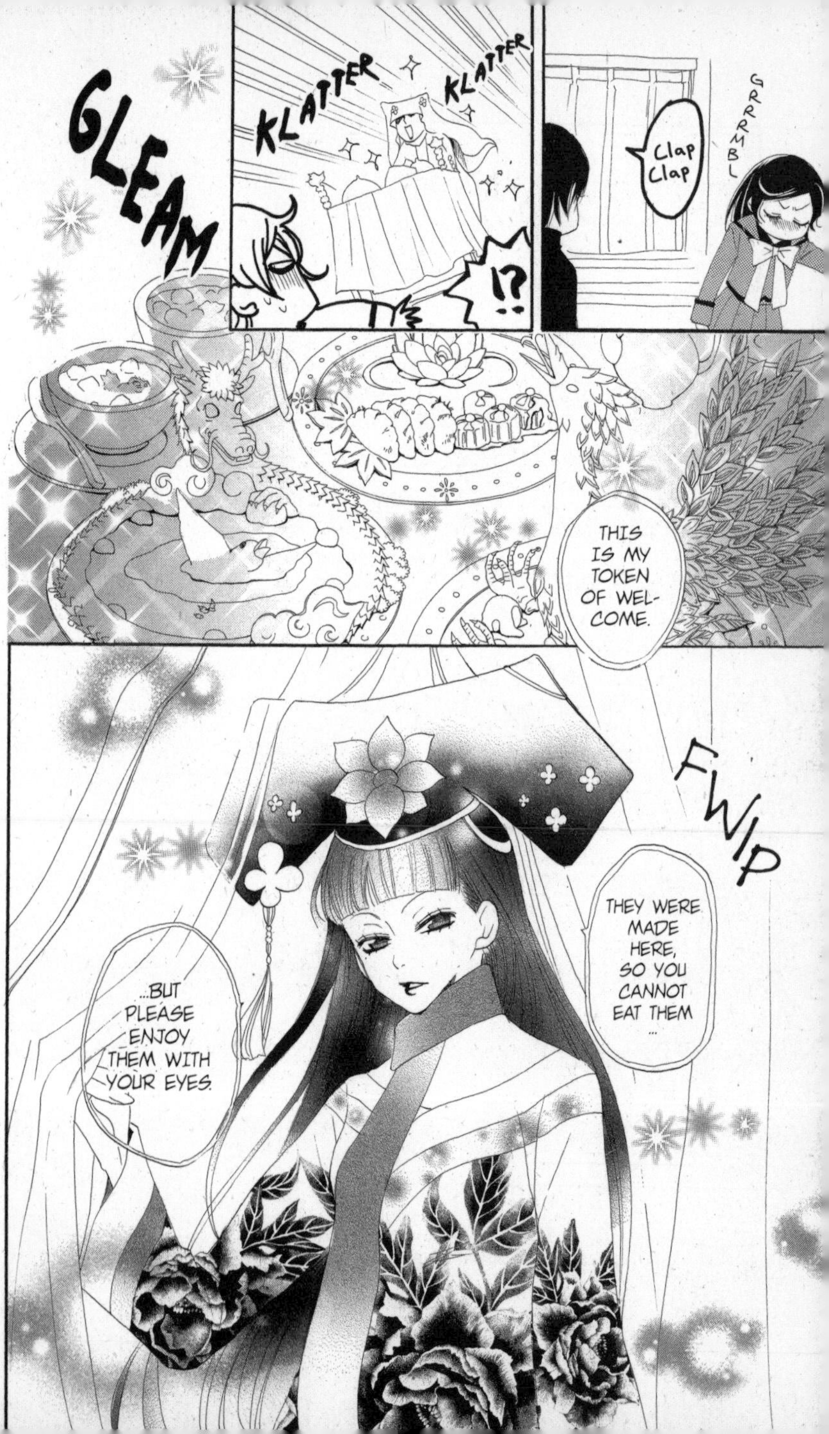
Clap Clap
GRRRMBL
KLATTER
KLATTER
!?
GLEAM
THIS IS MY TOKEN OF WEL-COME.
FWIP
THEY WERE MADE HERE, SO YOU CANNOT EAT THEM ...
...BUT PLEASE ENJOY THEM WITH YOUR EYES.

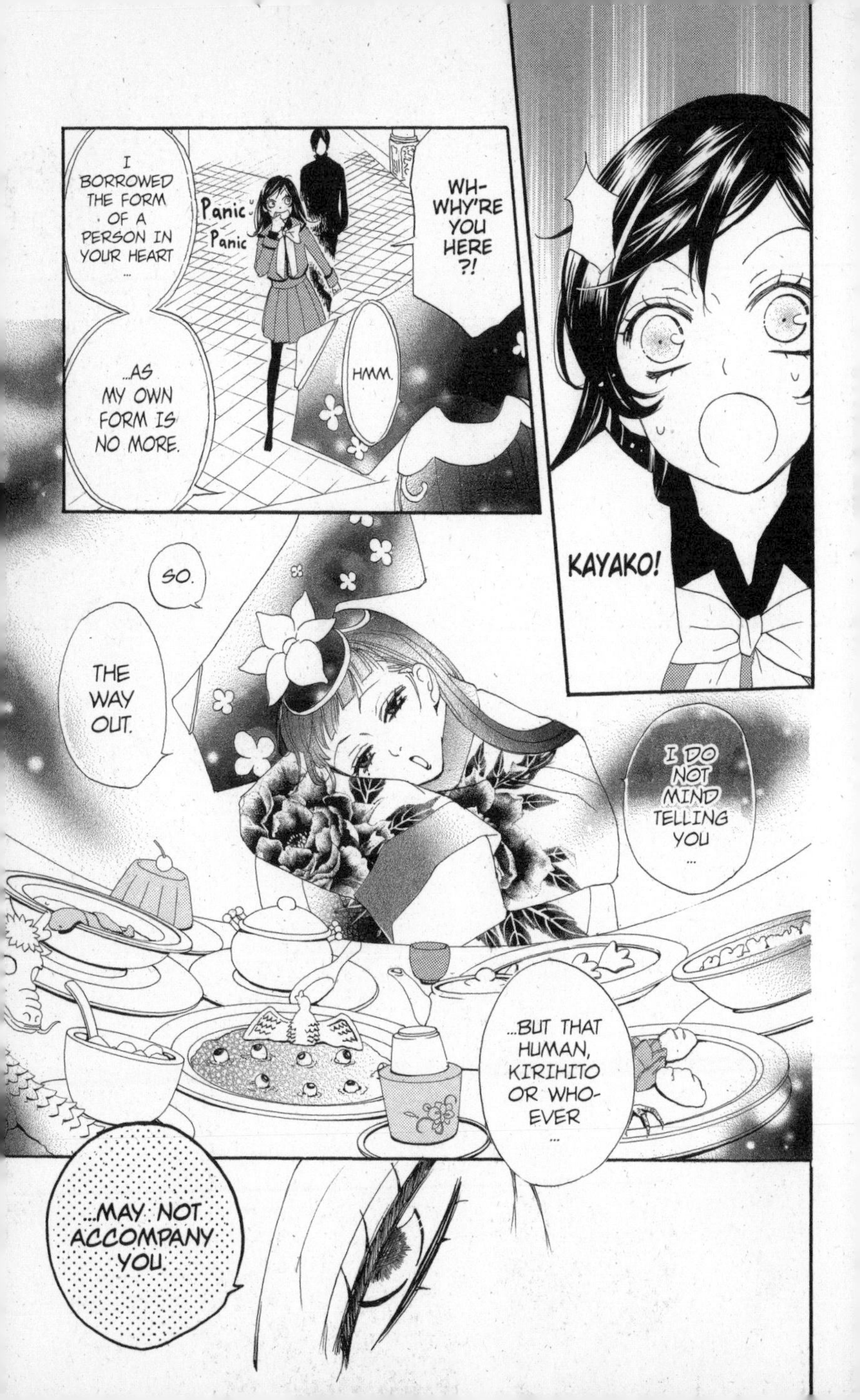
KAYAKO!
WH-WHY'RE YOU HERE?!
Panic Panic
I BORROWED THE FORM OF A PERSON IN YOUR HEART ...
...AS MY OWN FORM IS NO MORE.
HMM.
SO.
THE WAY OUT.
I DO NOT MIND TELLING YOU ...
...BUT THAT HUMAN, KIRIHITO OR WHO-EVER ...
...MAY NOT ACCOMPANY YOU.

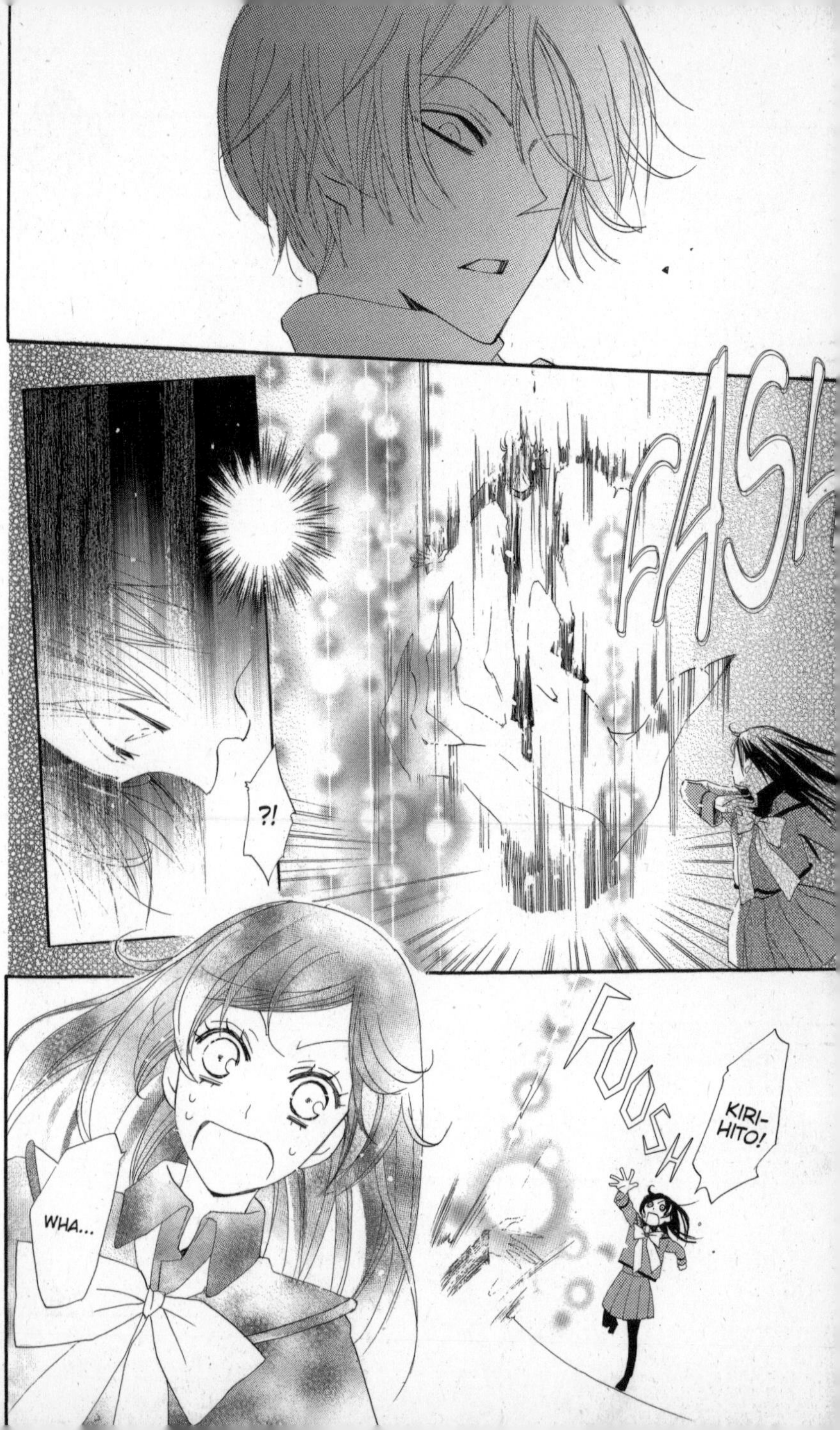
FASH
?!
FOOSH
KIRI-HITO!
WHA...

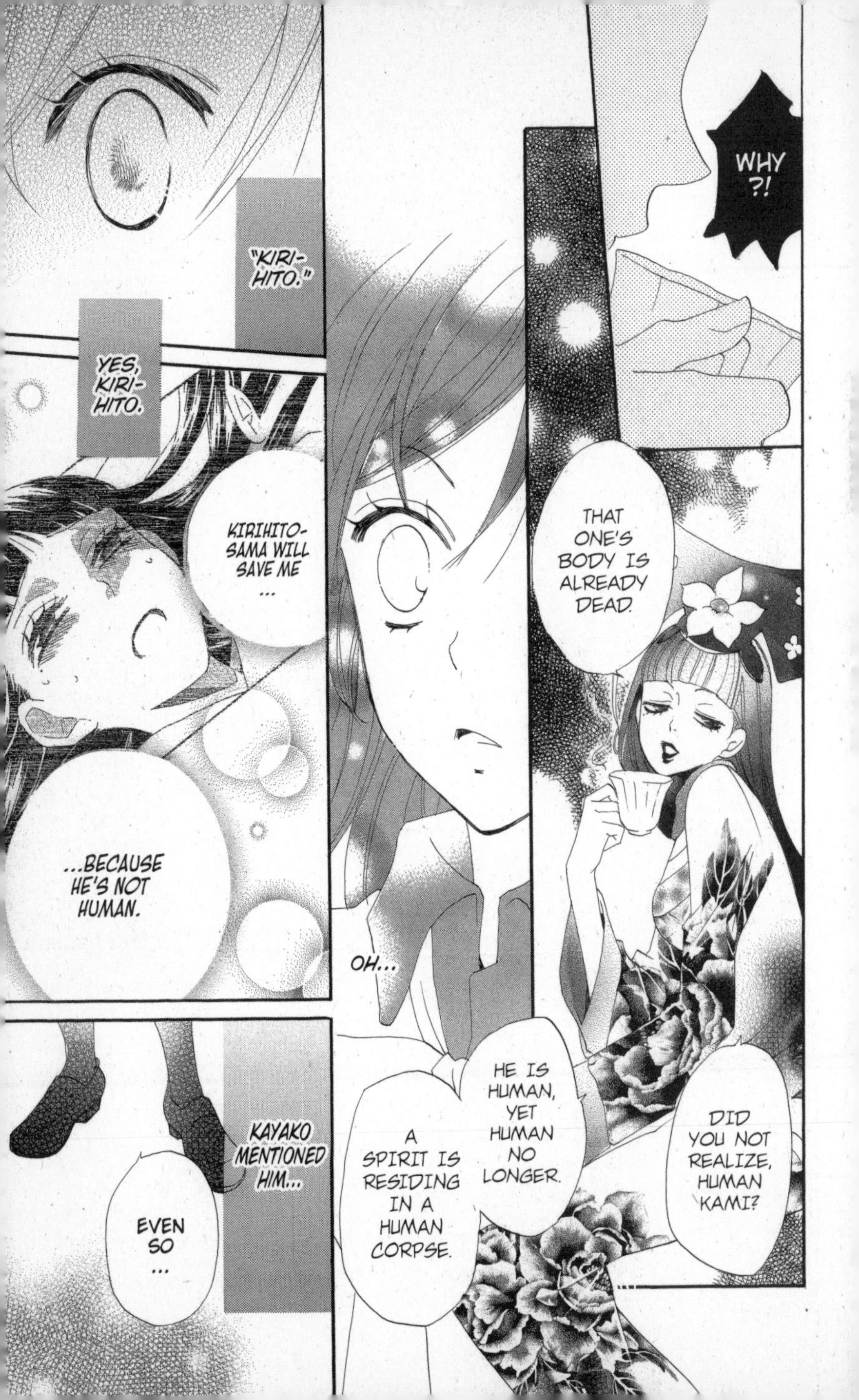
WHY ?!
THAT ONE'S BODY IS ALREADY DEAD.
DID YOU NOT REALIZE, HUMAN KAMI?
HE IS HUMAN, YET HUMAN NO LONGER.
A SPIRIT IS RESIDING IN A HUMAN CORPSE.
OH...
"KIRI-HITO."
YES, KIRI-HITO.
KIRIHITO-SAMA WILL SAVE ME ...
...BECAUSE HE'S NOT HUMAN.
KAYAKO MENTIONED HIM...
EVEN SO ...

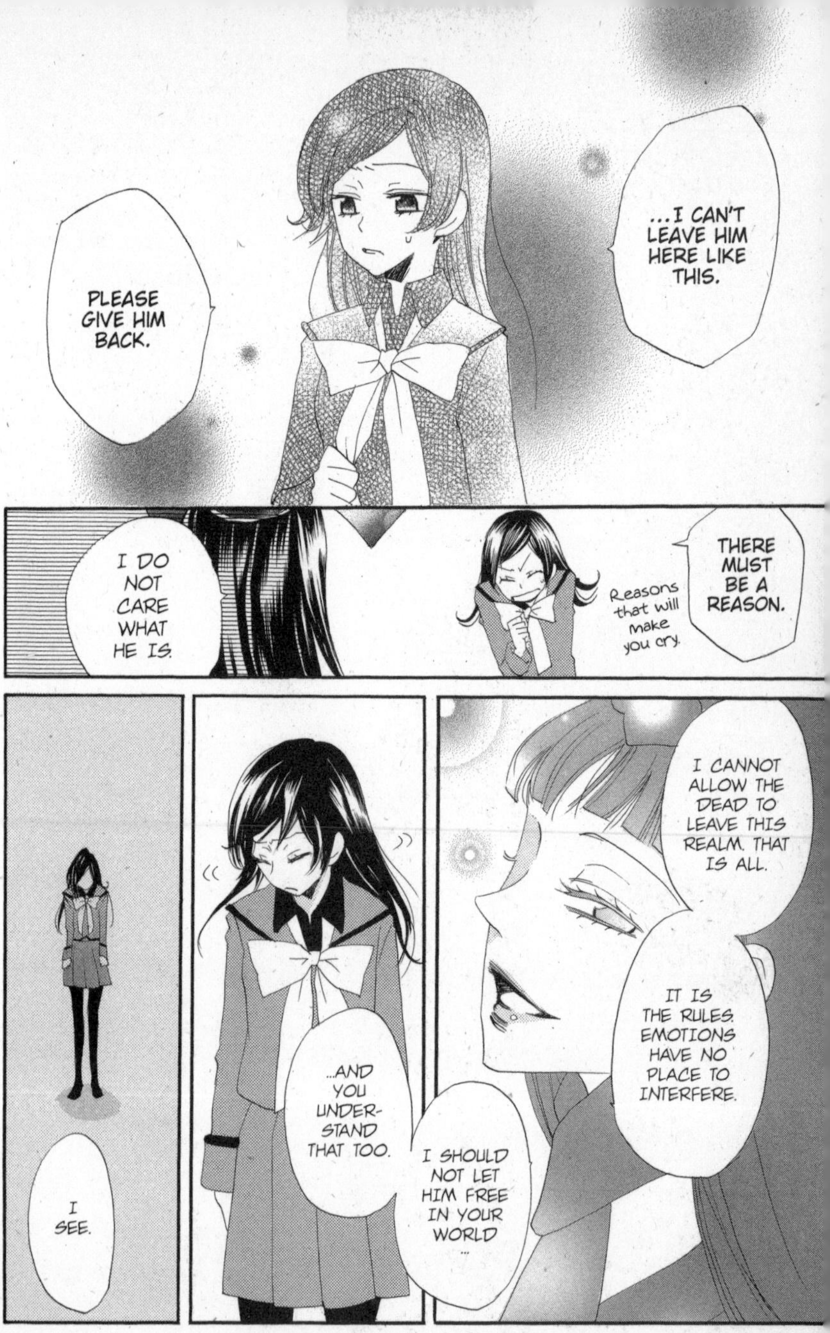
...I CAN'T LEAVE HIM HERE LIKE THIS.
PLEASE GIVE HIM BACK.
THERE MUST BE A REASON.
Reasons that will make you cry.
I DO NOT CARE WHAT HE IS.
I CANNOT ALLOW THE DEAD TO LEAVE THIS REALM. THAT IS ALL.
IT IS THE RULES. EMOTIONS HAVE NO PLACE TO INTERFERE.
I SHOULD NOT LET HIM FREE IN YOUR WORLD ...
...AND YOU UNDERSTAND THAT TOO.
I SEE.

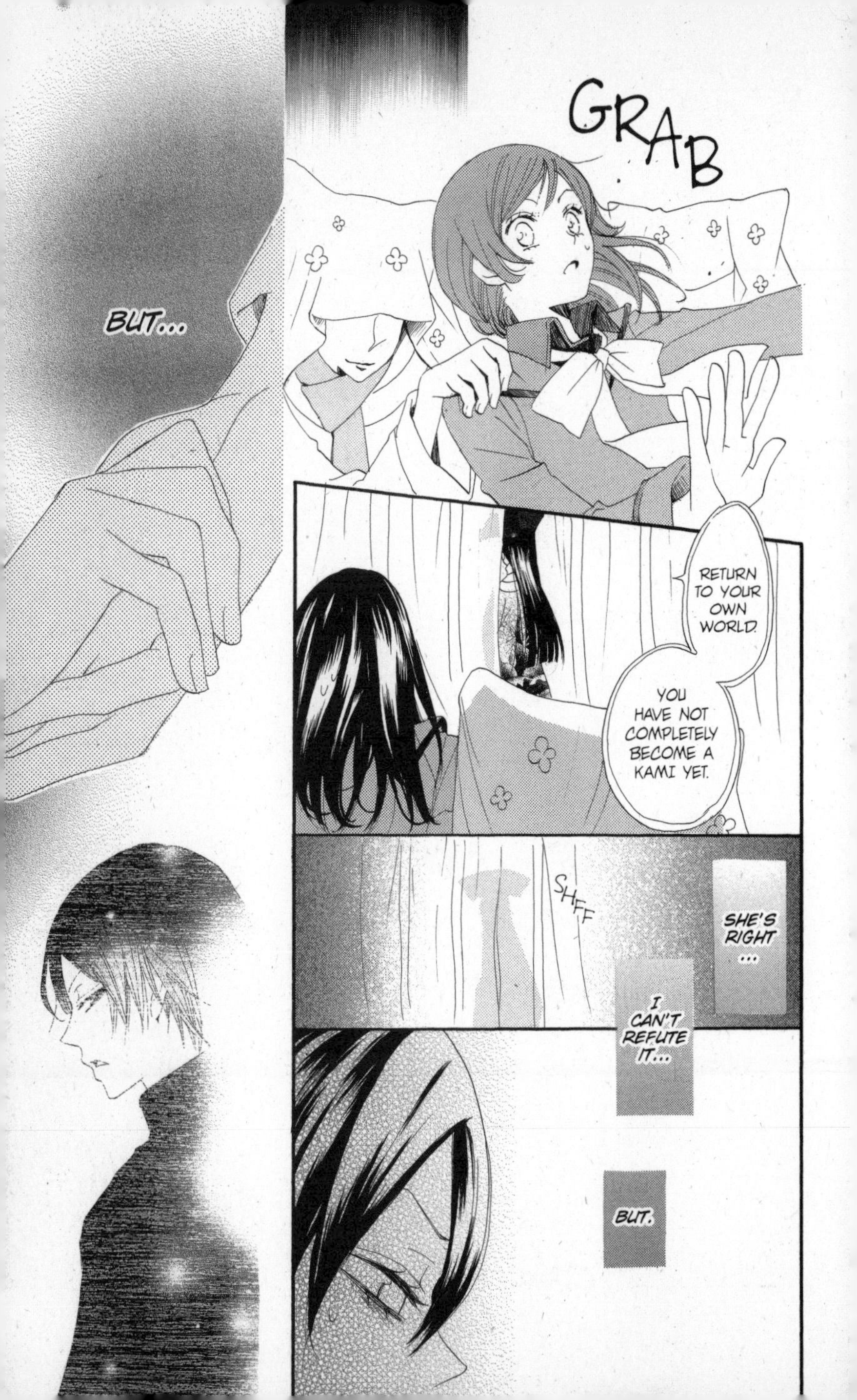
GRAB
RETURN TO YOUR OWN WORLD.
YOU HAVE NOT COMPLETELY BECOME A KAMI YET.
SHFF
SHE'S RIGHT...
I CAN'T REFUTE IT...
BUT.
BUT...

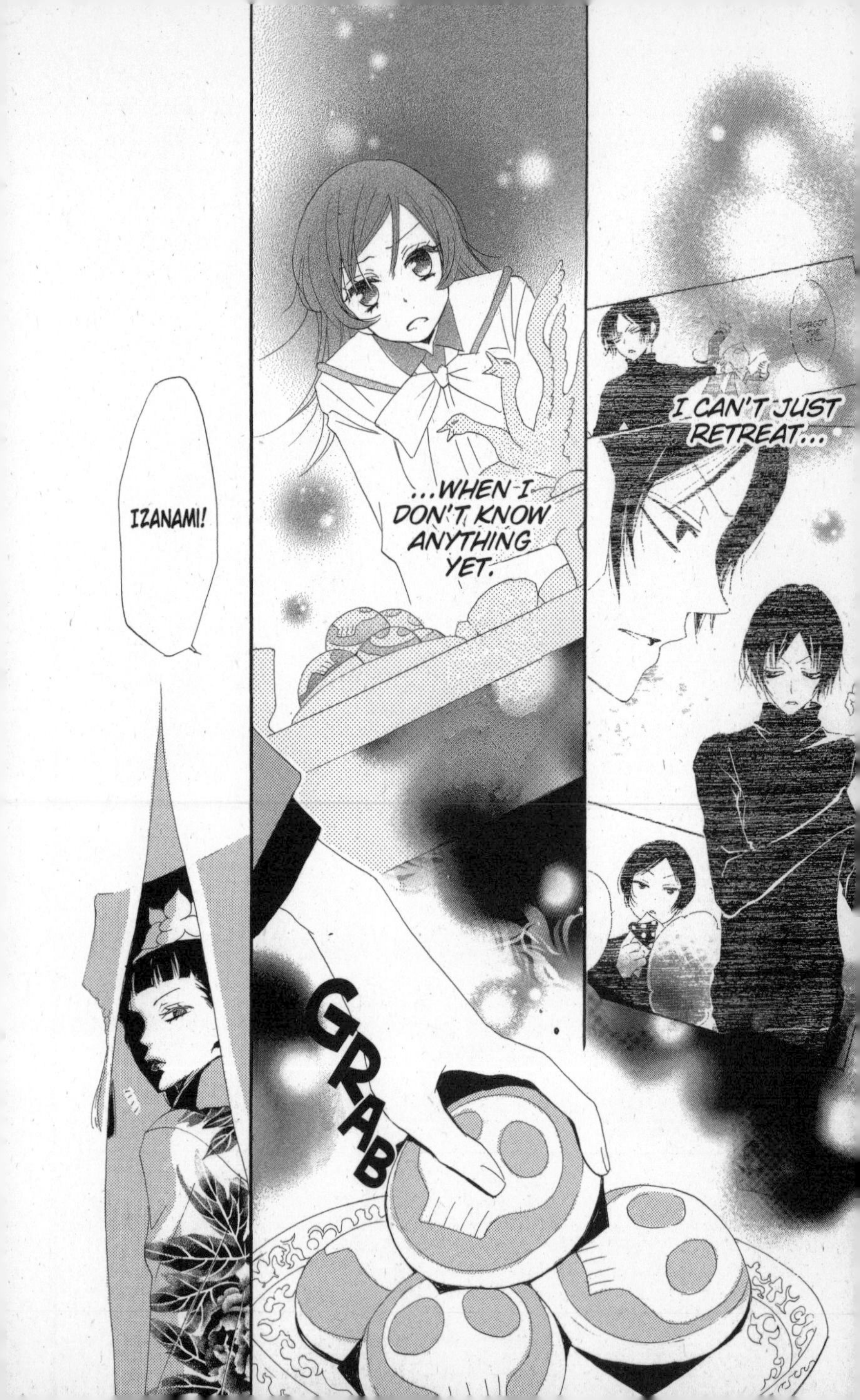
I CAN'T JUST RETREAT...
...WHEN I DON'T KNOW ANYTHING YET.
GRAB
IZANAMI!

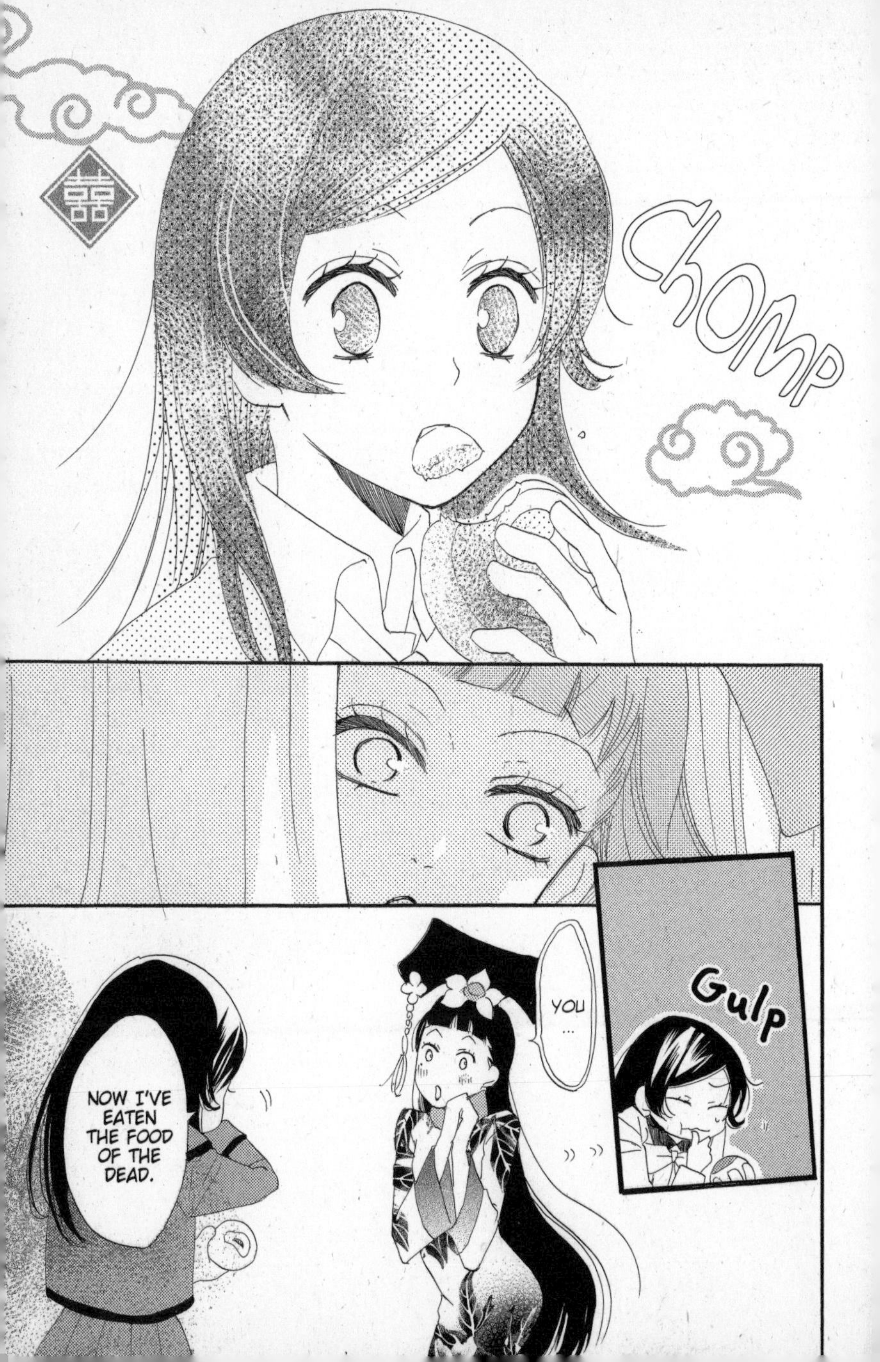
CHOMP
Gulp
YOU ...
NOW I'VE EATEN THE FOOD OF THE DEAD.

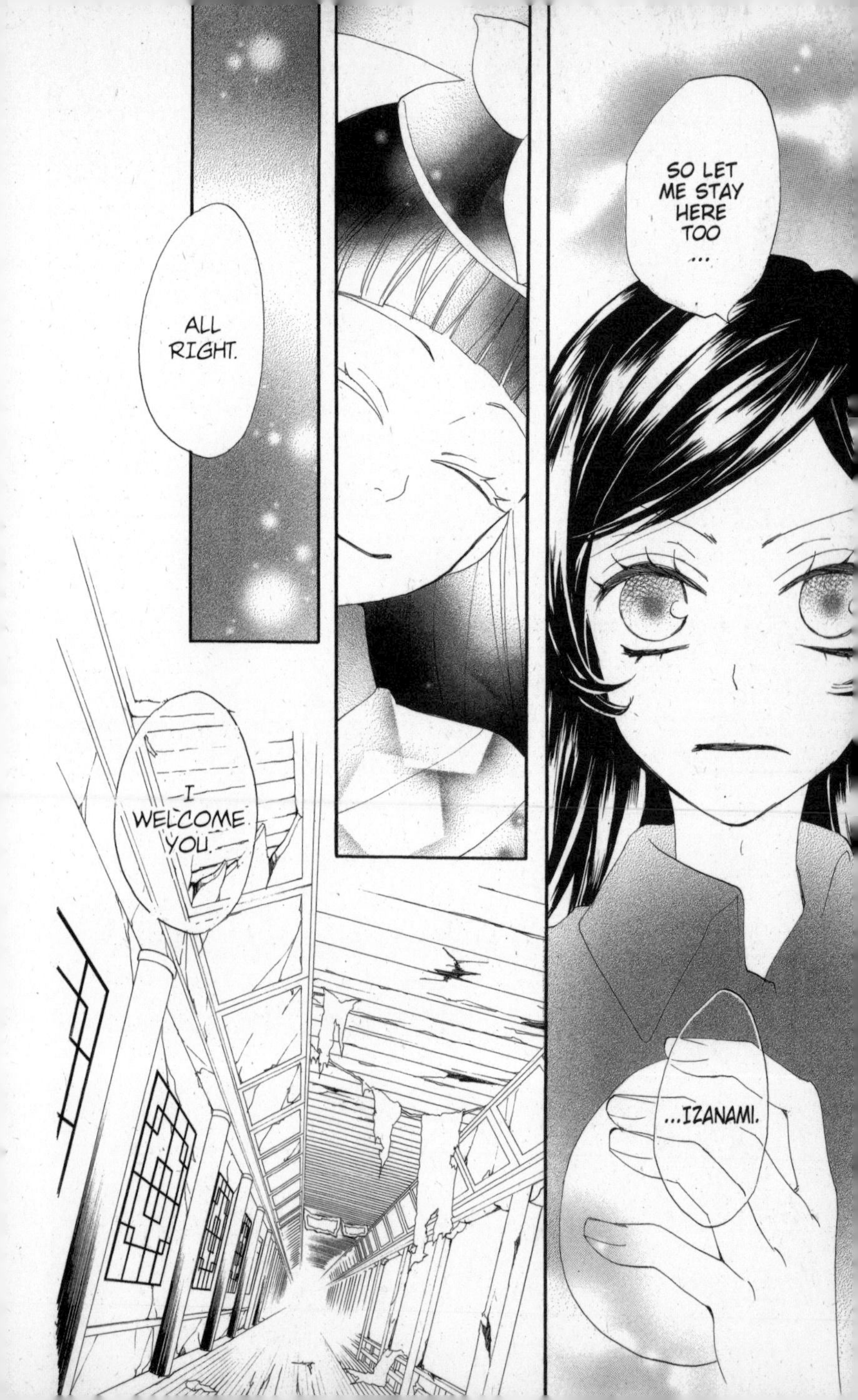
SO LET ME STAY HERE TOO ...
...IZANAMI.
ALL RIGHT.
I WELCOME YOU.

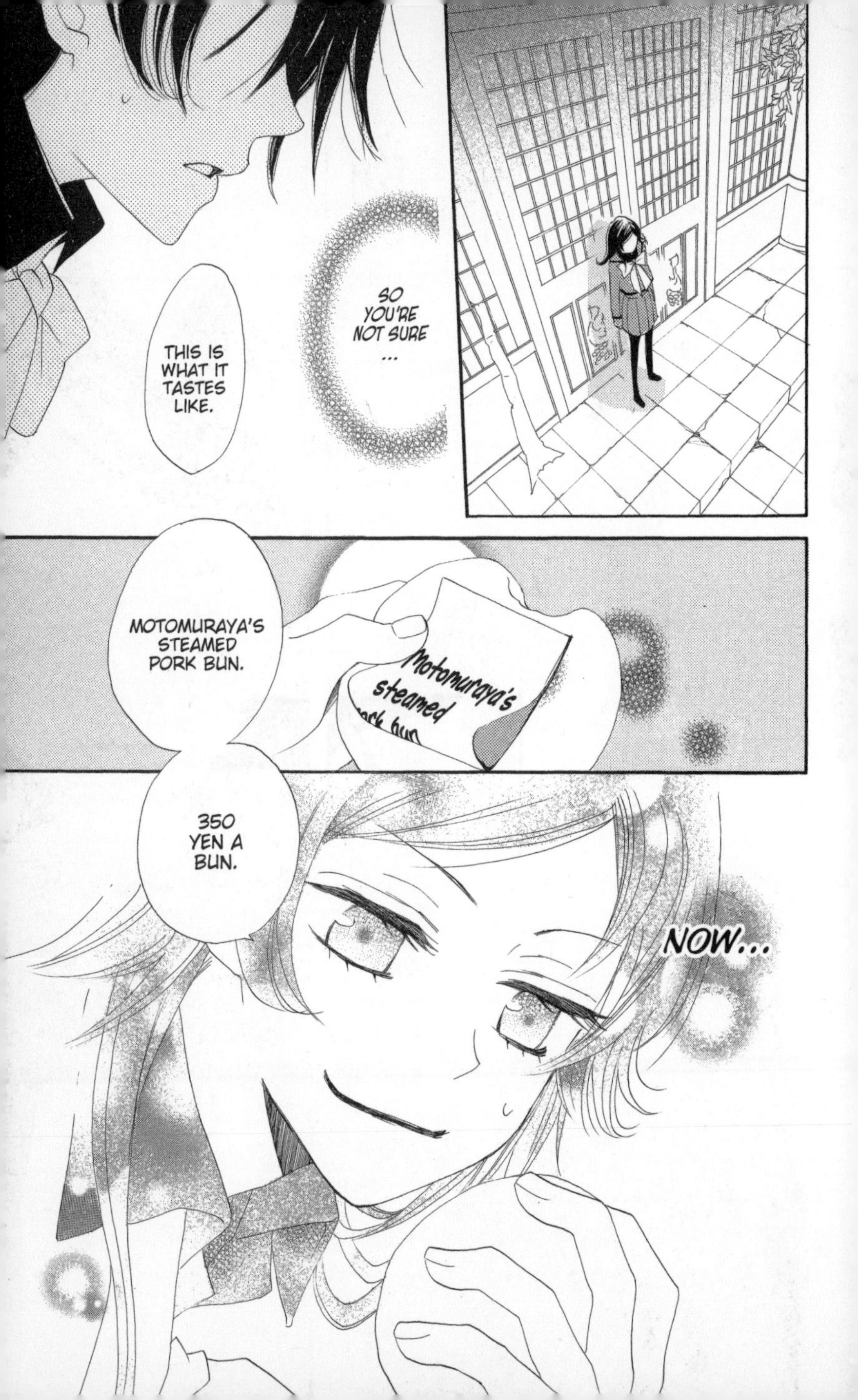
SO YOU'RE NOT SURE ...
THIS IS WHAT IT TASTES LIKE.
MOTOMURAYA'S STEAMED PORK BUN.
Motomuraya's steamed
350 YEN A BUN.
NOW...

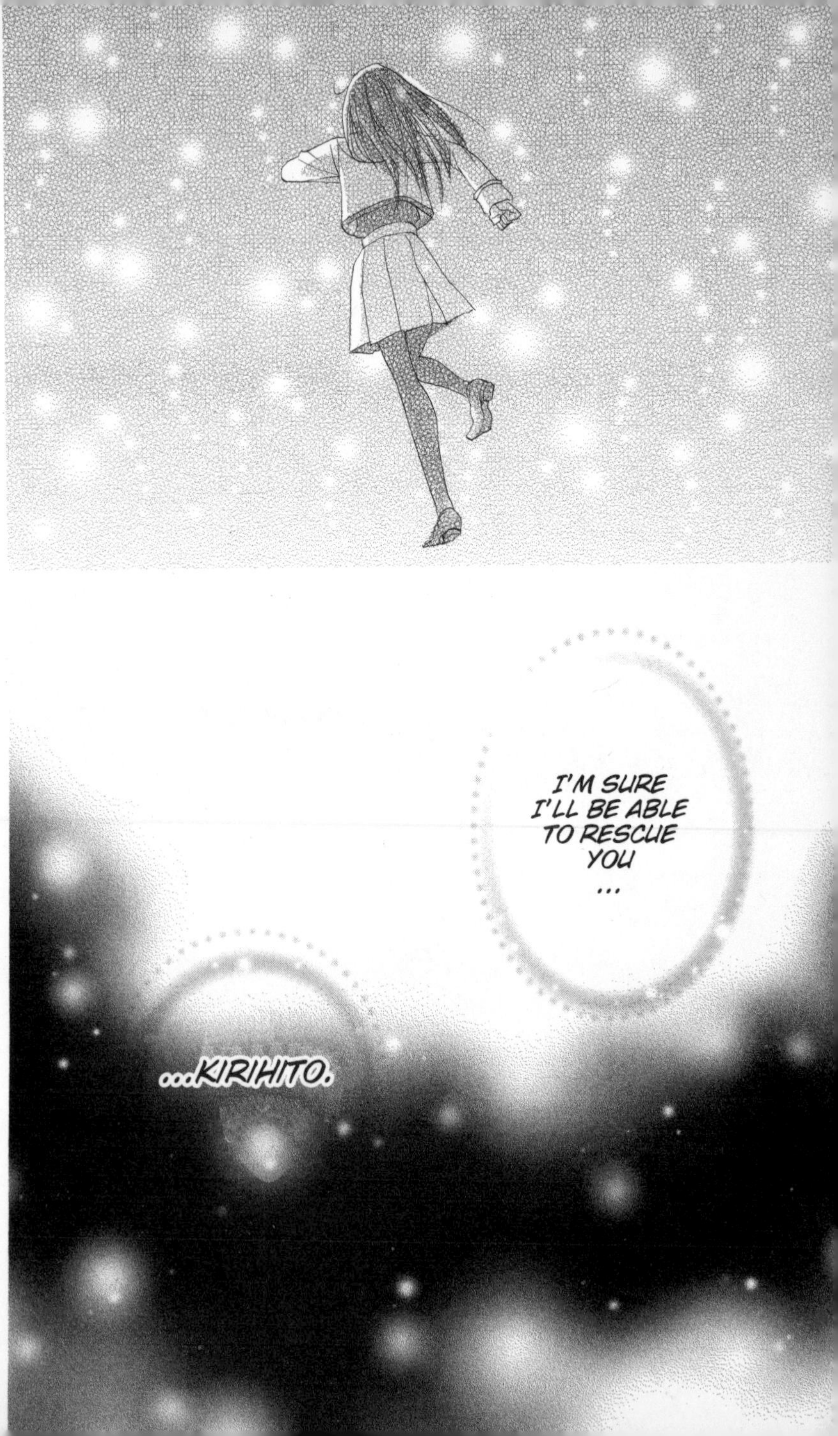
I'M SURE I'LL BE ABLE TO RESCUE YOU ...
...KIRIHITO.

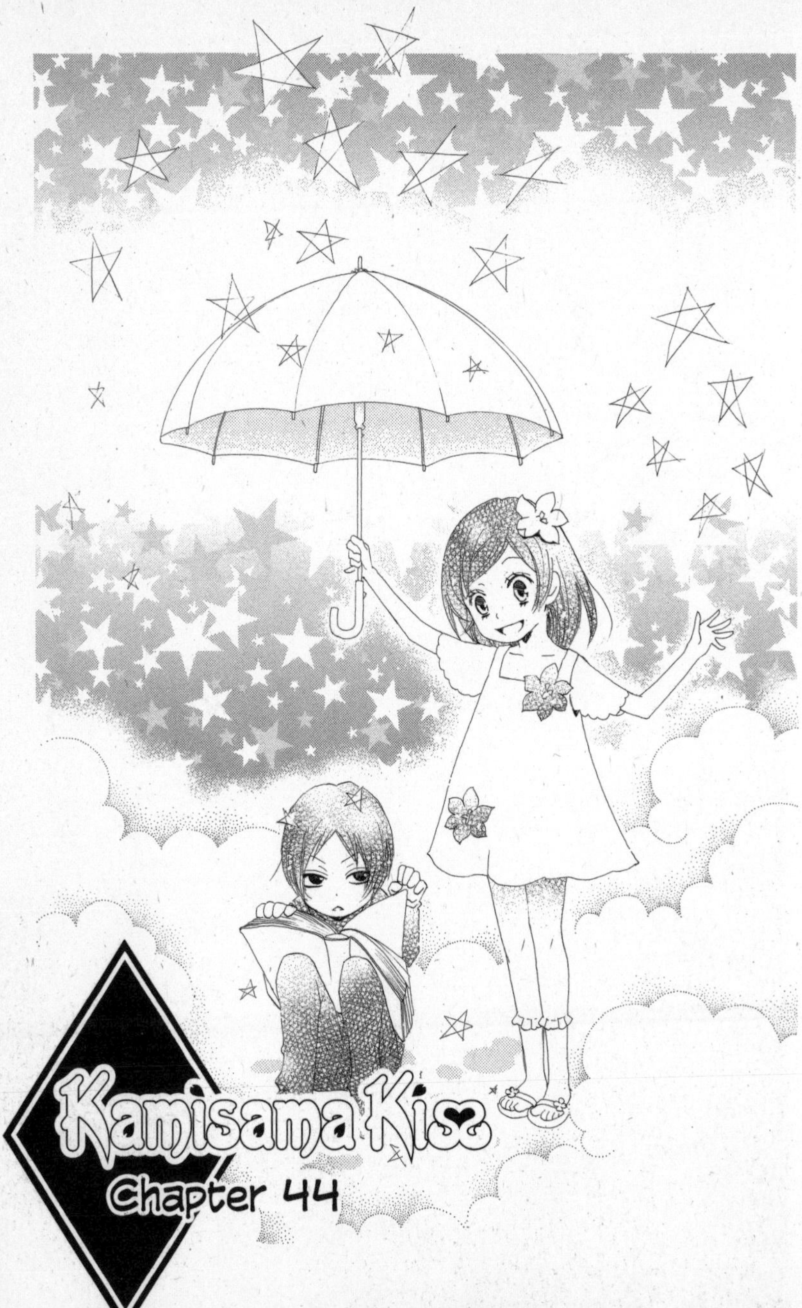
Kamisama Kiss
Chapter 44

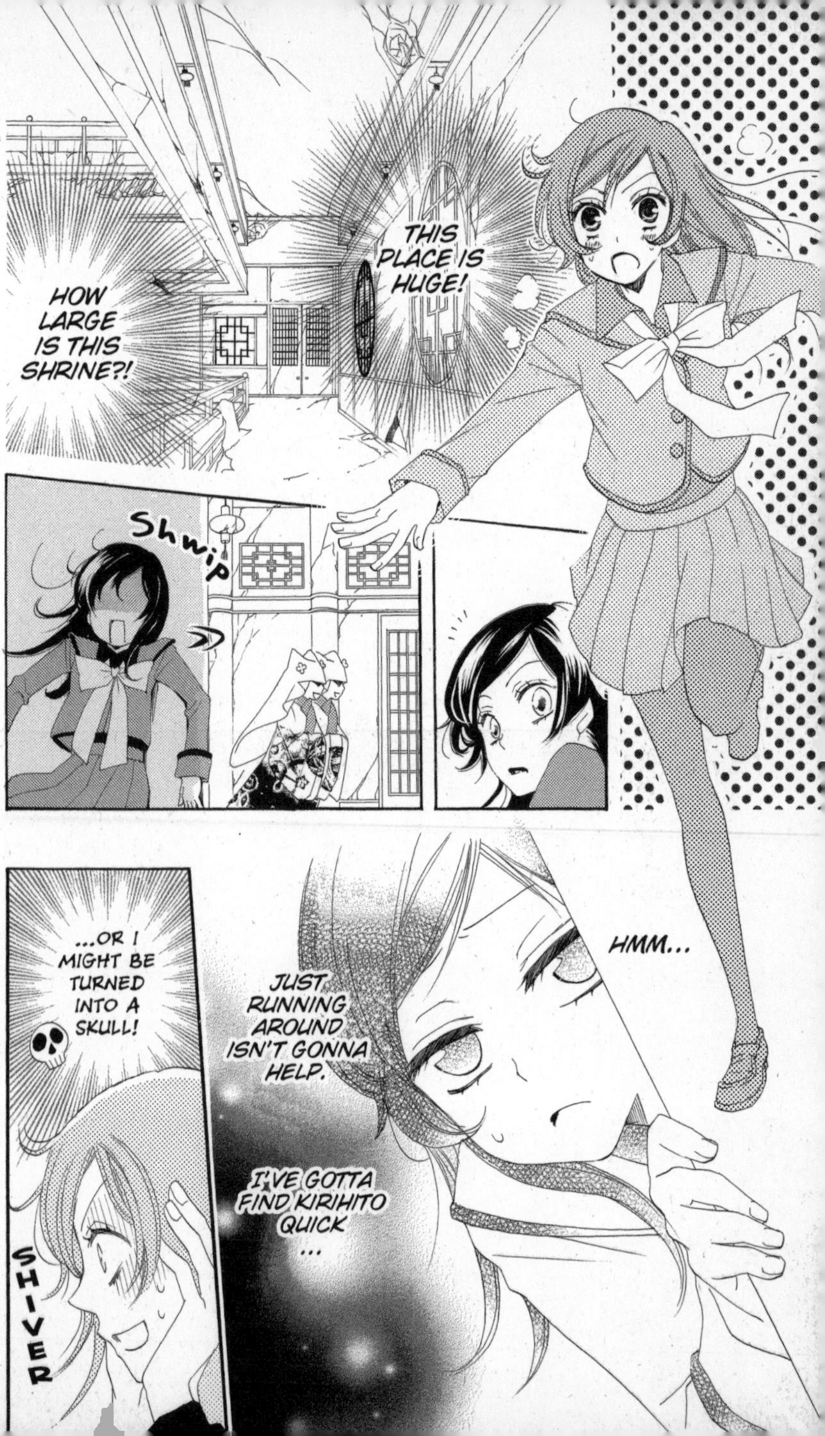
THIS PLACE IS HUGE!
HOW LARGE IS THIS SHRINE?!
Shwip
HMM...
JUST RUNNING AROUND ISN'T GONNA HELP.
I'VE GOTTA FIND KIRIHITO QUICK ...
...OR I MIGHT BE TURNED INTO A SKULL!
SHIVER

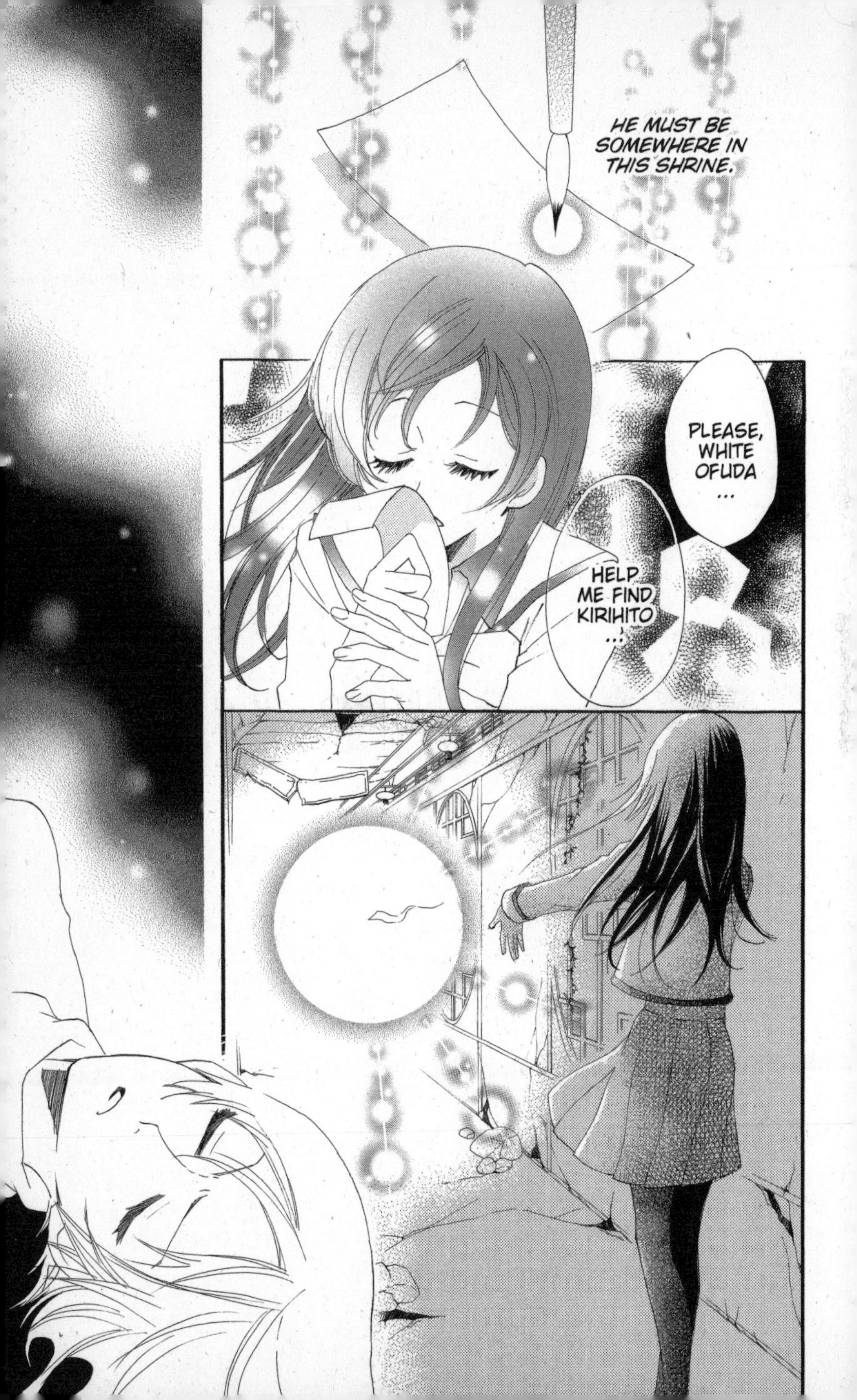
HE MUST BE SOMEWHERE IN THIS SHRINE.
PLEASE, WHITE OFUDA ...
HELP ME FIND KIRIHITO ...

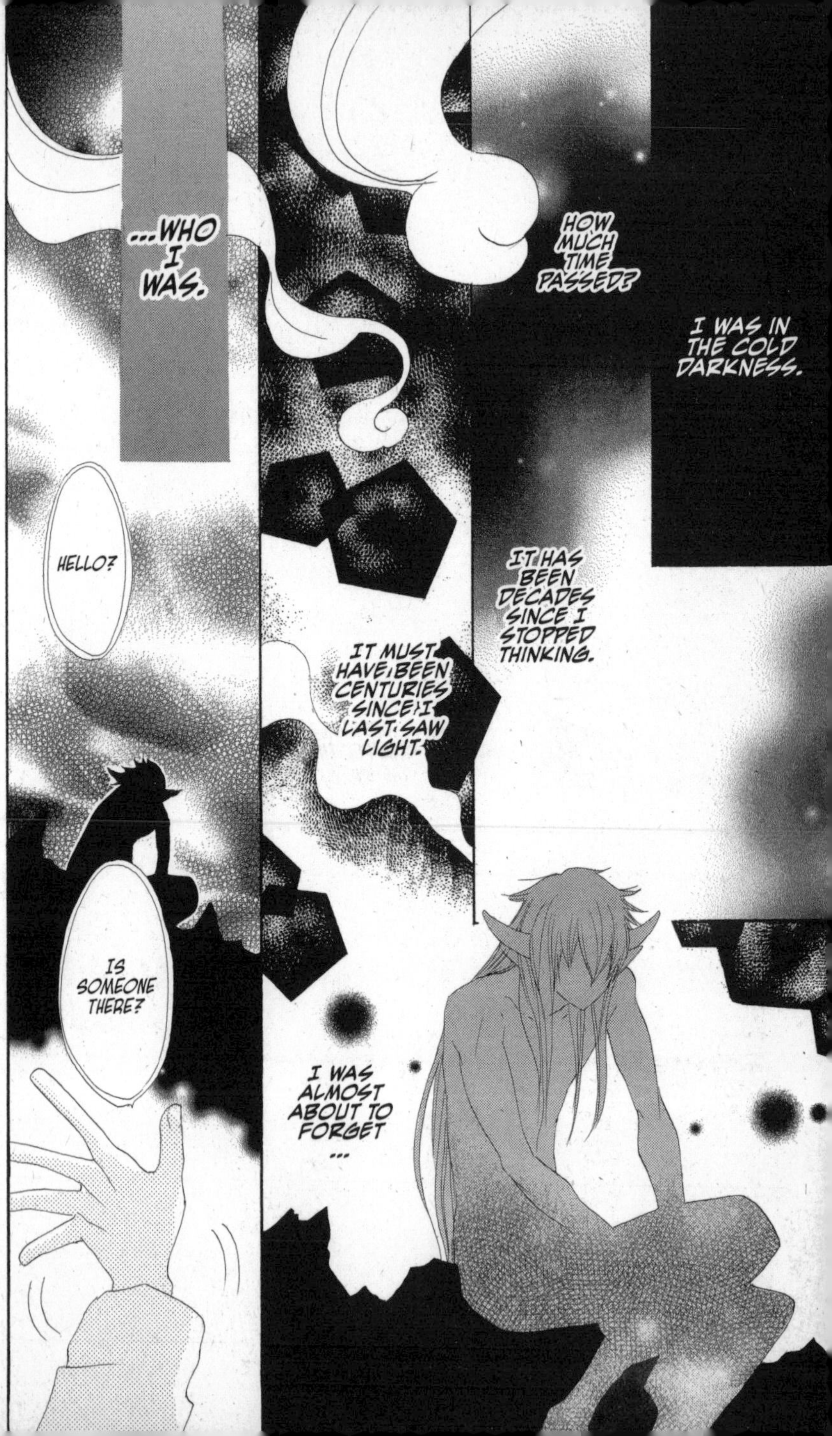
I WAS IN THE COLD DARKNESS.
HOW MUCH TIME PASSED?
IT HAS BEEN DECADES SINCE I STOPPED THINKING.
IT MUST HAVE BEEN CENTURIES SINCE I LAST SAW LIGHT.
I WAS ALMOST ABOUT TO FORGET ...
...WHO I WAS.
HELLO?
IS SOMEONE THERE?

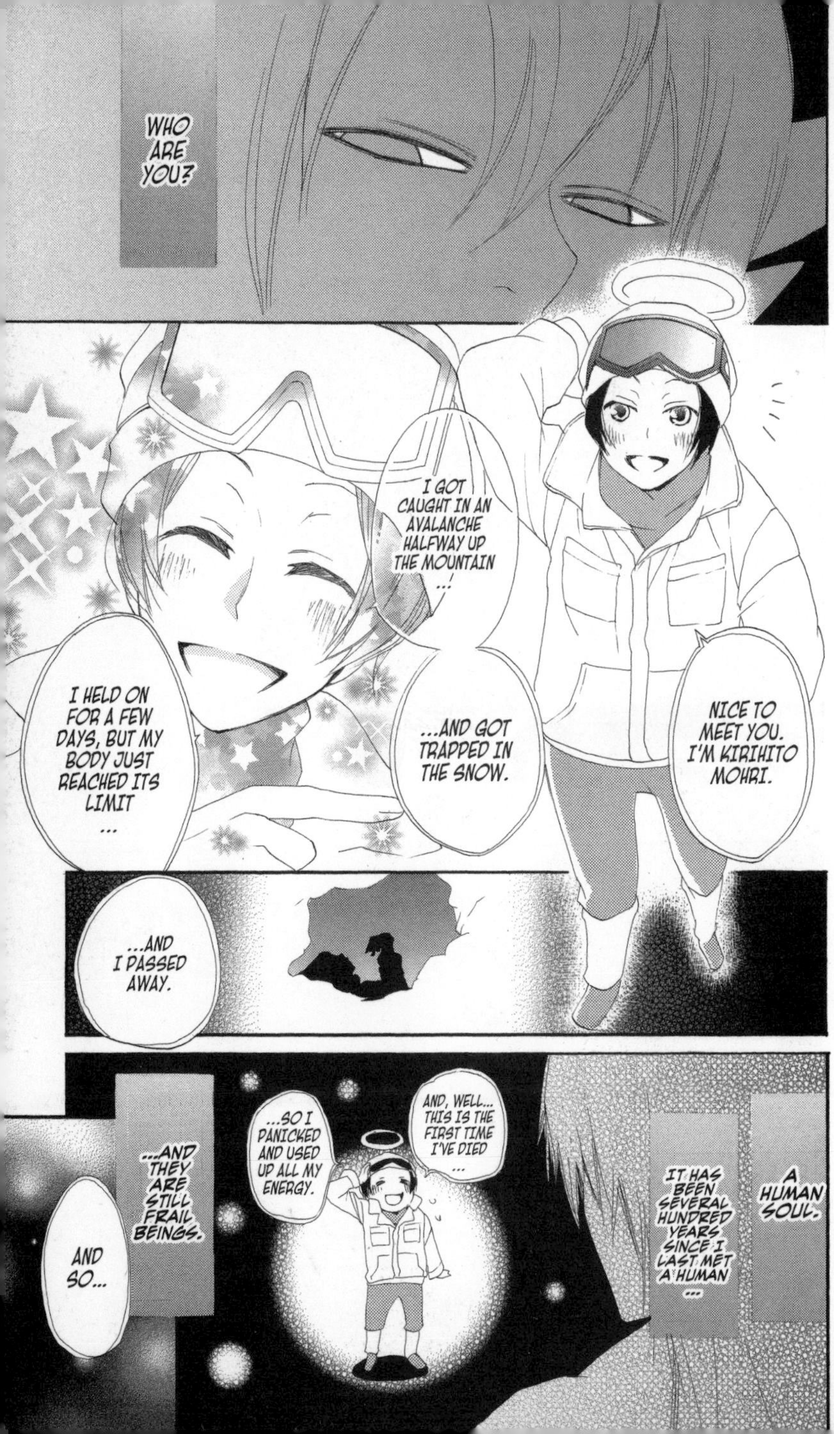
WHO ARE YOU?
NICE TO MEET YOU. I'M KIRIHITO MOHRI.
I GOT CAUGHT IN AN AVALANCHE HALFWAY UP THE MOUNTAIN...!
...AND GOT TRAPPED IN THE SNOW.
I HELD ON FOR A FEW DAYS, BUT MY BODY JUST REACHED ITS LIMIT...
...AND I PASSED AWAY.
A HUMAN SOUL.
IT HAS BEEN SEVERAL HUNDRED YEARS SINCE I LAST MET A HUMAN...
AND, WELL... THIS IS THE FIRST TIME I'VE DIED...
...SO I PANICKED AND USED UP ALL MY ENERGY.
...AND THEY ARE STILL FRAIL BEINGS.
AND SO...

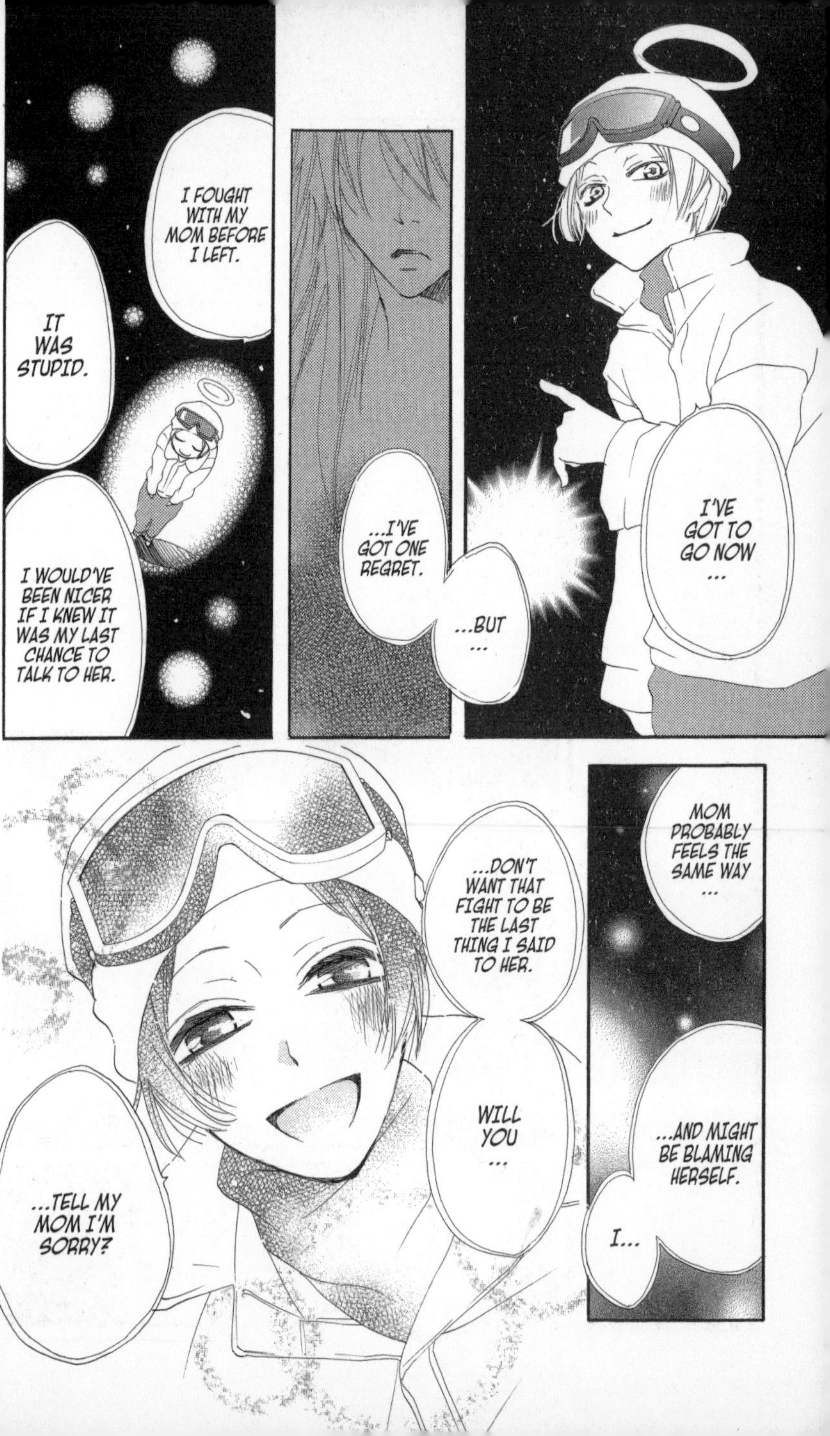
I'VE GOT TO GO NOW ...
...BUT ...
...I'VE GOT ONE REGRET.
I FOUGHT WITH MY MOM BEFORE I LEFT.
IT WAS STUPID.
I WOULD'VE BEEN NICER IF I KNEW IT WAS MY LAST CHANCE TO TALK TO HER.
MOM PROBABLY FEELS THE SAME WAY ...
...AND MIGHT BE BLAMING HERSELF.
I...
...DON'T WANT THAT FIGHT TO BE THE LAST THING I SAID TO HER.
WILL YOU ...
...TELL MY MOM I'M SORRY?

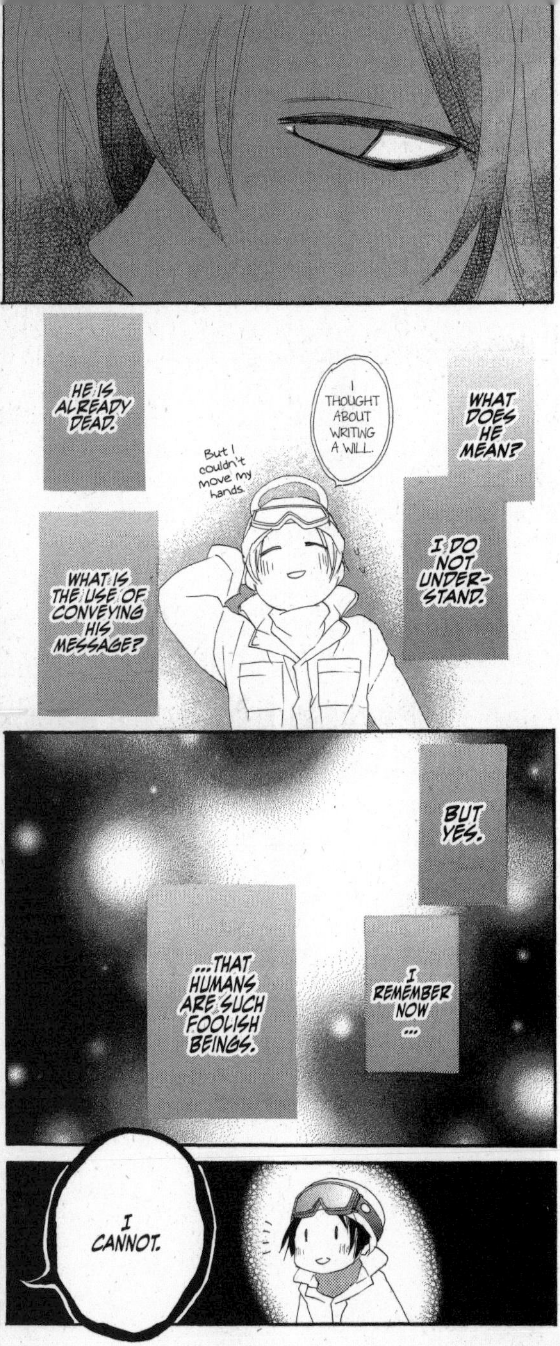
WHAT DOES HE MEAN?
I DO NOT UNDERSTAND.
I THOUGHT ABOUT WRITING A WILL.
But I couldn't move my hands.
HE IS ALREADY DEAD.
WHAT IS THE USE OF CONVEYING HIS MESSAGE?
BUT YES.
I REMEMBER NOW...
...THAT HUMANS ARE SUCH FOOLISH BEINGS.
I CANNOT.

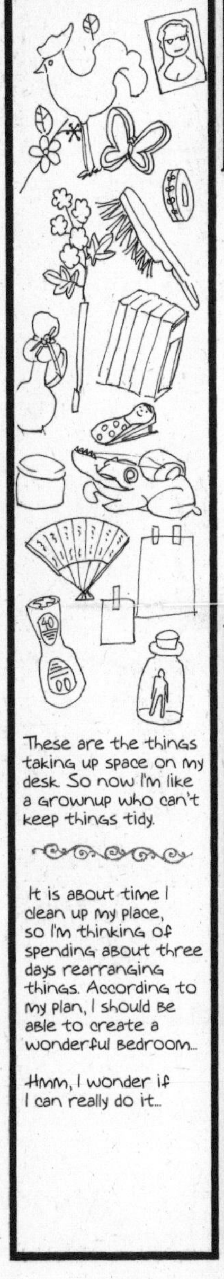

These are the things taking up space on my desk. So now I'm like a grownup who can't keep things tidy.

It is about time I clean up my place, so I'm thinking of spending about three days rearranging things. According to my plan, I should be able to create a wonderful bedroom...

Hmm, I wonder if I can really do it...

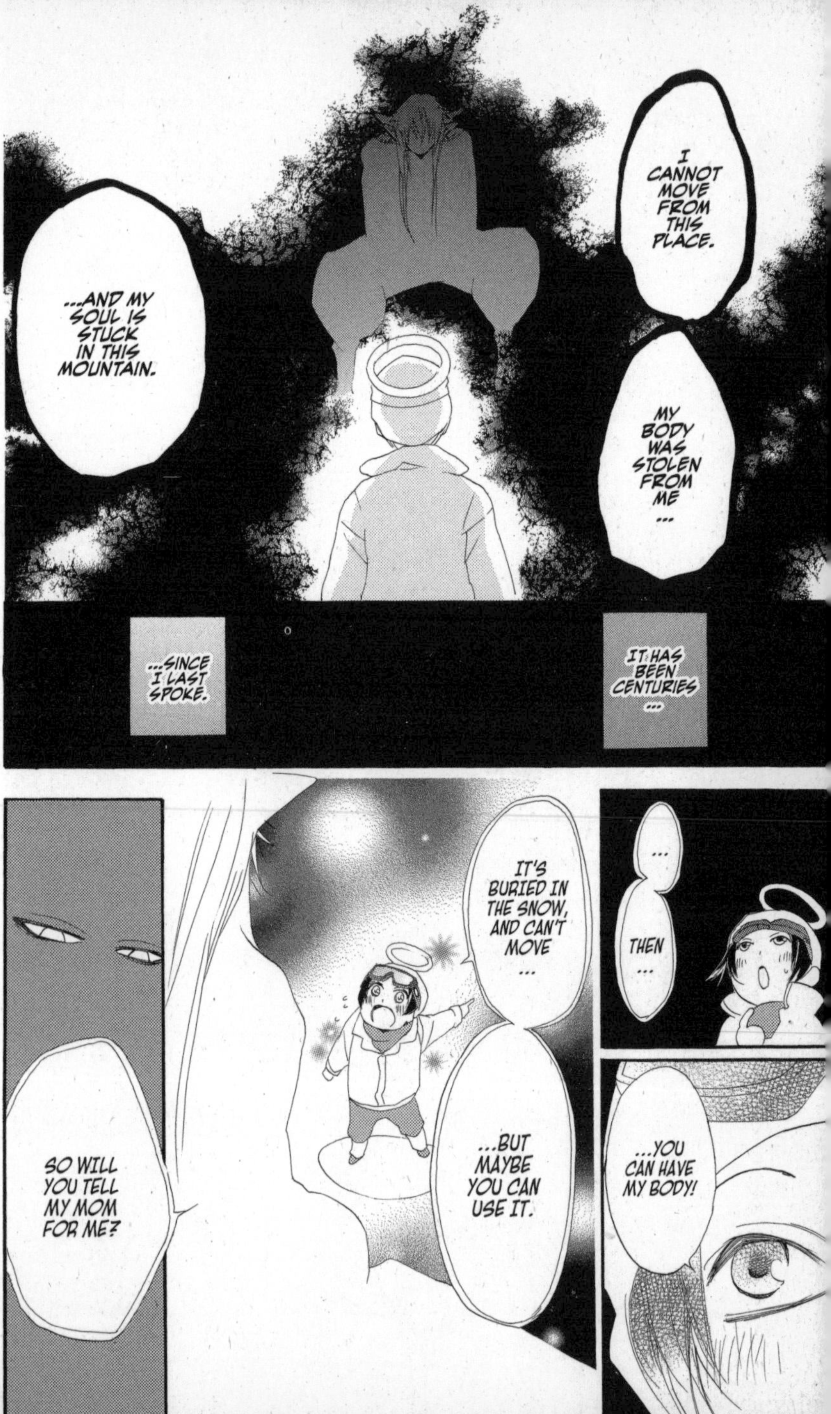
I CANNOT MOVE FROM THIS PLACE.
MY BODY WAS STOLEN FROM ME...
...AND MY SOUL IS STUCK IN THIS MOUNTAIN.
IT HAS BEEN CENTURIES...
...SINCE I LAST SPOKE.
...
THEN...
...YOU CAN HAVE MY BODY!
IT'S BURIED IN THE SNOW, AND CAN'T MOVE...
...BUT MAYBE YOU CAN USE IT.
SO WILL YOU TELL MY MOM FOR ME?

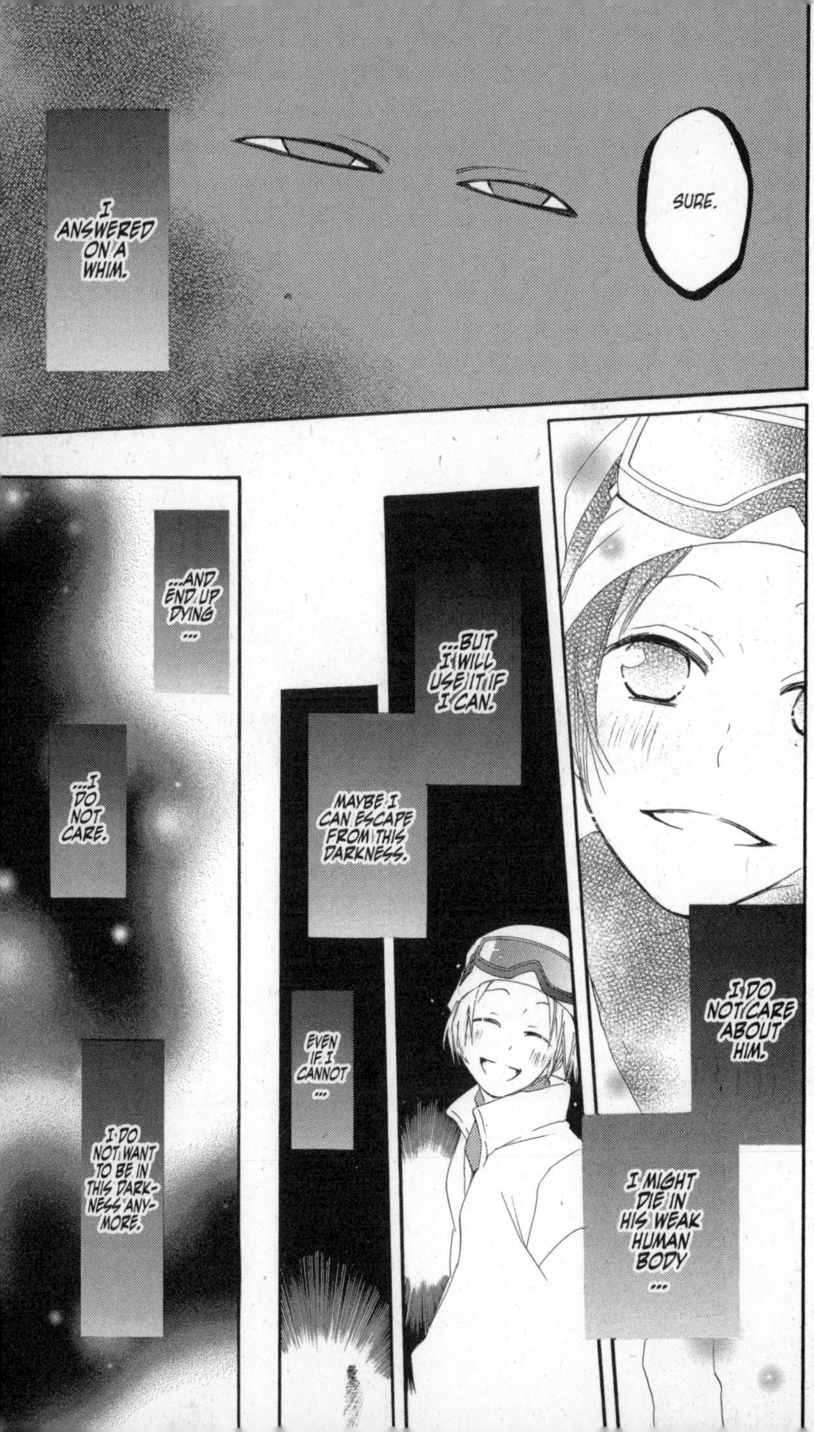
SURE.
I ANSWERED ON A WHIM.
I DO NOT CARE ABOUT HIM.
I MIGHT DIE IN HIS WEAK HUMAN BODY ...
...BUT I WILL USE IT IF I CAN.
MAYBE I CAN ESCAPE FROM THIS DARKNESS.
EVEN IF I CANNOT ...
...AND END UP DYING ...
...I DO NOT CARE.
I DO NOT WANT TO BE IN THIS DARK-NESS ANY-MORE.

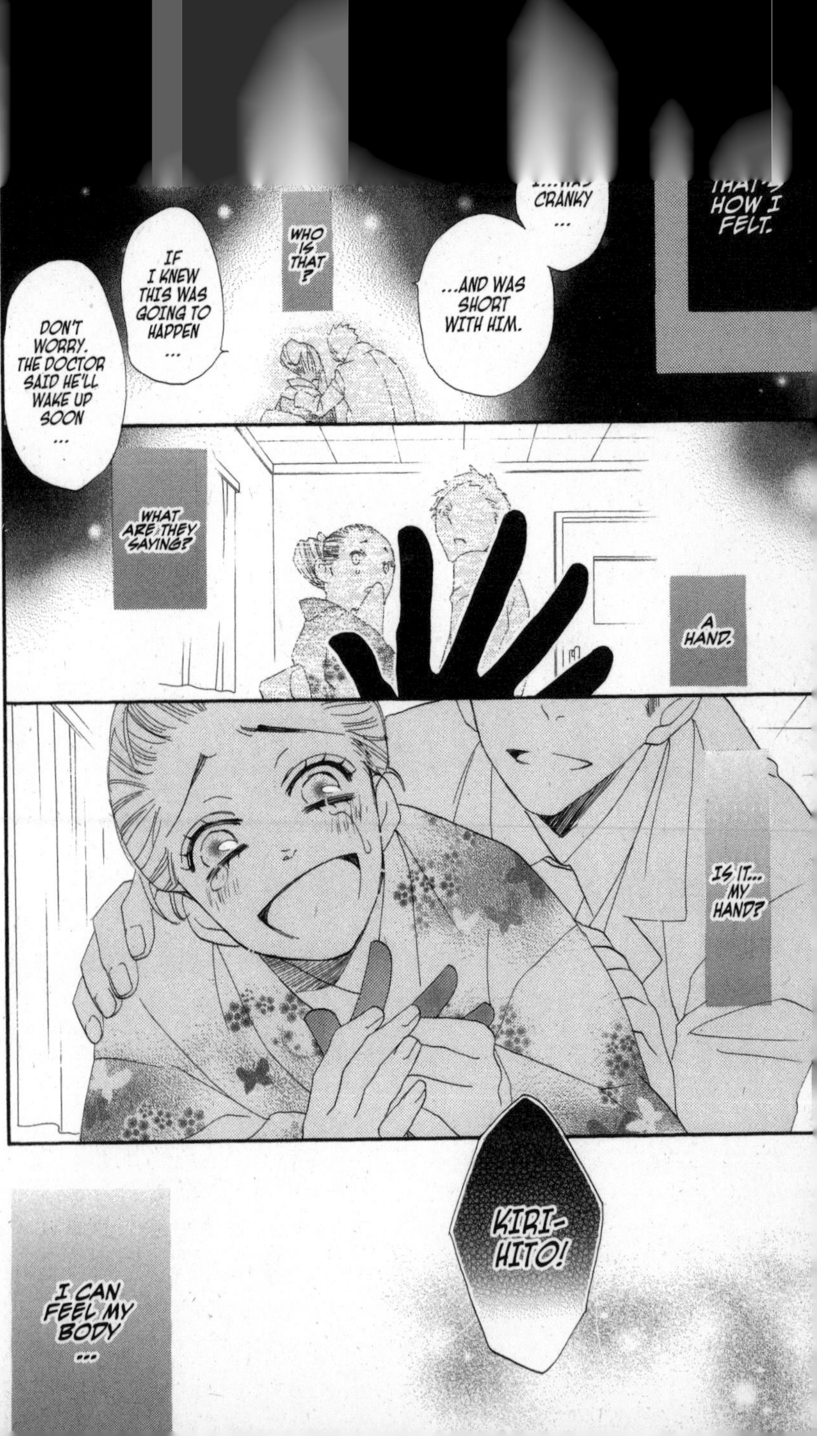
HOW I FELT.
CRANKY...
...AND WAS SHORT WITH HIM.
WHO IS THAT?
IF I KNEW THIS WAS GOING TO HAPPEN...
DON'T WORRY. THE DOCTOR SAID HE'LL WAKE UP SOON...
A HAND.
WHAT ARE THEY SAYING?
IS IT... MY HAND?
KIRI-HITO!
I CAN FEEL MY BODY...

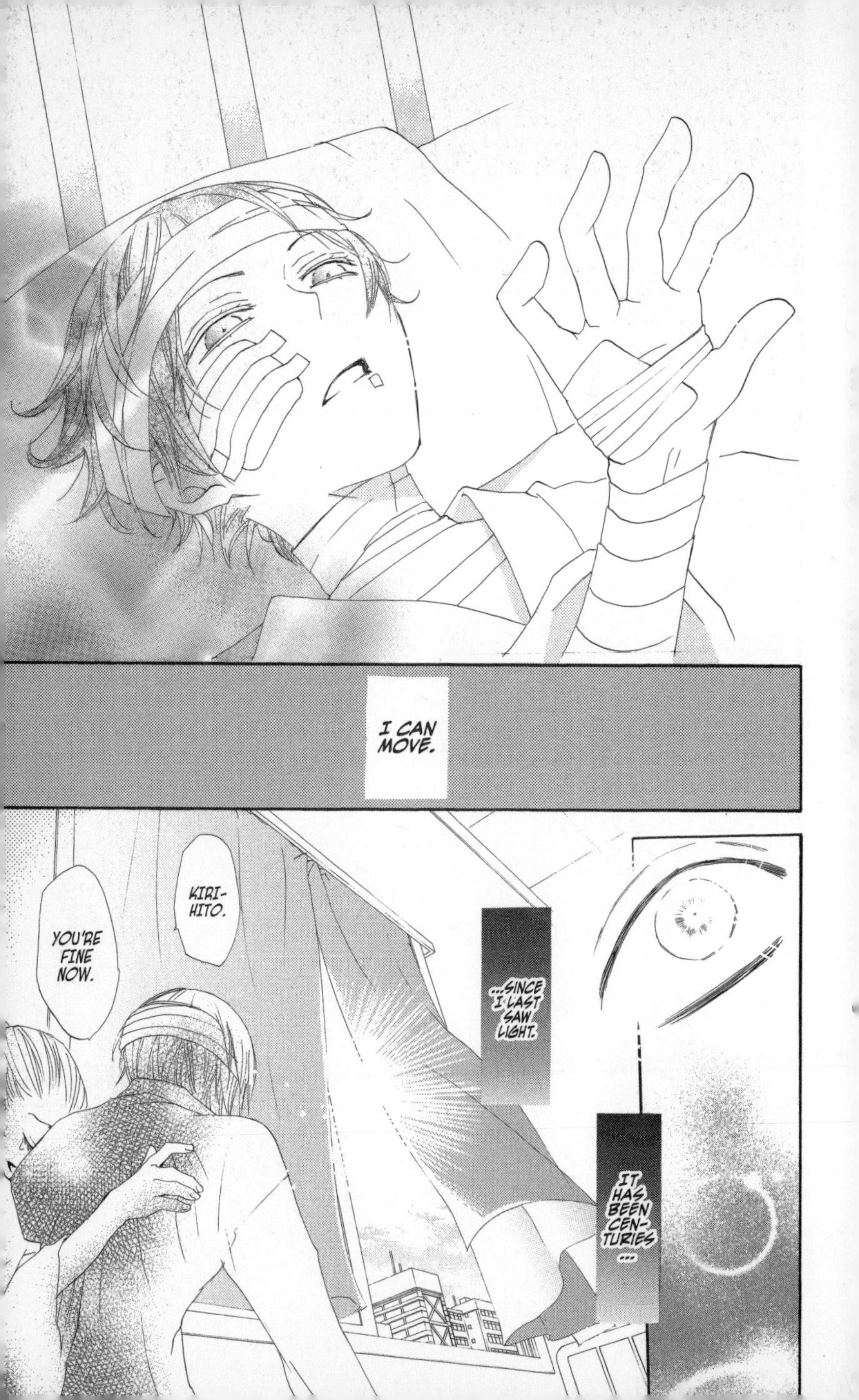
I CAN MOVE.
IT HAS BEEN CEN-TURIES...
...SINCE I LAST SAW LIGHT.
KIRI-HITO.
YOU'RE FINE NOW.

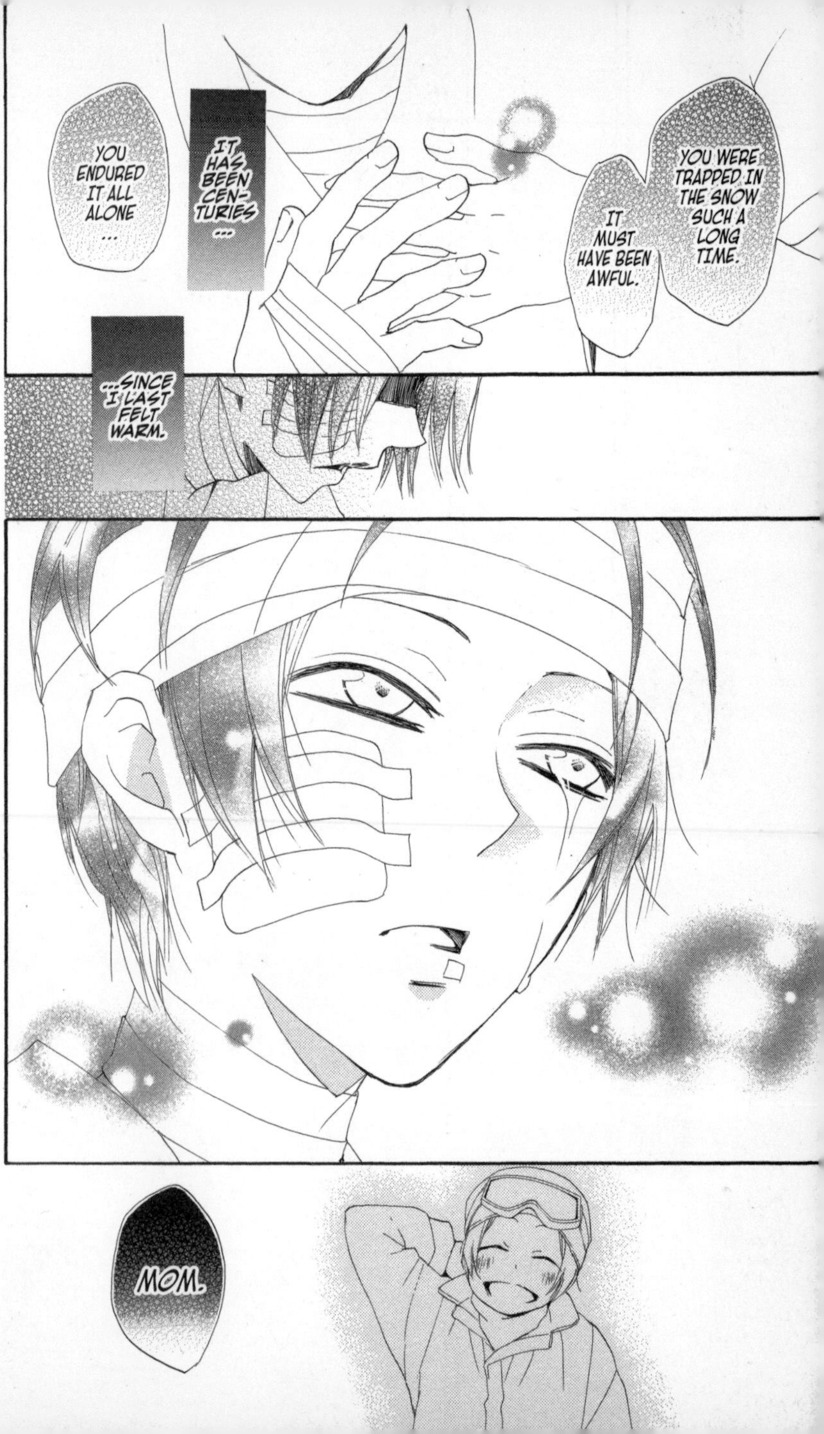
YOU WERE TRAPPED IN THE SNOW SUCH A LONG TIME.
IT MUST HAVE BEEN AWFUL.
IT HAS BEEN CENTURIES...
YOU ENDURED IT ALL ALONE...
...SINCE I LAST FELT WARM.
MOM.

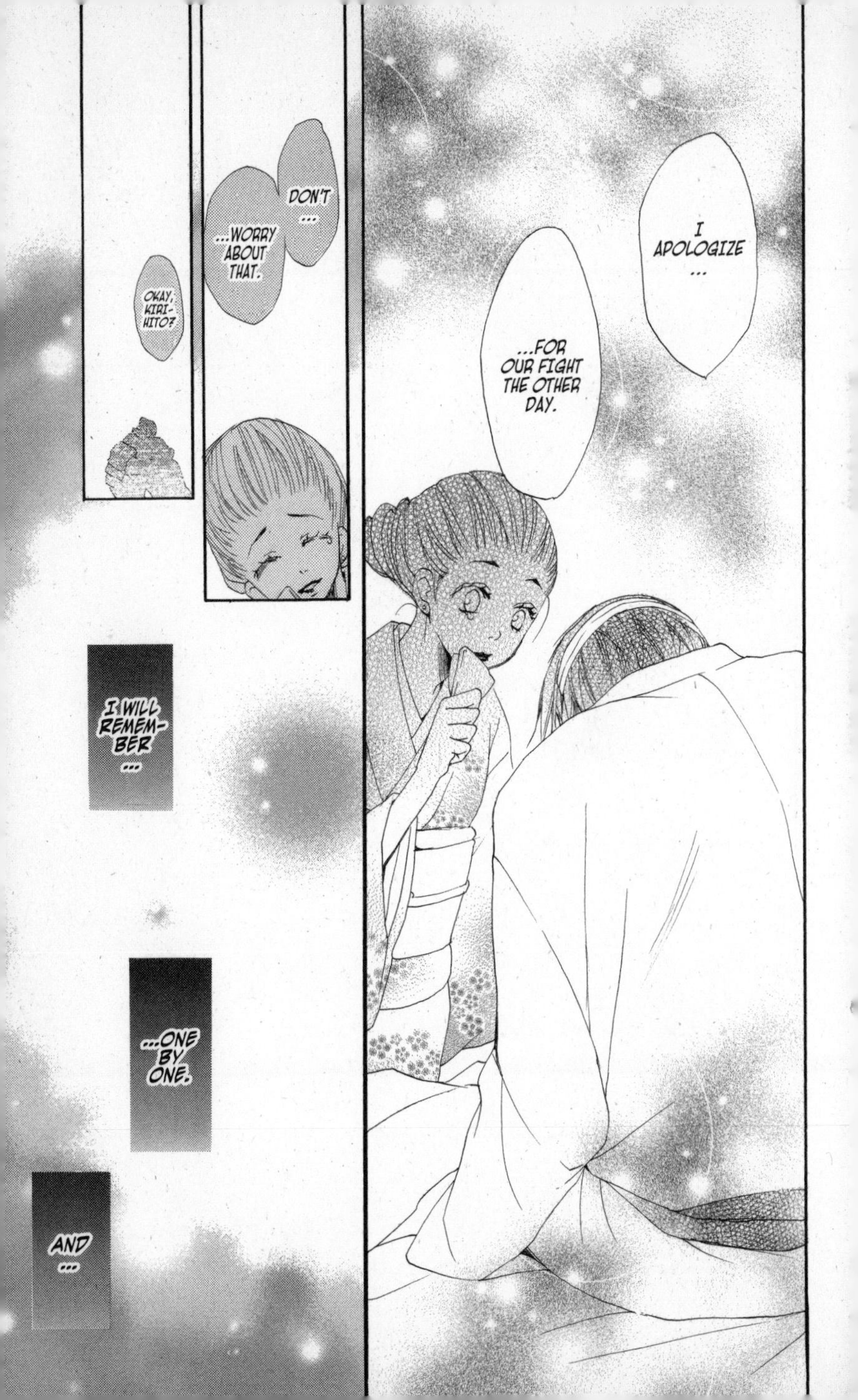
I APOLOGIZE ...
...FOR OUR FIGHT THE OTHER DAY.
DON'T ...
...WORRY ABOUT THAT.
OKAY, KIRI-HITO?
I WILL REMEMBER ...
...ONE BY ONE.
AND ...

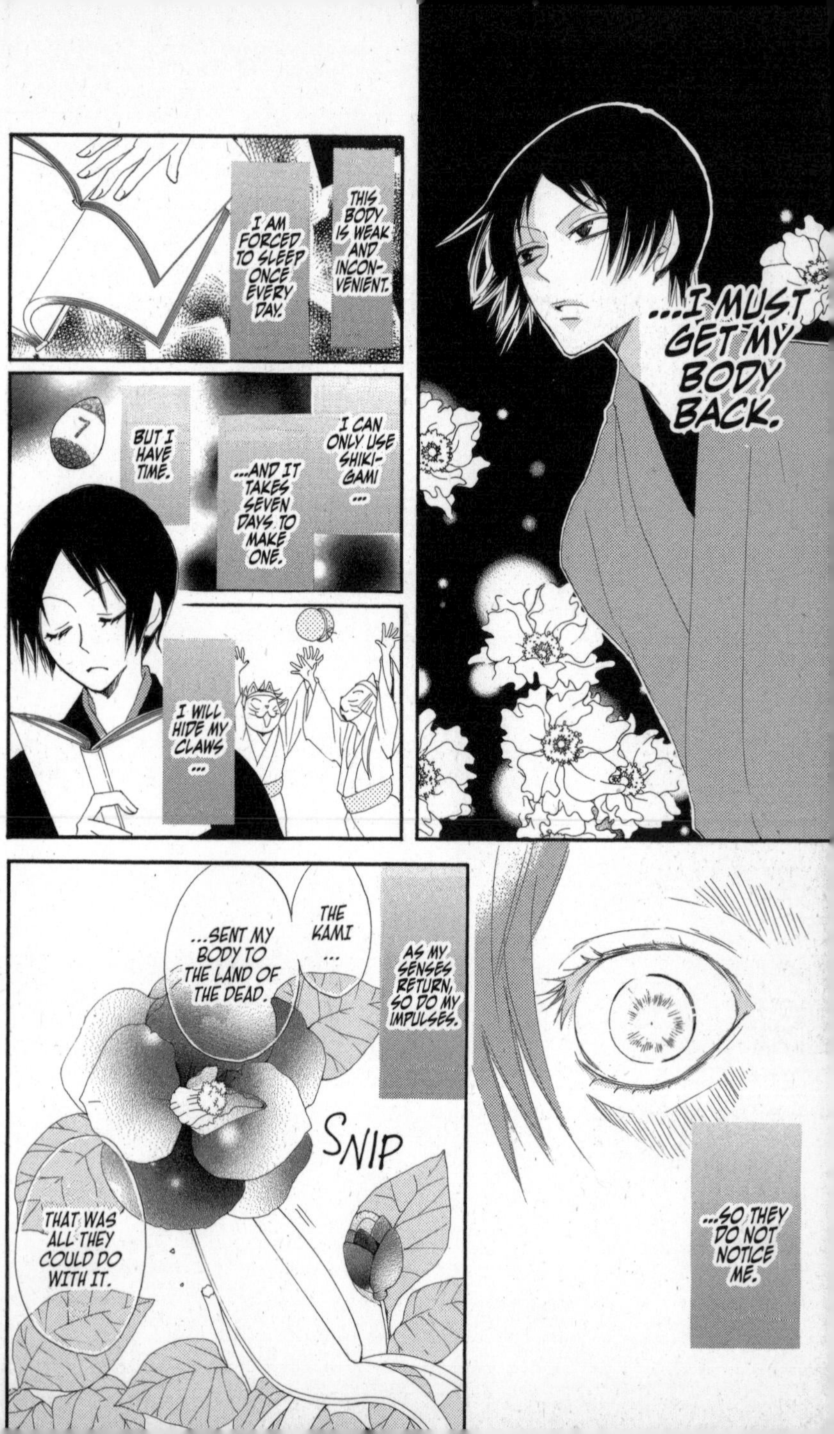
...I MUST GET MY BODY BACK.
THIS BODY IS WEAK AND INCONVENIENT.
I AM FORCED TO SLEEP ONCE EVERY DAY.
I CAN ONLY USE SHIKIGAMI...
...AND IT TAKES SEVEN DAYS TO MAKE ONE.
BUT I HAVE TIME.
I WILL HIDE MY CLAWS...
...SO THEY DO NOT NOTICE ME.
AS MY SENSES RETURN, SO DO MY IMPULSES.
THE KAMI...
...SENT MY BODY TO THE LAND OF THE DEAD.
SNIP
THAT WAS ALL THEY COULD DO WITH IT.

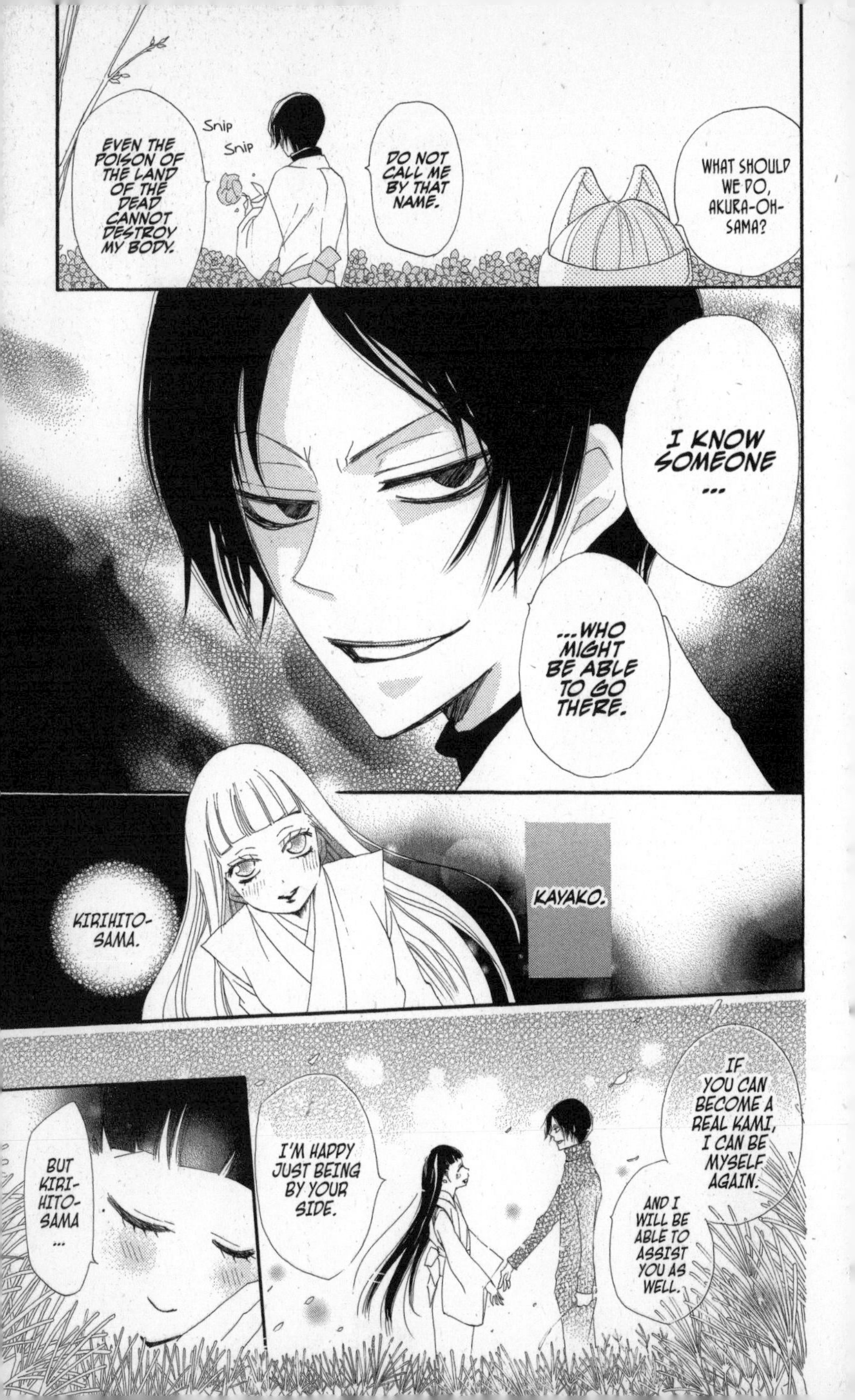
WHAT SHOULD WE DO, AKURA-OH-SAMA?
DO NOT CALL ME BY THAT NAME.
Snip
Snip
EVEN THE POISON OF THE LAND OF THE DEAD CANNOT DESTROY MY BODY.
I KNOW SOMEONE ...
...WHO MIGHT BE ABLE TO GO THERE.
KAYAKO.
KIRIHITO-SAMA.
IF YOU CAN BECOME A REAL KAMI, I CAN BE MYSELF AGAIN.
AND I WILL BE ABLE TO ASSIST YOU AS WELL.
I'M HAPPY JUST BEING BY YOUR SIDE.
BUT KIRIHITO-SAMA ...

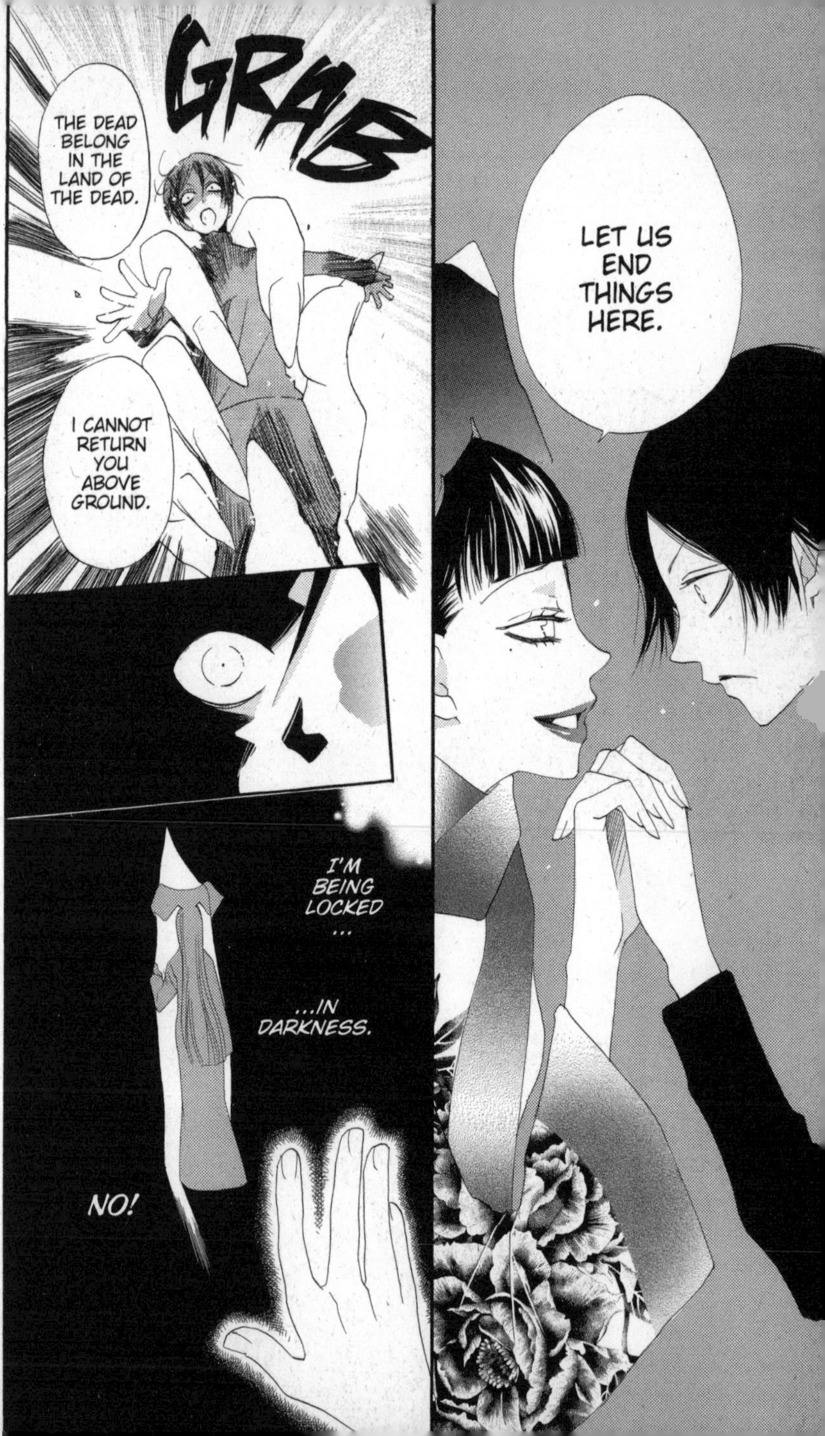
LET US END THINGS HERE.
GRAB
THE DEAD BELONG IN THE LAND OF THE DEAD.
I CANNOT RETURN YOU ABOVE GROUND.
I'M BEING LOCKED ...
...IN DARKNESS.
NO!

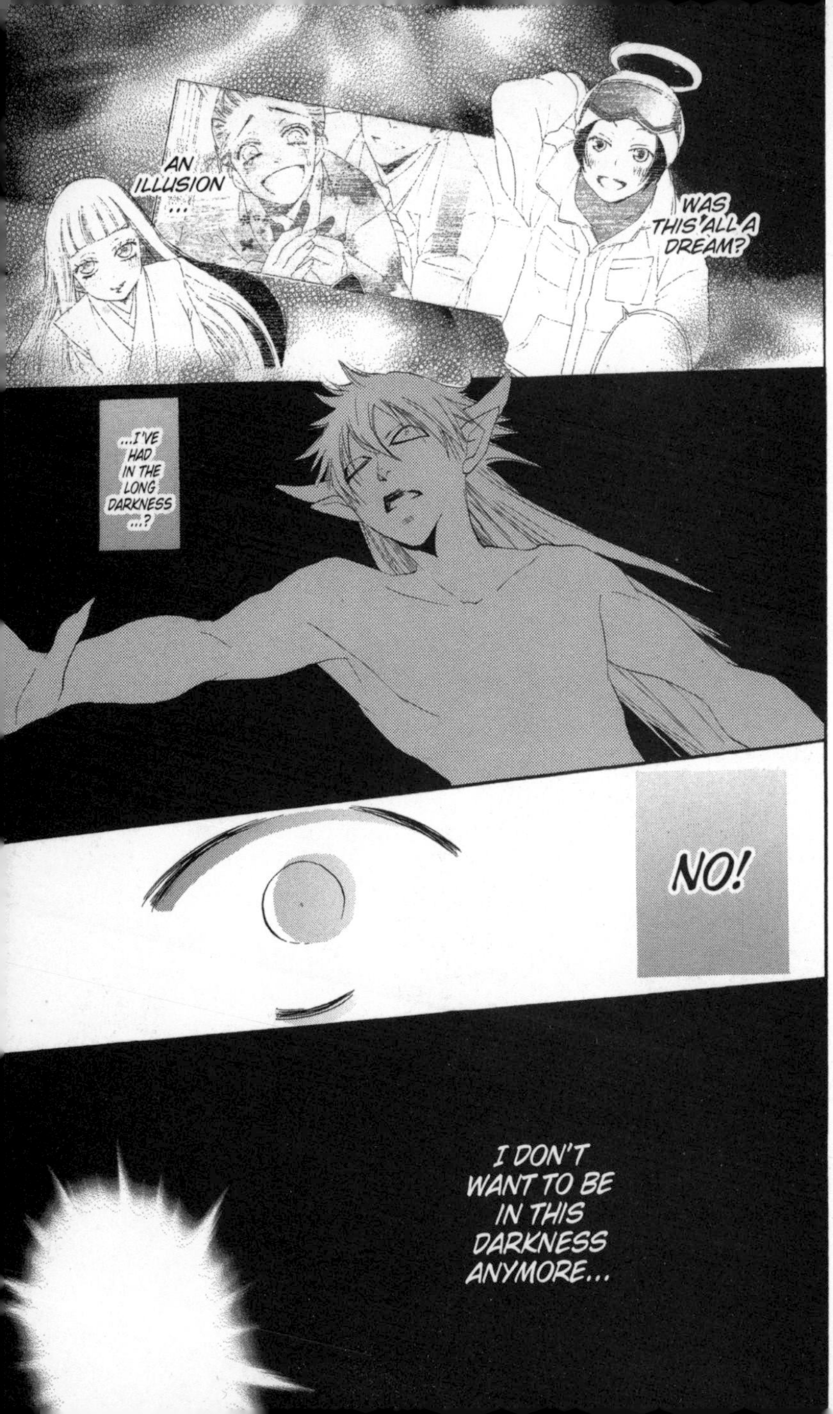
WAS THIS ALL A DREAM?
AN ILLUSION ...
...I'VE HAD IN THE LONG DARKNESS ...?
NO!
I DON'T WANT TO BE IN THIS DARKNESS ANYMORE...

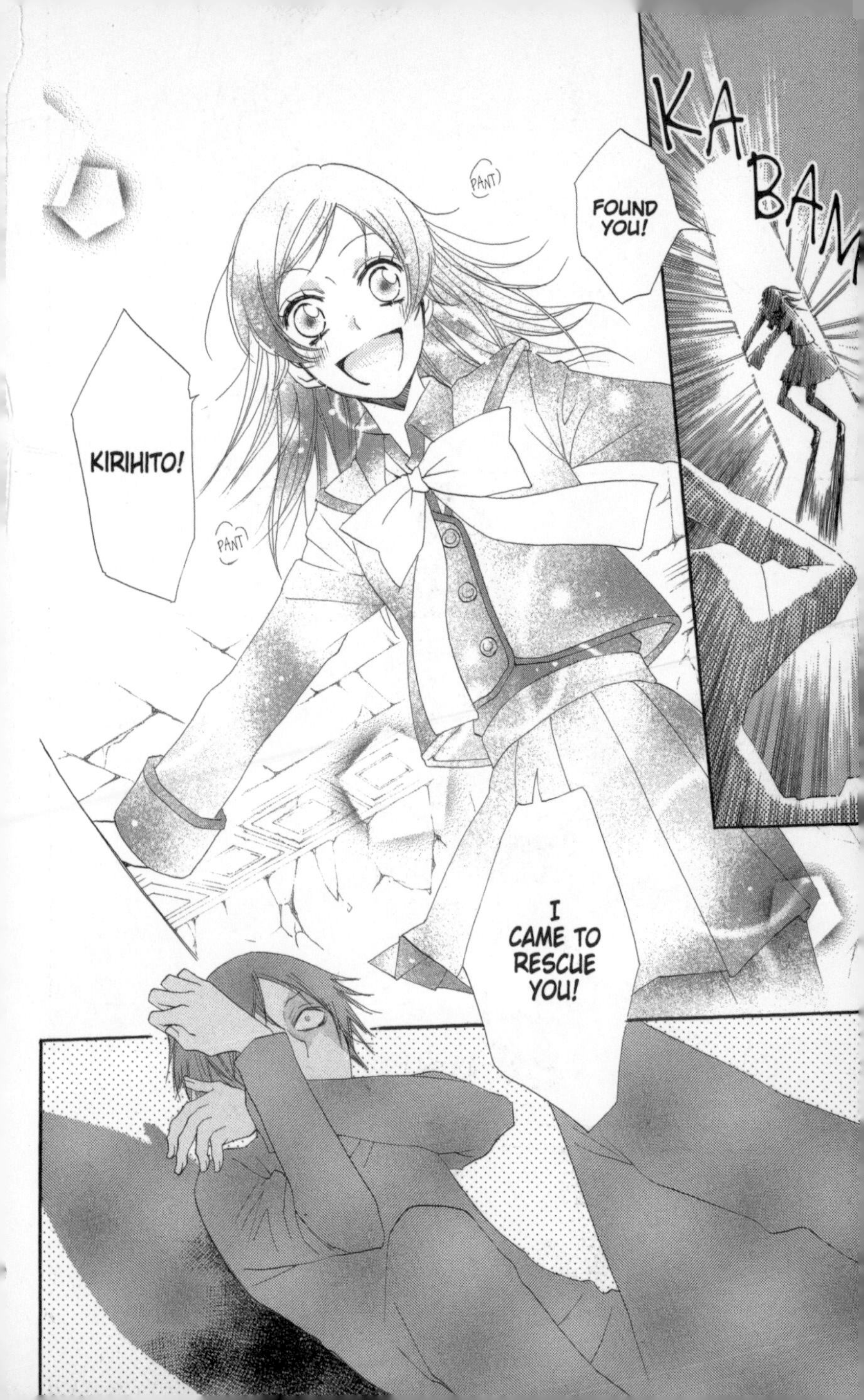
KA BAM
FOUND YOU!
PANT
KIRIHITO!
PANT
I CAME TO RESCUE YOU!

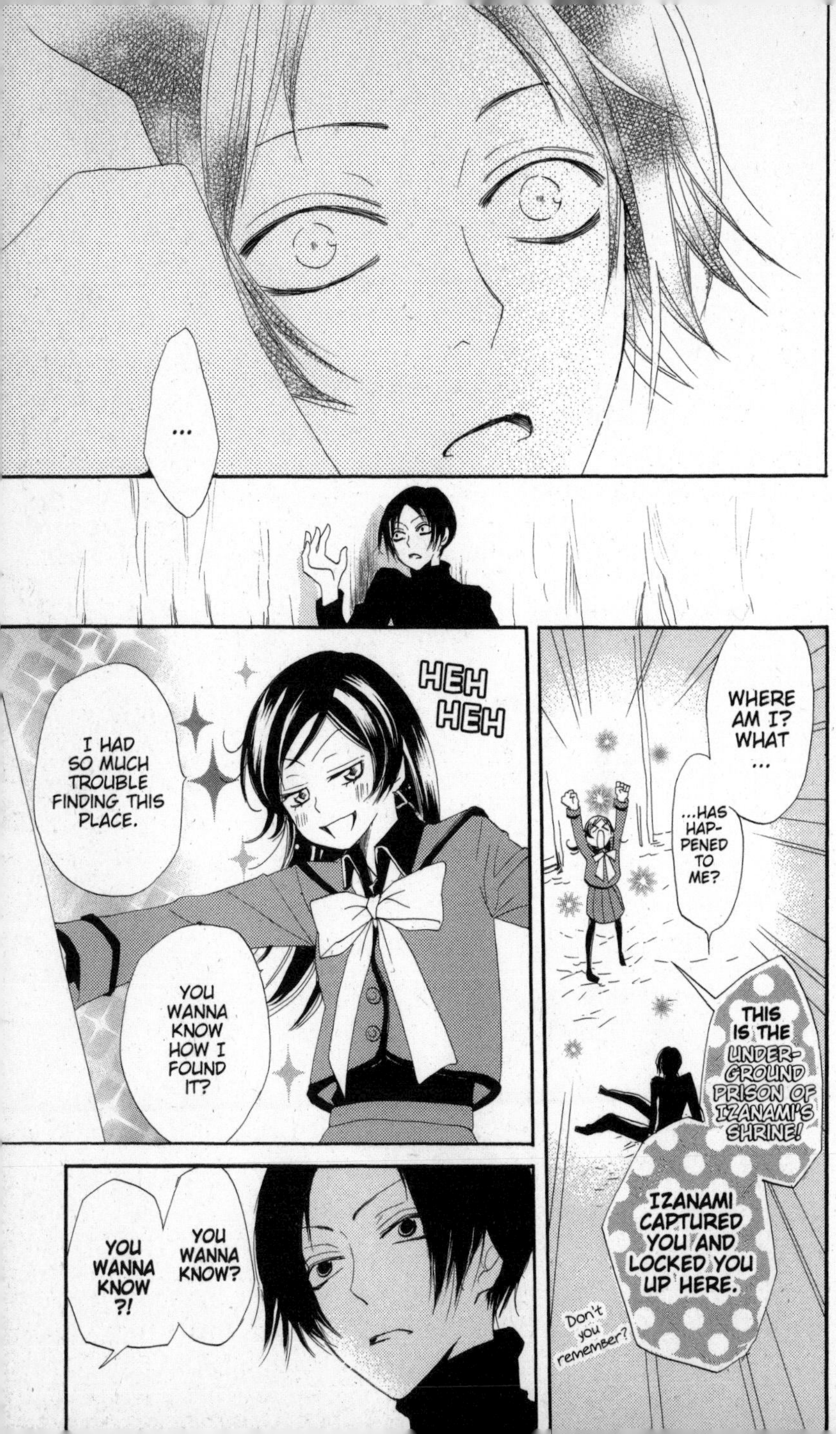
...
WHERE AM I? WHAT...
...HAS HAPPENED TO ME?
THIS IS THE UNDERGROUND PRISON OF IZANAMI'S SHRINE!
IZANAMI CAPTURED YOU AND LOCKED YOU UP HERE.
Don't you remember?
HEH HEH
I HAD SO MUCH TROUBLE FINDING THIS PLACE.
YOU WANNA KNOW HOW I FOUND IT?
YOU WANNA KNOW?
YOU WANNA KNOW?!

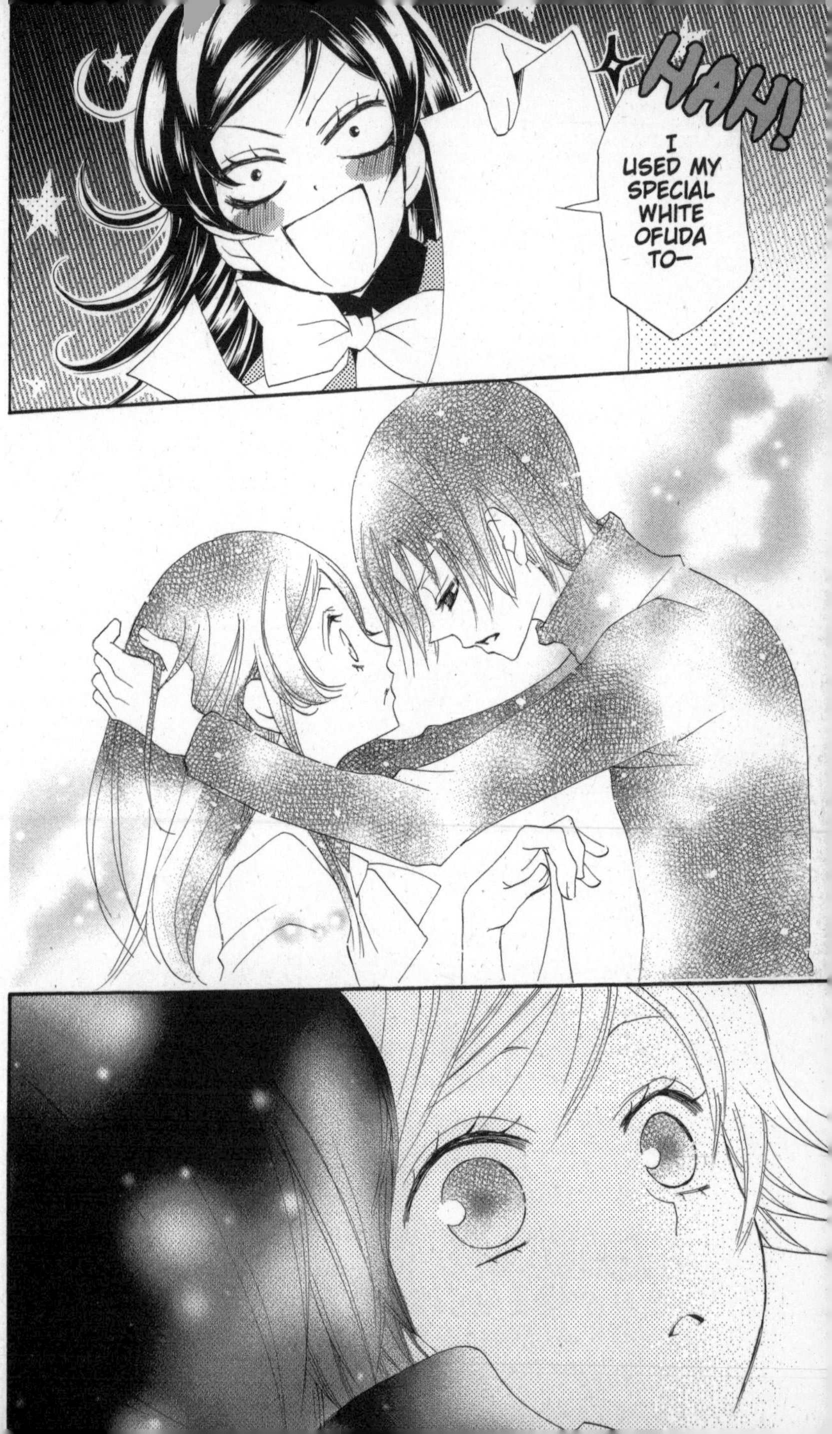
HAH!
I USED MY SPECIAL WHITE OFUDA TO—

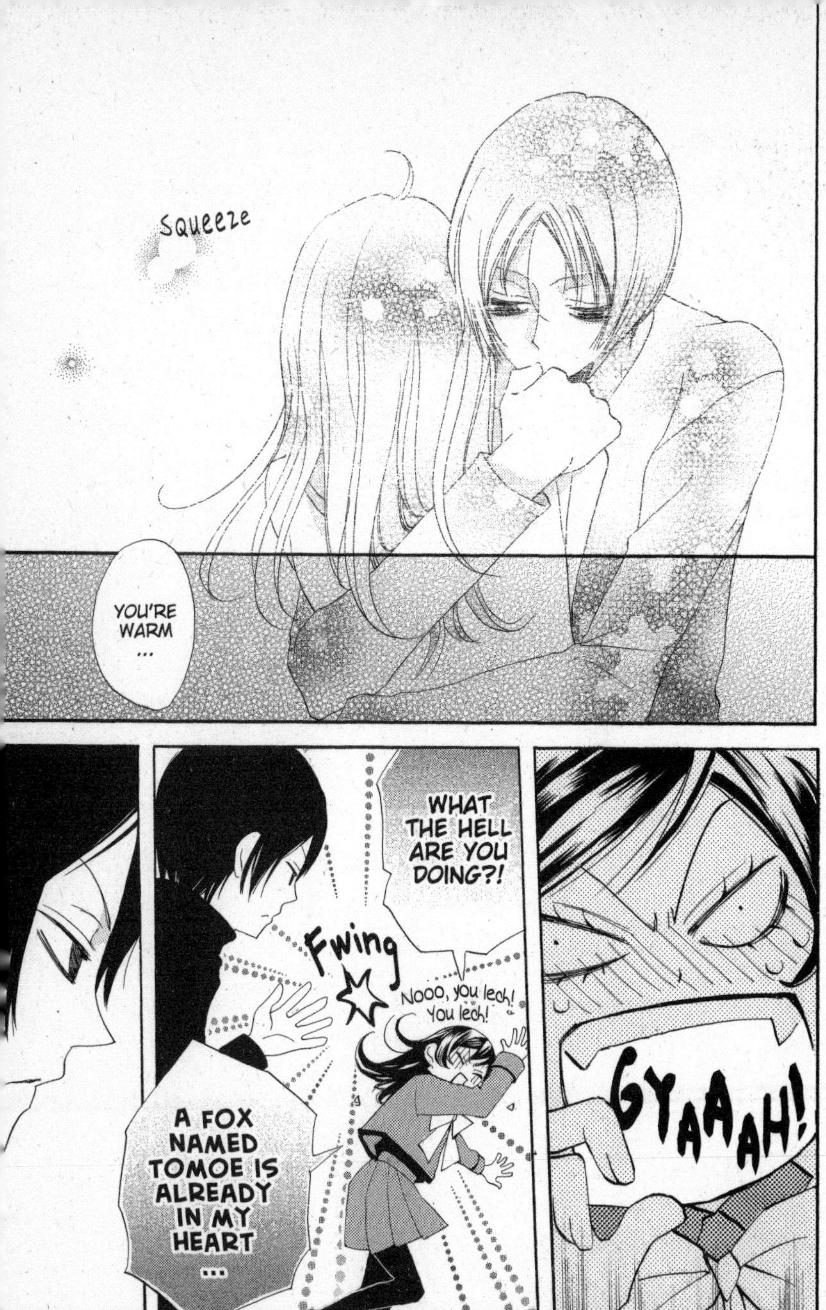
Squeeze
YOU'RE WARM ...
GYAAAH!
WHAT THE HELL ARE YOU DOING?!
Fwing
Nooo, you lech! You lech!
A FOX NAMED TOMOE IS ALREADY IN MY HEART ...

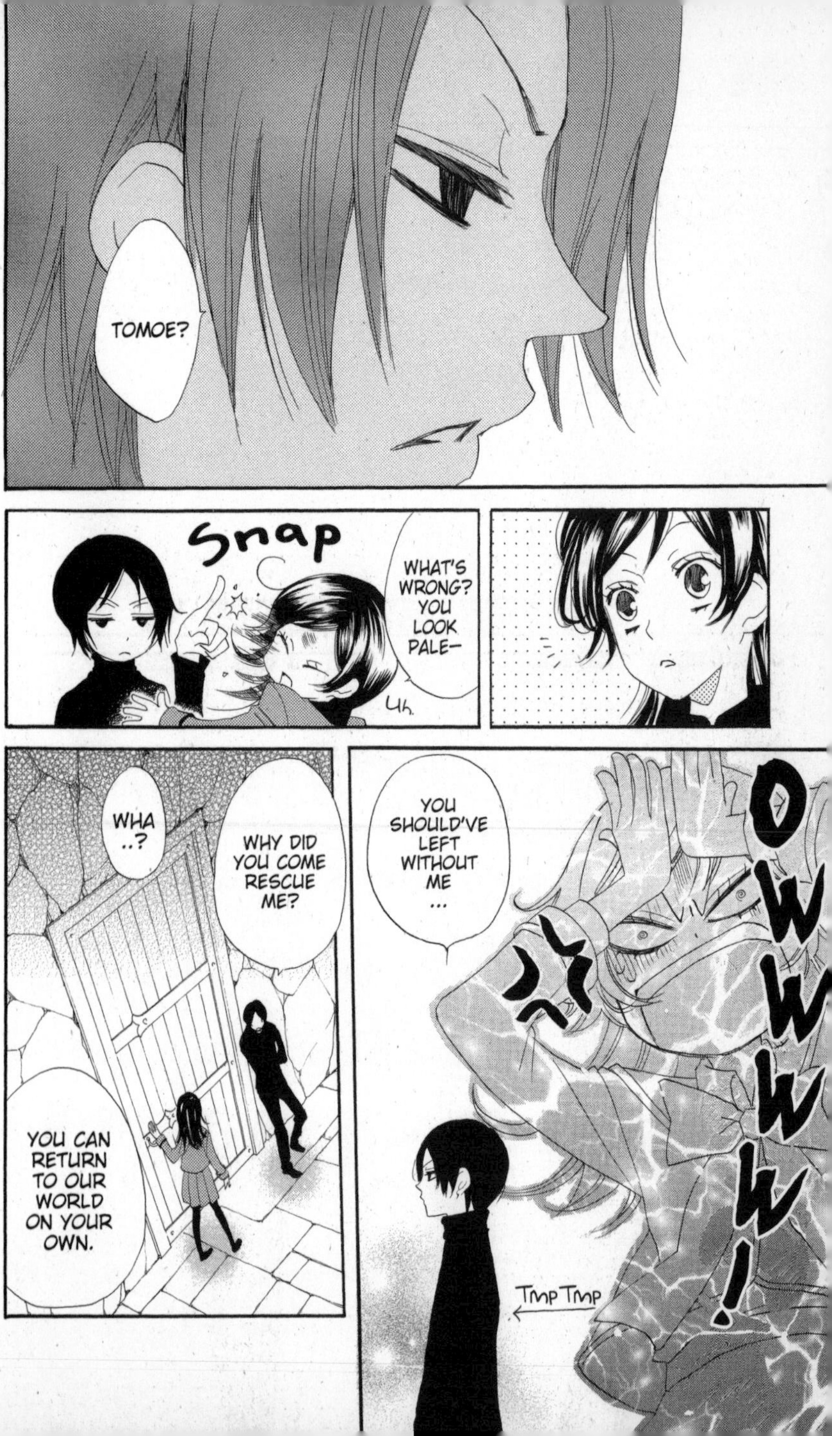
TOMOE?
WHAT'S WRONG? YOU LOOK PALE—
Snap
Uh.
YOU SHOULD'VE LEFT WITHOUT ME ...
OWWWW!
Tmp Tmp
WHY DID YOU COME RESCUE ME?
WHA ..?
YOU CAN RETURN TO OUR WORLD ON YOUR OWN.

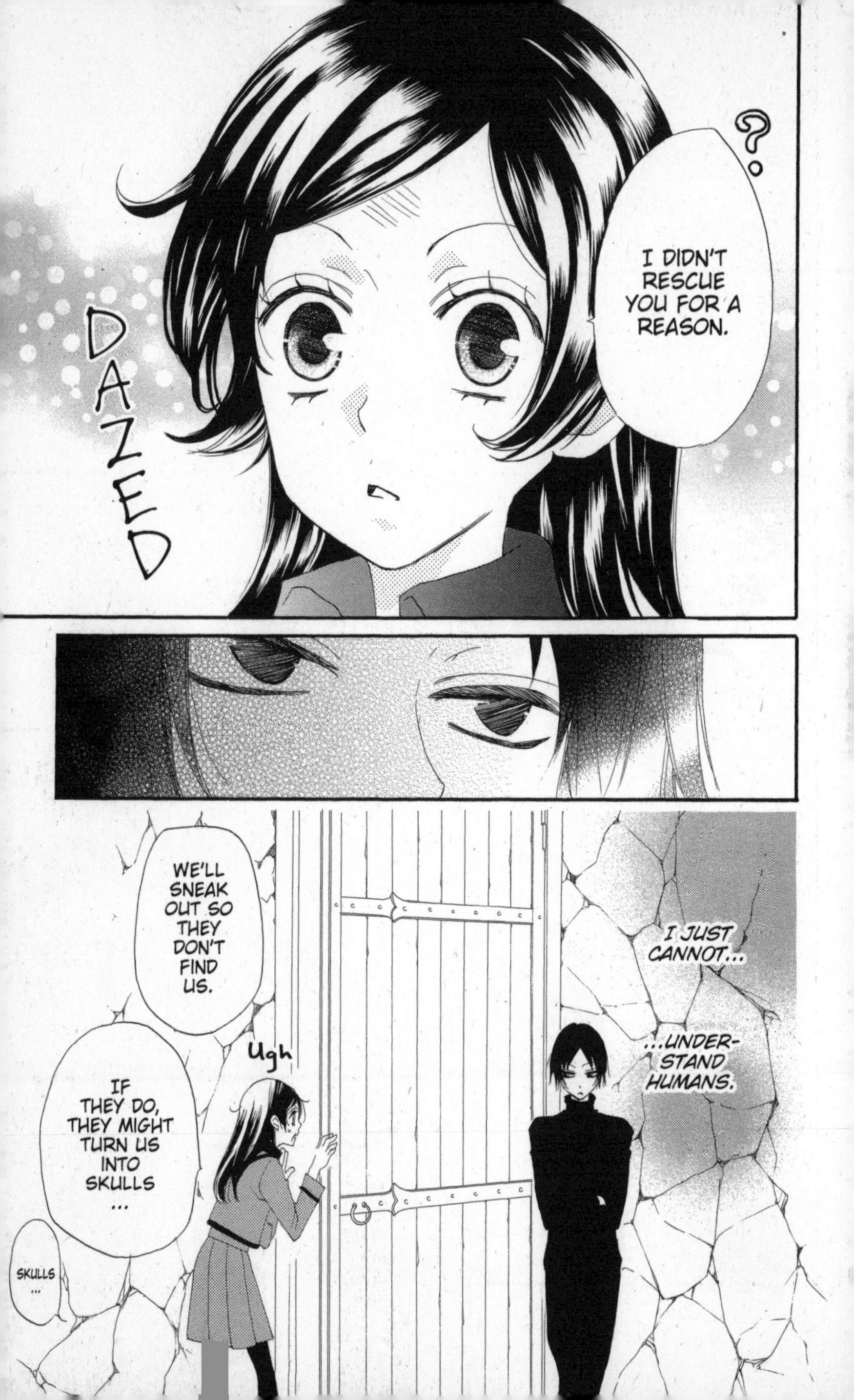

?
I DIDN'T RESCUE YOU FOR A REASON.
DAZED
I JUST CANNOT...
...UNDER-STAND HUMANS.
WE'LL SNEAK OUT SO THEY DON'T FIND US.
Ugh
IF THEY DO, THEY MIGHT TURN US INTO SKULLS ...
SKULLS ...

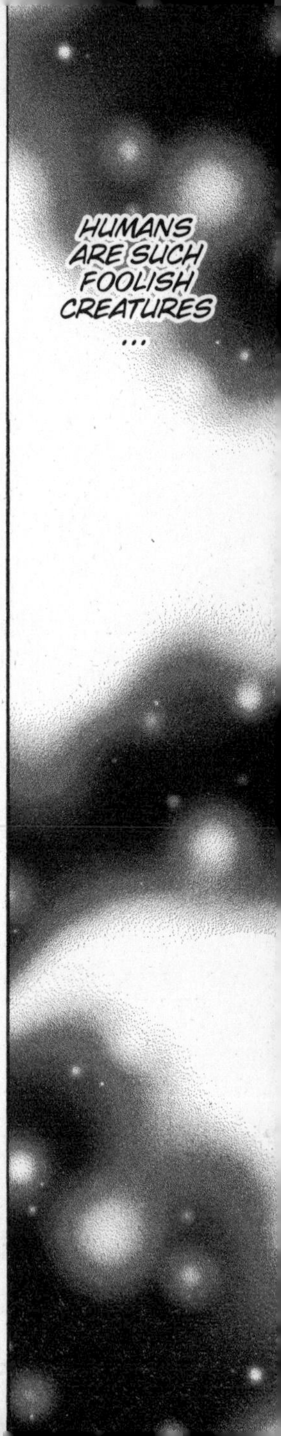
HUMANS ARE SUCH FOOLISH CREATURES...

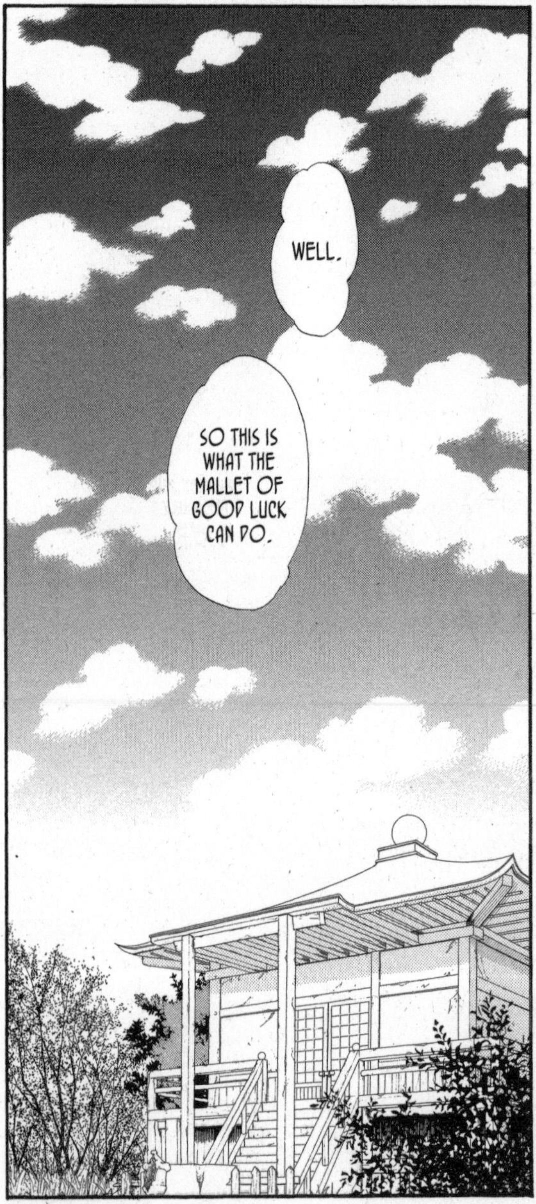
WELL.
SO THIS IS WHAT THE MALLET OF GOOD LUCK CAN DO.

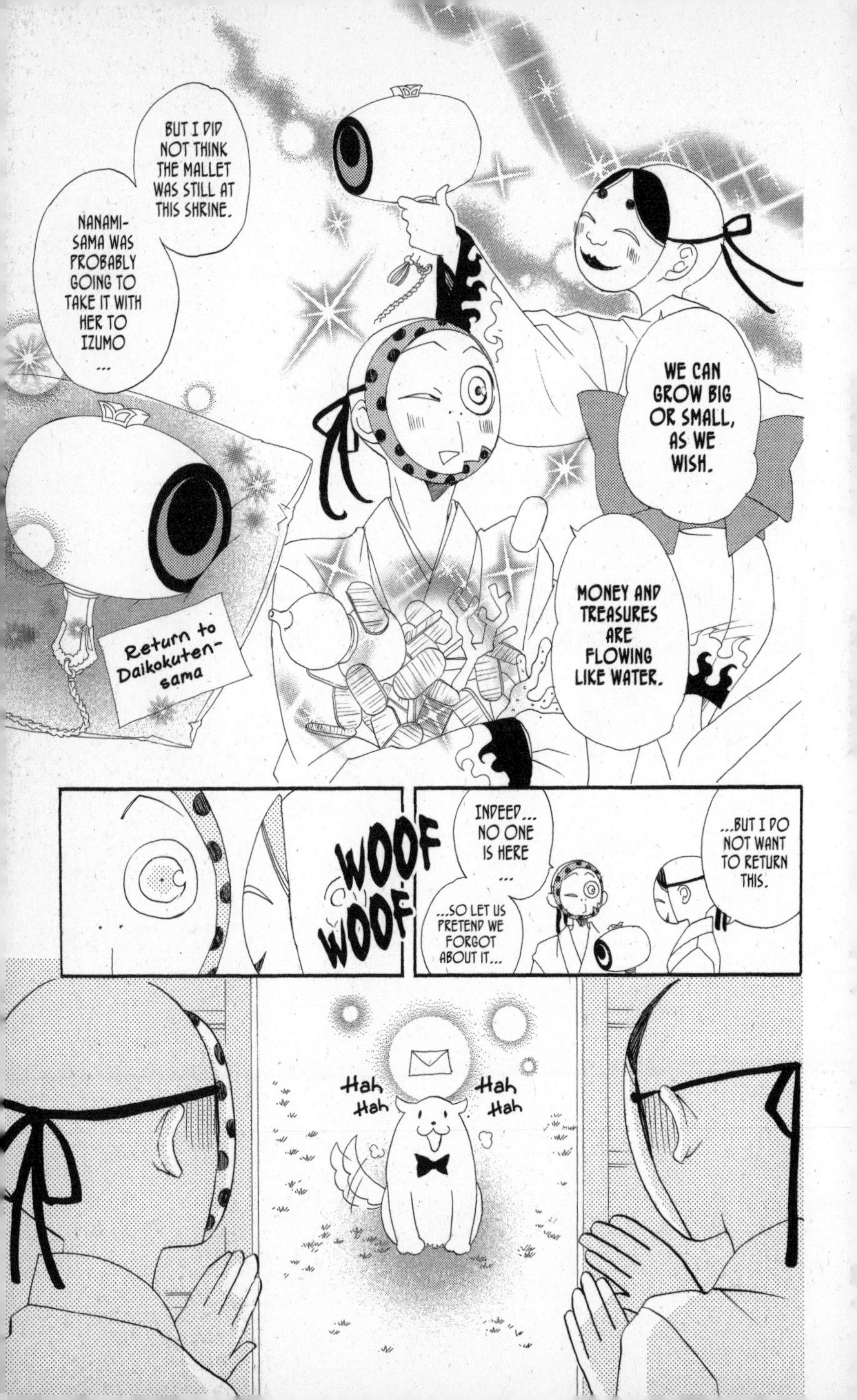
WE CAN GROW BIG OR SMALL, AS WE WISH.
MONEY AND TREASURES ARE FLOWING LIKE WATER.
BUT I DID NOT THINK THE MALLET WAS STILL AT THIS SHRINE.
NANAMI-SAMA WAS PROBABLY GOING TO TAKE IT WITH HER TO IZUMO ...
Return to Daikokuten-sama
...BUT I DO NOT WANT TO RETURN THIS.
INDEED... NO ONE IS HERE ...
...SO LET US PRETEND WE FORGOT ABOUT IT...
WOOF WOOF
Hah Hah
Hah Hah

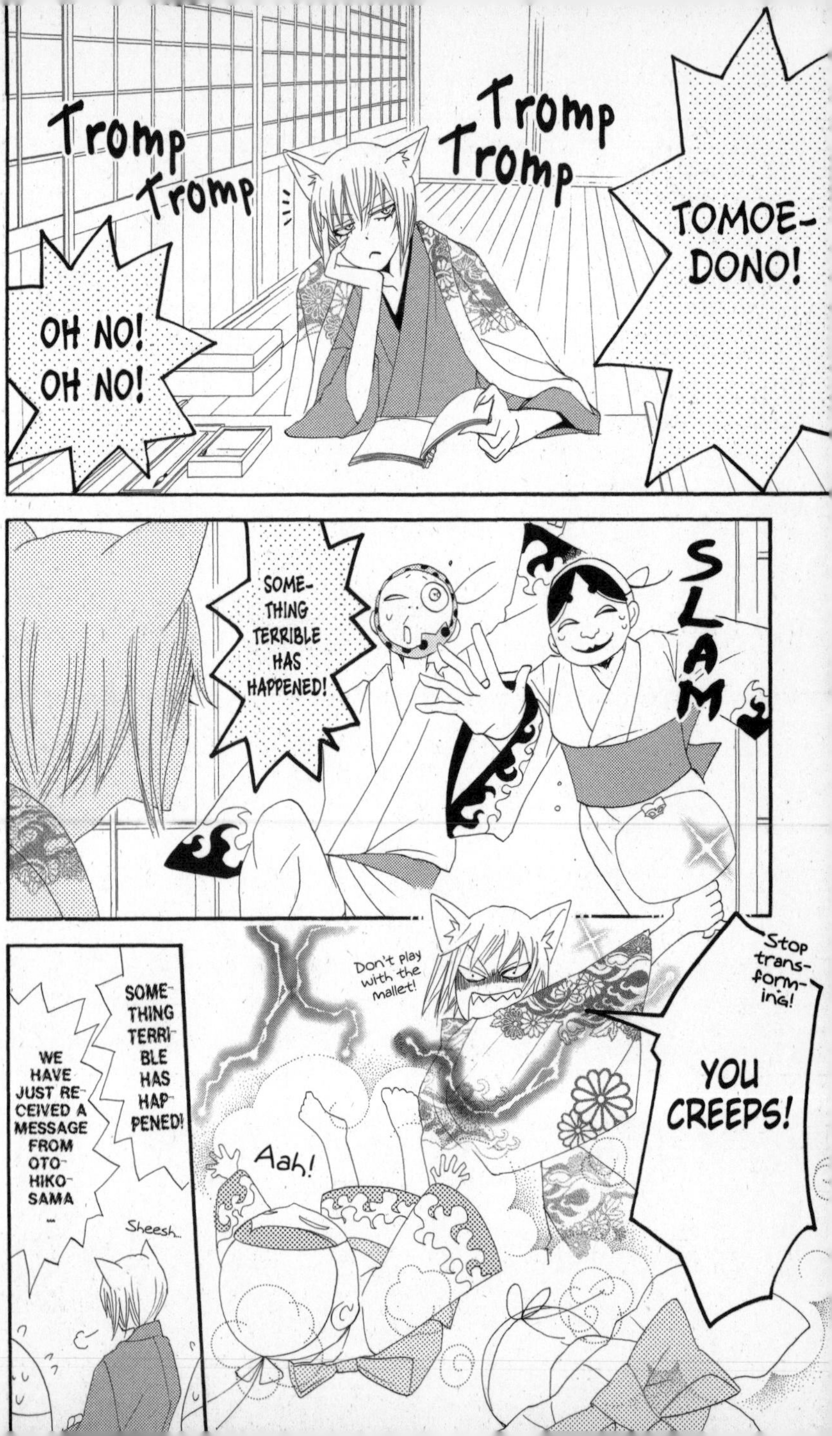
TOMOE-DONO!
Tromp Tromp
Tromp Tromp
OH NO! OH NO!
SLAM
SOMETHING TERRIBLE HAS HAPPENED!
Stop transforming!
YOU CREEPS!
Don't play with the mallet!
Aah!
SOMETHING TERRIBLE HAS HAPPENED!
WE HAVE JUST RECEIVED A MESSAGE FROM OTOHIKO-SAMA...
Sheesh...

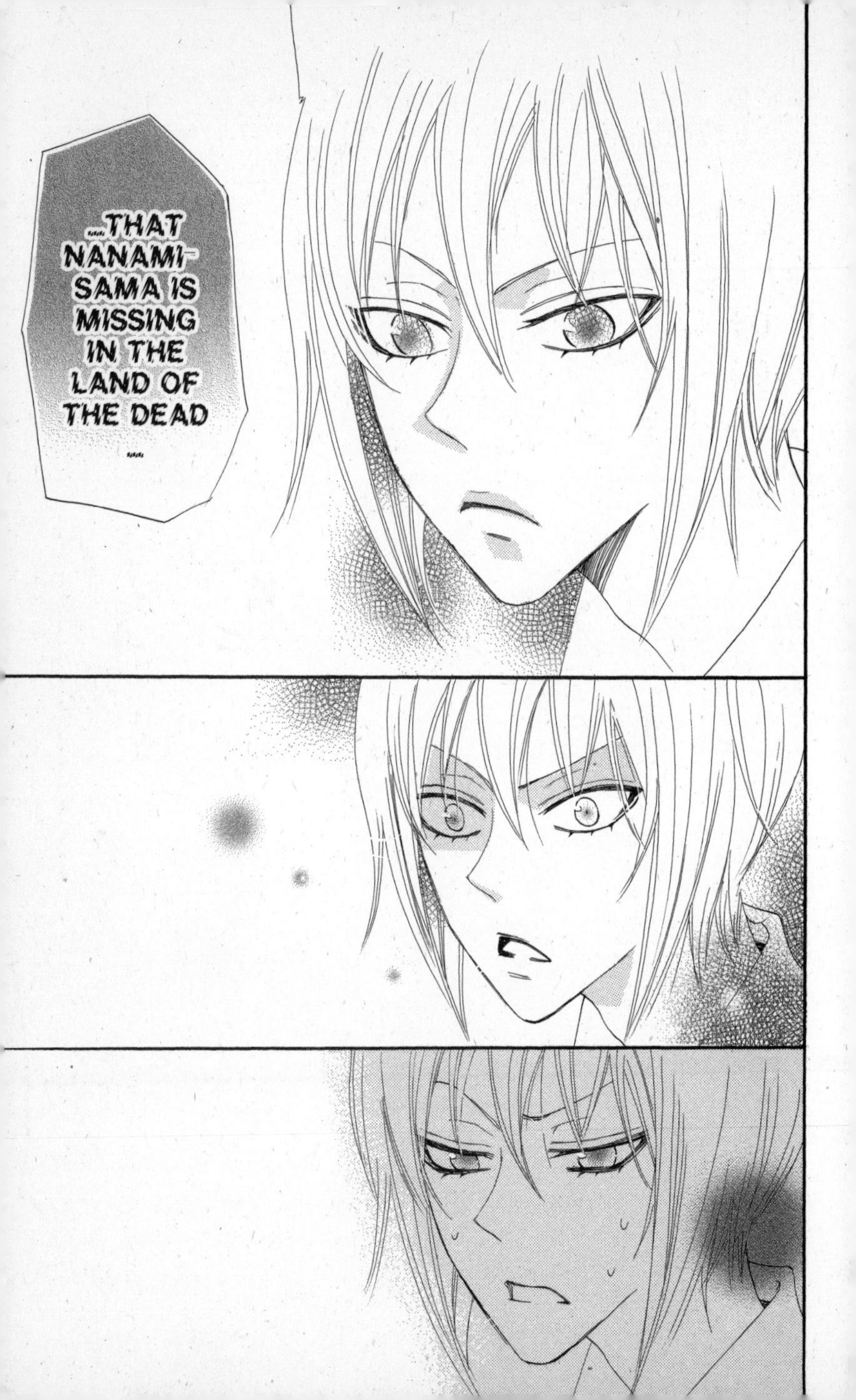
...THAT NANAMI-SAMA IS MISSING IN THE LAND OF THE DEAD
...

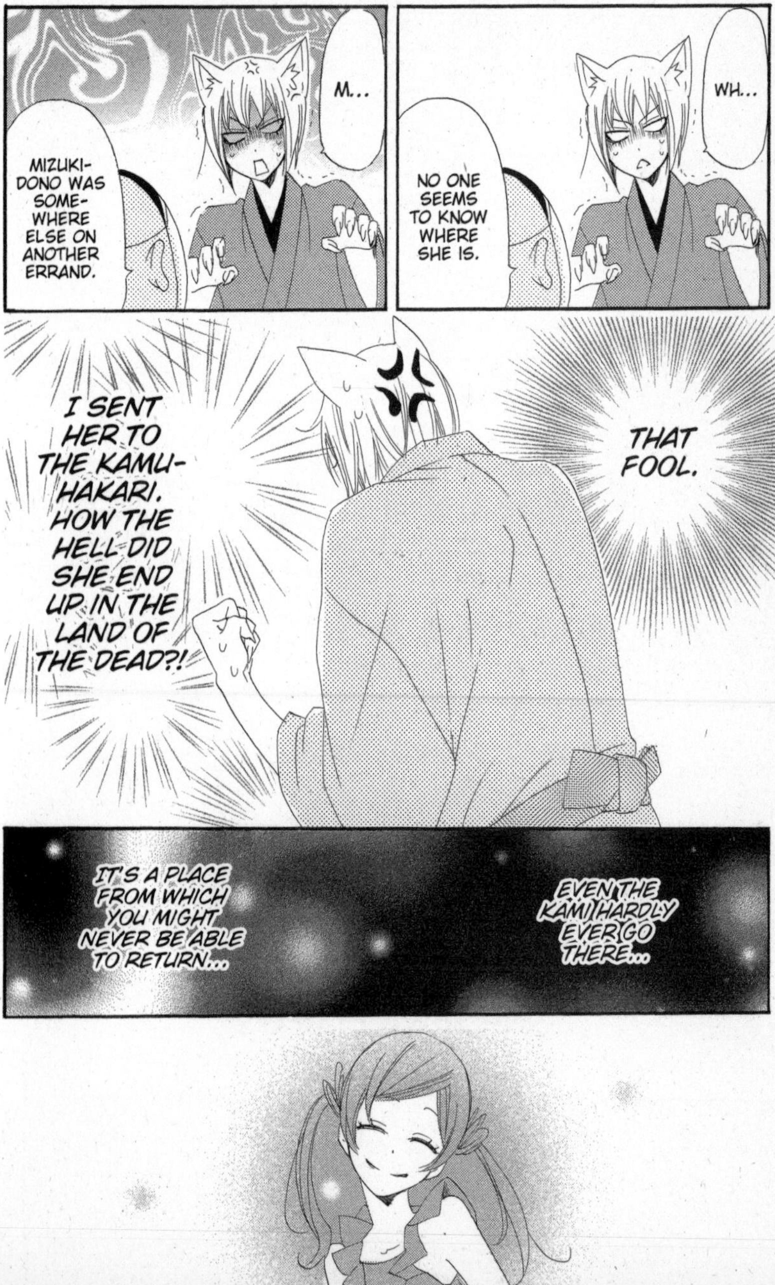
WH...
NO ONE SEEMS TO KNOW WHERE SHE IS.
M...
MIZUKI-DONO WAS SOME-WHERE ELSE ON ANOTHER ERRAND.
THAT FOOL.
I SENT HER TO THE KAMU-HAKARI. HOW THE HELL DID SHE END UP IN THE LAND OF THE DEAD?!
EVEN THE KAMI HARDLY EVER GO THERE...
IT'S A PLACE FROM WHICH YOU MIGHT NEVER BE ABLE TO RETURN...

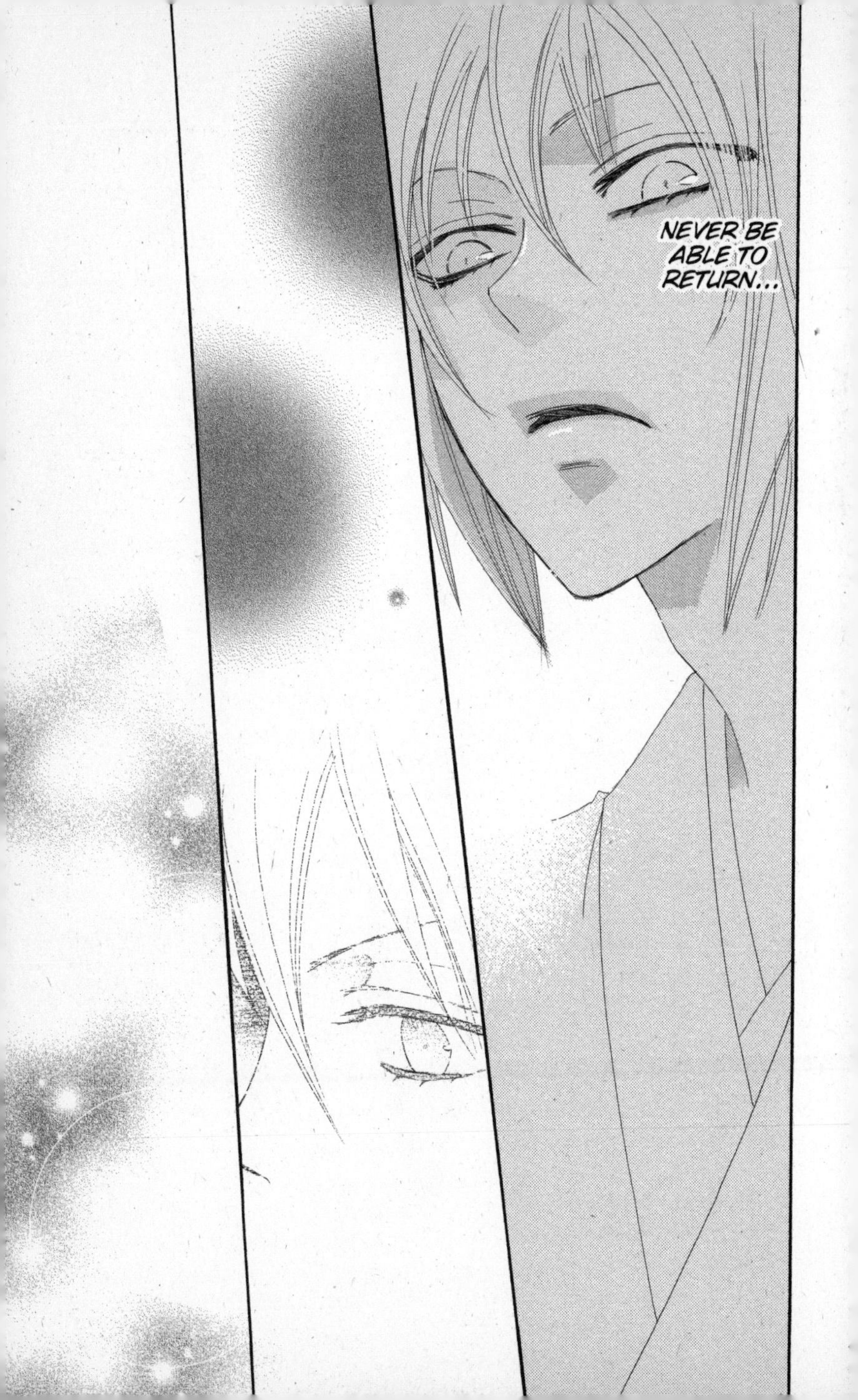
NEVER BE ABLE TO RETURN...

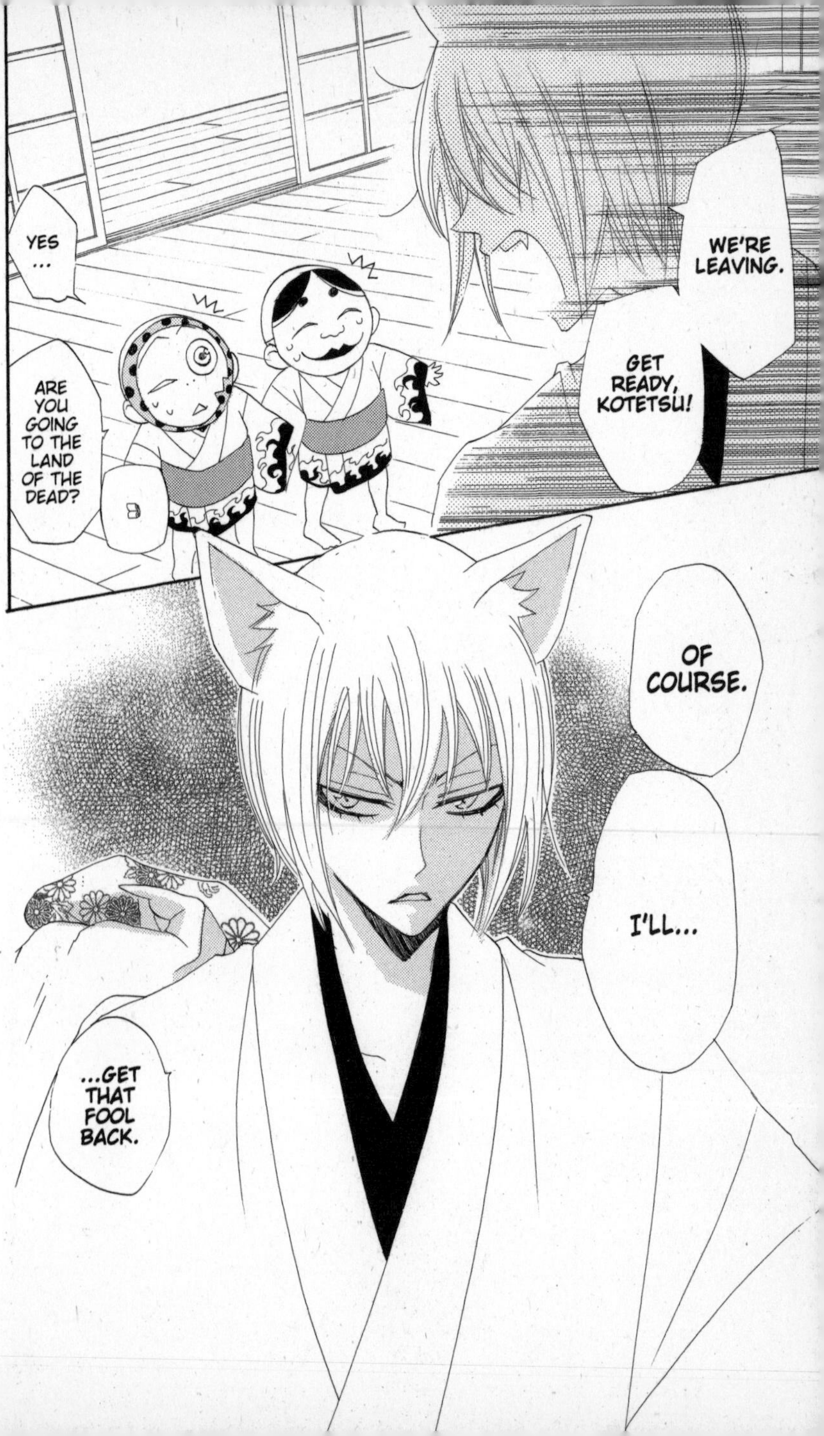
WE'RE LEAVING.
GET READY, KOTETSU!
YES...
ARE YOU GOING TO THE LAND OF THE DEAD?
OF COURSE.
I'LL...
...GET THAT FOOL BACK.

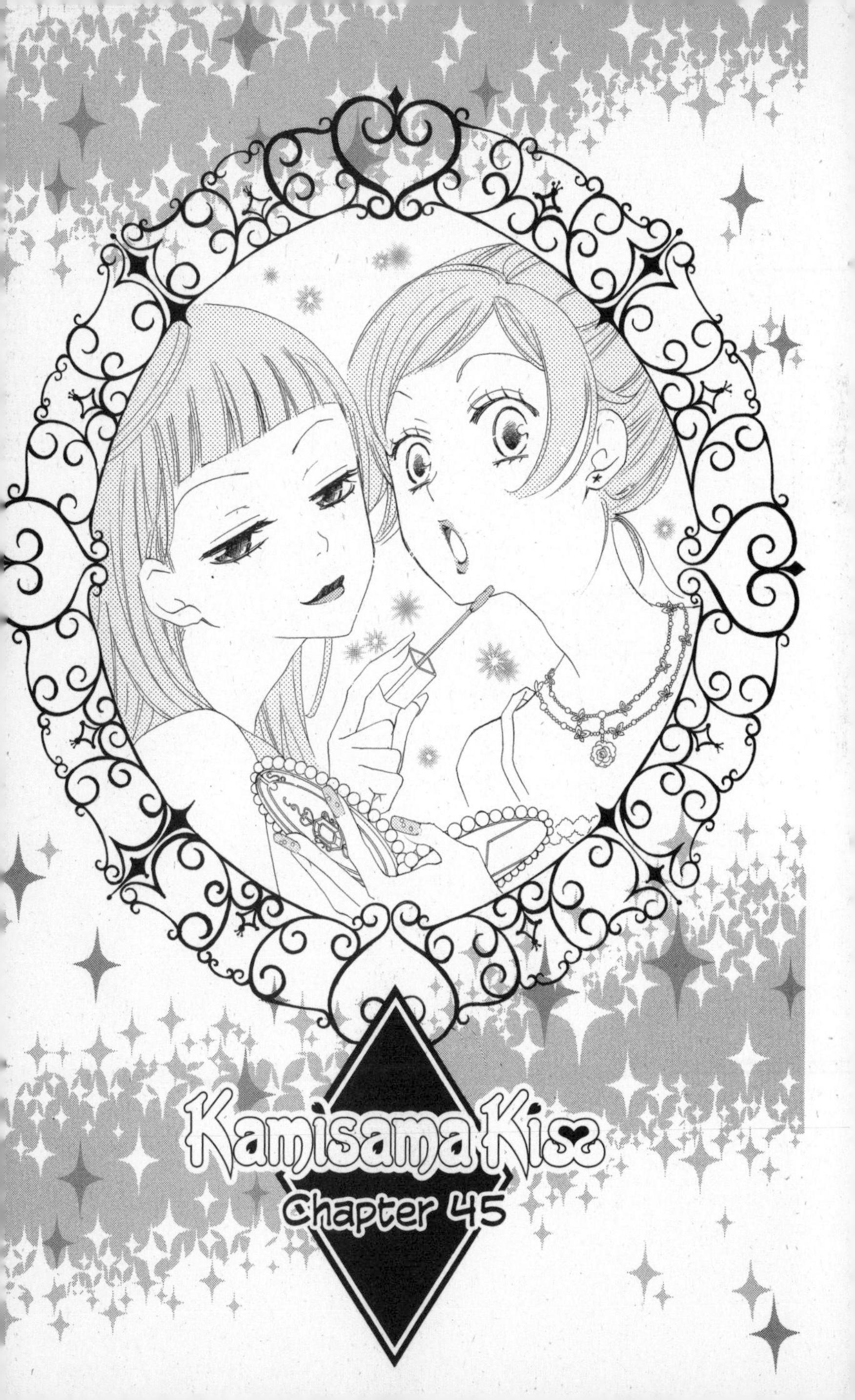
Kamisama Kiss
Chapter 45

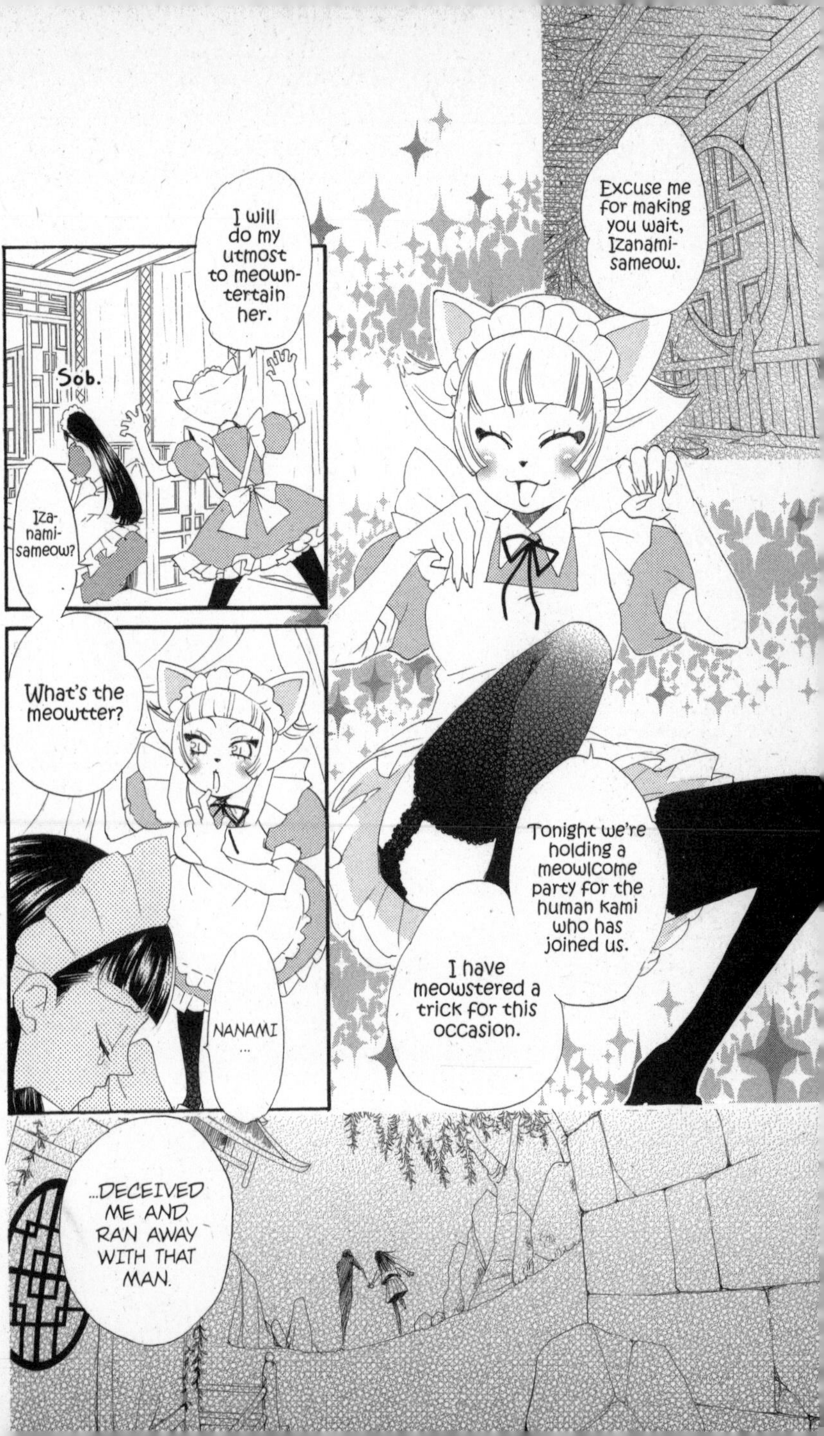

Excuse me for making you wait, Izanami-sameow.
Tonight we're holding a meowlcome party for the human kami who has joined us.
I have meowstered a trick for this occasion.
I will do my utmost to meowntertain her.
Sob.
Iza-nami-sameow?
What's the meowtter?
NANAMI...
...DECEIVED ME AND RAN AWAY WITH THAT MAN.

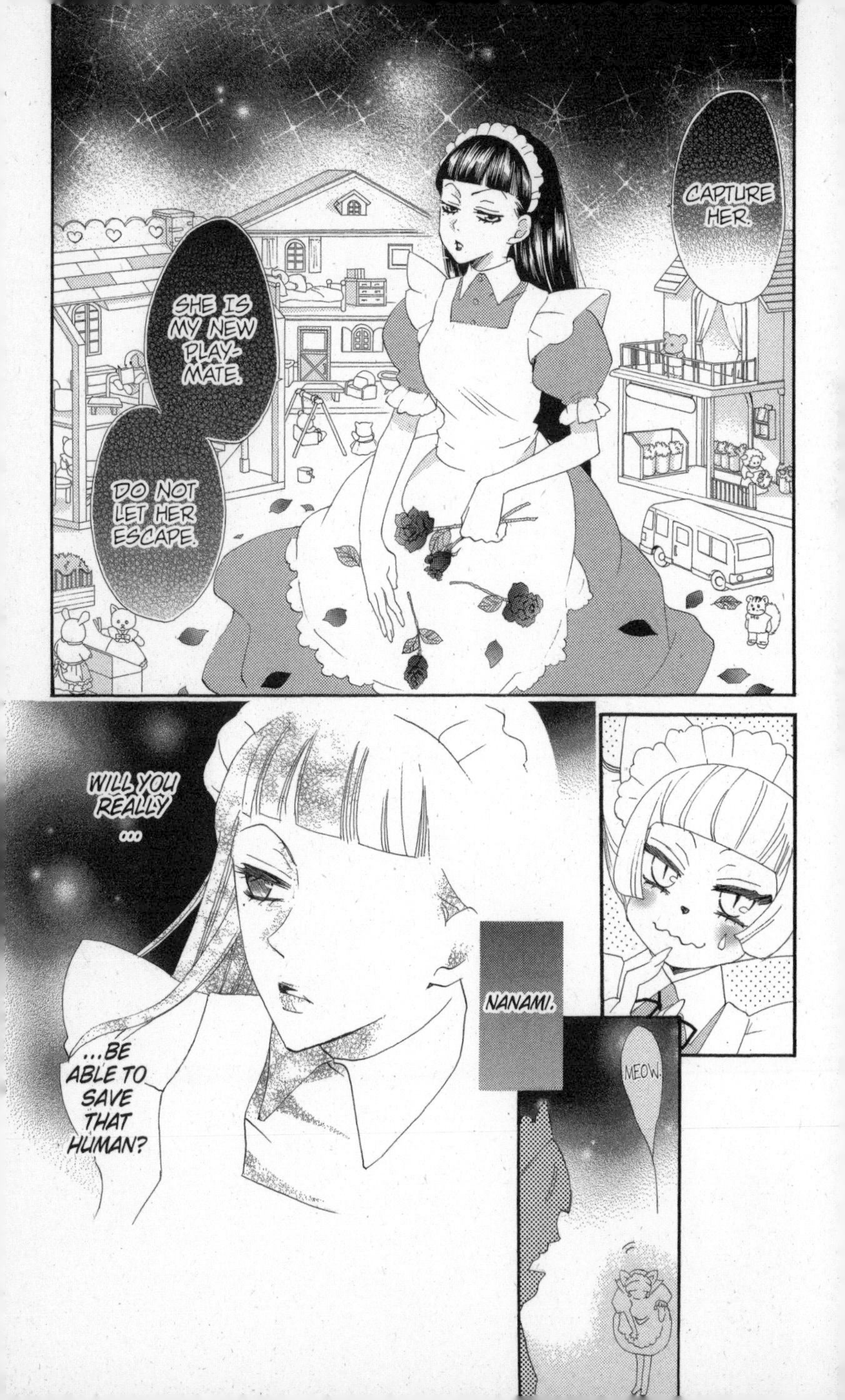
CAPTURE HER.
SHE IS MY NEW PLAY-MATE.
DO NOT LET HER ESCAPE.
NANAMI.
MEOW.
WILL YOU REALLY ...
...BE ABLE TO SAVE THAT HUMAN?

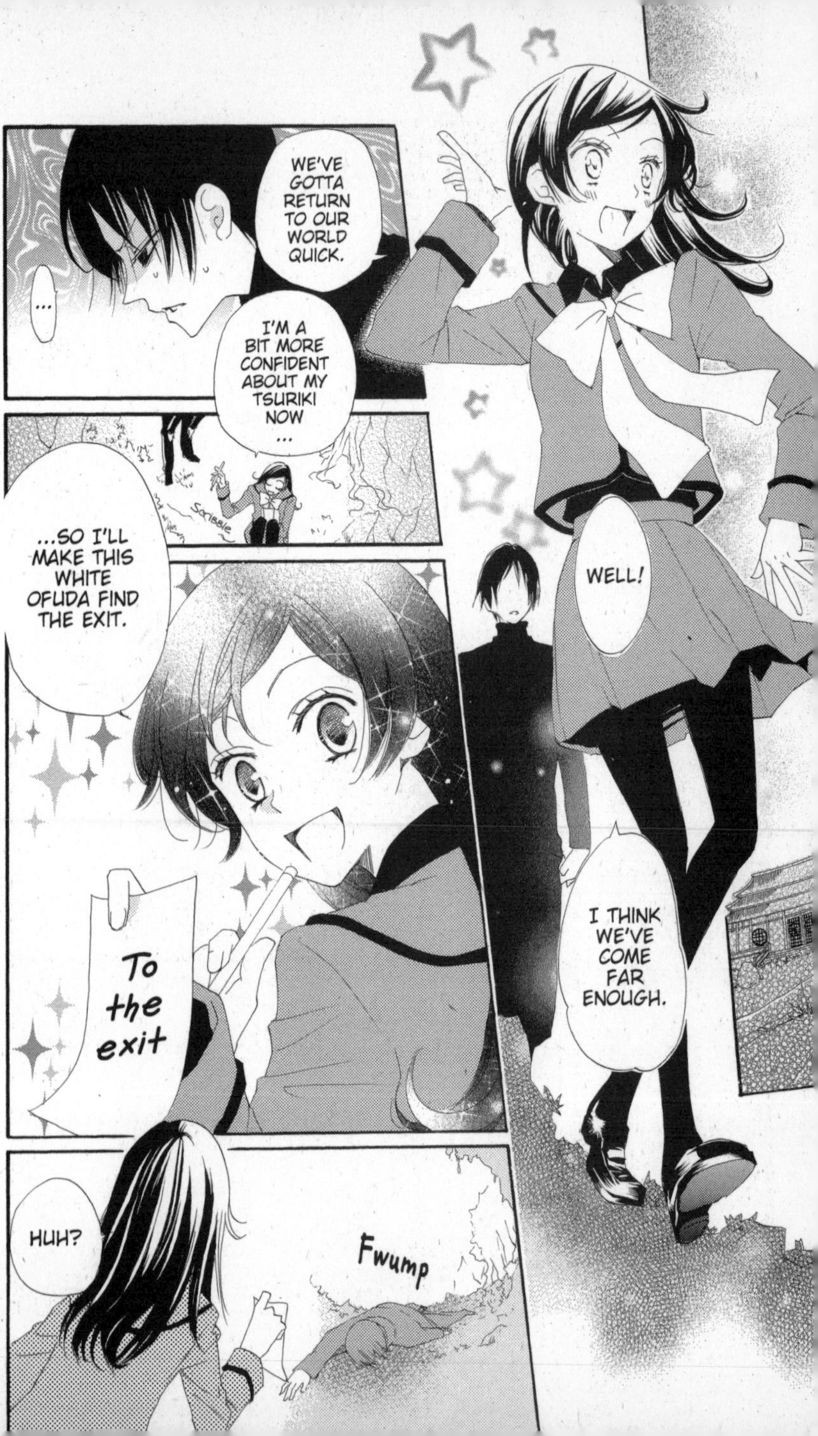
WELL!
I THINK WE'VE COME FAR ENOUGH.
WE'VE GOTTA RETURN TO OUR WORLD QUICK.
...
I'M A BIT MORE CONFIDENT ABOUT MY TSURIKI NOW...
Scribble
...SO I'LL MAKE THIS WHITE OFUDA FIND THE EXIT.
To the exit
HUH?
Fwump

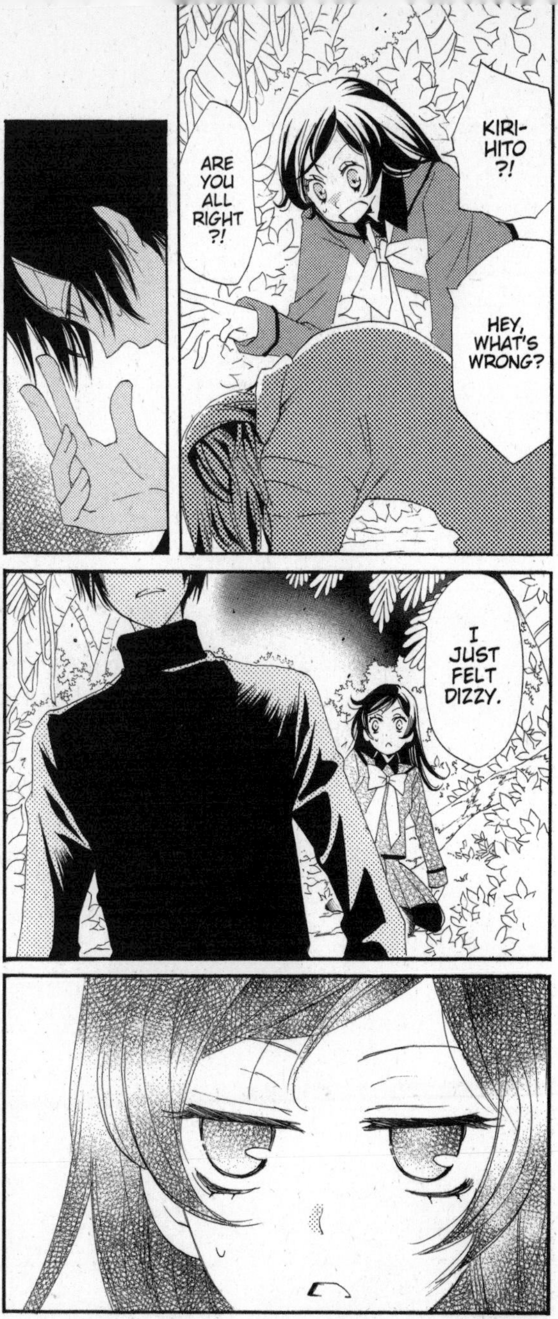
KIRI-HITO ?!
ARE YOU ALL RIGHT ?!
HEY, WHAT'S WRONG?
I JUST FELT DIZZY.

The other day, I went to Egypt, a place I've always wanted to go.

I was impressed a lot during my travels. My heart grew a little bigger, thinking things were all right even 4,000 years ago!

I went on a cruise for the first time in my life at Lake Nasser, the biggest man-made lake in the world. It was a lake, so it didn't smell like the sea at all. I was out on the decks every night and looked at the starry skies, and almost forgot about the everyday world. The ship was designed for 180 passengers, but there were only 18 people aboard, so it was almost as if we'd rented the entire ship, and I was able to spend my time very comfortably.

The last stop, the Abu Simbel temples, was really wonderful! I almost didn't want to return to Cairo! But Cairo has the Egyptian Museum. I almost cried when I saw King Tutankhamen's gold mask.

And that was my Egyptian trip!

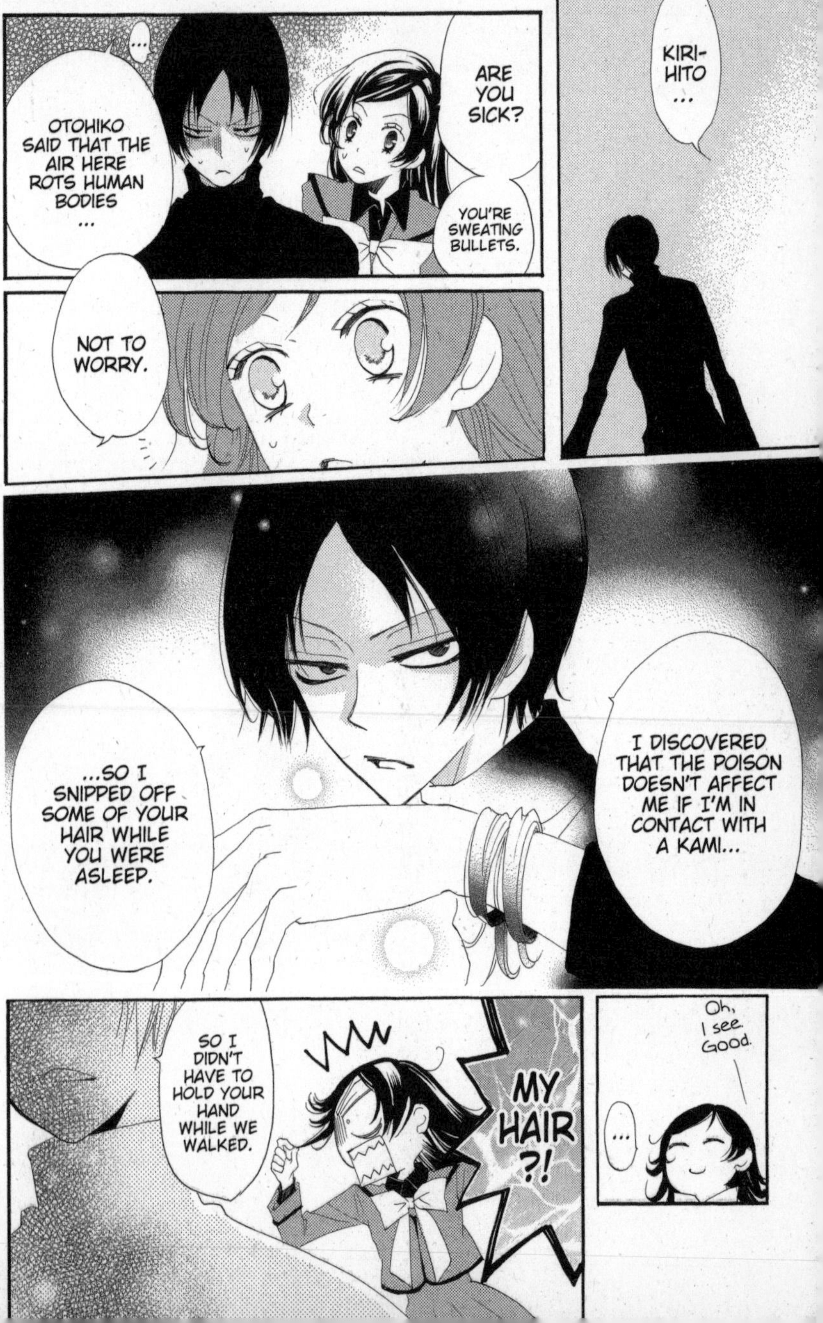
KIRI-HITO ...
ARE YOU SICK?
YOU'RE SWEATING BULLETS.
...
OTOHIKO SAID THAT THE AIR HERE ROTS HUMAN BODIES ...
NOT TO WORRY.
I DISCOVERED THAT THE POISON DOESN'T AFFECT ME IF I'M IN CONTACT WITH A KAMI...
...SO I SNIPPED OFF SOME OF YOUR HAIR WHILE YOU WERE ASLEEP.
Oh, I see. Good.
...
MY HAIR?!
SO I DIDN'T HAVE TO HOLD YOUR HAND WHILE WE WALKED.

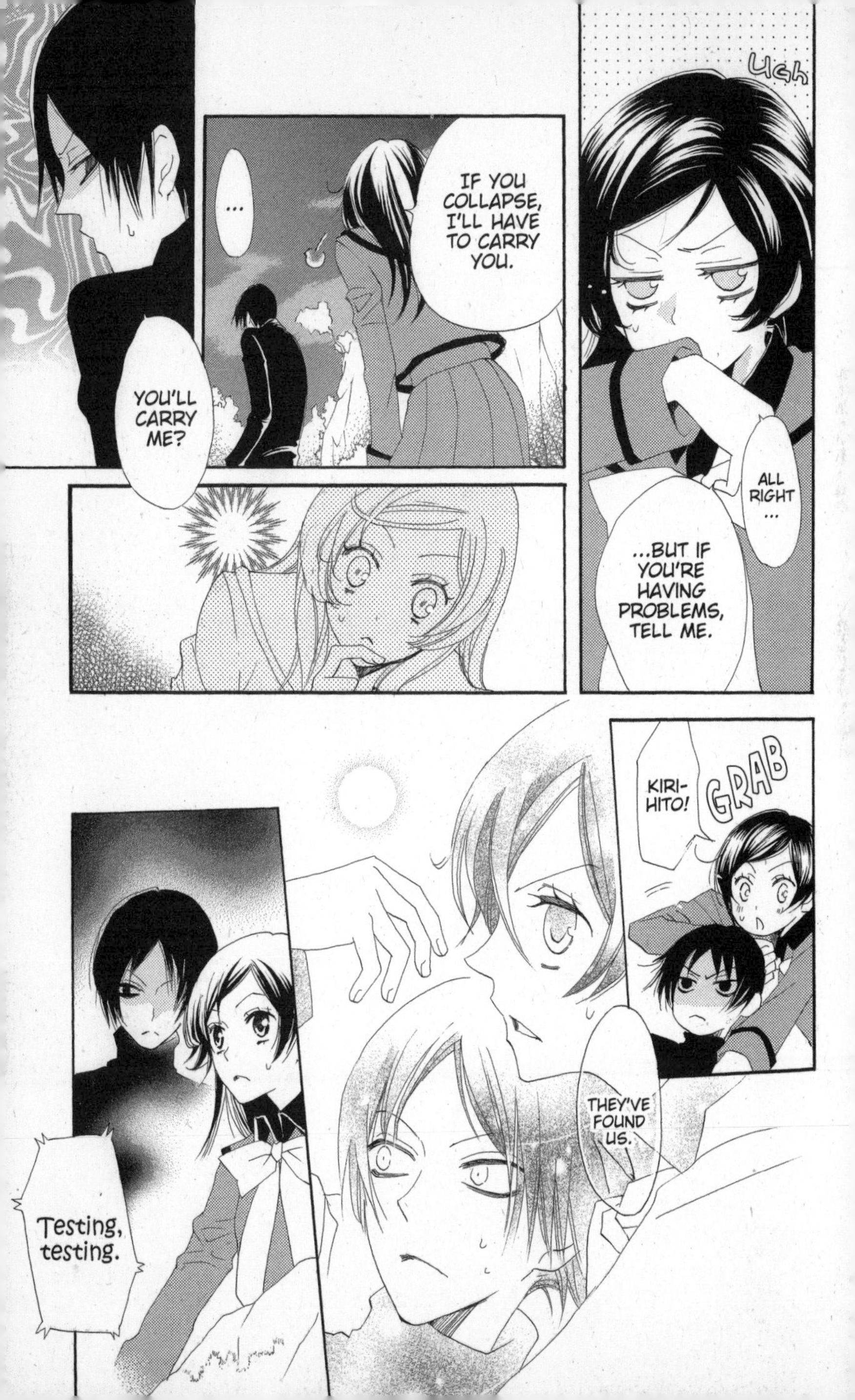
Ugh
ALL RIGHT ...
...BUT IF YOU'RE HAVING PROBLEMS, TELL ME.
...
IF YOU COLLAPSE, I'LL HAVE TO CARRY YOU.
YOU'LL CARRY ME?
KIRI-HITO!
GRAB
THEY'VE FOUND US.
Testing, testing.

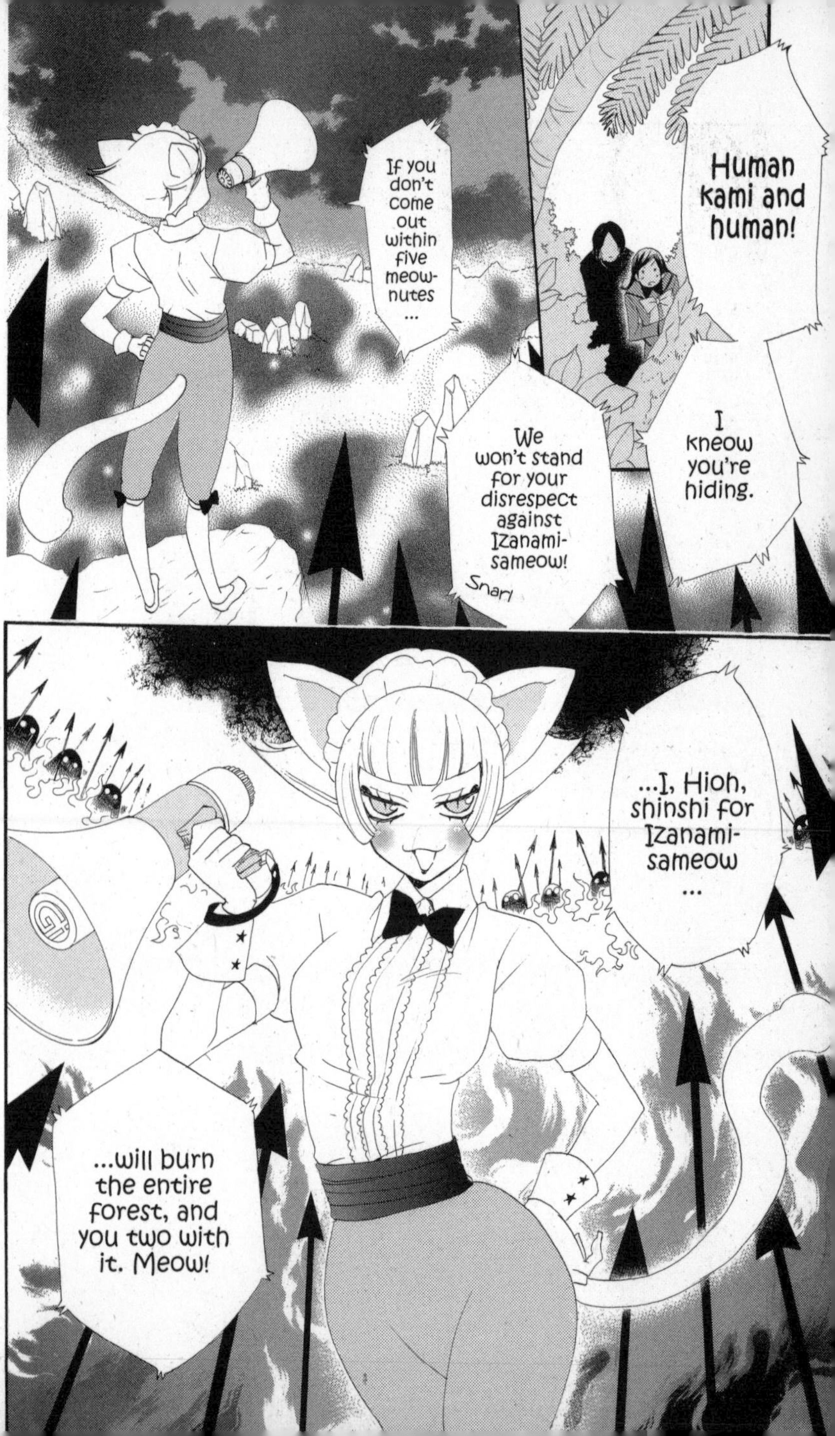
Human kami and human!
I kneow you're hiding.
We won't stand for your disrespect against Izanami-sameow!
Snarl
If you don't come out within five meow-nutes ...
...I, Hioh, shinshi for Izanami-sameow ...
...will burn the entire forest, and you two with it. Meow!

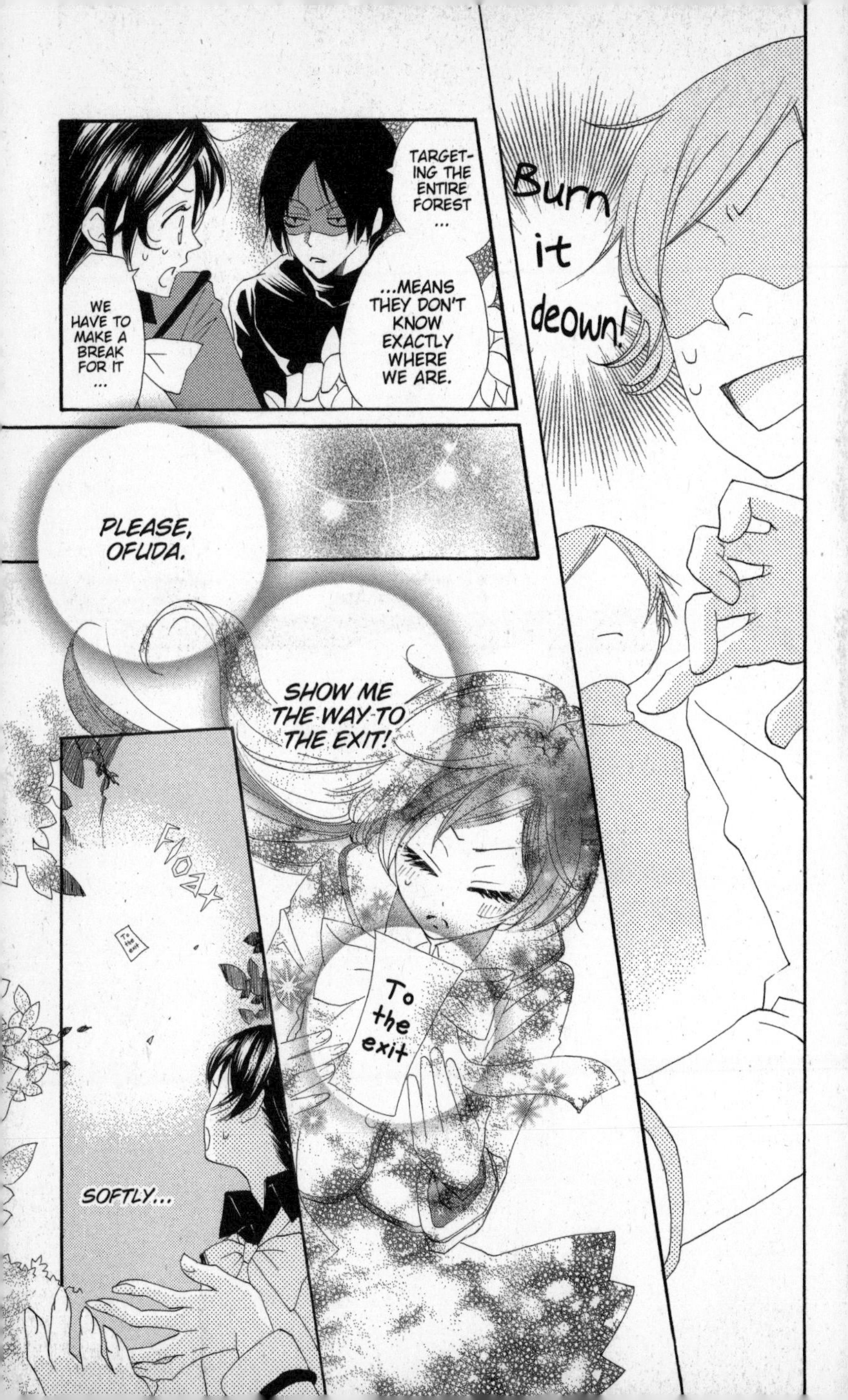
Burn it deown!
TARGET-ING THE ENTIRE FOREST...
...MEANS THEY DON'T KNOW EXACTLY WHERE WE ARE.
WE HAVE TO MAKE A BREAK FOR IT...
PLEASE, OFUDA.
SHOW ME THE WAY TO THE EXIT!
To the exit
Float
To the exit
SOFTLY...

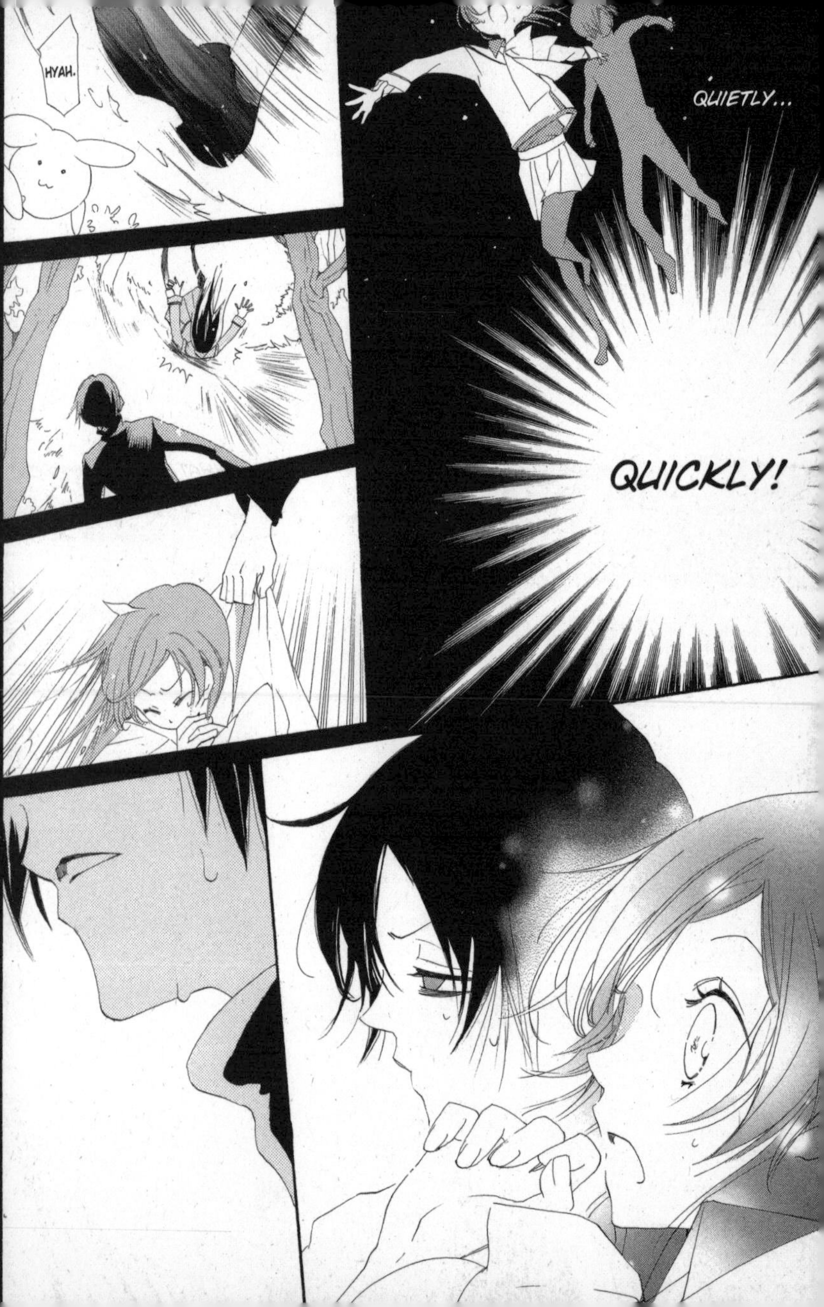
QUIETLY...
QUICKLY!
HYAH.

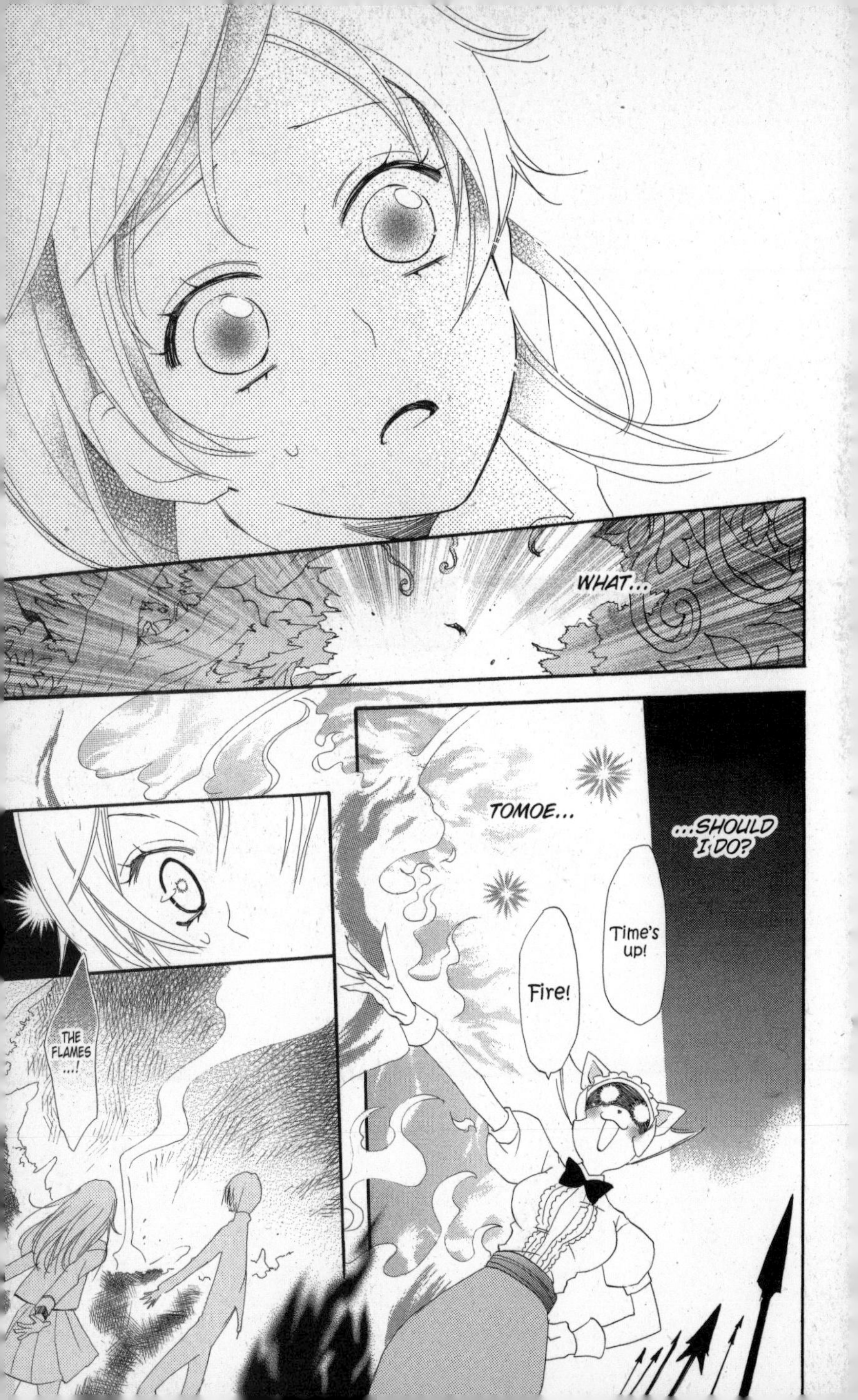
WHAT...
...SHOULD I DO?
TOMOE...
Time's up!
Fire!
THE FLAMES ...!

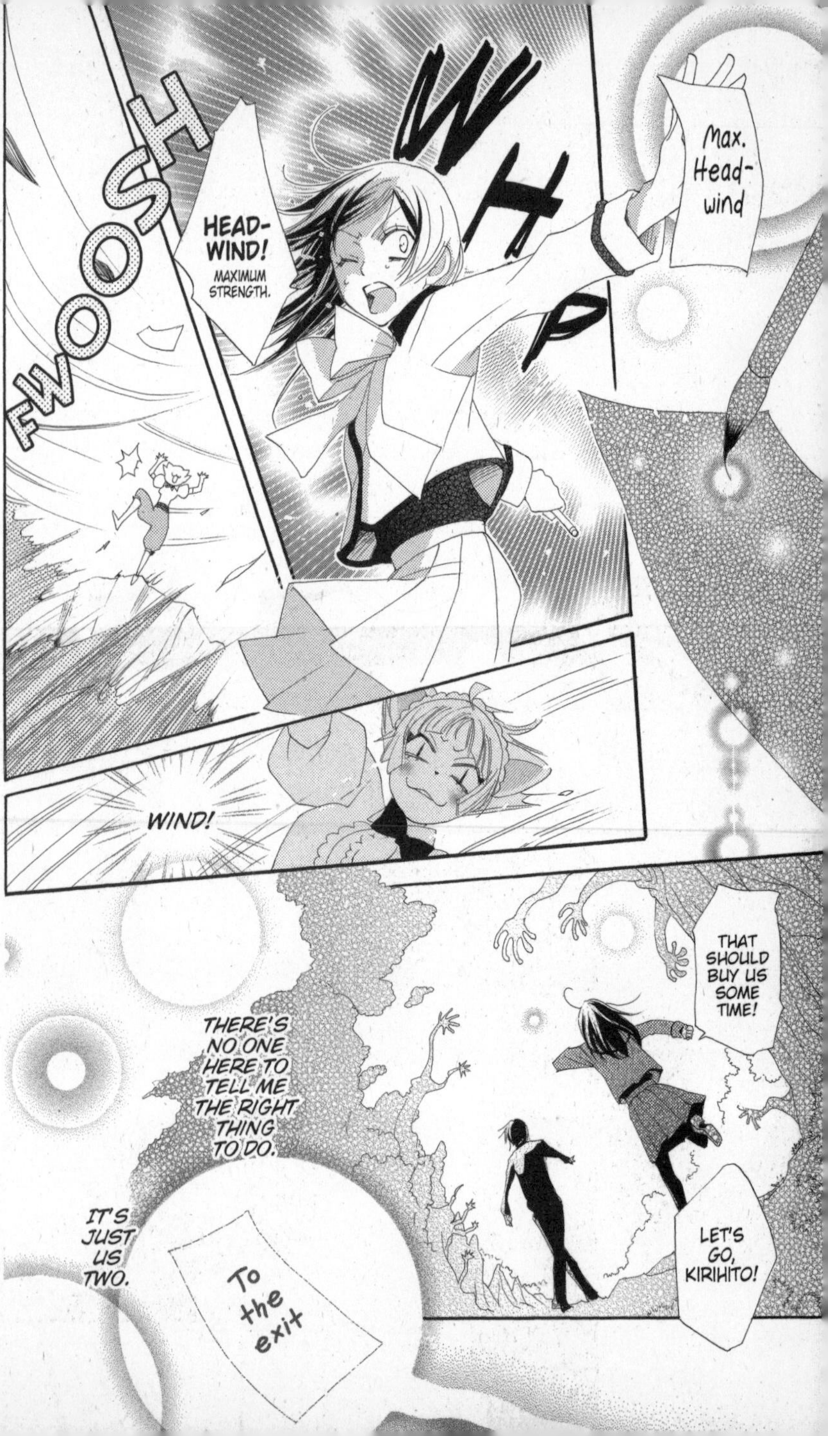
Max. Head-wind
WHIP
HEAD-WIND!
MAXIMUM STRENGTH.
FWOOSH
WIND!
THAT SHOULD BUY US SOME TIME!
LET'S GO, KIRIHITO!
THERE'S NO ONE HERE TO TELL ME THE RIGHT THING TO DO.
IT'S JUST US TWO.
To the exit

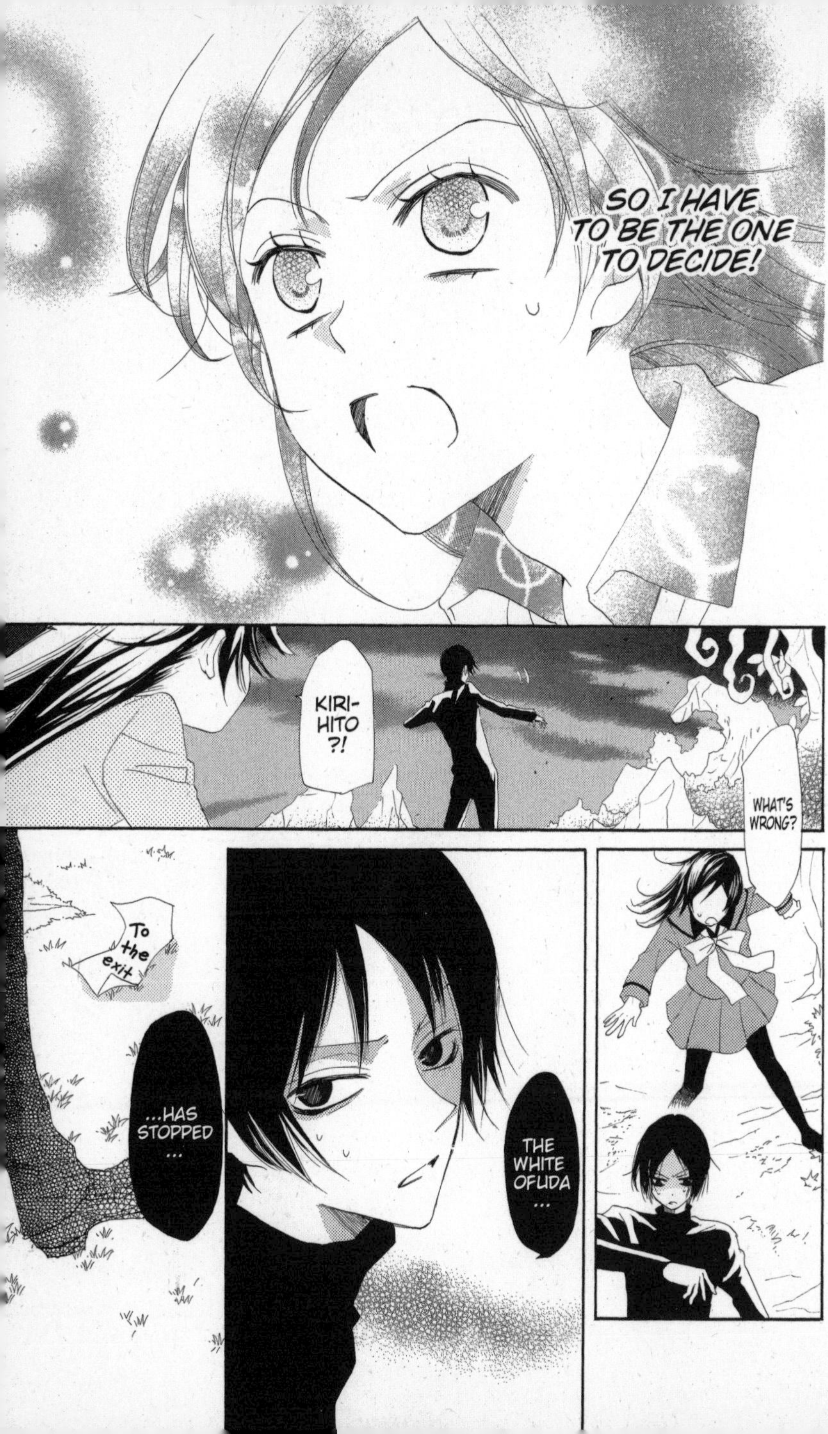
SO I HAVE TO BE THE ONE TO DECIDE!
KIRI-HITO ?!
WHAT'S WRONG?
THE WHITE OFUDA ...
...HAS STOPPED ...
To the exit

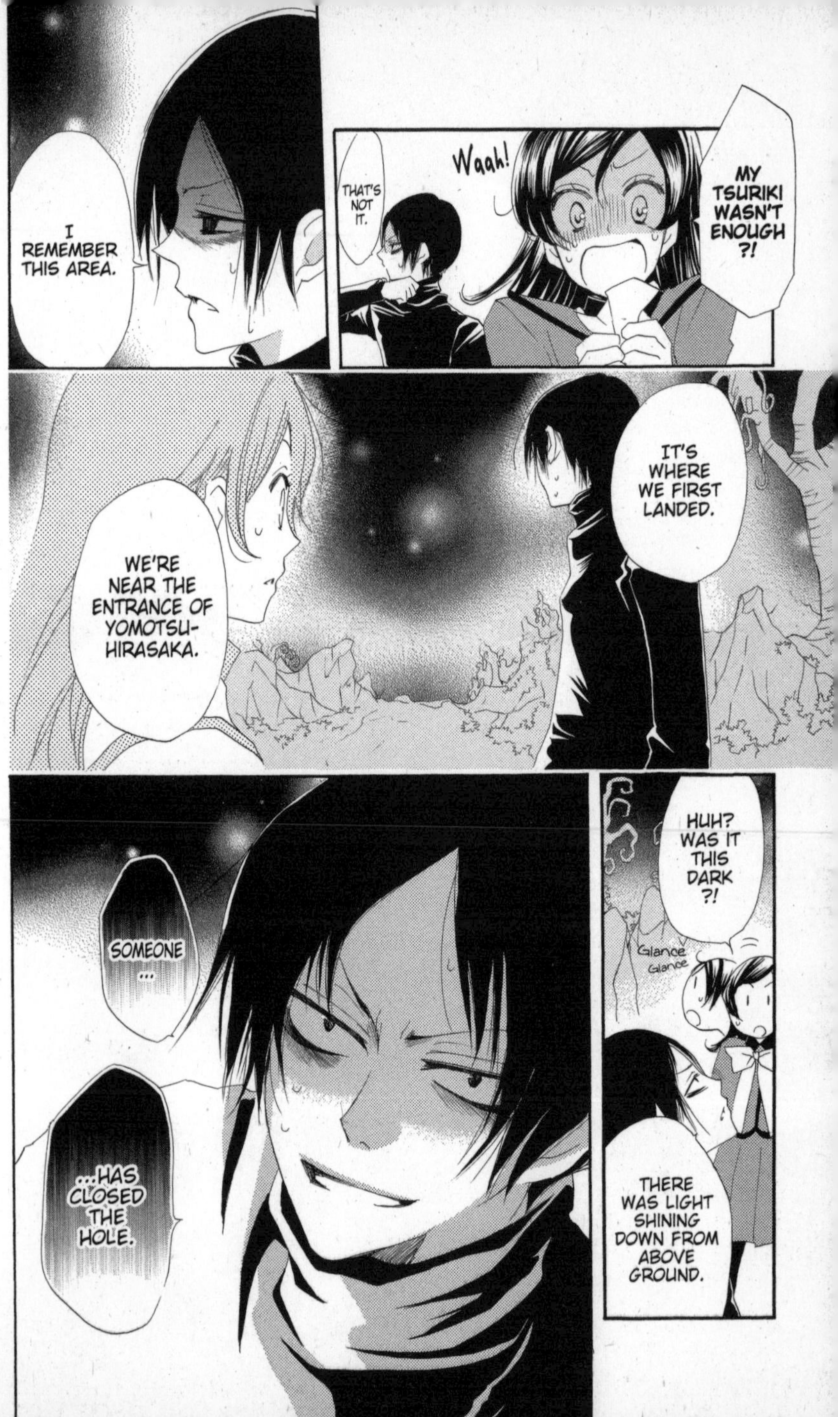
MY TSURIKI WASN'T ENOUGH ?!
Waah!
THAT'S NOT IT.
I REMEMBER THIS AREA.
IT'S WHERE WE FIRST LANDED.
WE'RE NEAR THE ENTRANCE OF YOMOTSU-HIRASAKA.
HUH? WAS IT THIS DARK ?!
Glance Glance
THERE WAS LIGHT SHINING DOWN FROM ABOVE GROUND.
SOMEONE ...
...HAS CLOSED THE HOLE.

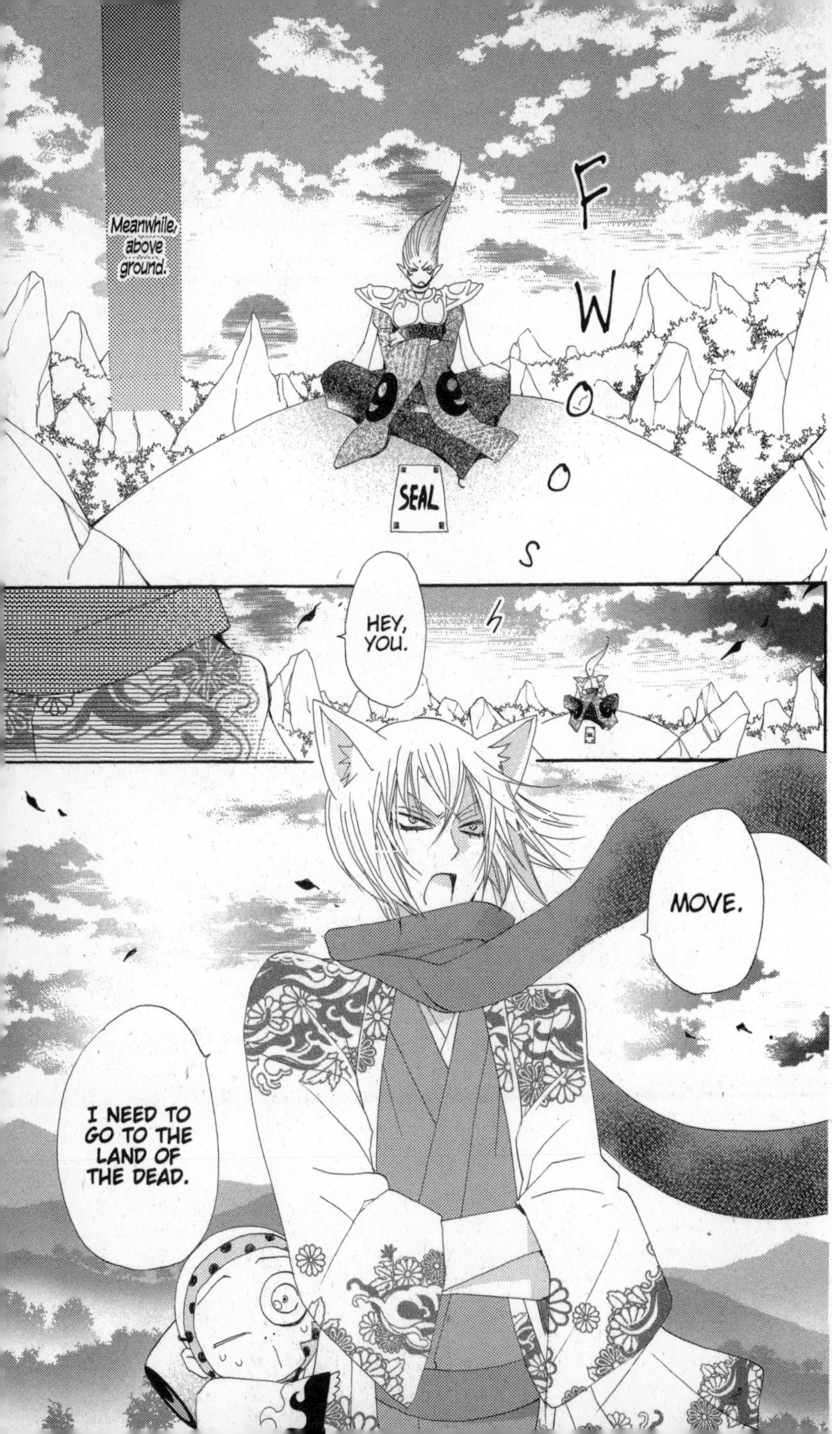
Meanwhile, above ground.
FWOOSH
SEAL
HEY, YOU.
MOVE.
I NEED TO GO TO THE LAND OF THE DEAD.

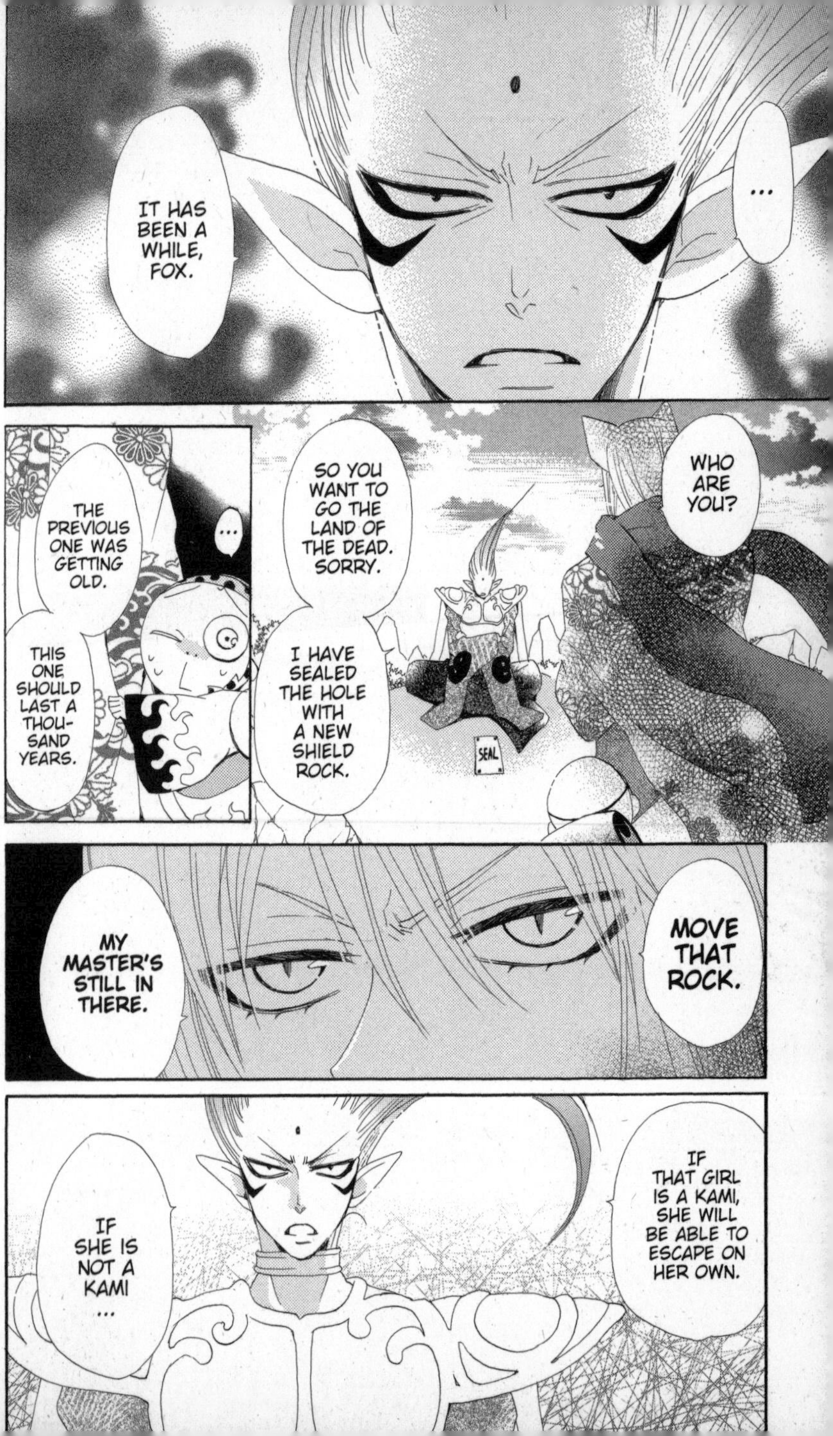
...
IT HAS BEEN A WHILE, FOX.
WHO ARE YOU?
SO YOU WANT TO GO THE LAND OF THE DEAD. SORRY.
I HAVE SEALED THE HOLE WITH A NEW SHIELD ROCK.
SEAL
...
THE PREVIOUS ONE WAS GETTING OLD.
THIS ONE SHOULD LAST A THOU-SAND YEARS.
MOVE THAT ROCK.
MY MASTER'S STILL IN THERE.
IF THAT GIRL IS A KAMI, SHE WILL BE ABLE TO ESCAPE ON HER OWN.
IF SHE IS NOT A KAMI ...

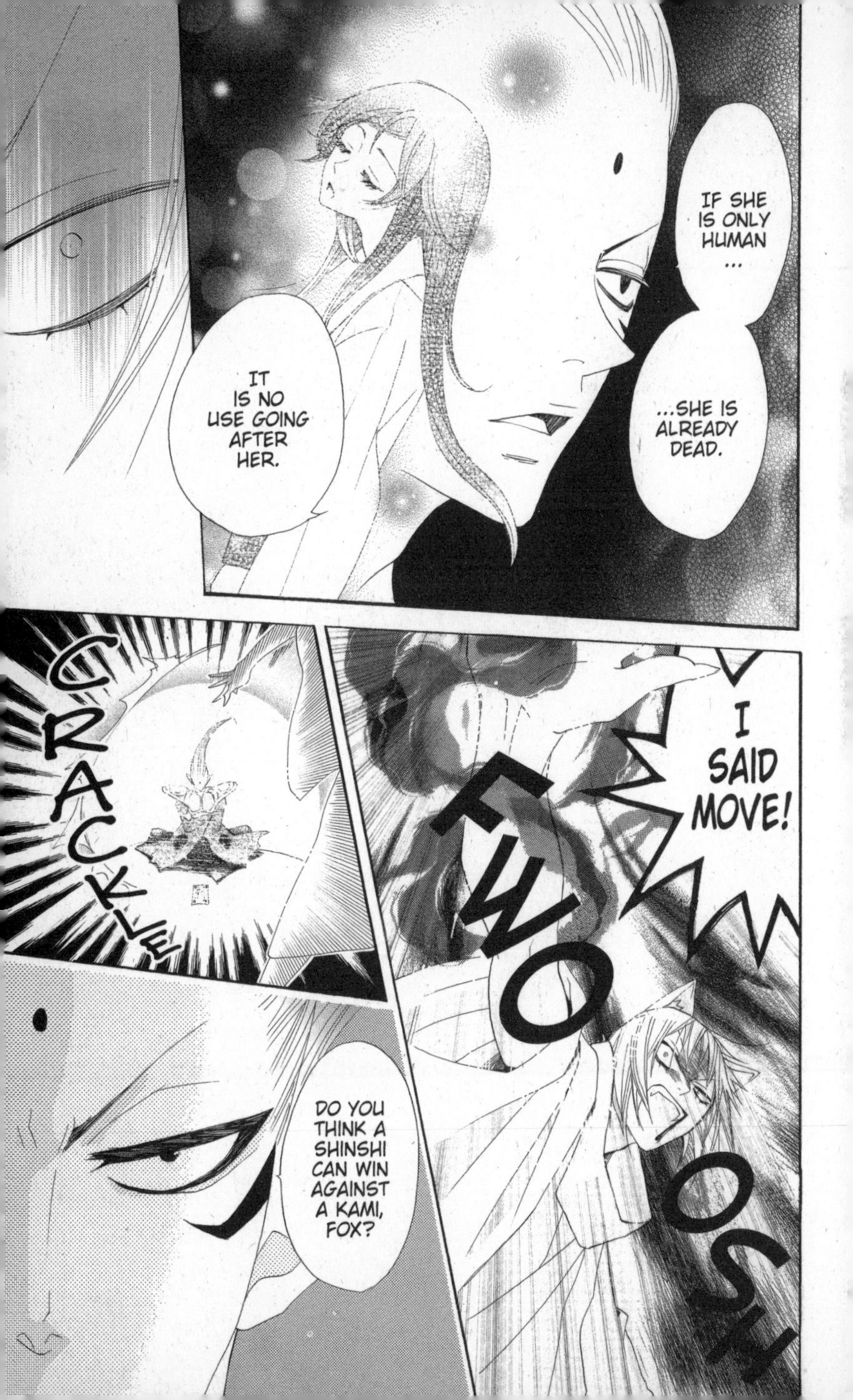
IF SHE IS ONLY HUMAN ...
...SHE IS ALREADY DEAD.
IT IS NO USE GOING AFTER HER.
I SAID MOVE!
FWOOSH
CRACKLE
DO YOU THINK A SHINSHI CAN WIN AGAINST A KAMI, FOX?

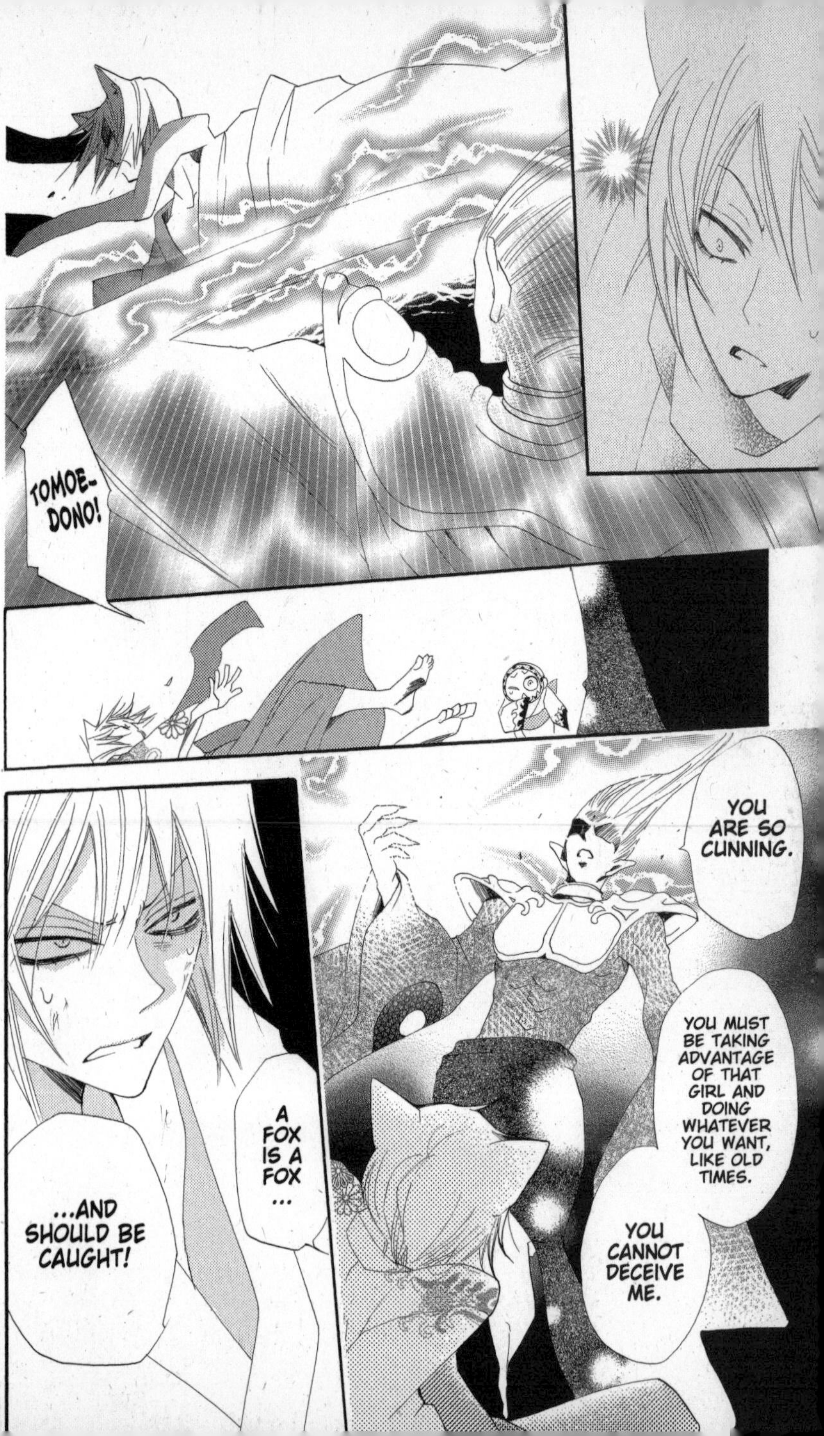
TOMOE-DONO!
YOU ARE SO CUNNING.
YOU MUST BE TAKING ADVANTAGE OF THAT GIRL AND DOING WHATEVER YOU WANT, LIKE OLD TIMES.
YOU CANNOT DECEIVE ME.
A FOX IS A FOX...
...AND SHOULD BE CAUGHT!

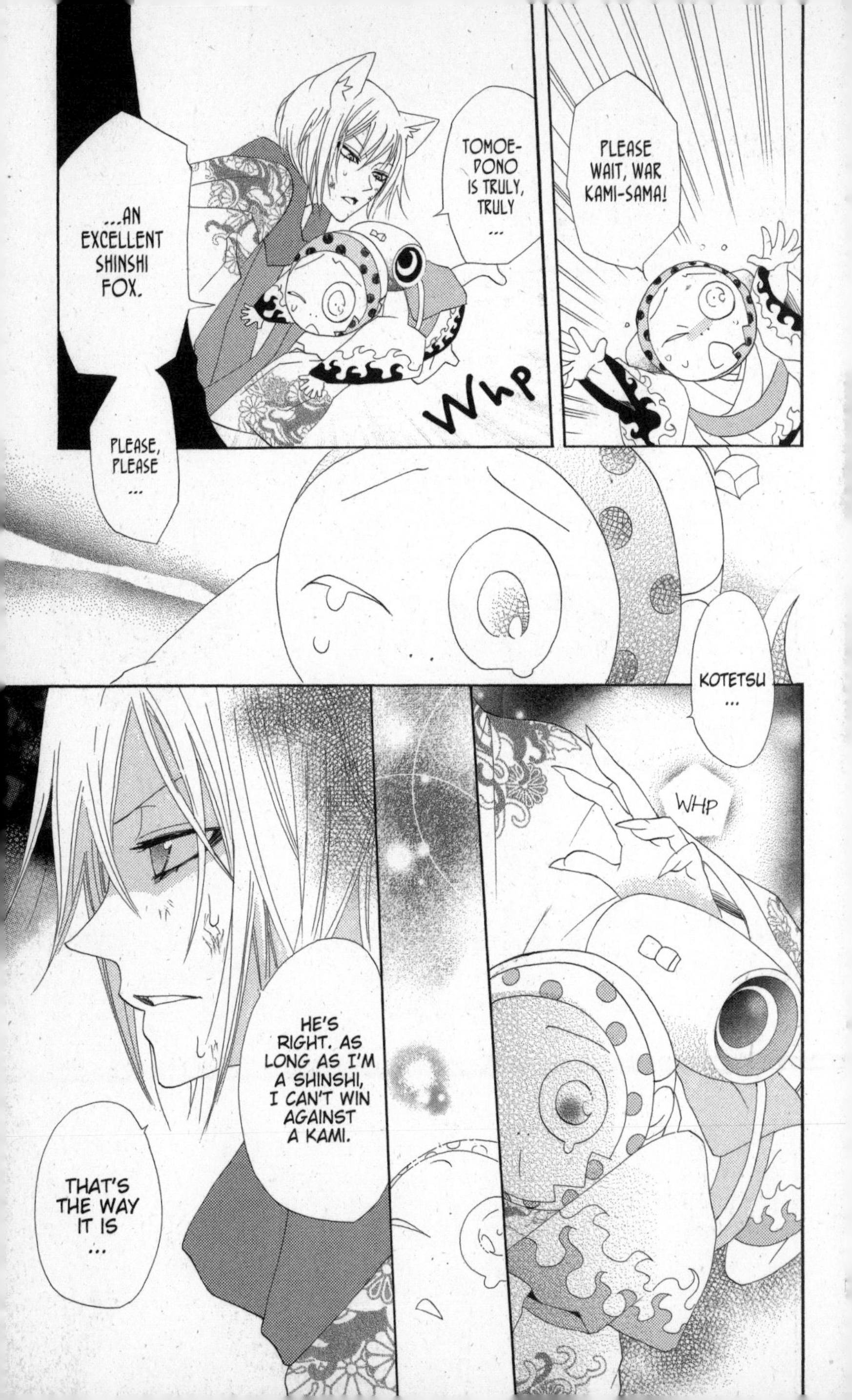
PLEASE WAIT, WAR KAMI-SAMA!
TOMOE-DONO IS TRULY, TRULY ...
...AN EXCELLENT SHINSHI FOX.
Whp
PLEASE, PLEASE ...
KOTETSU ...
WHP
HE'S RIGHT. AS LONG AS I'M A SHINSHI, I CAN'T WIN AGAINST A KAMI.
THAT'S THE WAY IT IS ...

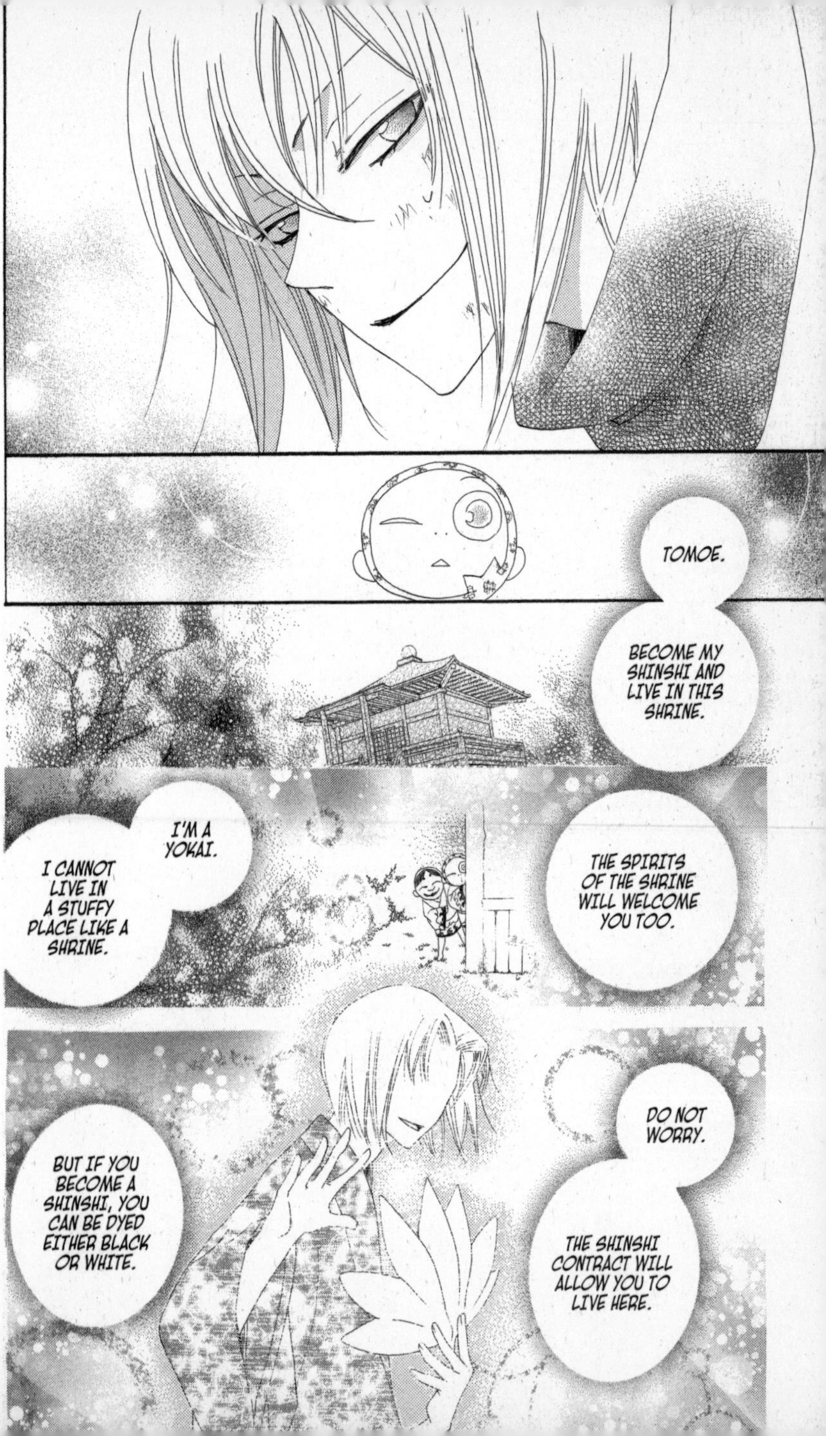
TOMOE.
BECOME MY SHINSHI AND LIVE IN THIS SHRINE.
THE SPIRITS OF THE SHRINE WILL WELCOME YOU TOO.
I'M A YOKAI.
I CANNOT LIVE IN A STUFFY PLACE LIKE A SHRINE.
DO NOT WORRY.
THE SHINSHI CONTRACT WILL ALLOW YOU TO LIVE HERE.
BUT IF YOU BECOME A SHINSHI, YOU CAN BE DYED EITHER BLACK OR WHITE.

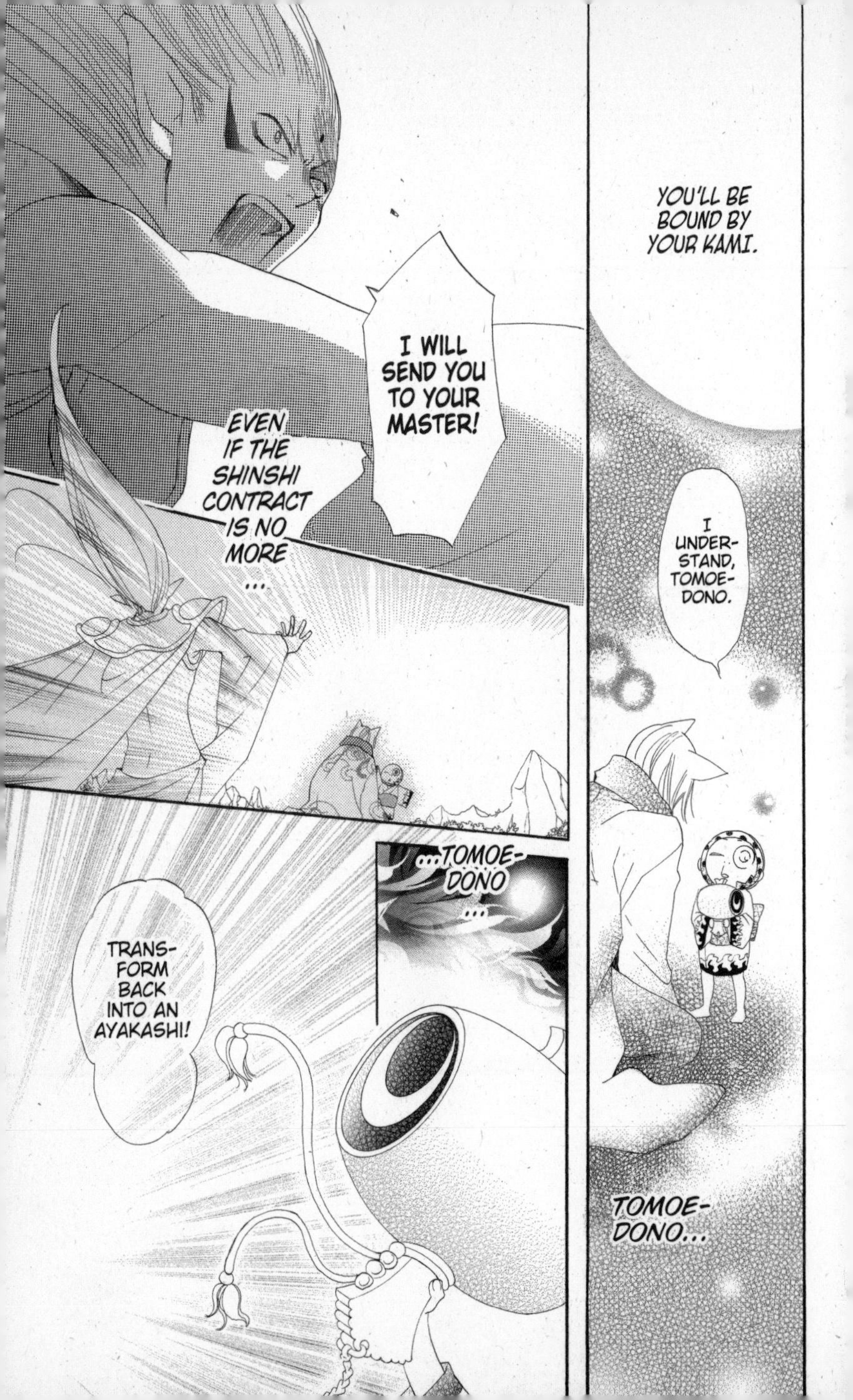
YOU'LL BE BOUND BY YOUR KAMI.
I UNDER-STAND, TOMOE-DONO.
TOMOE-DONO...
I WILL SEND YOU TO YOUR MASTER!
EVEN IF THE SHINSHI CONTRACT IS NO MORE...
...TOMOE-DONO...
TRANS-FORM BACK INTO AN AYAKASHI!

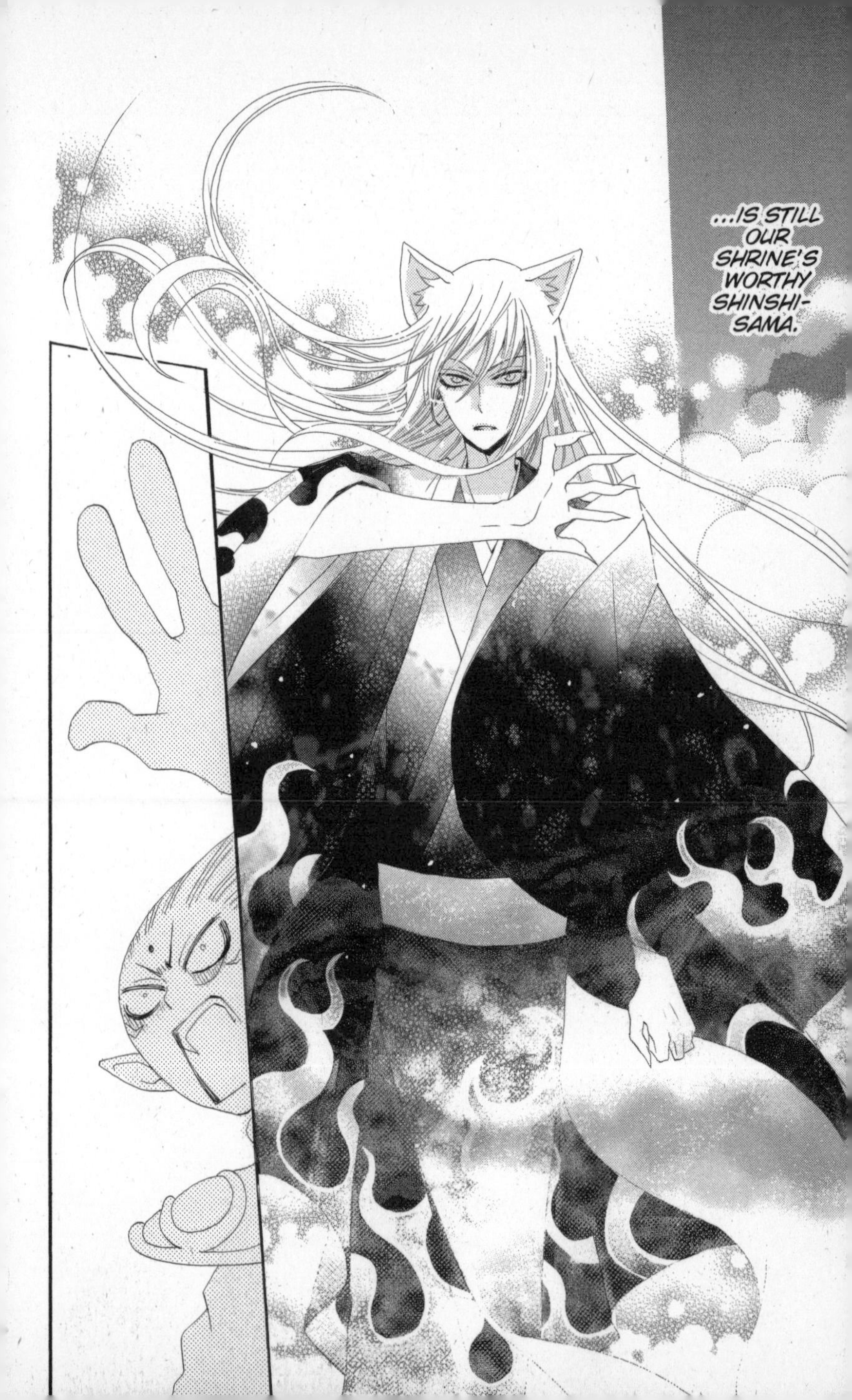
...IS STILL OUR SHRINE'S WORTHY SHINSHI-SAMA.

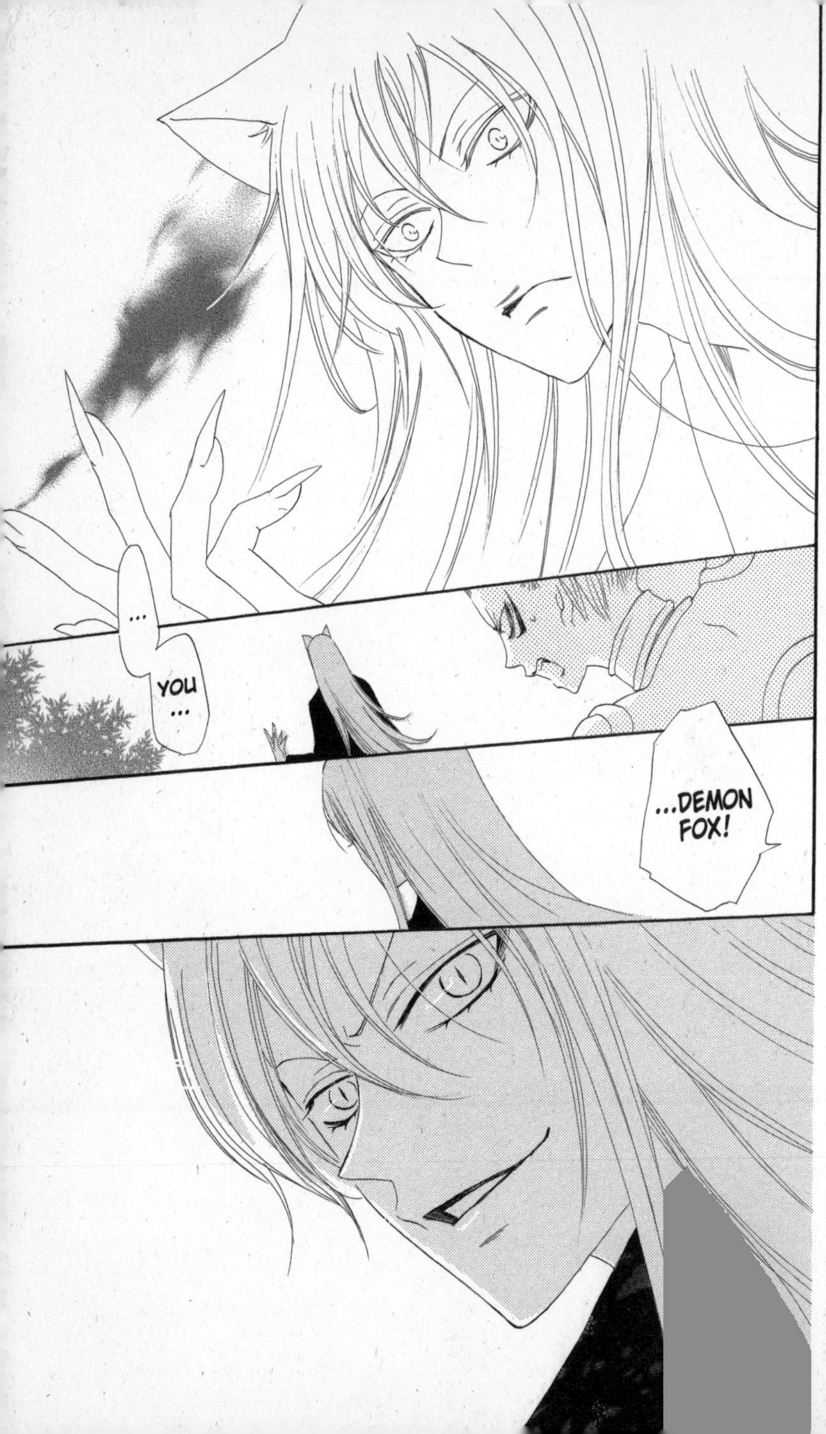
...YOU...
...DEMON FOX!

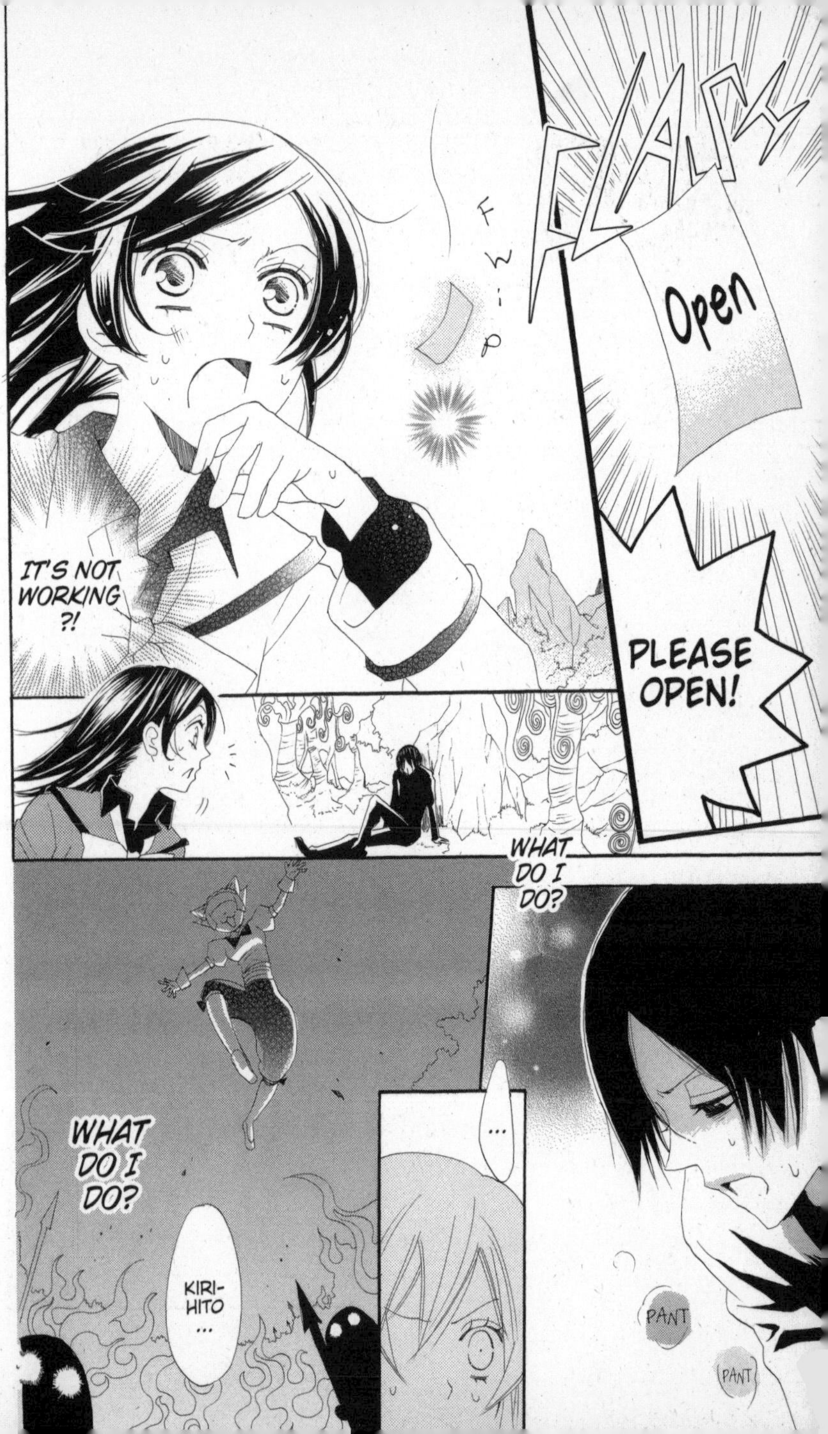
FLASH
Open
FWIP
IT'S NOT WORKING?!
PLEASE OPEN!
WHAT DO I DO?
...
PANT
PANT
WHAT DO I DO?
KIRI-HITO...

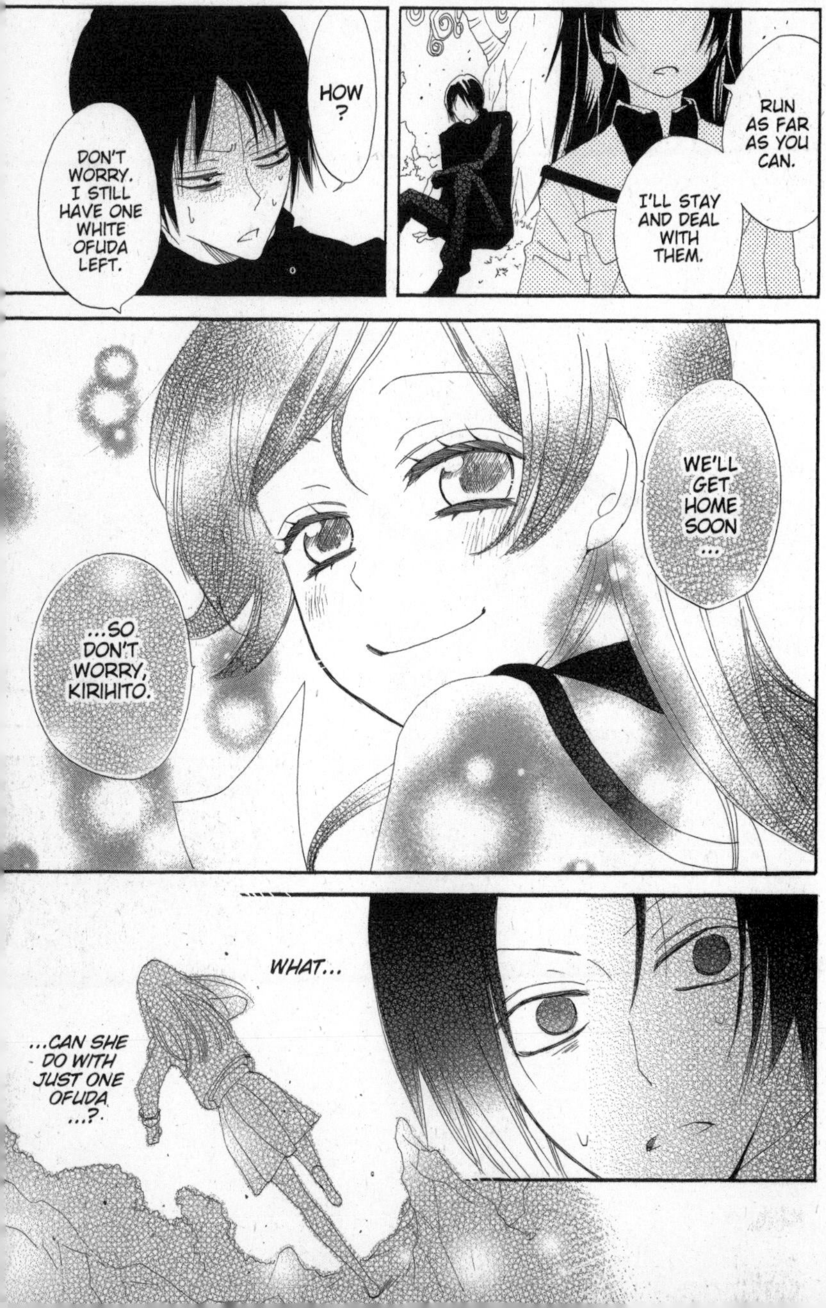
RUN AS FAR AS YOU CAN.
I'LL STAY AND DEAL WITH THEM.
HOW?
DON'T WORRY. I STILL HAVE ONE WHITE OFUDA LEFT.
WE'LL GET HOME SOON...
...SO DON'T WORRY, KIRIHITO.
WHAT...
...CAN SHE DO WITH JUST ONE OFUDA...?

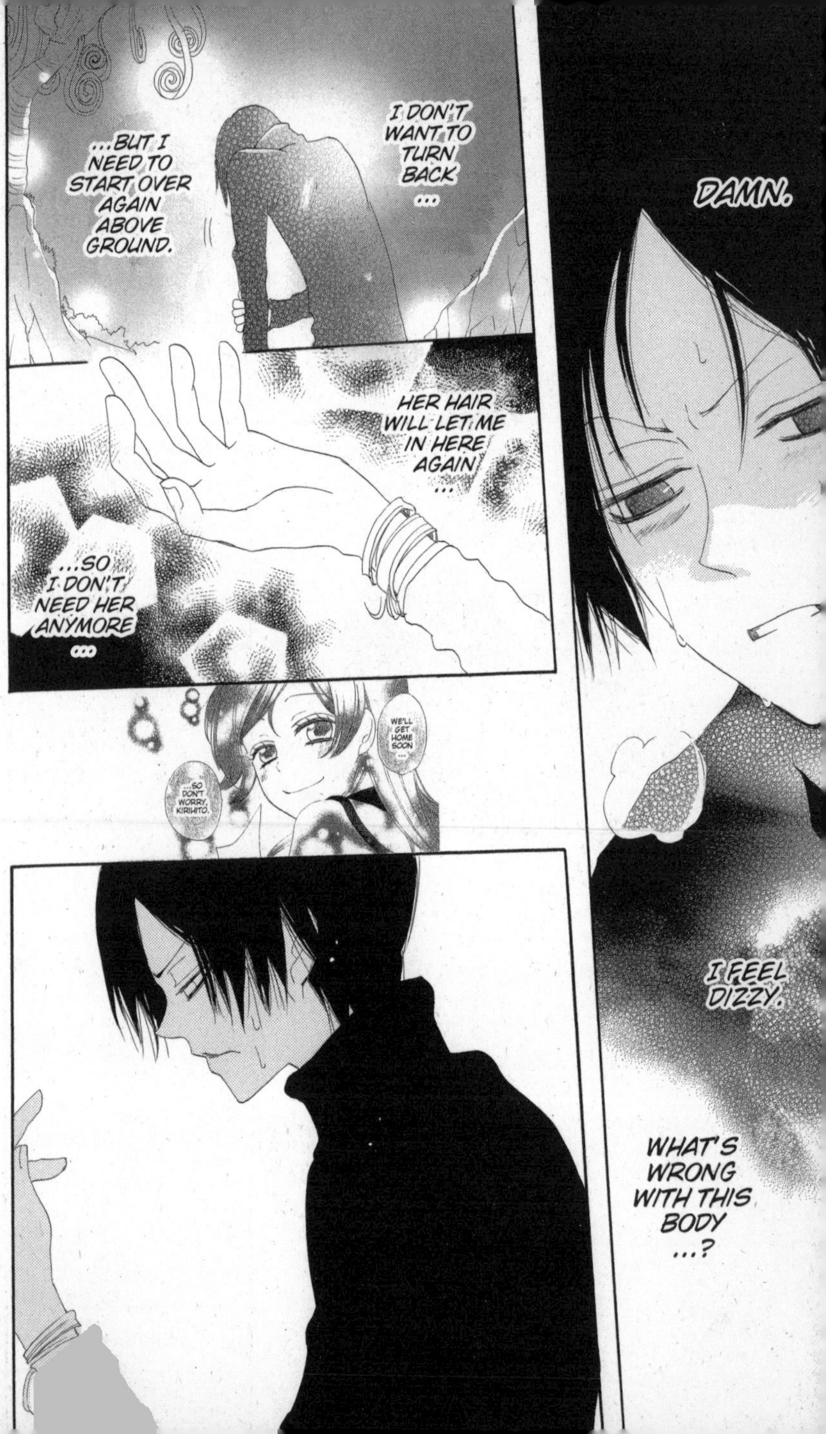
DAMN.
I FEEL DIZZY.
WHAT'S WRONG WITH THIS BODY ...?
I DON'T WANT TO TURN BACK ...
...BUT I NEED TO START OVER AGAIN ABOVE GROUND.
HER HAIR WILL LET ME IN HERE AGAIN ...
...SO I DON'T NEED HER ANYMORE ...
WE'LL GET HOME SOON ...
...SO DON'T WORRY, KIRIHITO.

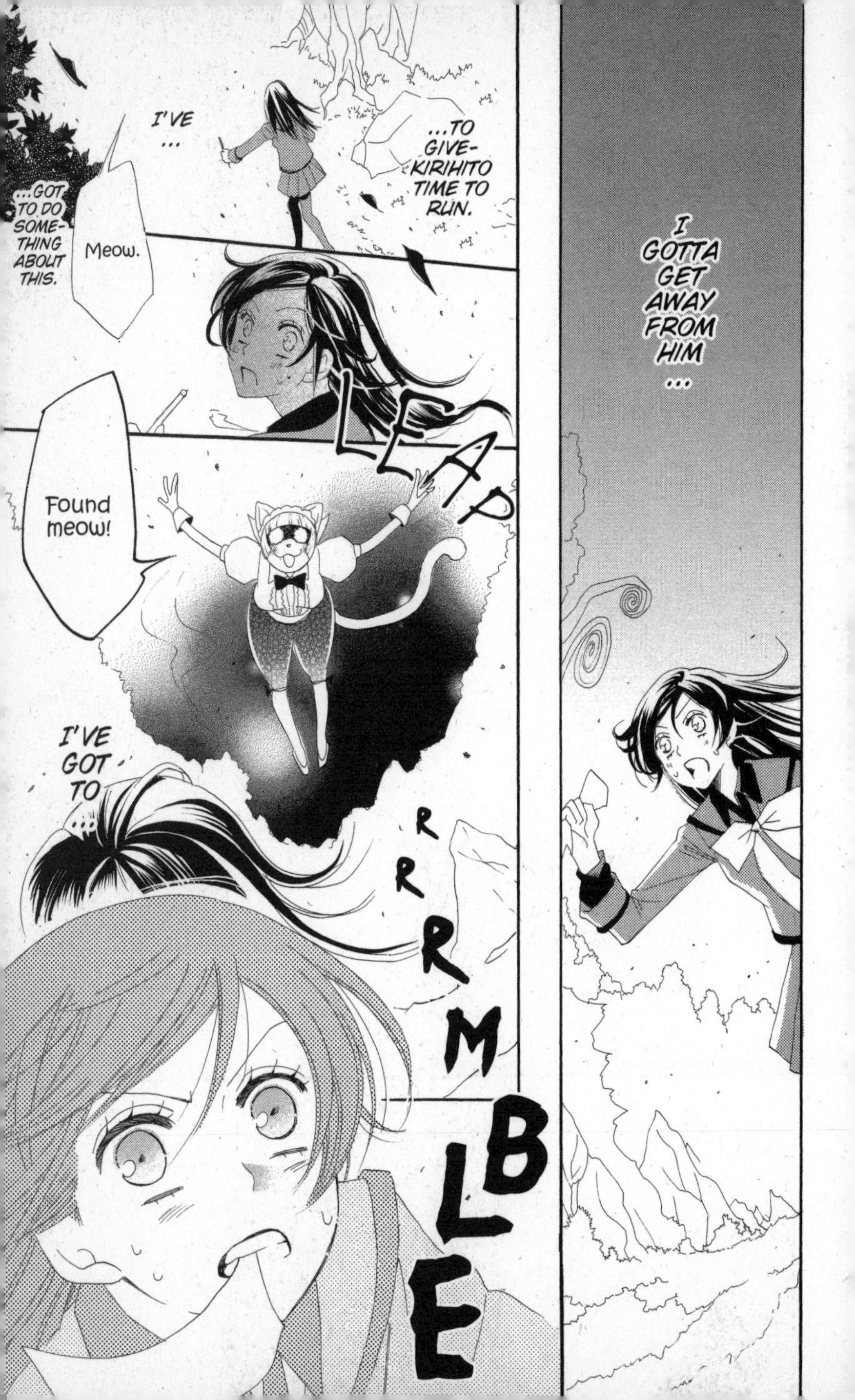
I GOTTA GET AWAY FROM HIM...
I'VE...
...GOT TO DO SOME-THING ABOUT THIS.
...TO GIVE-KIRIHITO TIME TO RUN.
Meow.
LEAP
Found meow!
I'VE GOT TO...
RRRRMBLE

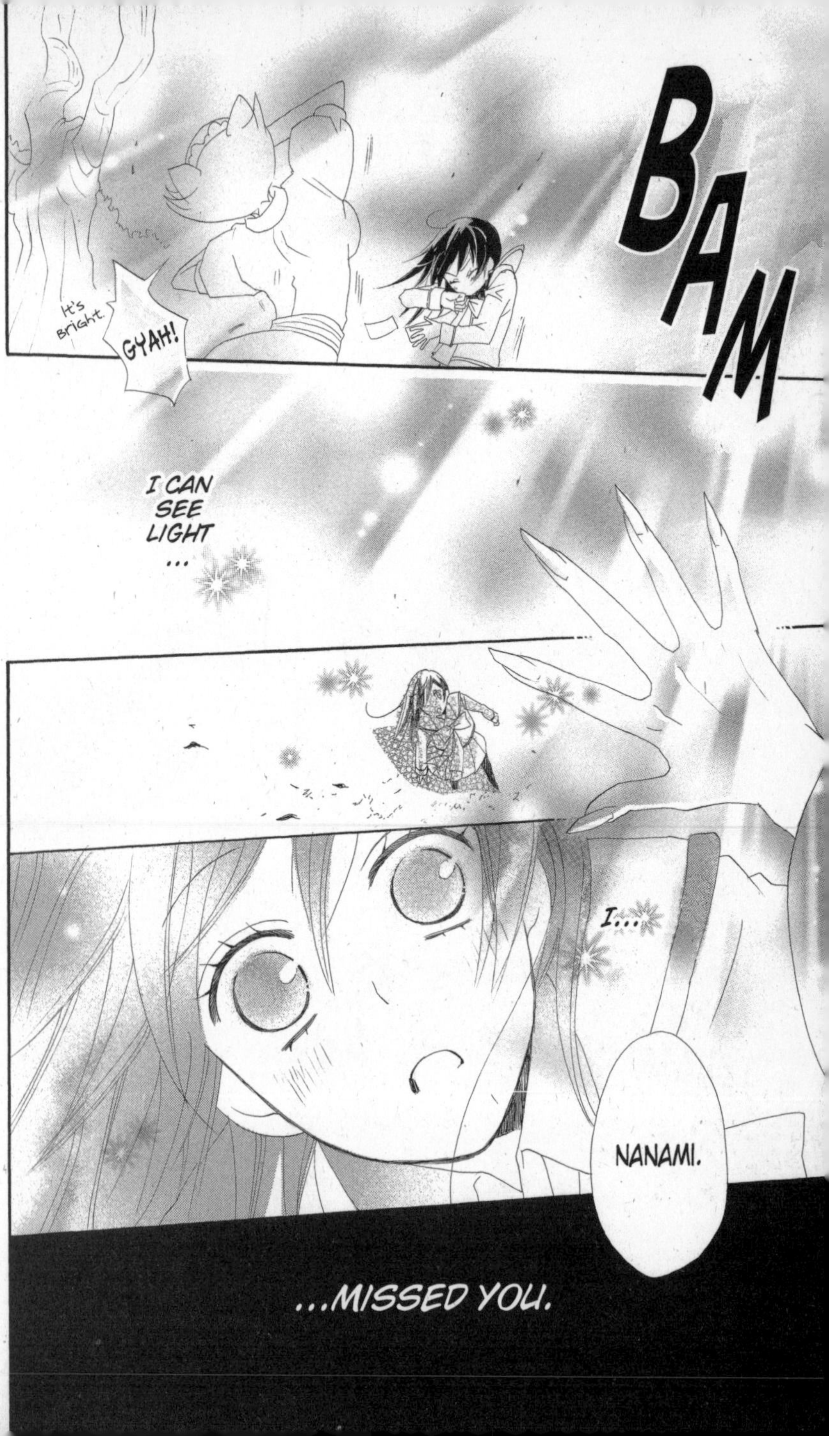
BAM
GYAH!
It's bright.
I CAN SEE LIGHT ...
I...
NANAMI.
...MISSED YOU.

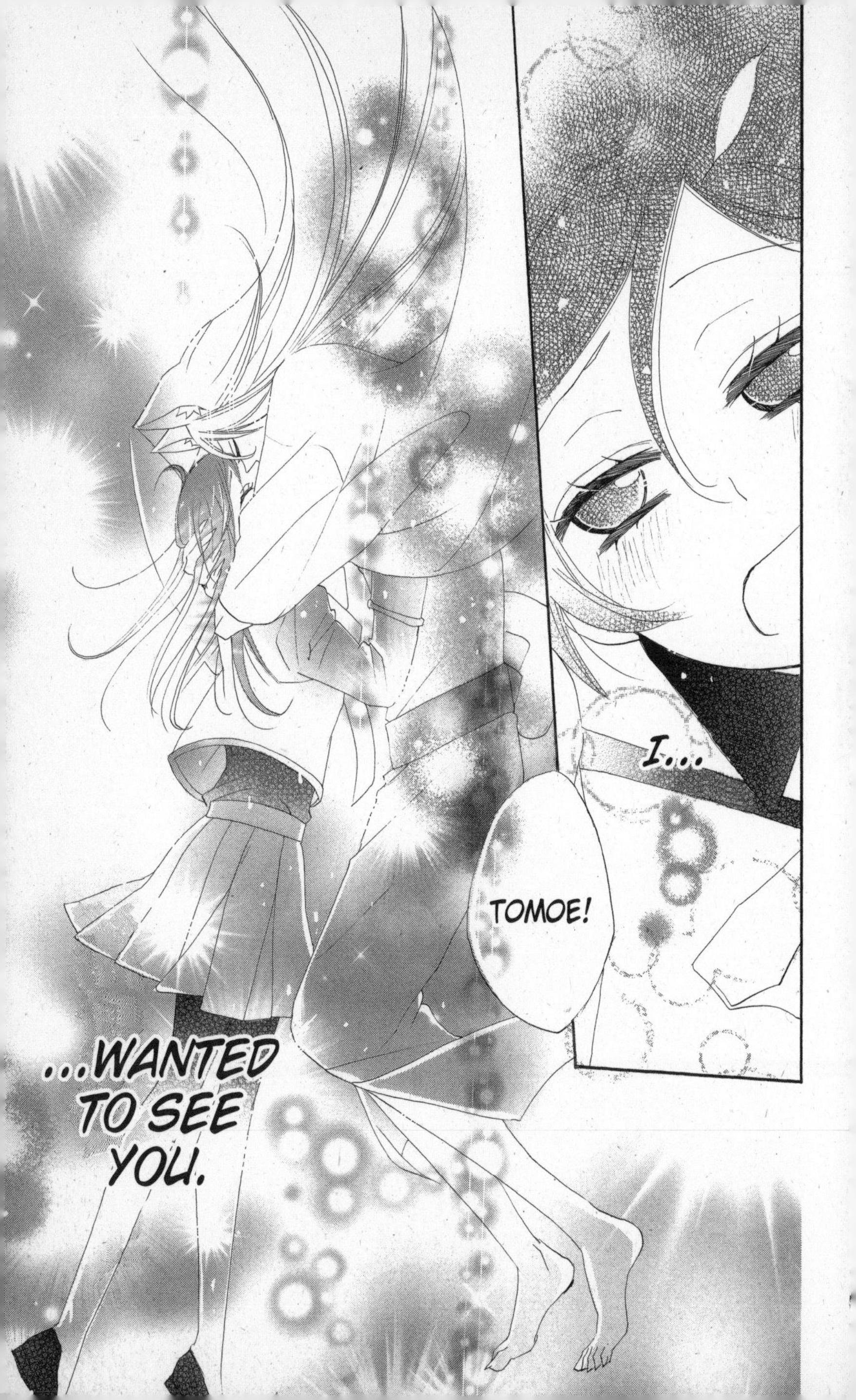
I...
TOMOE!
...WANTED TO SEE YOU.

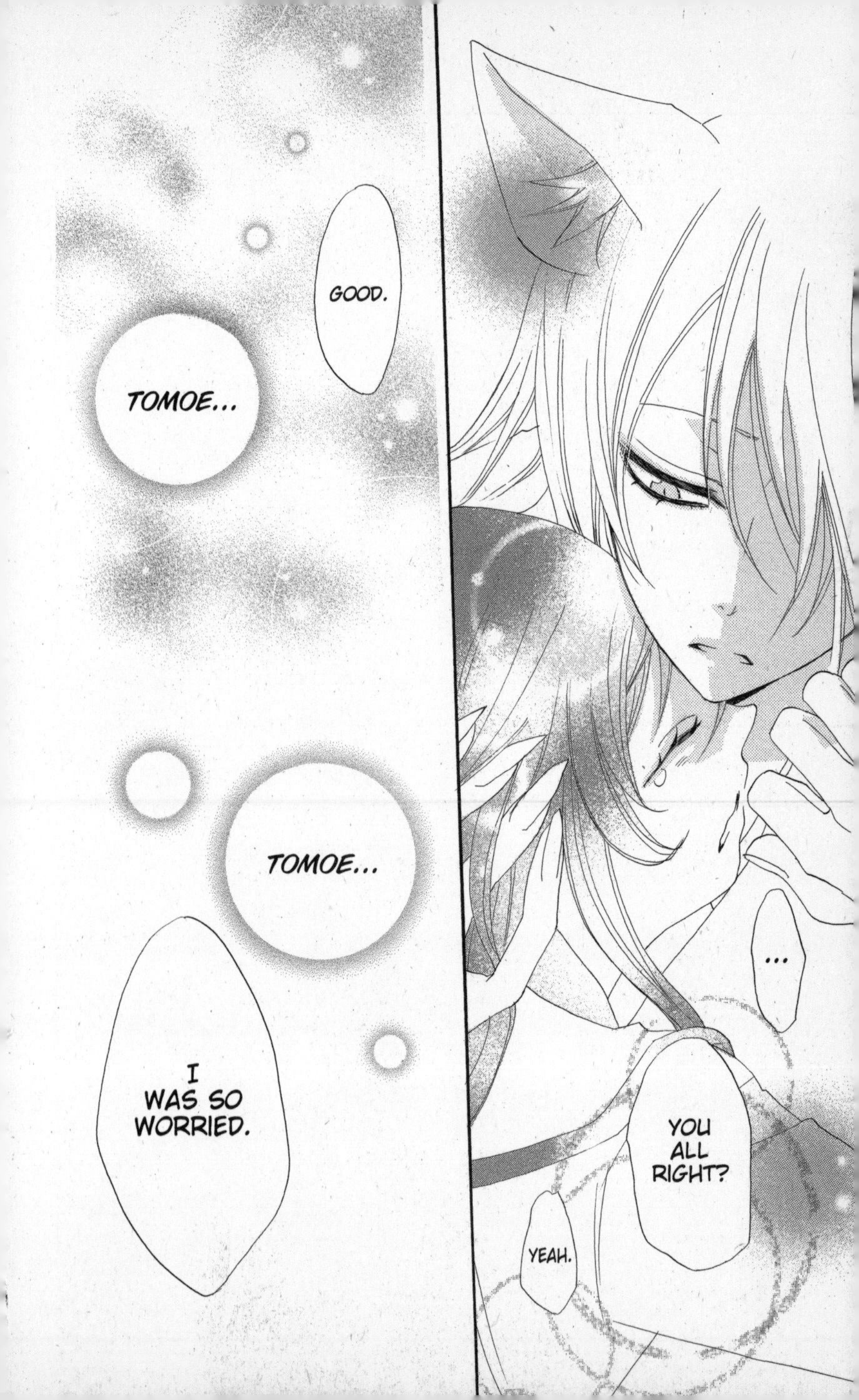
...
YOU ALL RIGHT?
YEAH.
GOOD.
TOMOE...
TOMOE...
I WAS SO WORRIED.

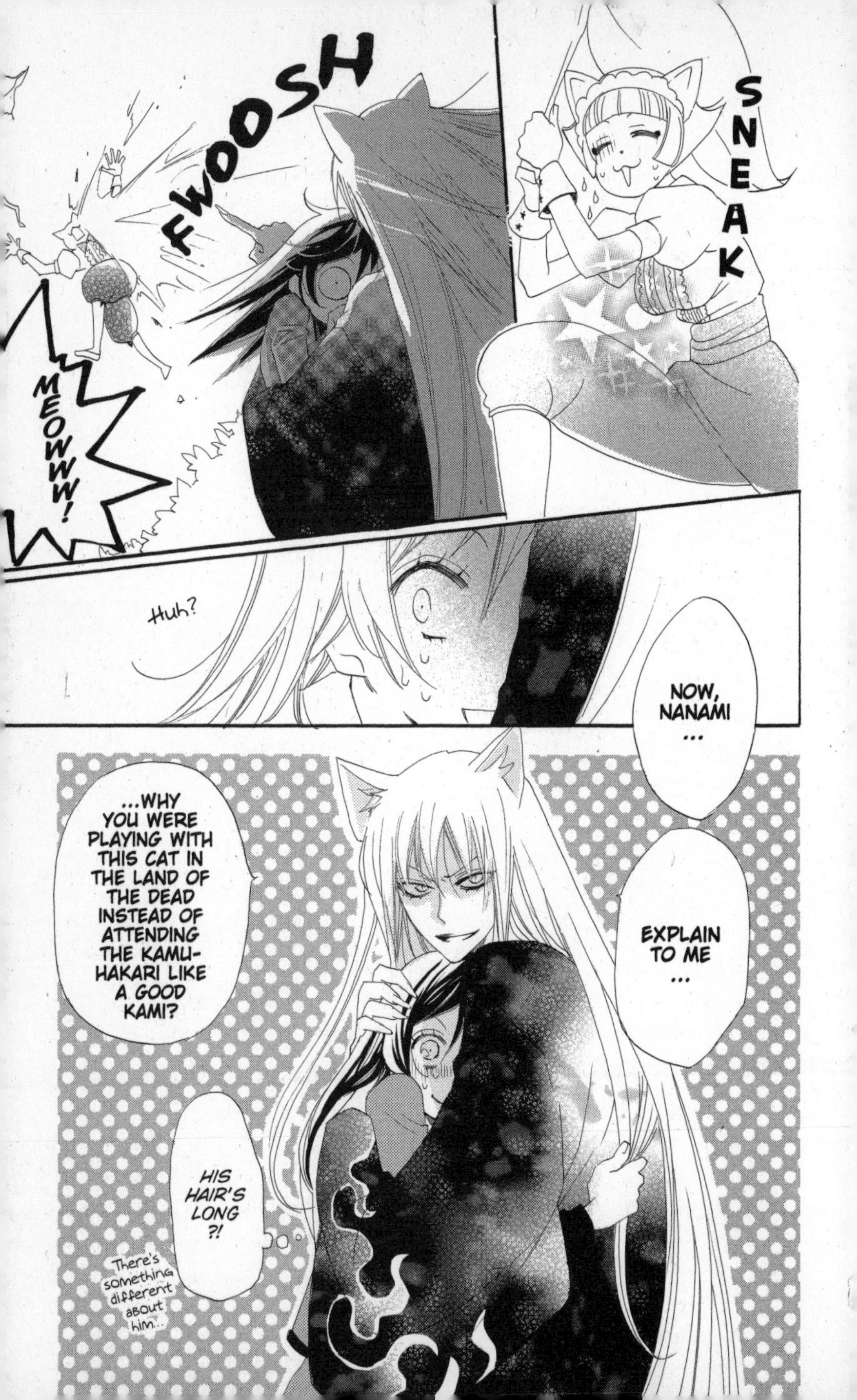
SNEAK
FWOOSH
MEOWWW!
Huh?
NOW, NANAMI ...
EXPLAIN TO ME ...
...WHY YOU WERE PLAYING WITH THIS CAT IN THE LAND OF THE DEAD INSTEAD OF ATTENDING THE KAMU-HAKARI LIKE A GOOD KAMI?
HIS HAIR'S LONG?!
There's something different about him...

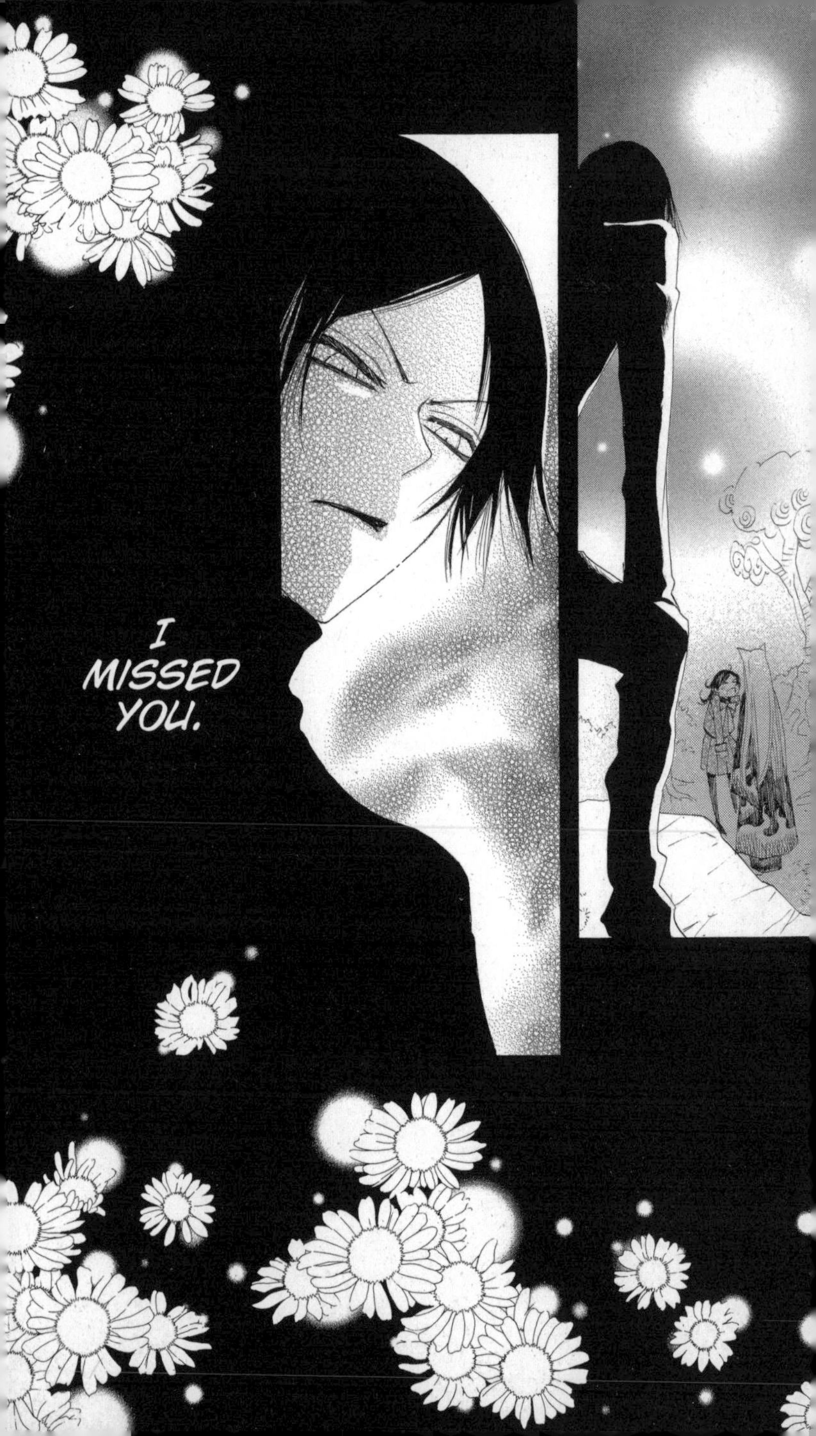
I MISSED YOU.

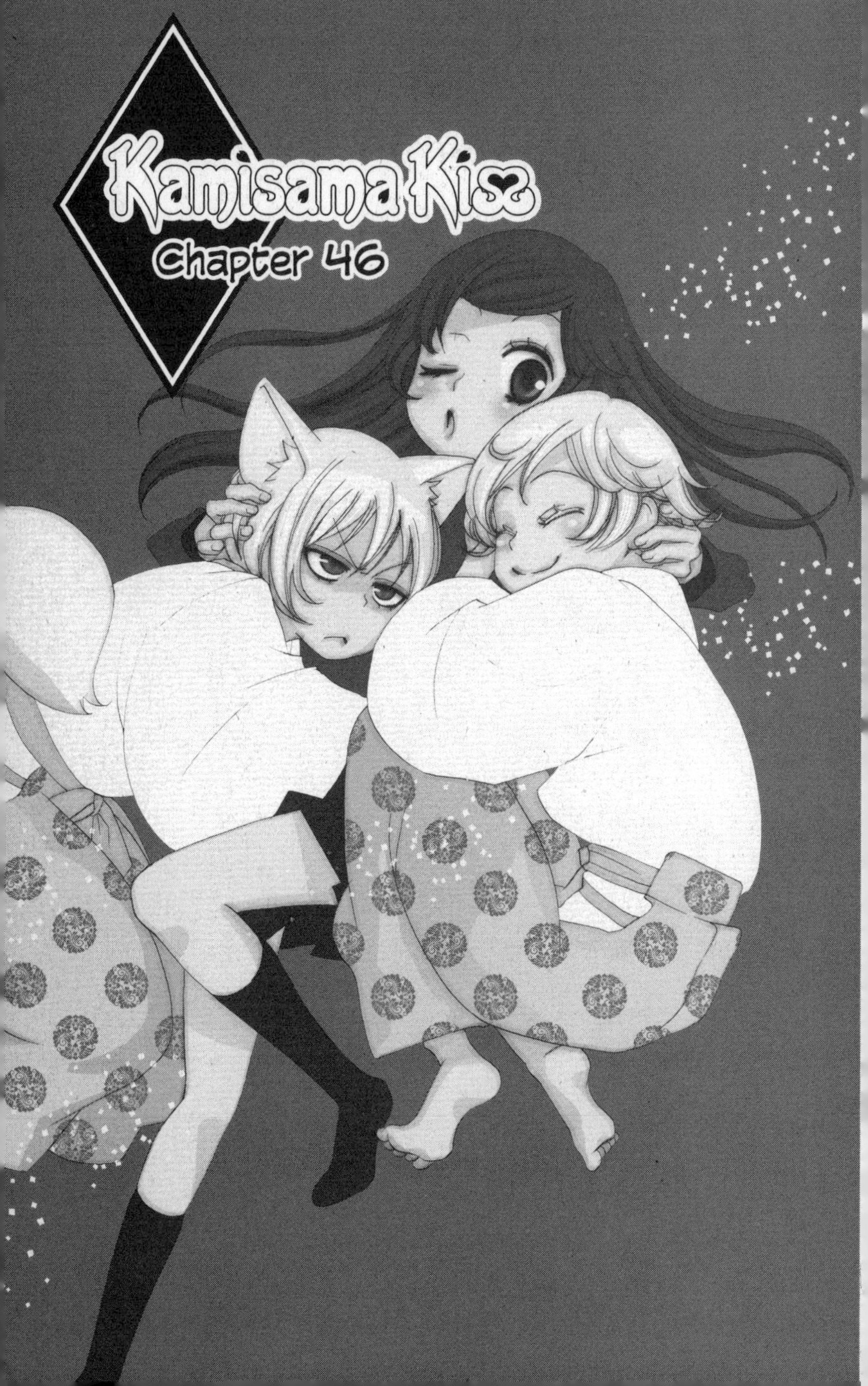
Kamisama Kiss
Chapter 46

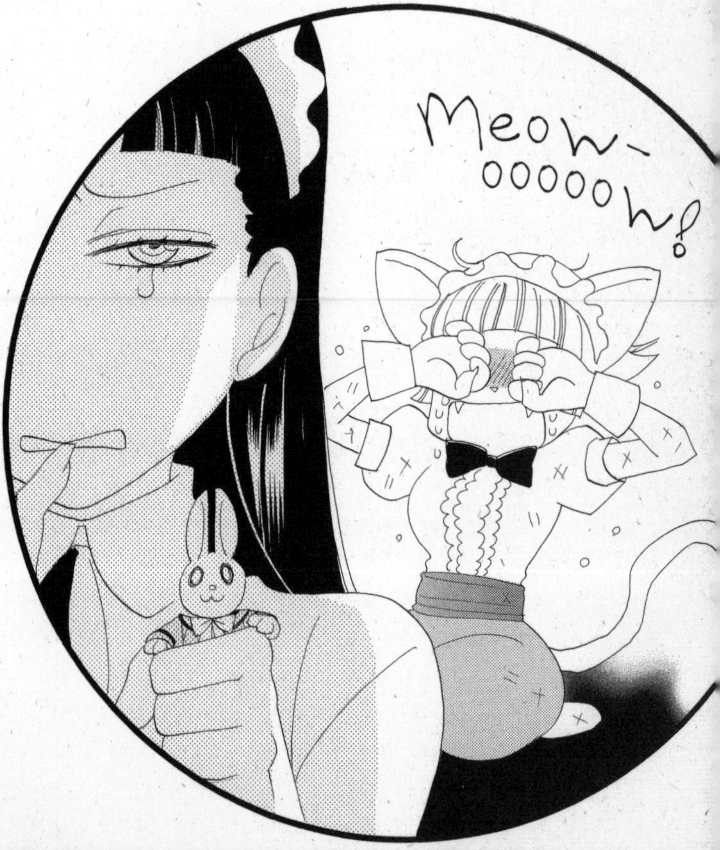
Meow-oooooow!

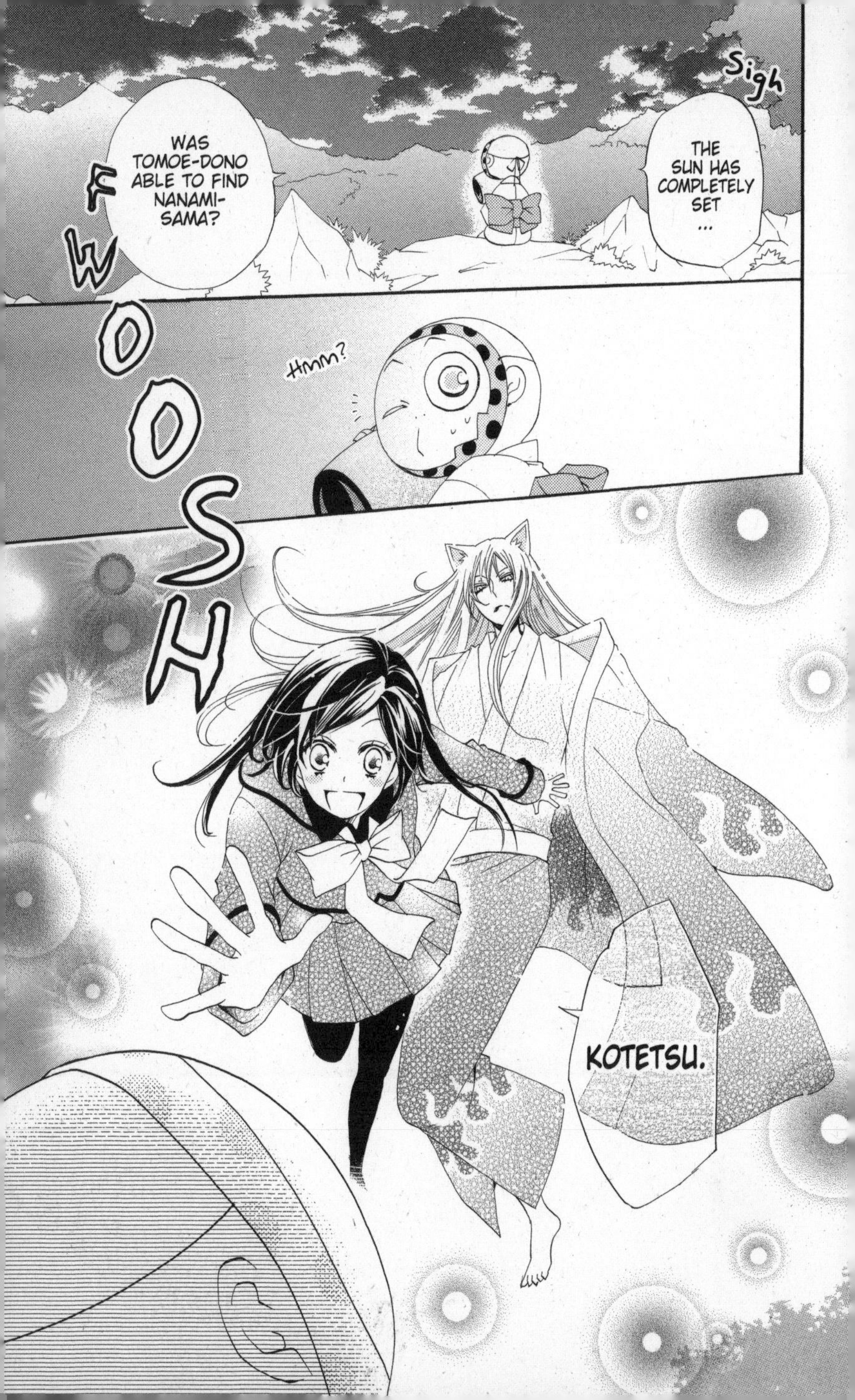
Sigh
THE SUN HAS COMPLETELY SET ...
WAS TOMOE-DONO ABLE TO FIND NANAMI-SAMA?
FWOOSH
Hmm?
KOTETSU.

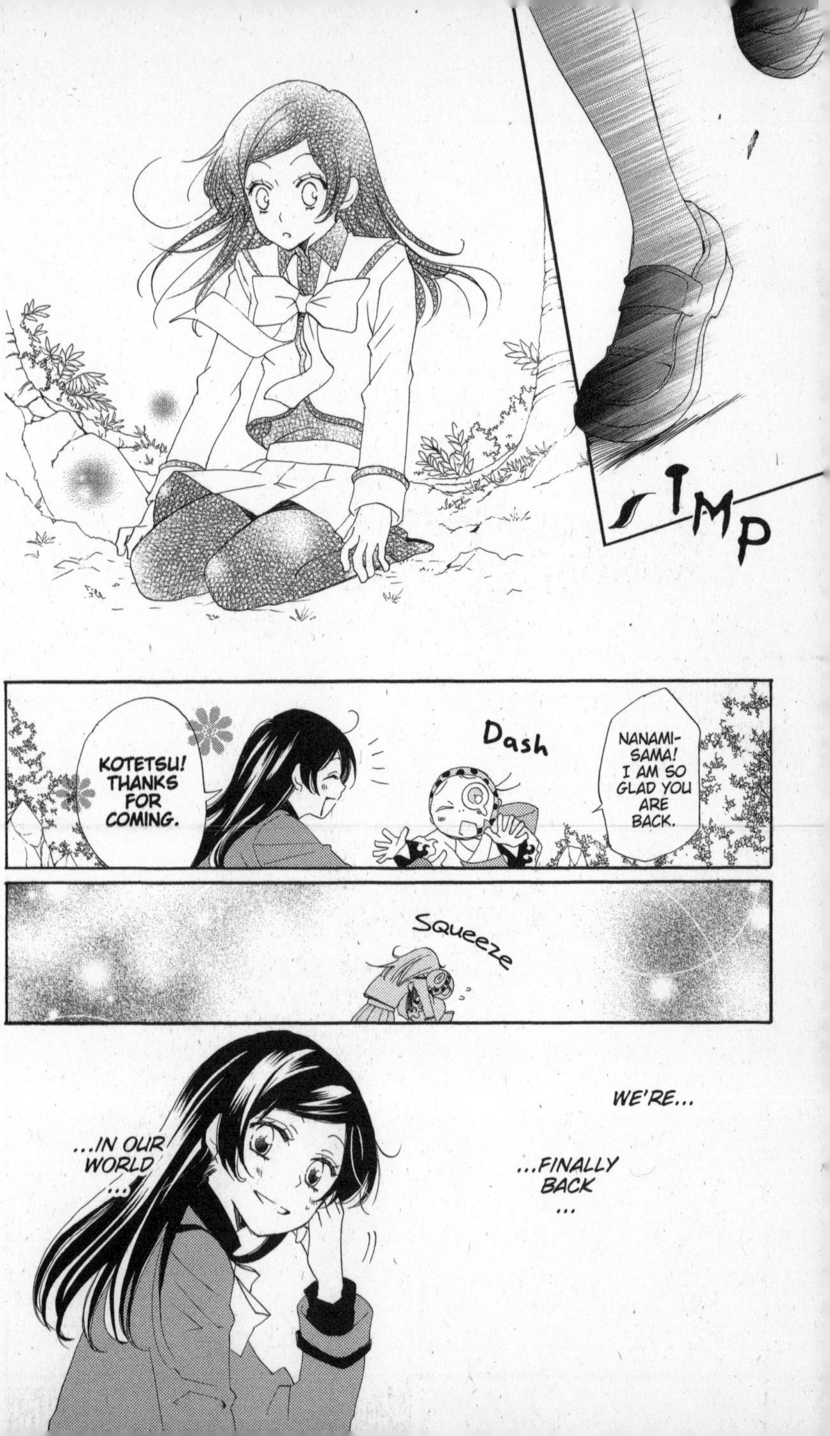
STMP
NANAMI-SAMA! I AM SO GLAD YOU ARE BACK.
Dash
KOTETSU! THANKS FOR COMING.
Squeeze
WE'RE...
...FINALLY BACK ...
...IN OUR WORLD ...

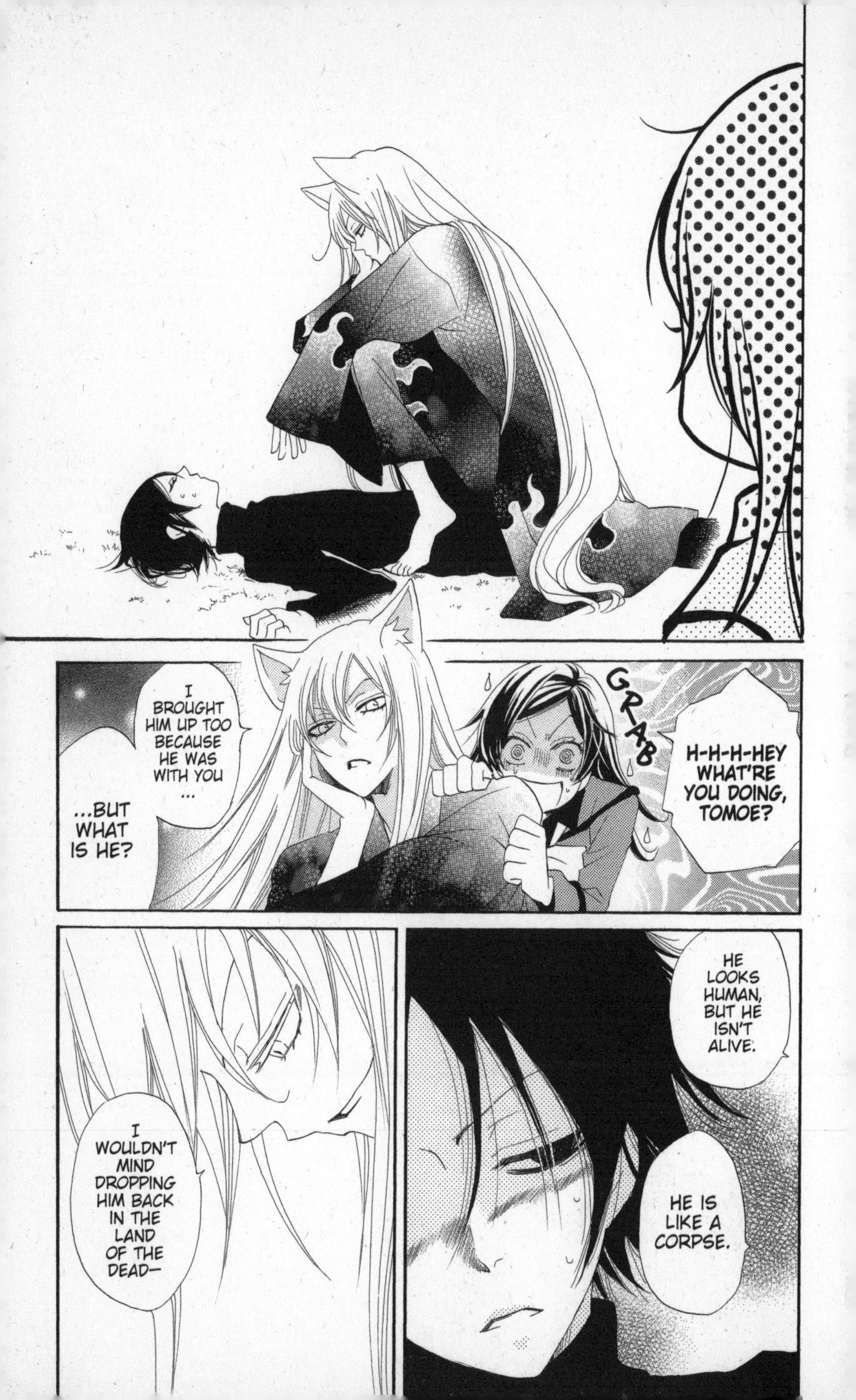
GRAB
H-H-H-HEY WHAT'RE YOU DOING, TOMOE?
I BROUGHT HIM UP TOO BECAUSE HE WAS WITH YOU ...
...BUT WHAT IS HE?
HE LOOKS HUMAN, BUT HE ISN'T ALIVE.
HE IS LIKE A CORPSE.
I WOULDN'T MIND DROPPING HIM BACK IN THE LAND OF THE DEAD—

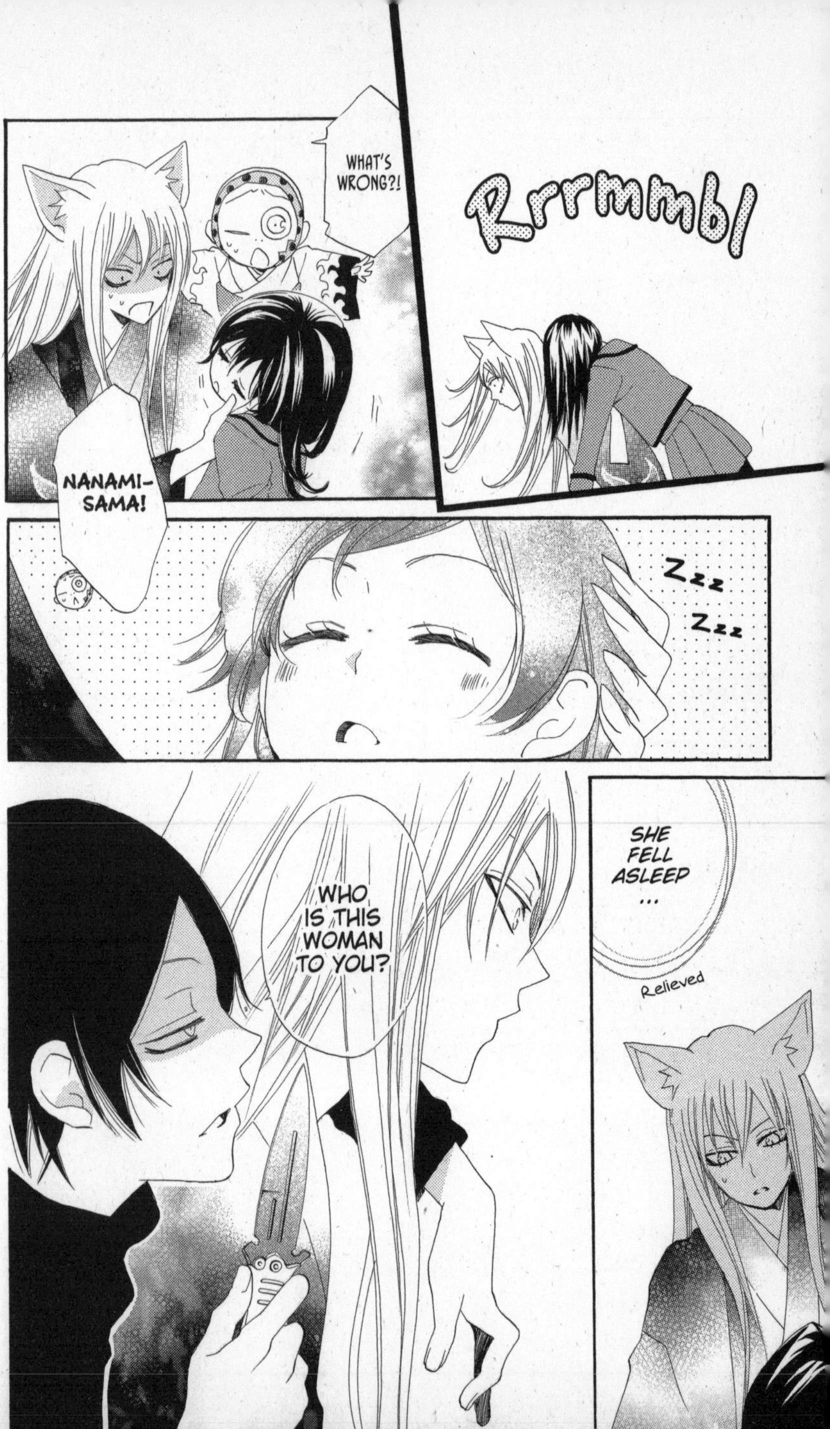
Rrrmmbl
WHAT'S WRONG?!
NANAMI-SAMA!
Zzz
Zzz
SHE FELL ASLEEP ...
Relieved
WHO IS THIS WOMAN TO YOU?

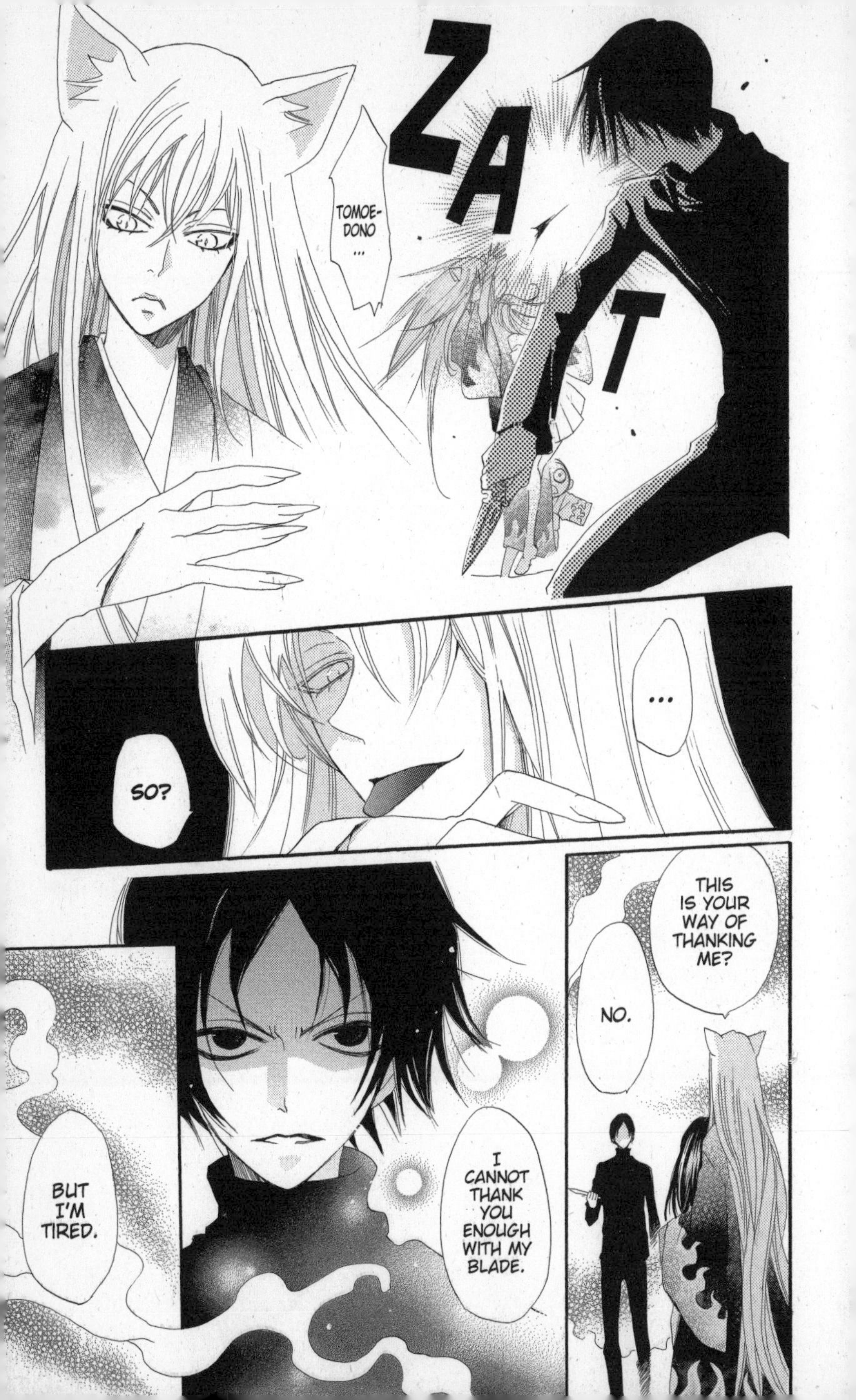
ZAT
TOMOE-DONO ...
...
SO?
THIS IS YOUR WAY OF THANKING ME?
NO.
I CANNOT THANK YOU ENOUGH WITH MY BLADE.
BUT I'M TIRED.

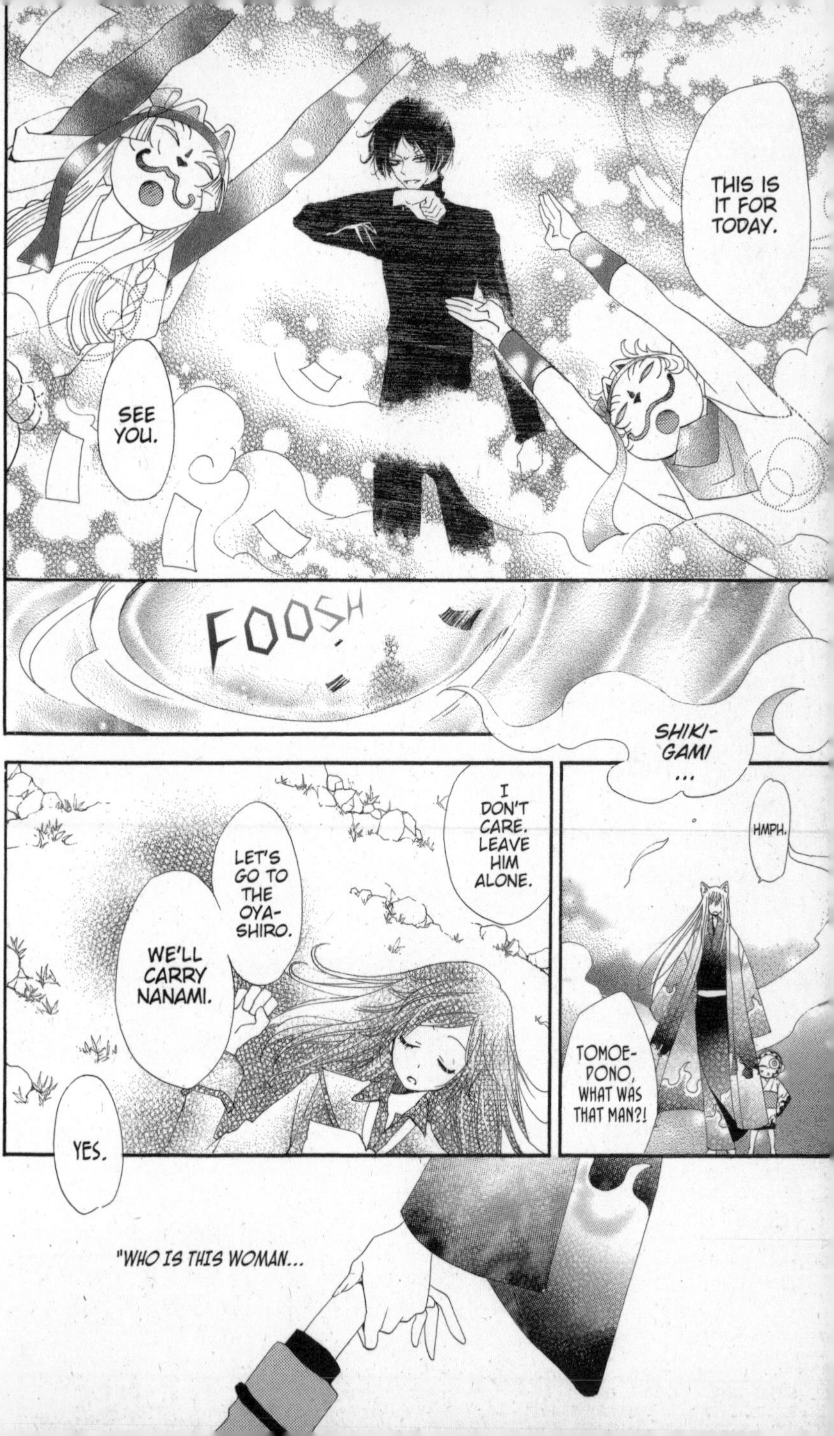
THIS IS IT FOR TODAY.
SEE YOU.
FOOSH
SHIKI-GAMI...
HMPH.
TOMOE-DONO, WHAT WAS THAT MAN?!
I DON'T CARE. LEAVE HIM ALONE.
LET'S GO TO THE OYA-SHIRO.
WE'LL CARRY NANAMI.
YES.
"WHO IS THIS WOMAN...

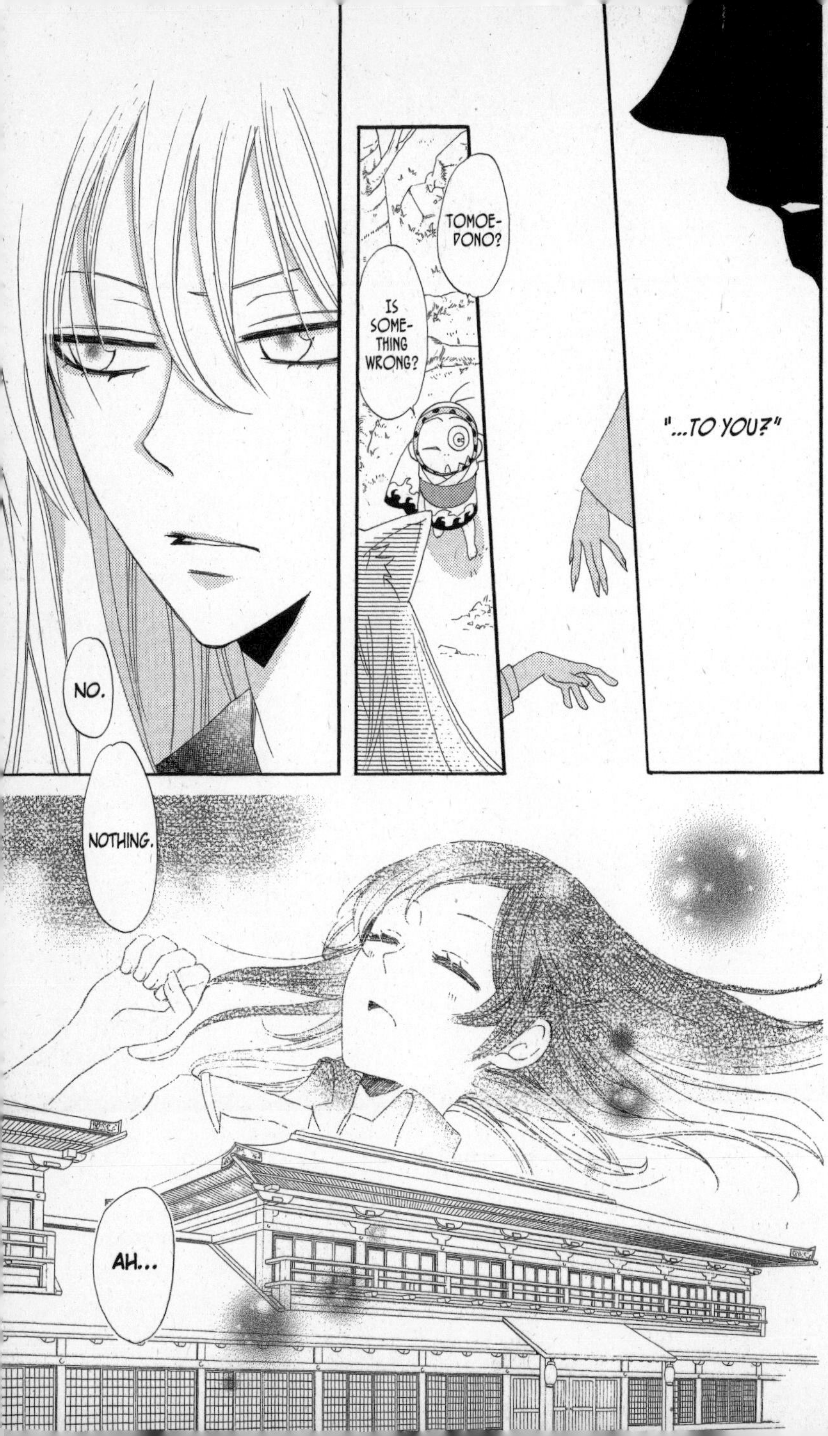
"...TO YOU?"
TOMOE-DONO?
IS SOME-THING WRONG?
NO.
NOTHING.
AH...

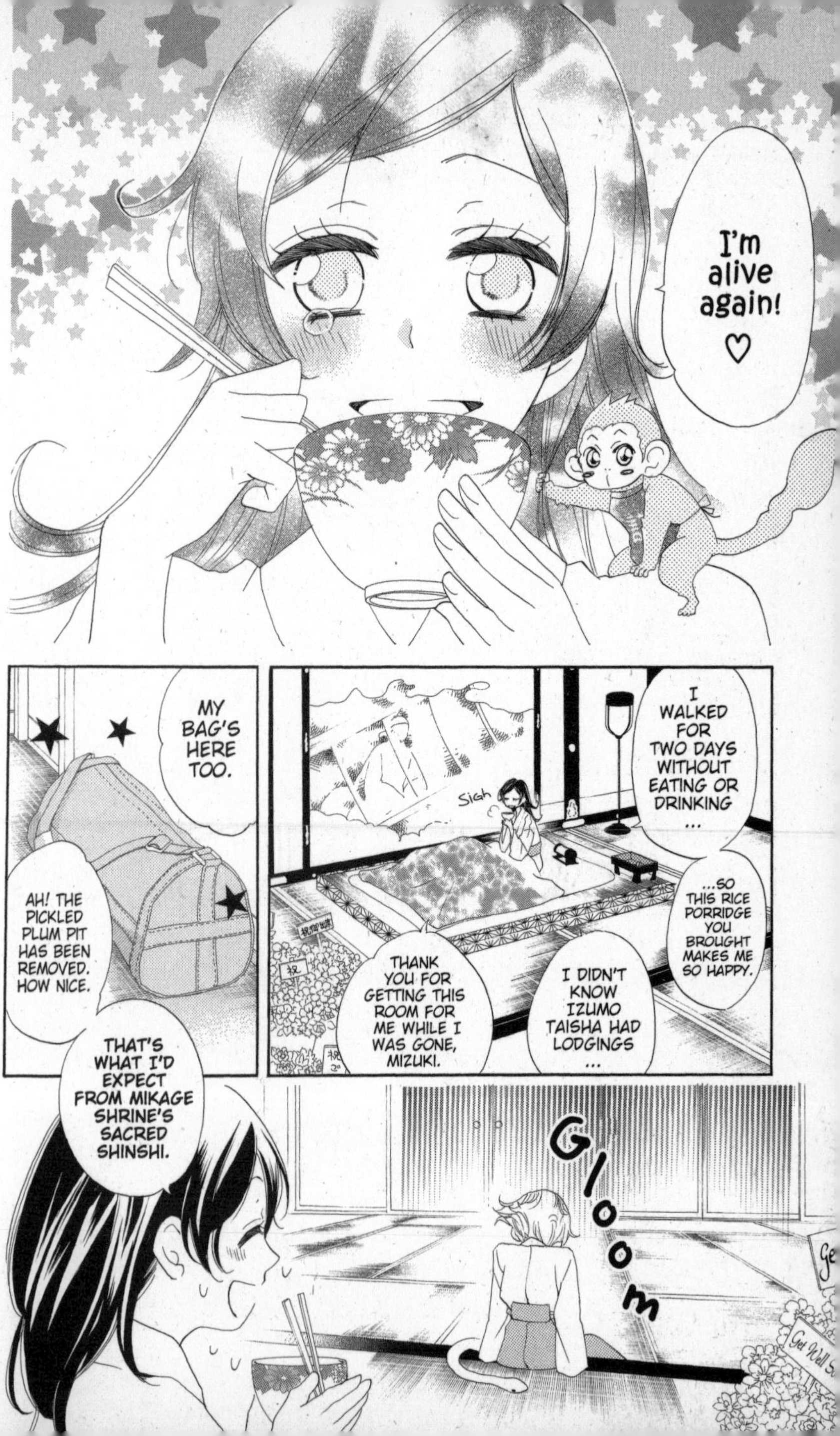
I'm alive again! ♡
I WALKED FOR TWO DAYS WITHOUT EATING OR DRINKING ...
...SO THIS RICE PORRIDGE YOU BROUGHT MAKES ME SO HAPPY.
Sigh
I DIDN'T KNOW IZUMO TAISHA HAD LODGINGS ...
THANK YOU FOR GETTING THIS ROOM FOR ME WHILE I WAS GONE, MIZUKI.
MY BAG'S HERE TOO.
AH! THE PICKLED PLUM PIT HAS BEEN REMOVED. HOW NICE.
THAT'S WHAT I'D EXPECT FROM MIKAGE SHRINE'S SACRED SHINSHI.
Gloom

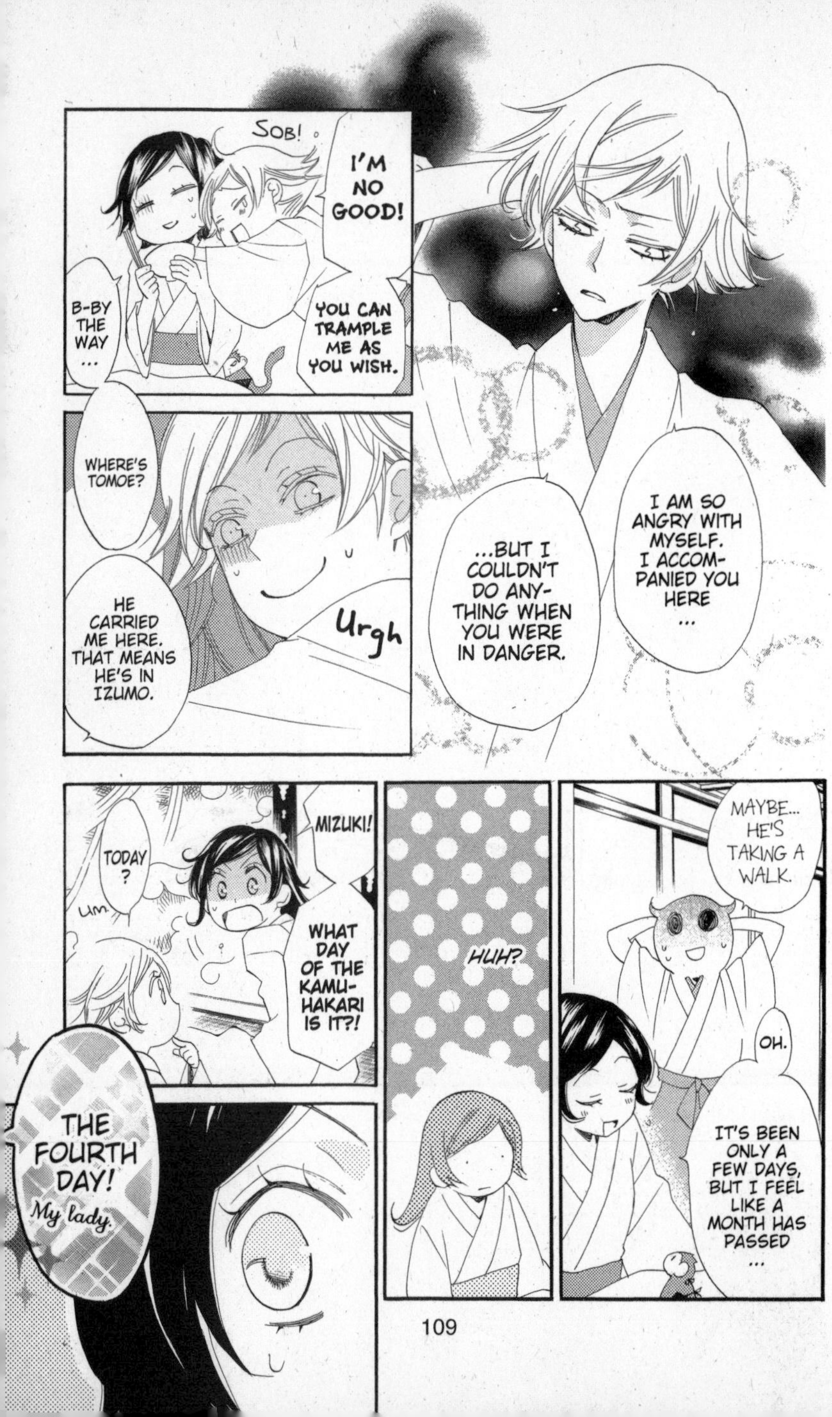
I AM SO ANGRY WITH MYSELF. I ACCOMPANIED YOU HERE...
...BUT I COULDN'T DO ANYTHING WHEN YOU WERE IN DANGER.
SOB!
I'M NO GOOD!
YOU CAN TRAMPLE ME AS YOU WISH.
B-BY THE WAY...
WHERE'S TOMOE?
Urgh
HE CARRIED ME HERE. THAT MEANS HE'S IN IZUMO.
MAYBE... HE'S TAKING A WALK.
OH.
IT'S BEEN ONLY A FEW DAYS, BUT I FEEL LIKE A MONTH HAS PASSED...
HUH?
MIZUKI!
WHAT DAY OF THE KAMUHAKARI IS IT?!
TODAY?
Um.
THE FOURTH DAY! My lady.

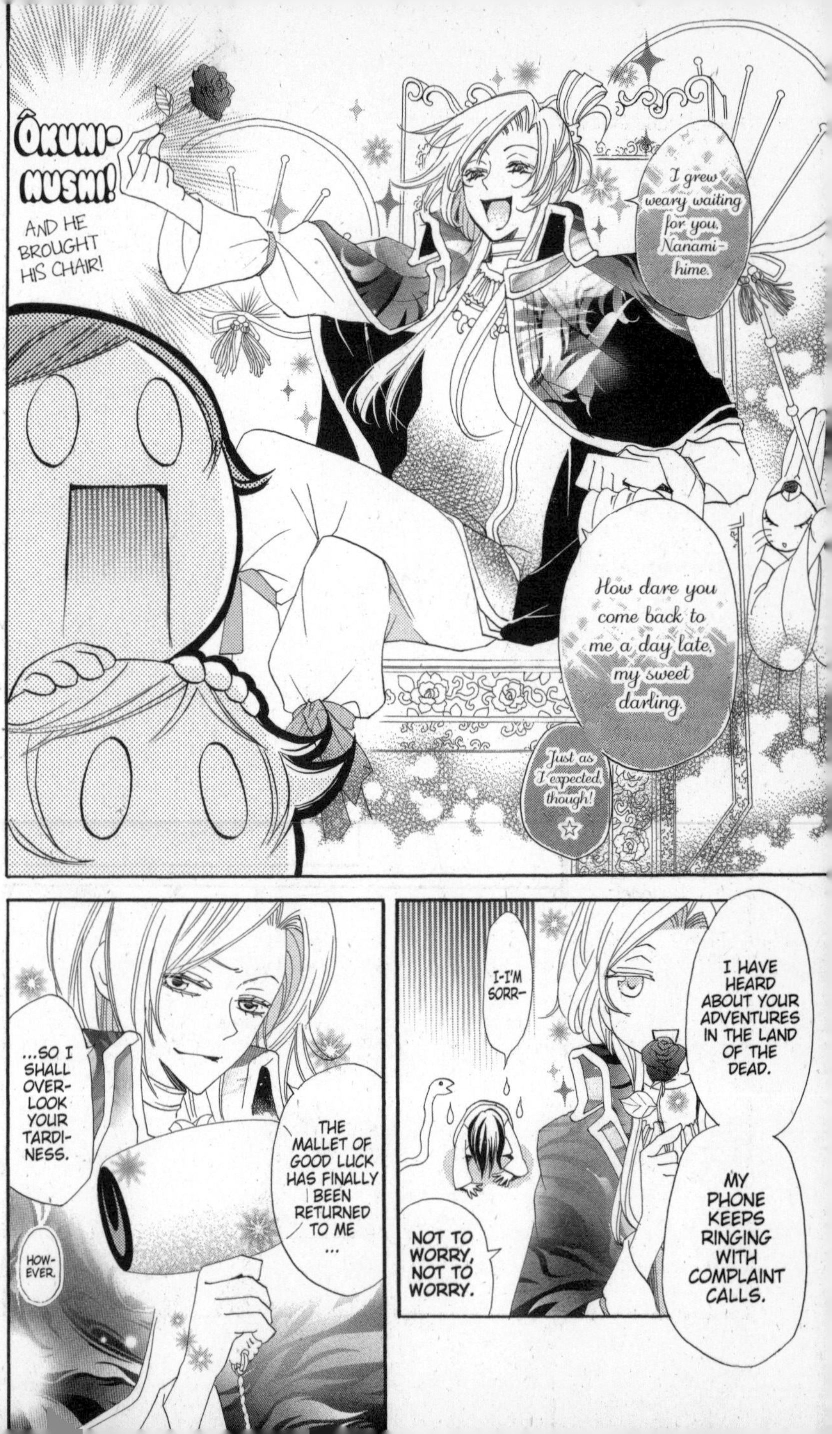
I grew weary waiting for you, Nanami-hime.
ÔKUNI-NUSHI!
AND HE BROUGHT HIS CHAIR!
How dare you come back to me a day late, my sweet darling.
Just as I expected, though! ☆
I HAVE HEARD ABOUT YOUR ADVENTURES IN THE LAND OF THE DEAD.
I-I'M SORR–
MY PHONE KEEPS RINGING WITH COMPLAINT CALLS.
NOT TO WORRY, NOT TO WORRY.
THE MALLET OF GOOD LUCK HAS FINALLY BEEN RETURNED TO ME...
HOW-EVER.
...SO I SHALL OVER-LOOK YOUR TARDI-NESS.

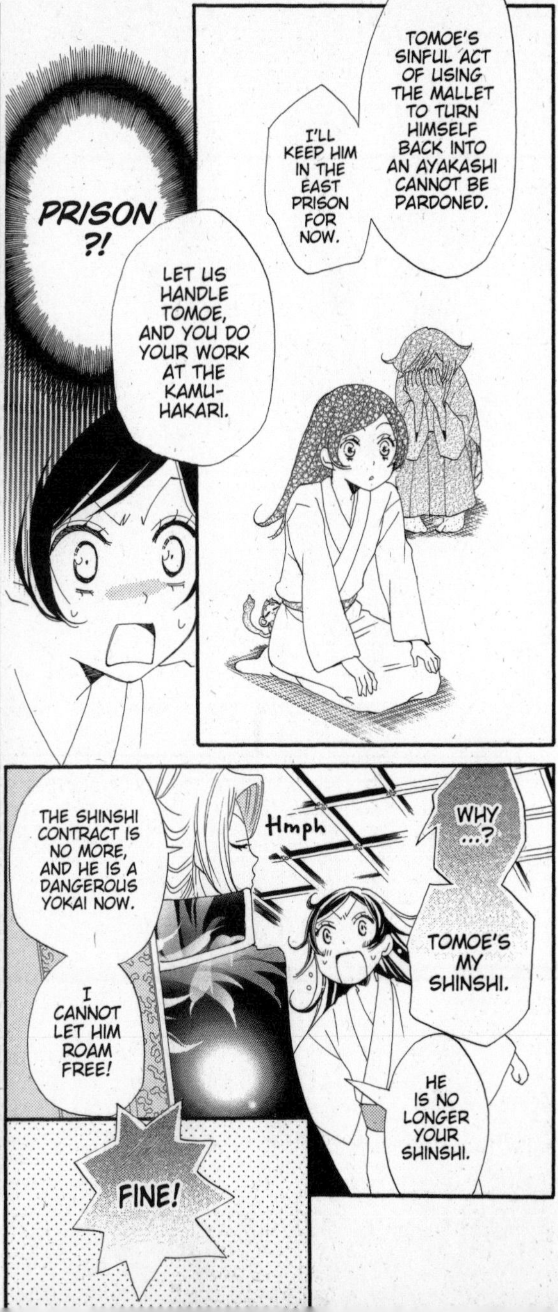
TOMOE'S SINFUL ACT OF USING THE MALLET TO TURN HIMSELF BACK INTO AN AYAKASHI CANNOT BE PARDONED.
I'LL KEEP HIM IN THE EAST PRISON FOR NOW.
LET US HANDLE TOMOE, AND YOU DO YOUR WORK AT THE KAMU-HAKARI.
PRISON ?!
WHY ...?
TOMOE'S MY SHINSHI.
Hmph
THE SHINSHI CONTRACT IS NO MORE, AND HE IS A DANGEROUS YOKAI NOW.
I CANNOT LET HIM ROAM FREE!
HE IS NO LONGER YOUR SHINSHI.
FINE!

About the manga

Chapter 43
My editor always told me how stubborn Nanami is, and I always thought "Really?" But she is stubborn! Really!

Chapter 44
The human Kirihito is a college student. He's about 21 years old.

Chapter 45
I drew 32 pages for this chapter. Noooooo!

Chapter 46
Because Ôkuninushi is a real kami, I take care when drawing him.... I wonder whether my version is acceptable? I had Izumo soba too, and it was delicious. I'd like to thank my editor who took me there!

Uh, I should've written this for Chapter 47. I'm sorry.

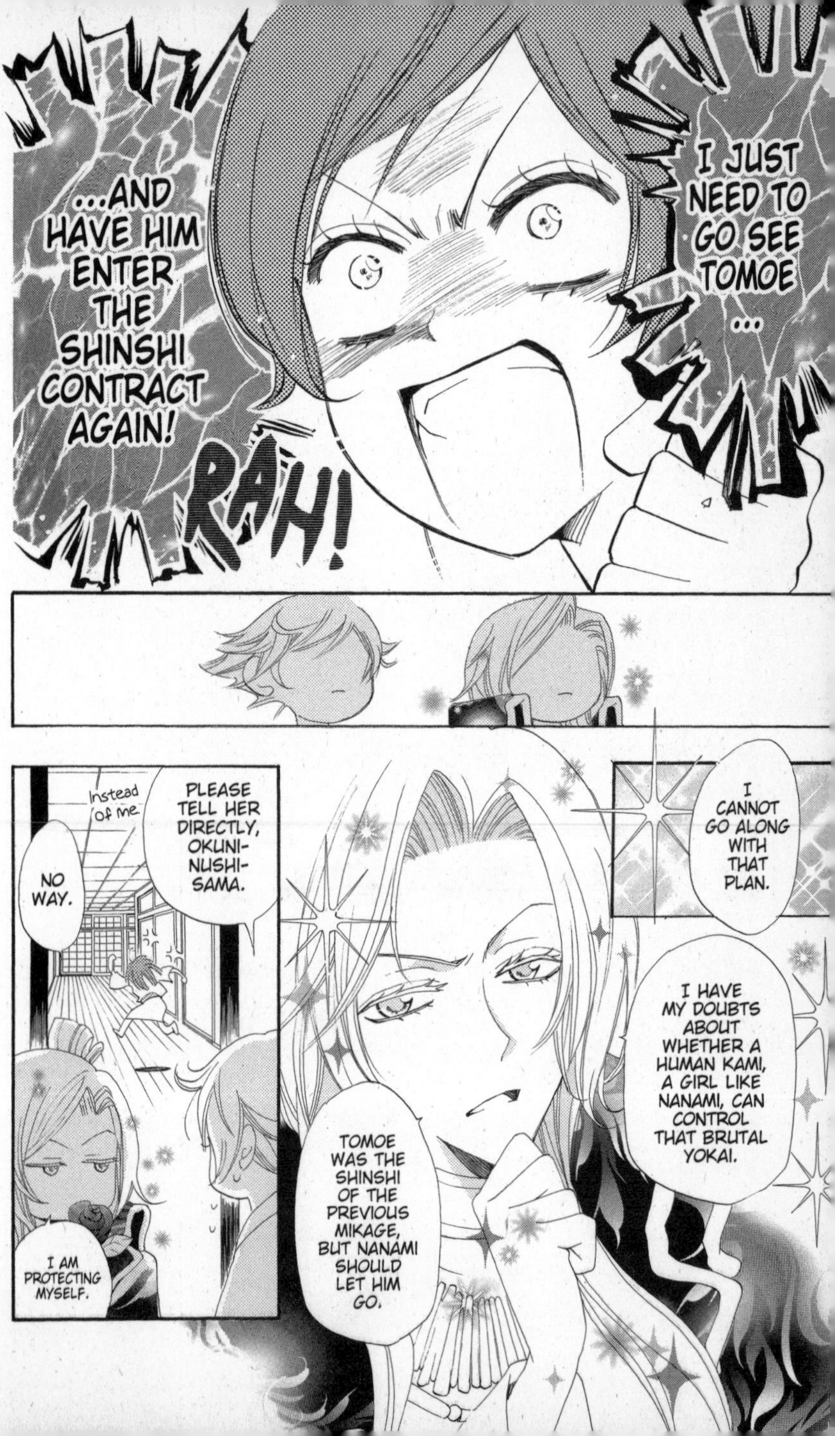
I JUST NEED TO GO SEE TOMOE ...
...AND HAVE HIM ENTER THE SHINSHI CONTRACT AGAIN!
RAH!
I CANNOT GO ALONG WITH THAT PLAN.
I HAVE MY DOUBTS ABOUT WHETHER A HUMAN KAMI, A GIRL LIKE NANAMI, CAN CONTROL THAT BRUTAL YOKAI.
TOMOE WAS THE SHINSHI OF THE PREVIOUS MIKAGE, BUT NANAMI SHOULD LET HIM GO.
PLEASE TELL HER DIRECTLY, OKUNI-NUSHI-SAMA.
Instead of me.
NO WAY.
I AM PROTECTING MYSELF.

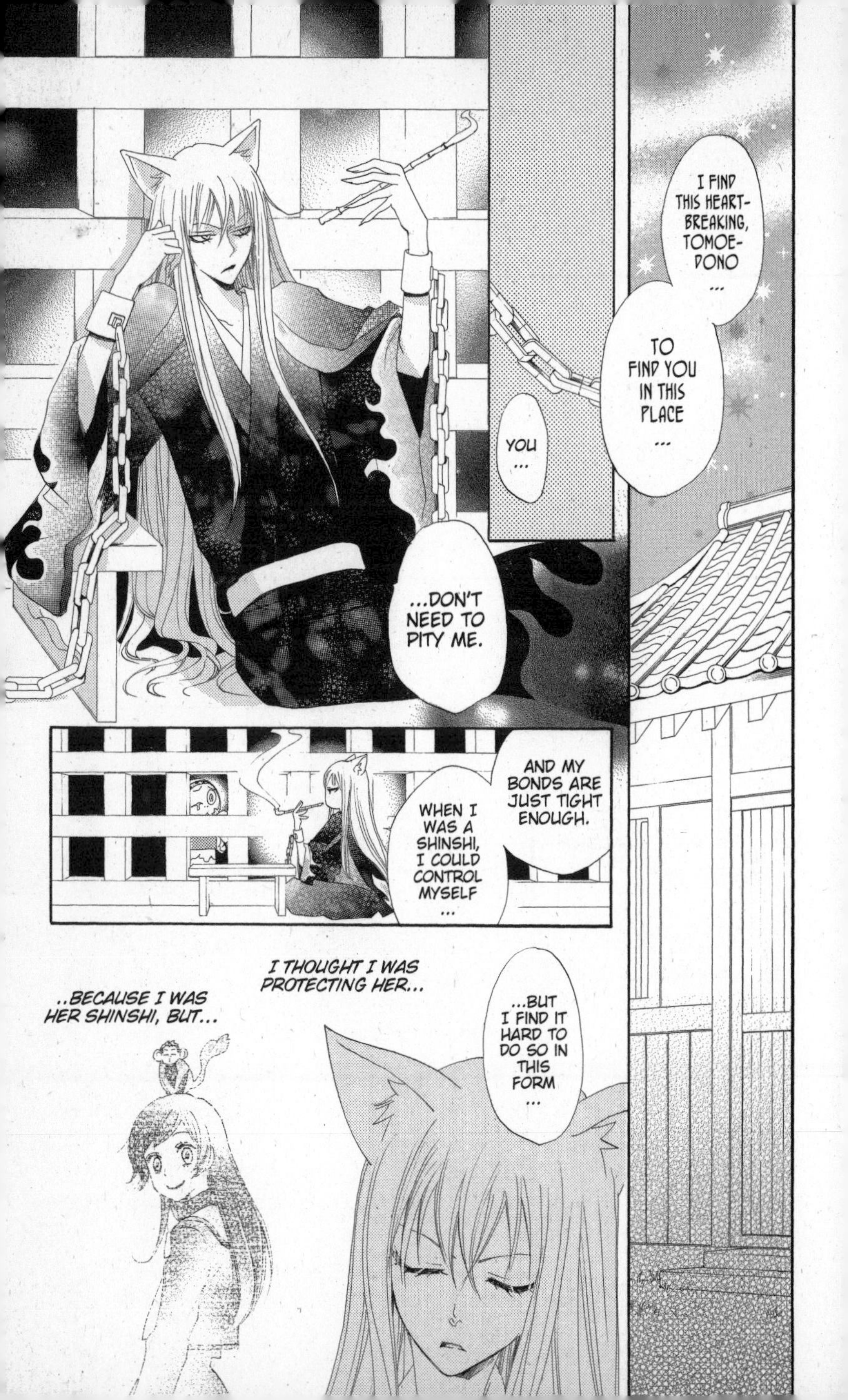
I FIND THIS HEART-BREAKING, TOMOE-DONO ...
TO FIND YOU IN THIS PLACE ...
YOU ...
...DON'T NEED TO PITY ME.
AND MY BONDS ARE JUST TIGHT ENOUGH.
WHEN I WAS A SHINSHI, I COULD CONTROL MYSELF ...
...BUT I FIND IT HARD TO DO SO IN THIS FORM ...
I THOUGHT I WAS PROTECTING HER...
..BECAUSE I WAS HER SHINSHI, BUT...

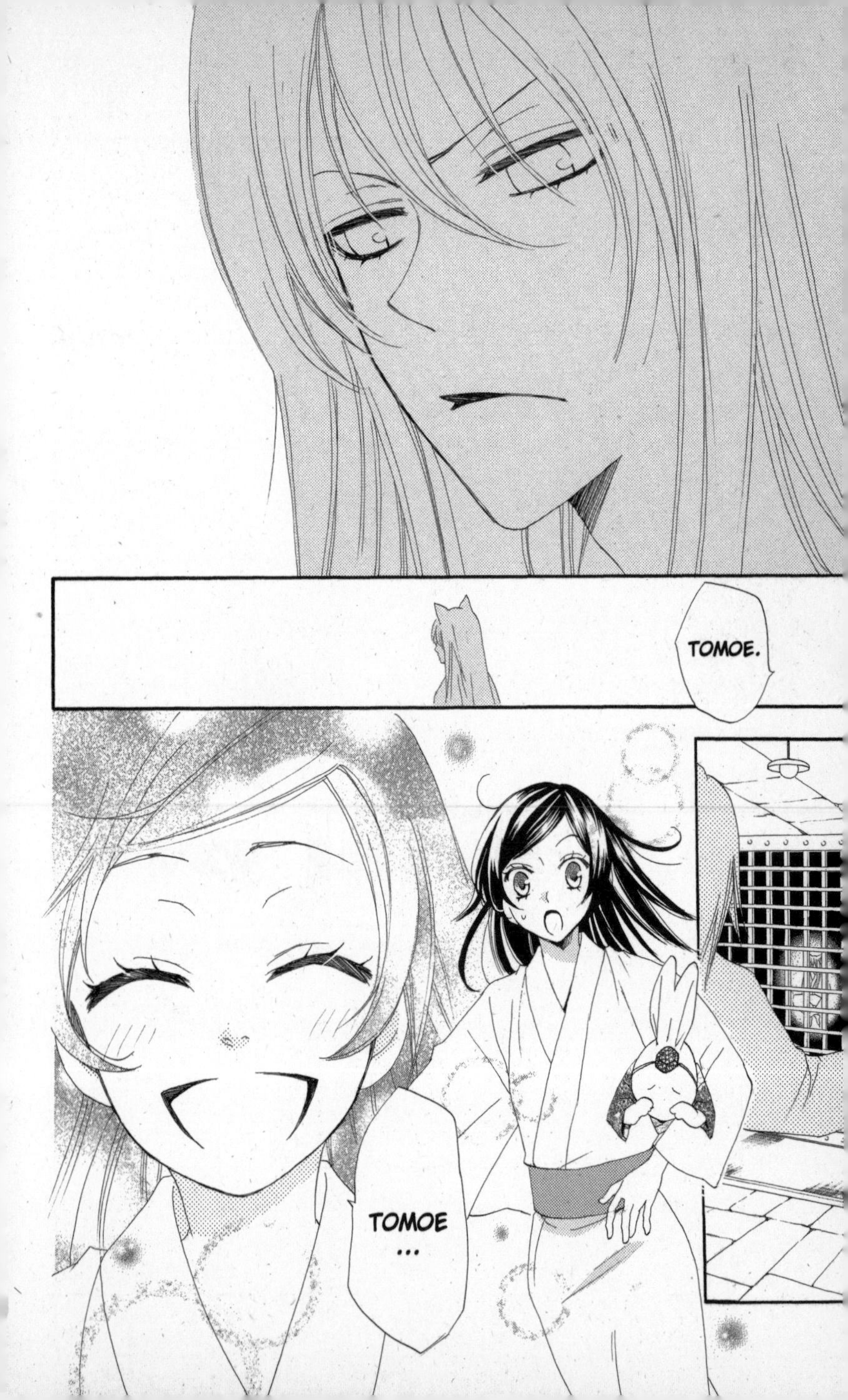
TOMOE.
TOMOE
...

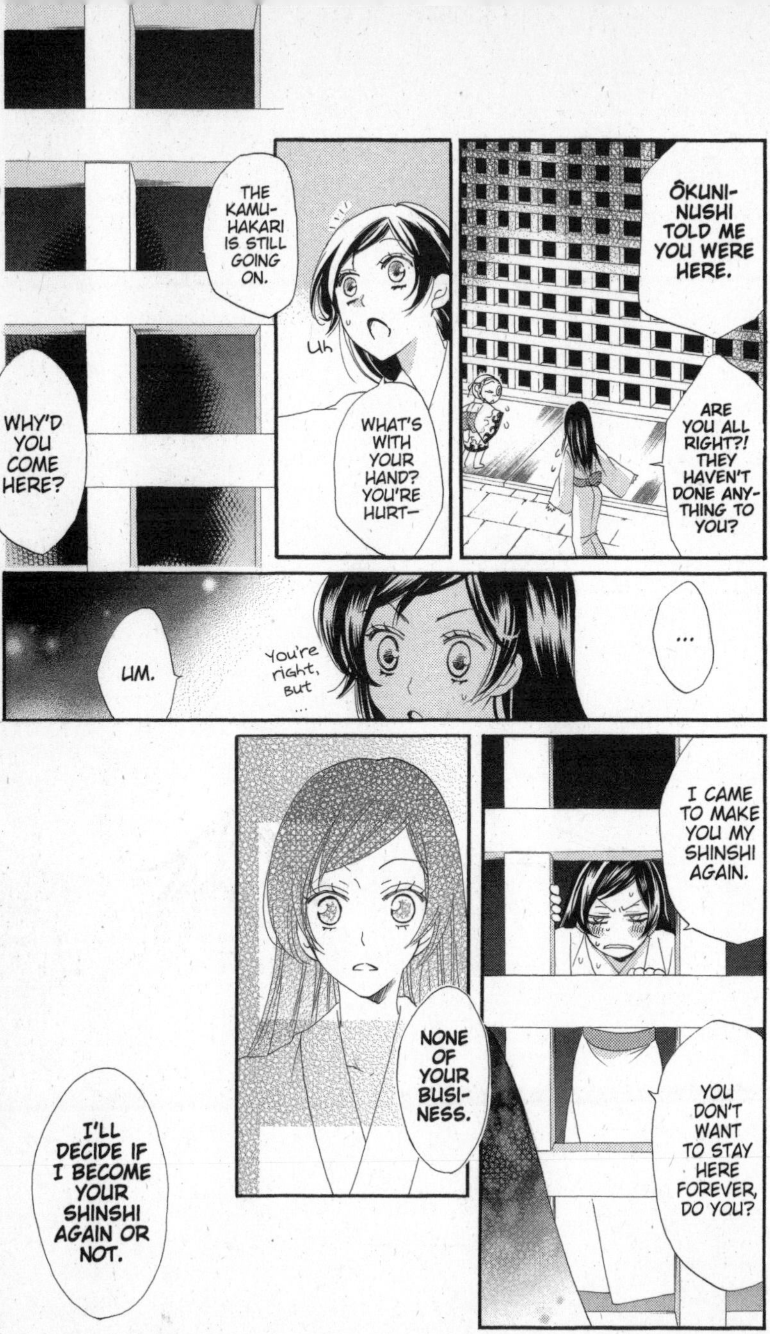
ÔKUNI-NUSHI TOLD ME YOU WERE HERE.
ARE YOU ALL RIGHT?! THEY HAVEN'T DONE ANY-THING TO YOU?
THE KAMU-HAKARI IS STILL GOING ON.
Uh
WHAT'S WITH YOUR HAND? YOU'RE HURT—
WHY'D YOU COME HERE?
...
You're right, but ...
UM.
I CAME TO MAKE YOU MY SHINSHI AGAIN.
YOU DON'T WANT TO STAY HERE FOREVER, DO YOU?
NONE OF YOUR BUSI-NESS.
I'LL DECIDE IF I BECOME YOUR SHINSHI AGAIN OR NOT.

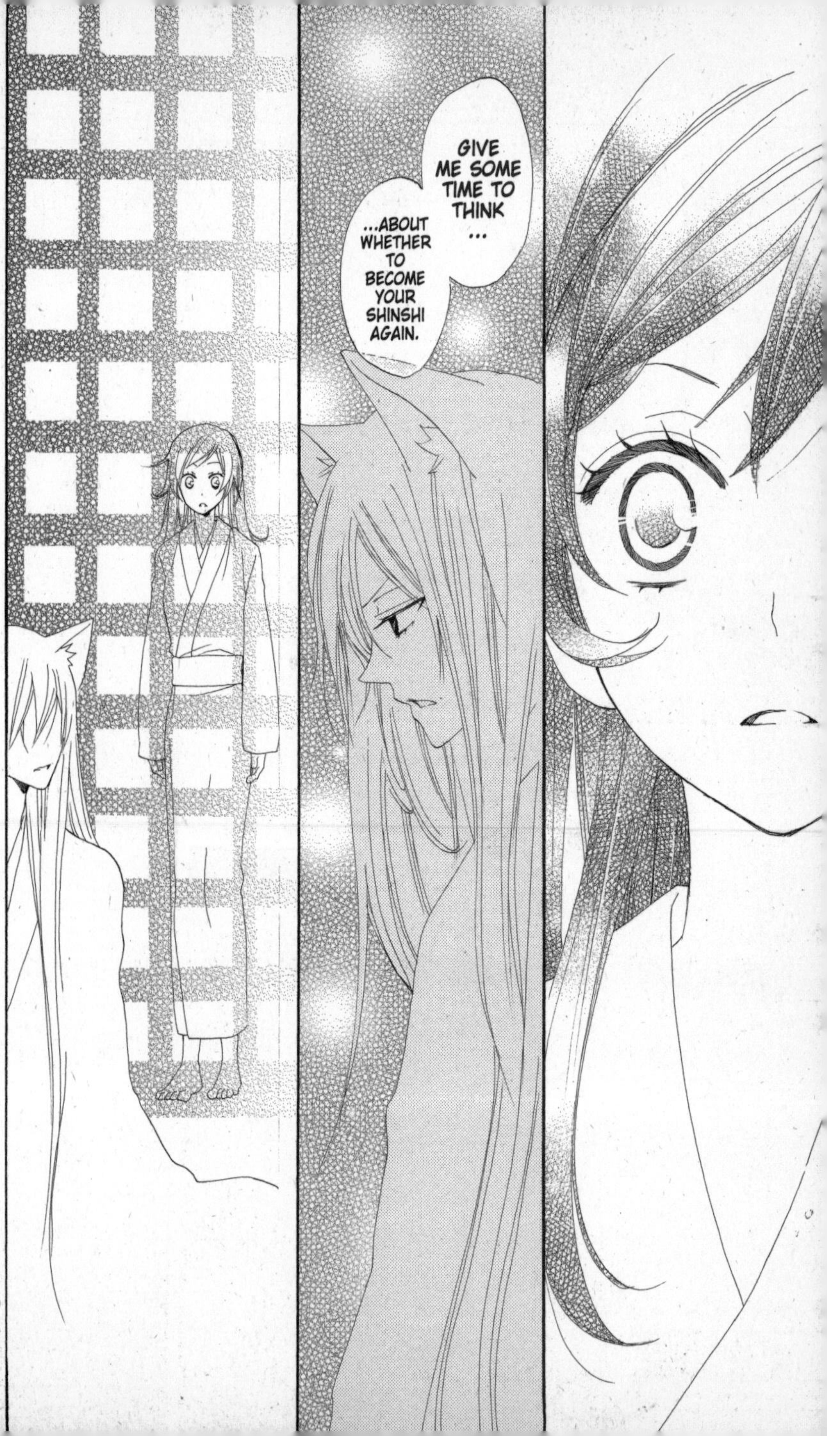
GIVE ME SOME TIME TO THINK ...
...ABOUT WHETHER TO BECOME YOUR SHINSHI AGAIN.

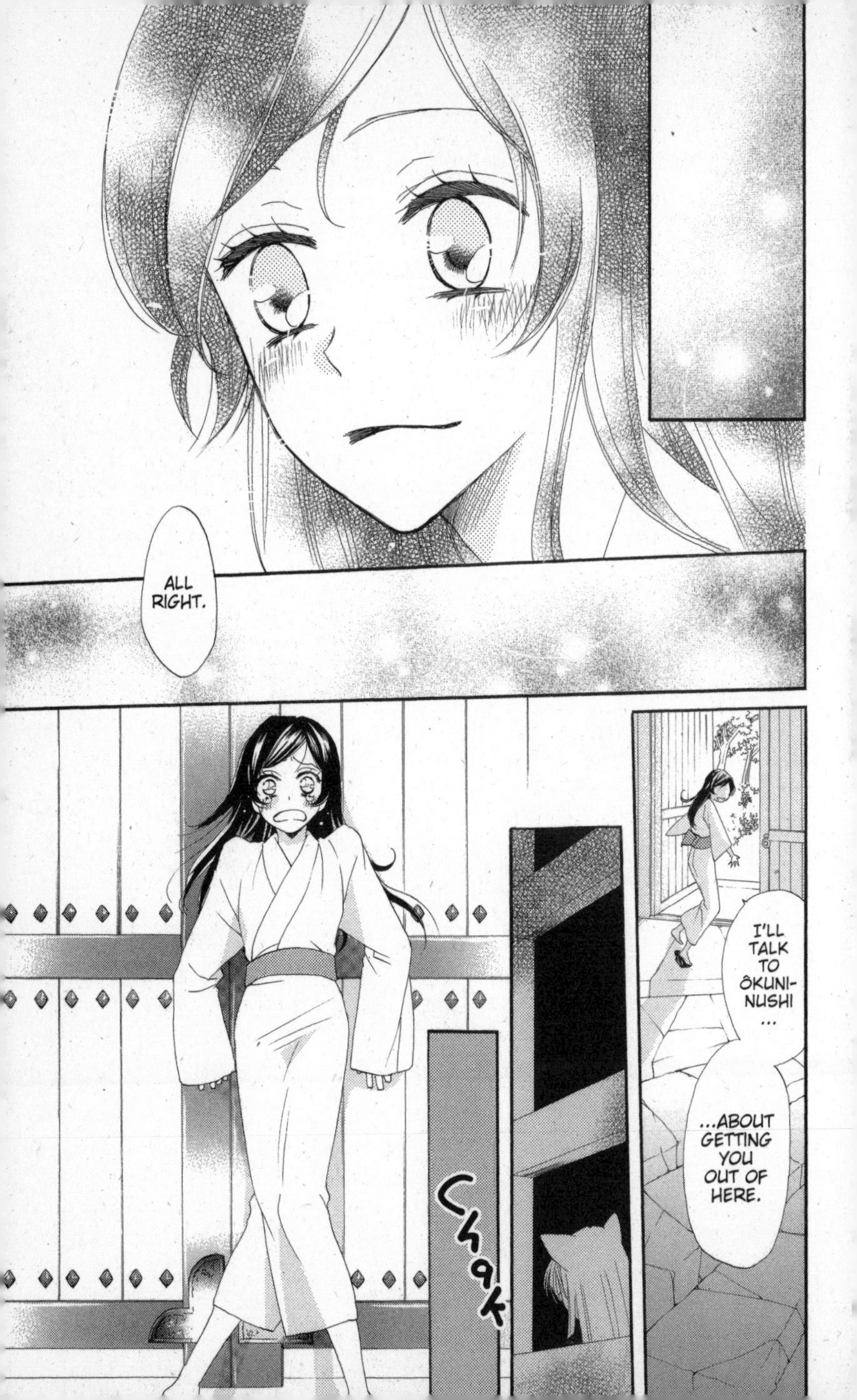
ALL RIGHT.
I'LL TALK TO ÔKUNI-NUSHI...
...ABOUT GETTING YOU OUT OF HERE.
Chak

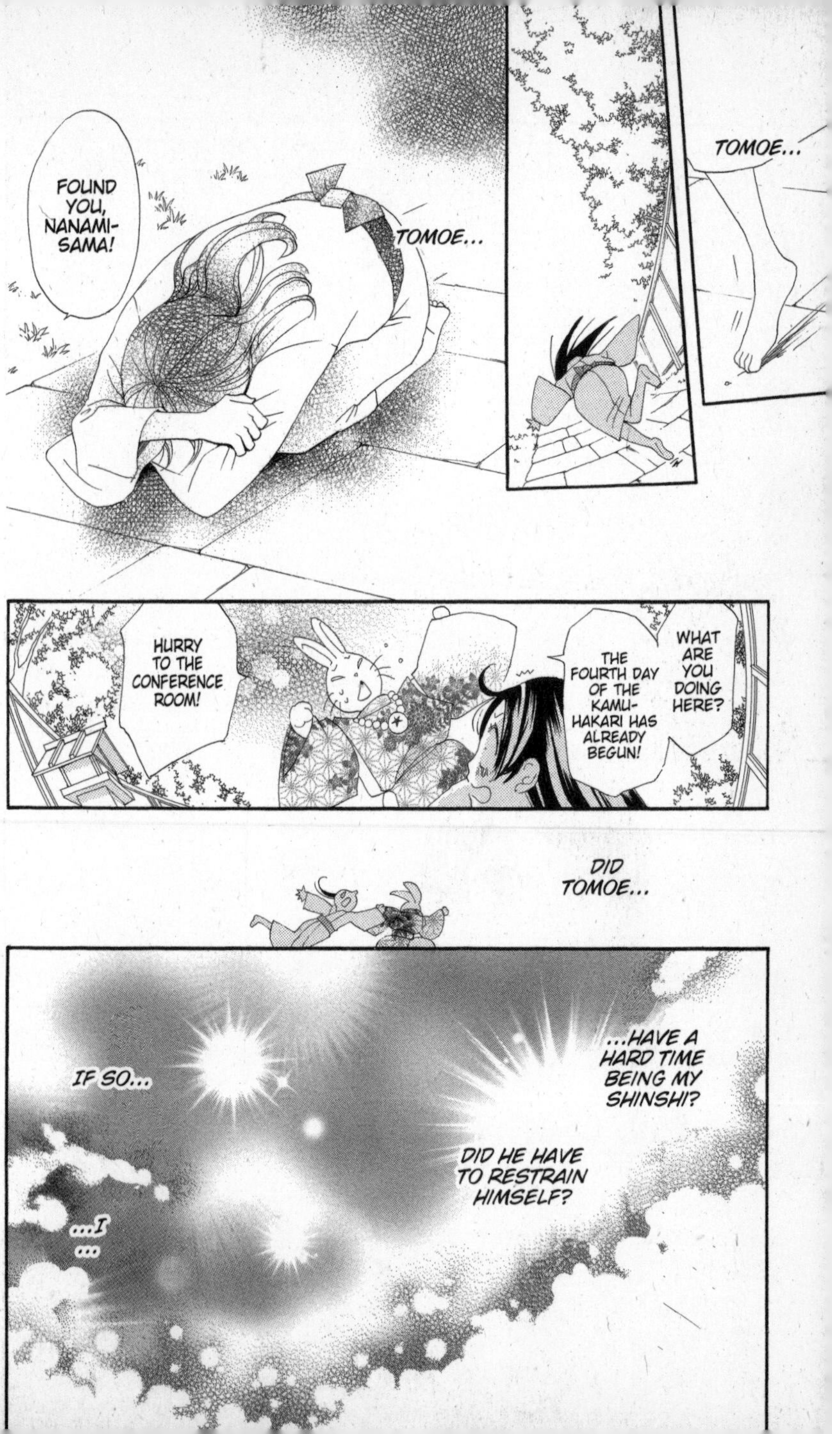
TOMOE...
TOMOE...
FOUND YOU, NANAMI-SAMA!
WHAT ARE YOU DOING HERE?
THE FOURTH DAY OF THE KAMU-HAKARI HAS ALREADY BEGUN!
HURRY TO THE CONFERENCE ROOM!
DID TOMOE...
...HAVE A HARD TIME BEING MY SHINSHI?
DID HE HAVE TO RESTRAIN HIMSELF?
IF SO...
...I
...

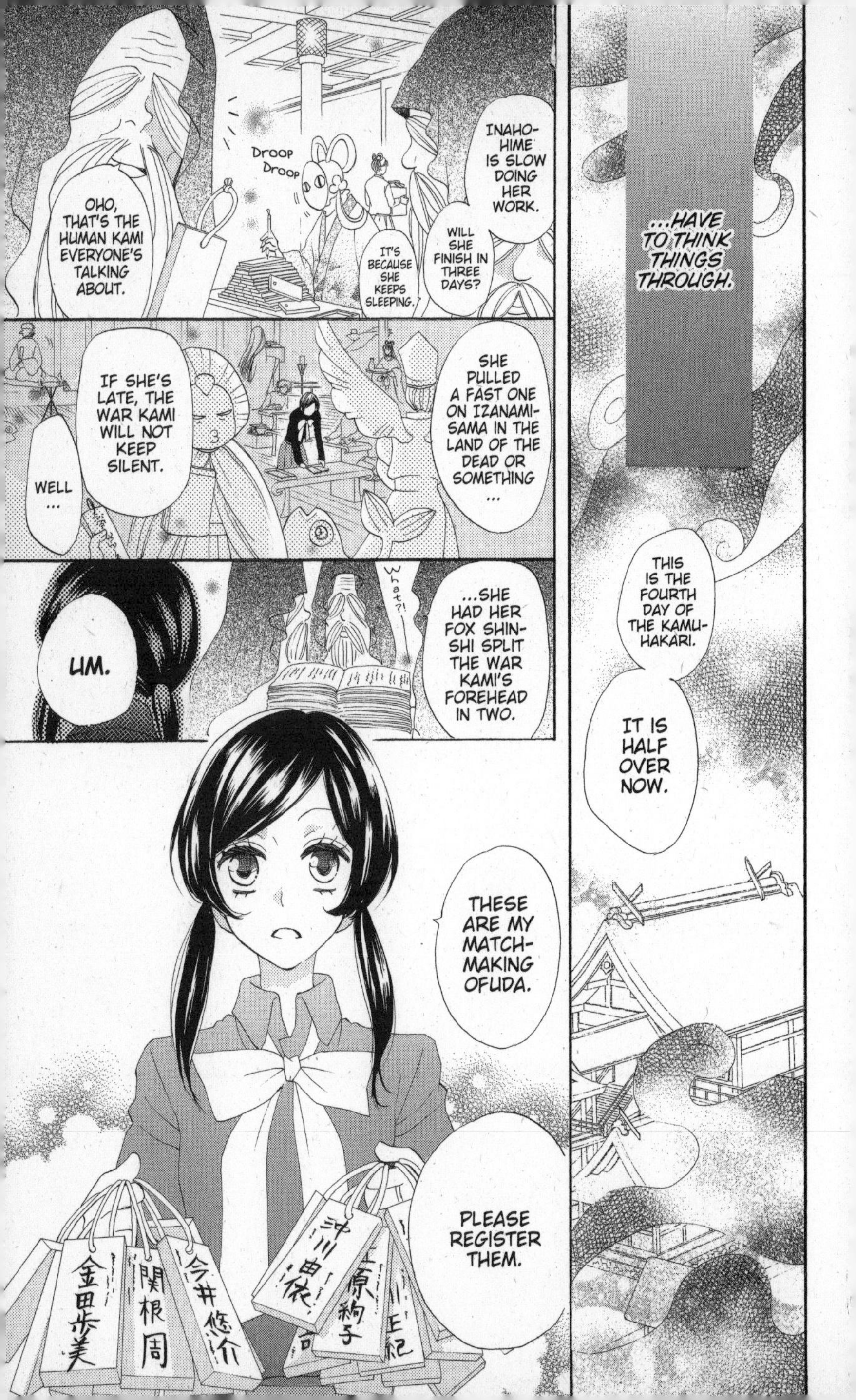
...HAVE TO THINK THINGS THROUGH.
THIS IS THE FOURTH DAY OF THE KAMU-HAKARI.
IT IS HALF OVER NOW.
INAHO-HIME IS SLOW DOING HER WORK.
WILL SHE FINISH IN THREE DAYS?
IT'S BECAUSE SHE KEEPS SLEEPING.
Droop Droop
OHO, THAT'S THE HUMAN KAMI EVERYONE'S TALKING ABOUT.
SHE PULLED A FAST ONE ON IZANAMI-SAMA IN THE LAND OF THE DEAD OR SOMETHING ...
IF SHE'S LATE, THE WAR KAMI WILL NOT KEEP SILENT.
WELL ...
...SHE HAD HER FOX SHIN-SHI SPLIT THE WAR KAMI'S FOREHEAD IN TWO.
What?!
UM.
THESE ARE MY MATCH-MAKING OFUDA.
PLEASE REGISTER THEM.
沖川由依
今井悠介
関根周
金田歩美

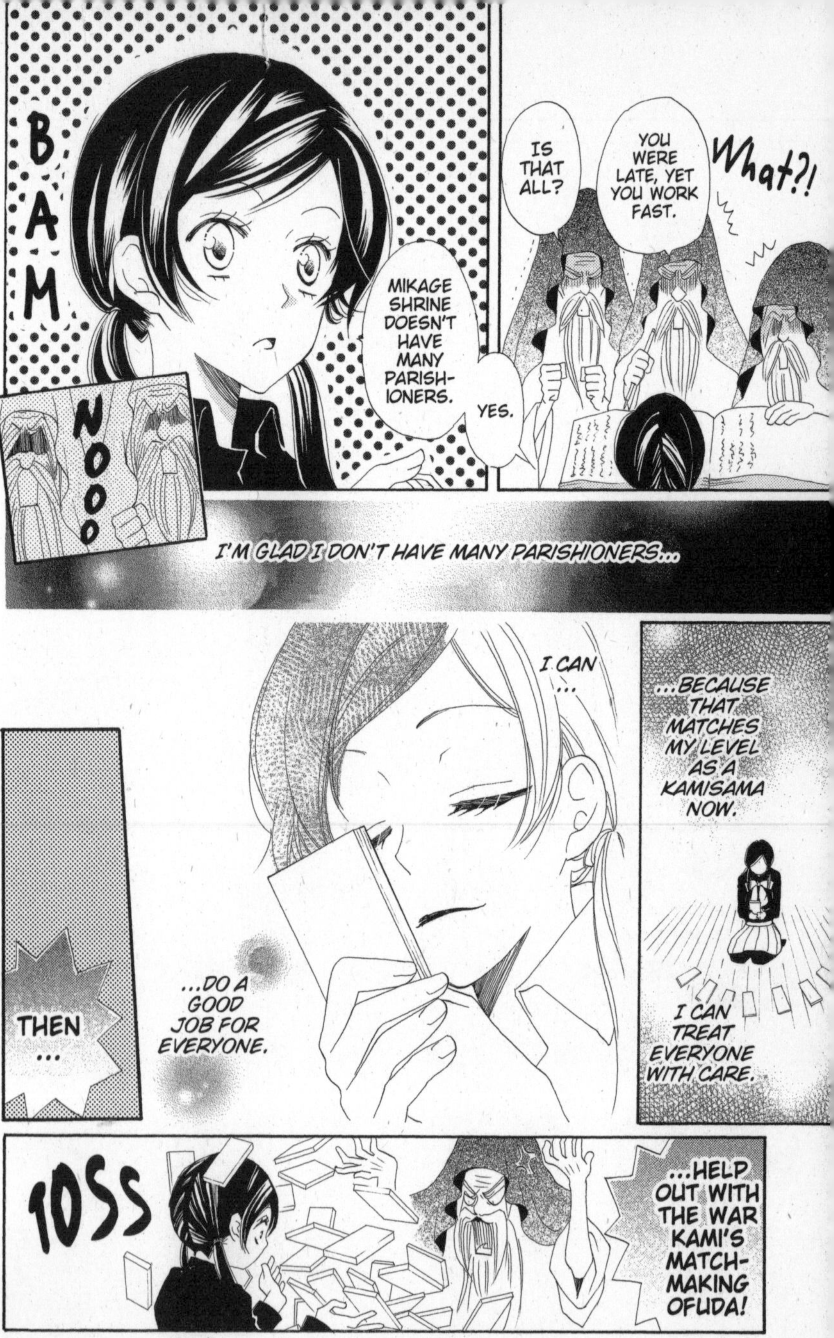
What?!
YOU WERE LATE, YET YOU WORK FAST.
IS THAT ALL?
YES.
MIKAGE SHRINE DOESN'T HAVE MANY PARISH-IONERS.
BAM
NOOO
I'M GLAD I DON'T HAVE MANY PARISHIONERS...
...BECAUSE THAT MATCHES MY LEVEL AS A KAMISAMA NOW.
I CAN TREAT EVERYONE WITH CARE.
I CAN ...
...DO A GOOD JOB FOR EVERYONE.
THEN ...
...HELP OUT WITH THE WAR KAMI'S MATCH-MAKING OFUDA!
TOSS

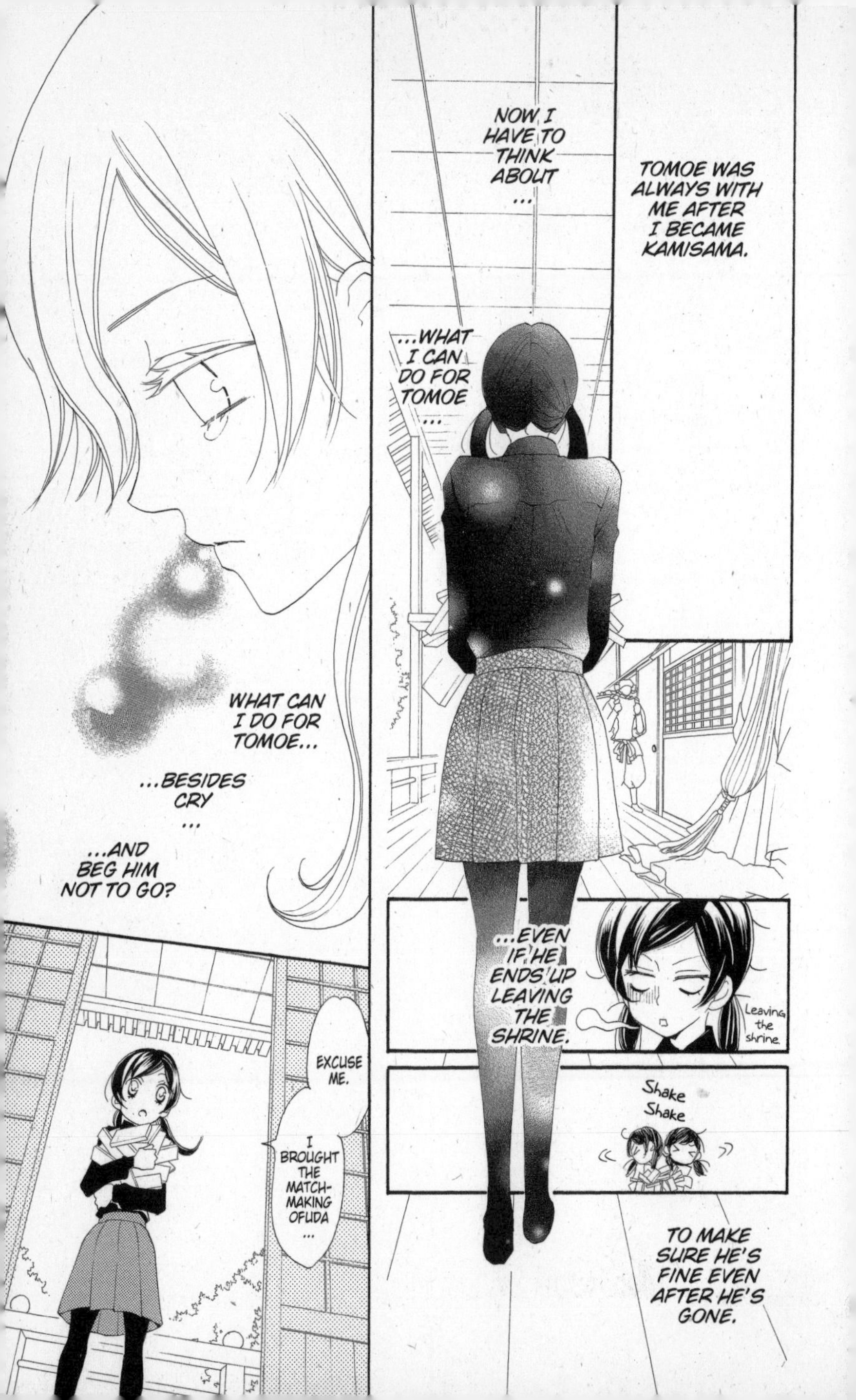
TOMOE WAS ALWAYS WITH ME AFTER I BECAME KAMISAMA.
NOW I HAVE TO THINK ABOUT...
...WHAT I CAN DO FOR TOMOE...
...EVEN IF HE ENDS UP LEAVING THE SHRINE.
Leaving the shrine.
Shake Shake
TO MAKE SURE HE'S FINE EVEN AFTER HE'S GONE.
WHAT CAN I DO FOR TOMOE...
...BESIDES CRY...
...AND BEG HIM NOT TO GO?
EXCUSE ME.
I BROUGHT THE MATCH-MAKING OFUDA...

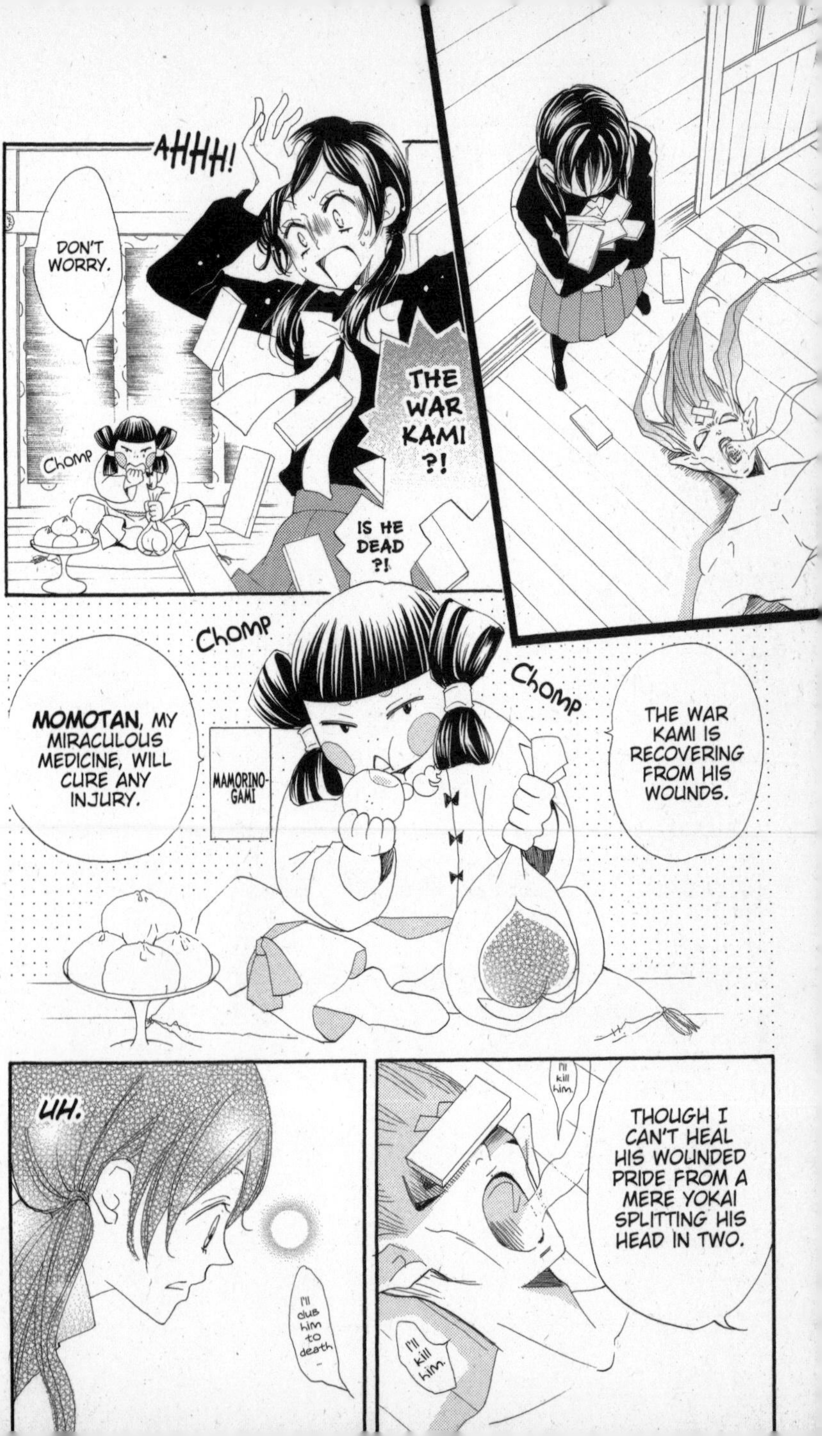
AHHH!
THE WAR KAMI ?!
DON'T WORRY.
IS HE DEAD ?!
Chomp
Chomp
Chomp
THE WAR KAMI IS RECOVERING FROM HIS WOUNDS.
MAMORINO-GAMI
MOMOTAN, MY MIRACULOUS MEDICINE, WILL CURE ANY INJURY.
THOUGH I CAN'T HEAL HIS WOUNDED PRIDE FROM A MERE YOKAI SPLITTING HIS HEAD IN TWO.
I'll kill him.
I'll kill him.
UH.
I'll club him to death...

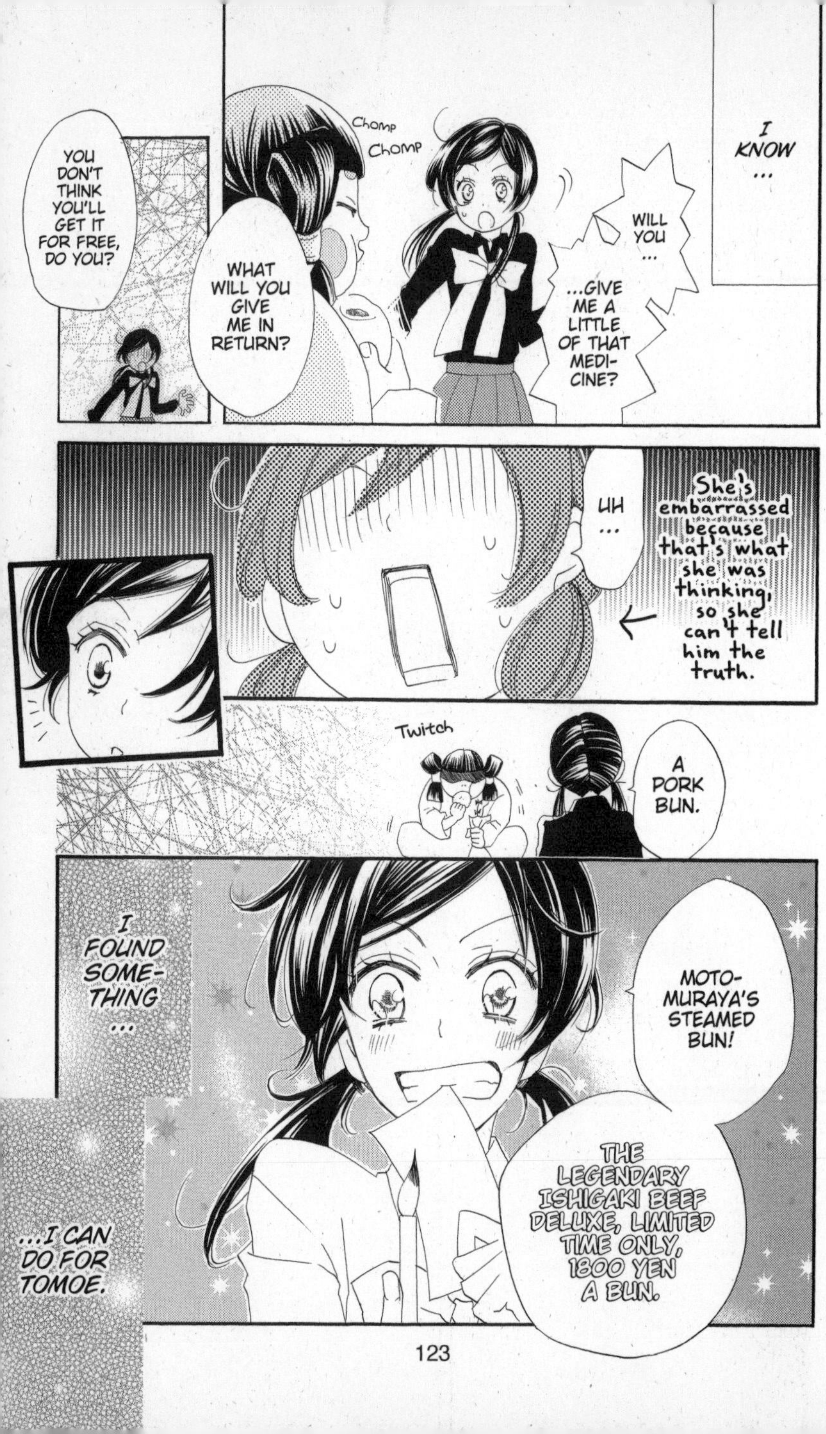
I KNOW ...
WILL YOU ...
...GIVE ME A LITTLE OF THAT MEDICINE?
Chomp
Chomp
WHAT WILL YOU GIVE ME IN RETURN?
YOU DON'T THINK YOU'LL GET IT FOR FREE, DO YOU?
UH ...
She's embarrassed because that's what she was thinking, so she can't tell him the truth.
A PORK BUN.
Twitch
MOTO-MURAYA'S STEAMED BUN!
THE LEGENDARY ISHIGAKI BEEF DELUXE, LIMITED TIME ONLY, 1800 YEN A BUN.
I FOUND SOMETHING ...
...I CAN DO FOR TOMOE.

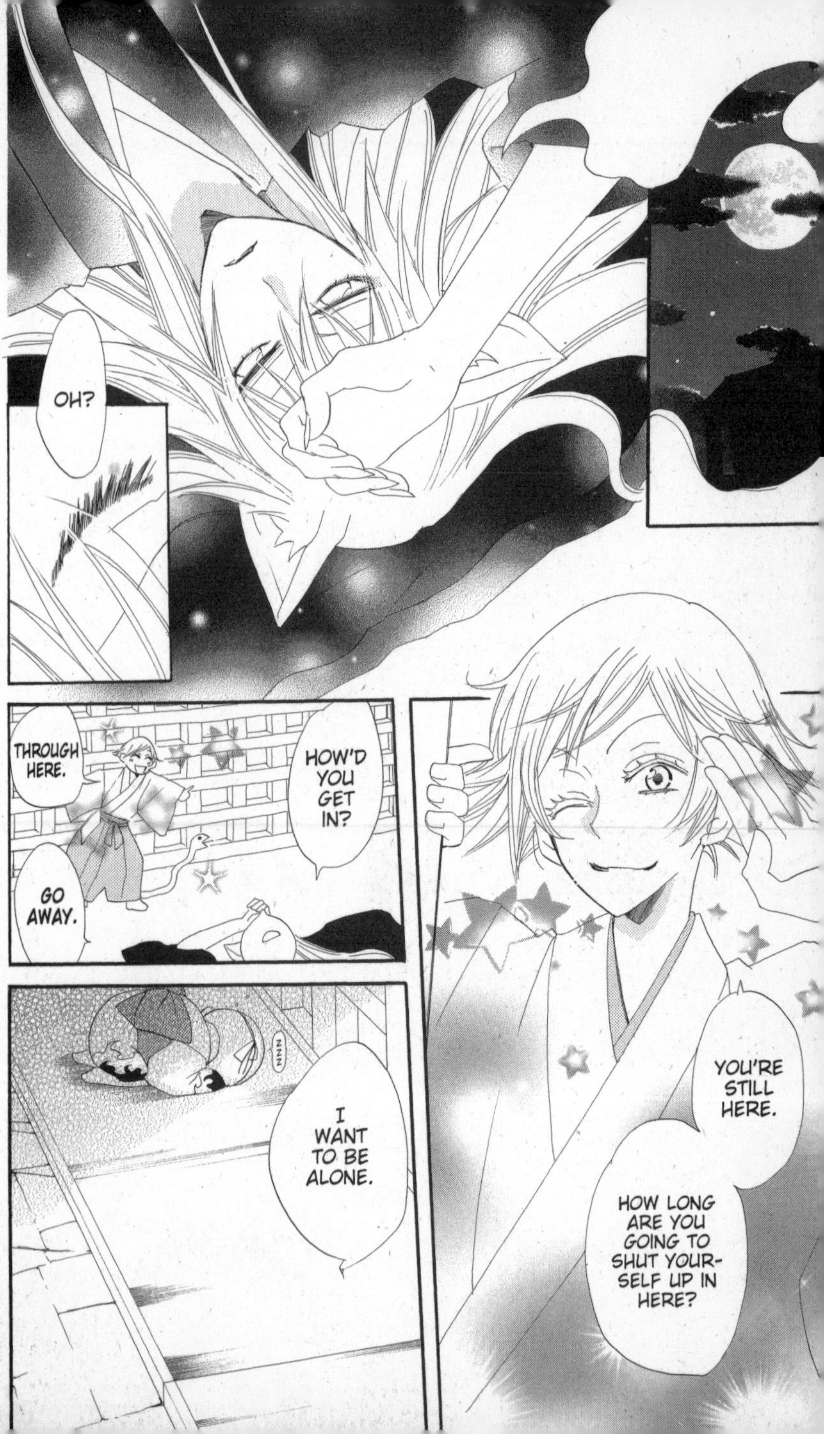
OH?
YOU'RE STILL HERE.
HOW LONG ARE YOU GOING TO SHUT YOURSELF UP IN HERE?
HOW'D YOU GET IN?
THROUGH HERE.
GO AWAY.
ZZZ
I WANT TO BE ALONE.

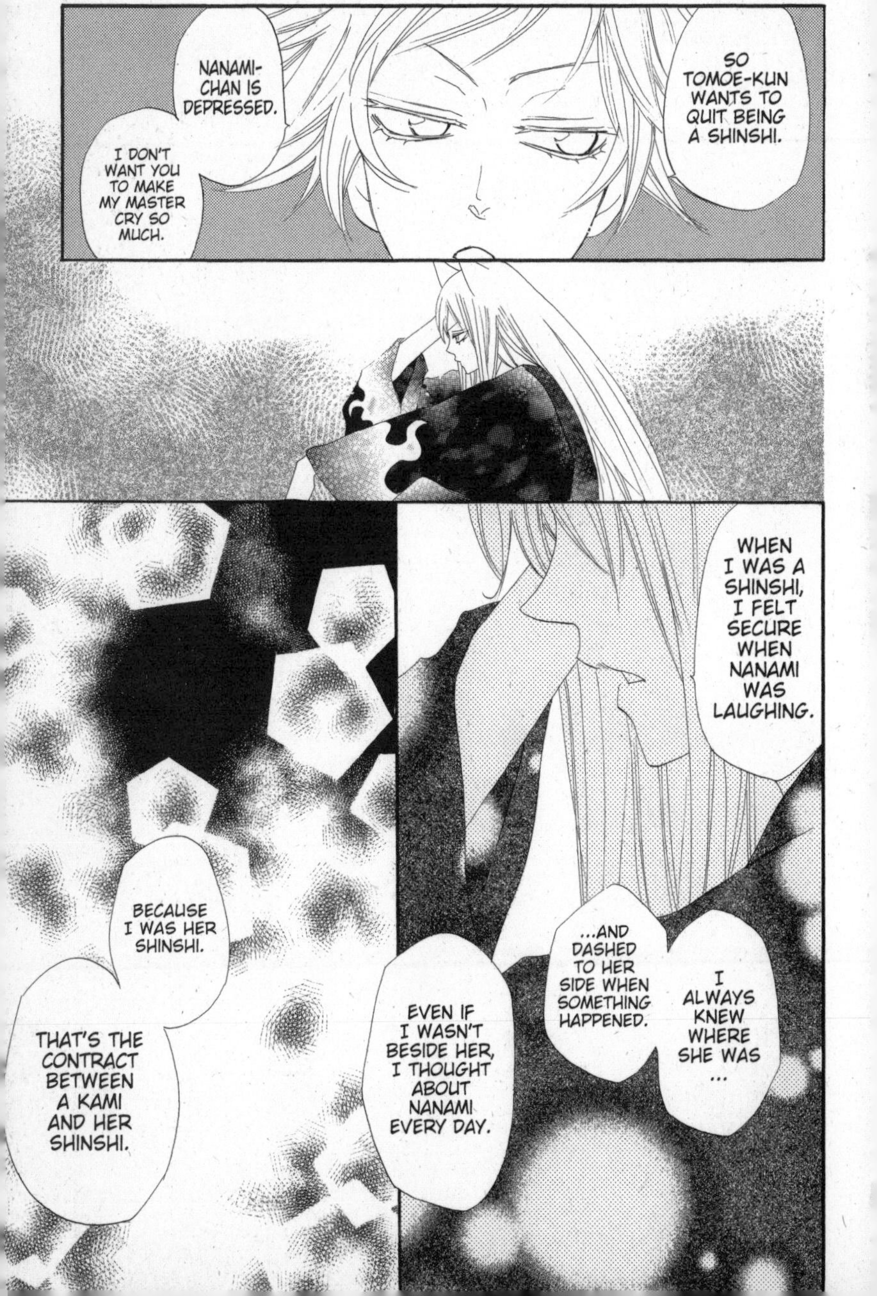
SO TOMOE-KUN WANTS TO QUIT BEING A SHINSHI.
NANAMI-CHAN IS DEPRESSED.
I DON'T WANT YOU TO MAKE MY MASTER CRY SO MUCH.
WHEN I WAS A SHINSHI, I FELT SECURE WHEN NANAMI WAS LAUGHING.
I ALWAYS KNEW WHERE SHE WAS ...
...AND DASHED TO HER SIDE WHEN SOMETHING HAPPENED.
EVEN IF I WASN'T BESIDE HER, I THOUGHT ABOUT NANAMI EVERY DAY.
BECAUSE I WAS HER SHINSHI.
THAT'S THE CONTRACT BETWEEN A KAMI AND HER SHINSHI.

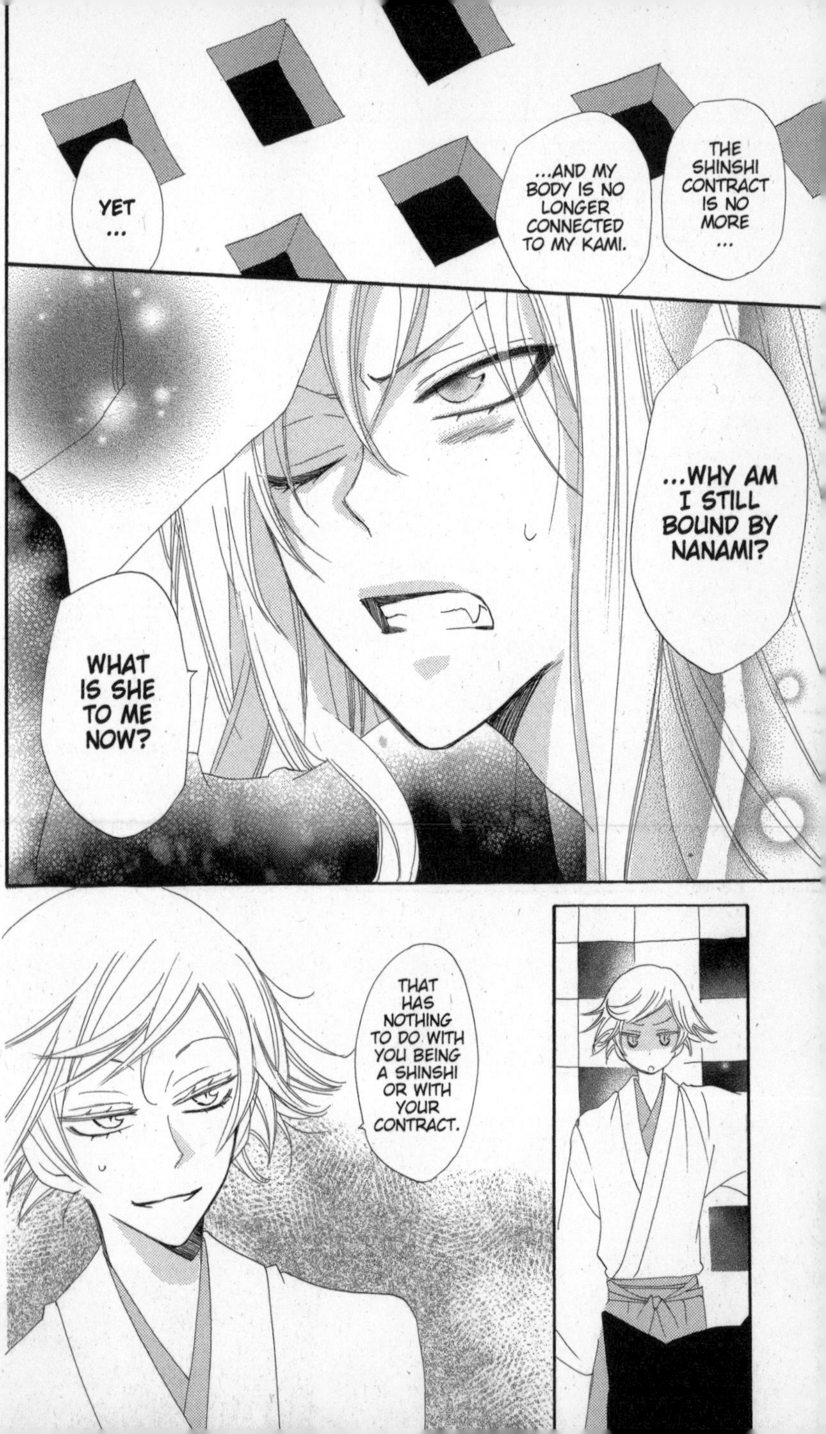
THE SHINSHI CONTRACT IS NO MORE ...
...AND MY BODY IS NO LONGER CONNECTED TO MY KAMI.
YET ...
...WHY AM I STILL BOUND BY NANAMI?
WHAT IS SHE TO ME NOW?
THAT HAS NOTHING TO DO WITH YOU BEING A SHINSHI OR WITH YOUR CONTRACT.

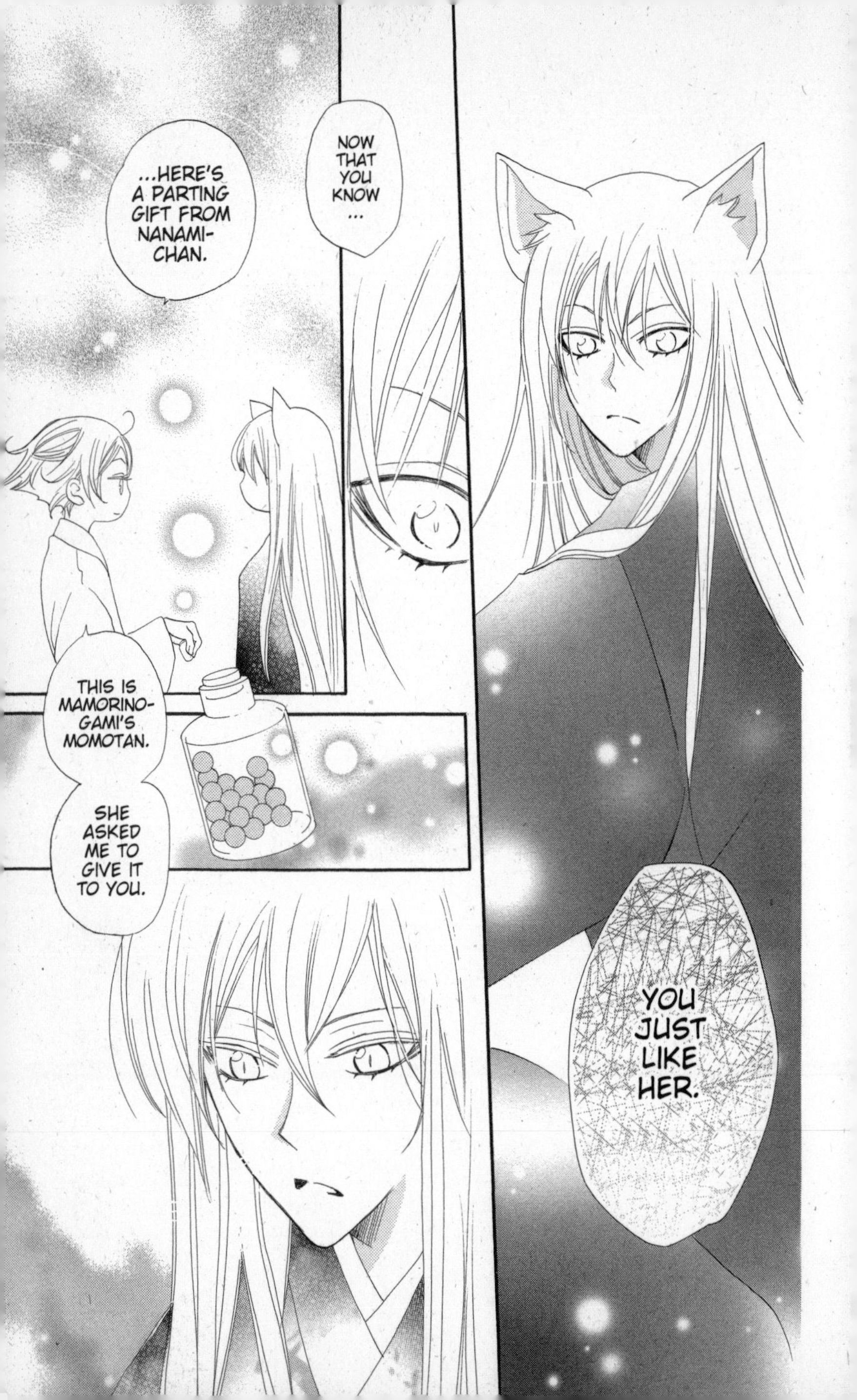
NOW THAT YOU KNOW ...
...HERE'S A PARTING GIFT FROM NANAMI-CHAN.
THIS IS MAMORINO-GAMI'S MOMOTAN.
SHE ASKED ME TO GIVE IT TO YOU.
YOU JUST LIKE HER.

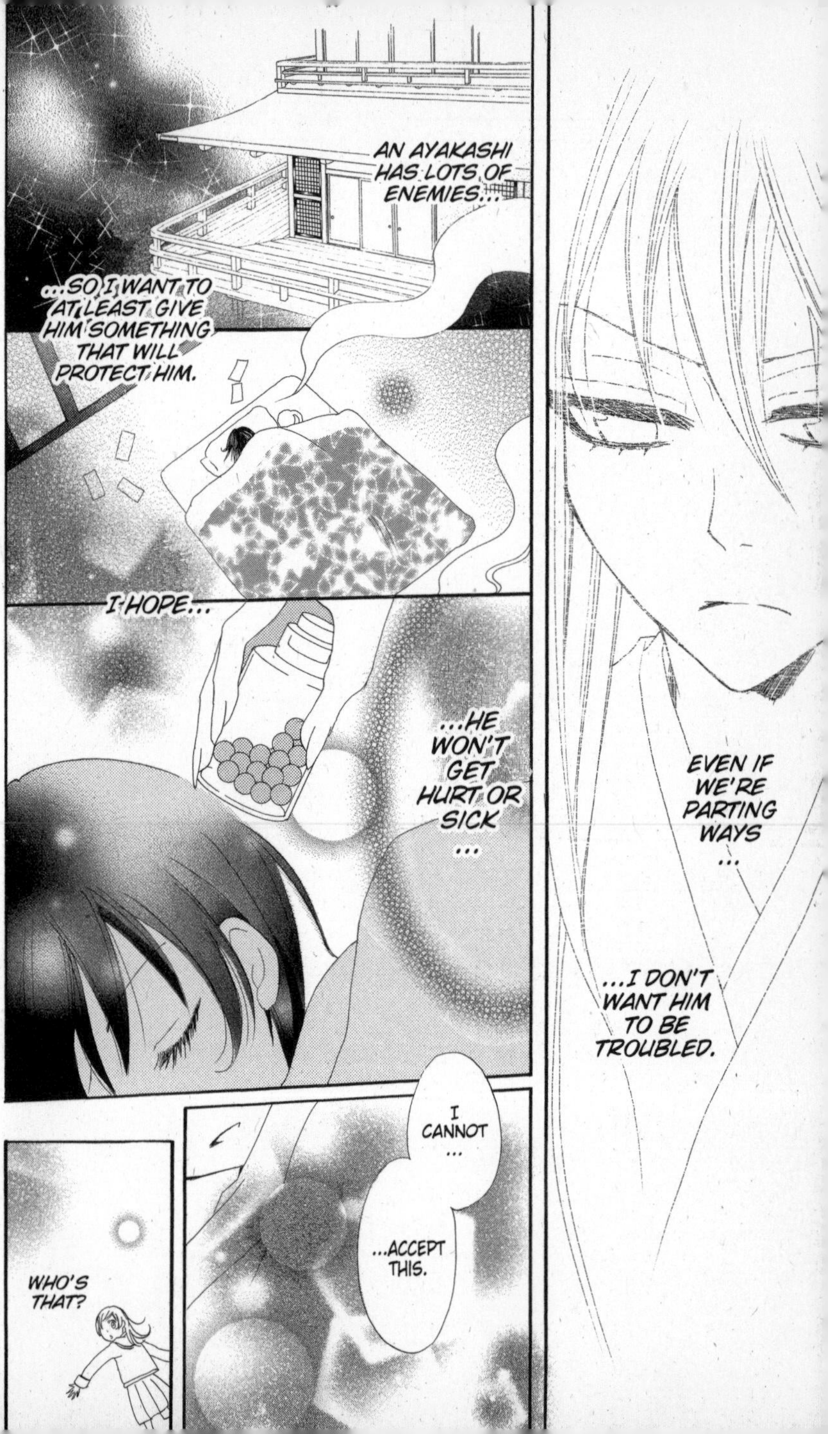
EVEN IF WE'RE PARTING WAYS...
...I DON'T WANT HIM TO BE TROUBLED.
AN AYAKASHI HAS LOTS OF ENEMIES...
...SO I WANT TO AT LEAST GIVE HIM SOMETHING THAT WILL PROTECT HIM.
I HOPE...
...HE WON'T GET HURT OR SICK...
I CANNOT...
...ACCEPT THIS.
WHO'S THAT?

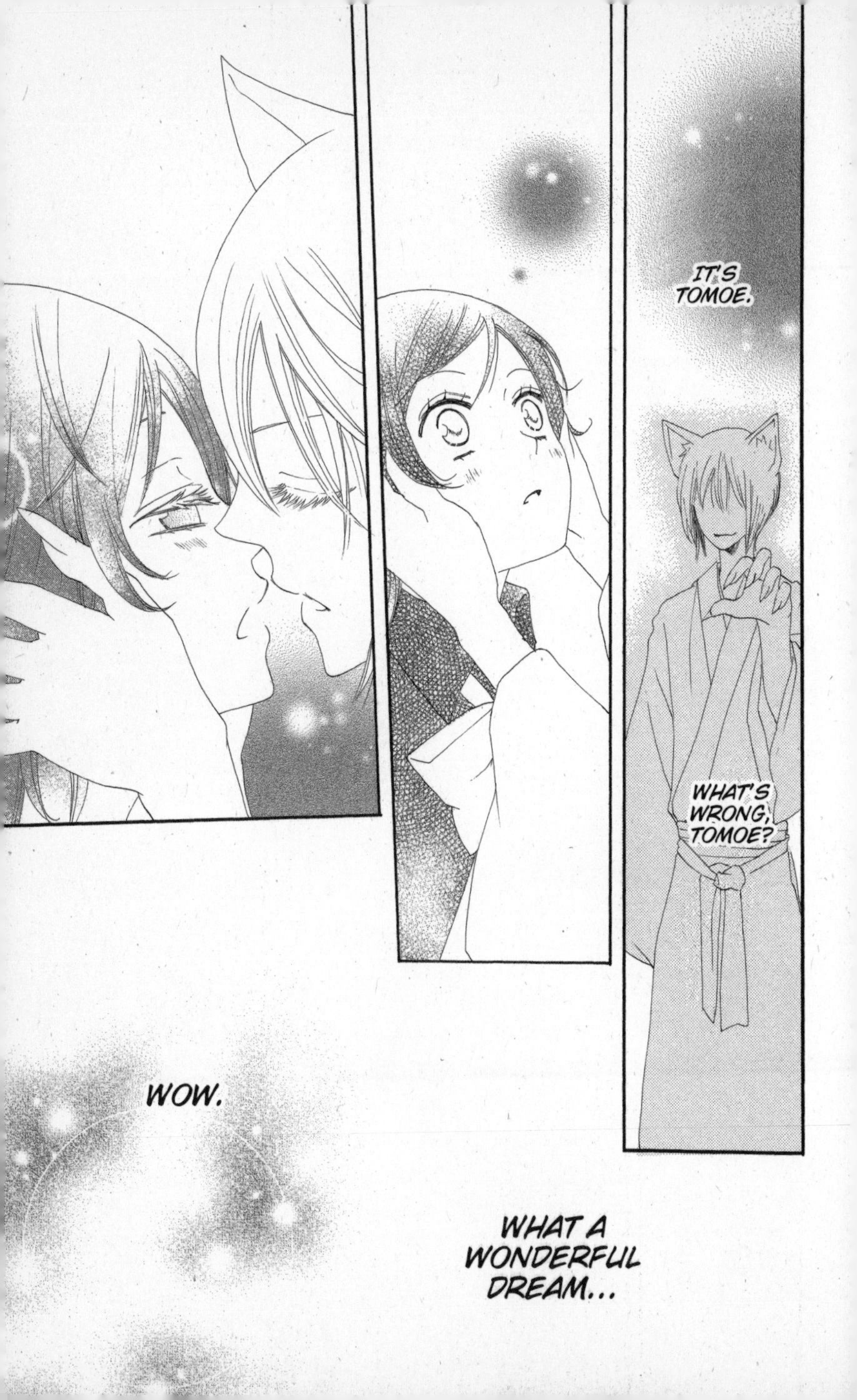
IT'S TOMOE.
WHAT'S WRONG, TOMOE?
WOW.
WHAT A WONDERFUL DREAM...

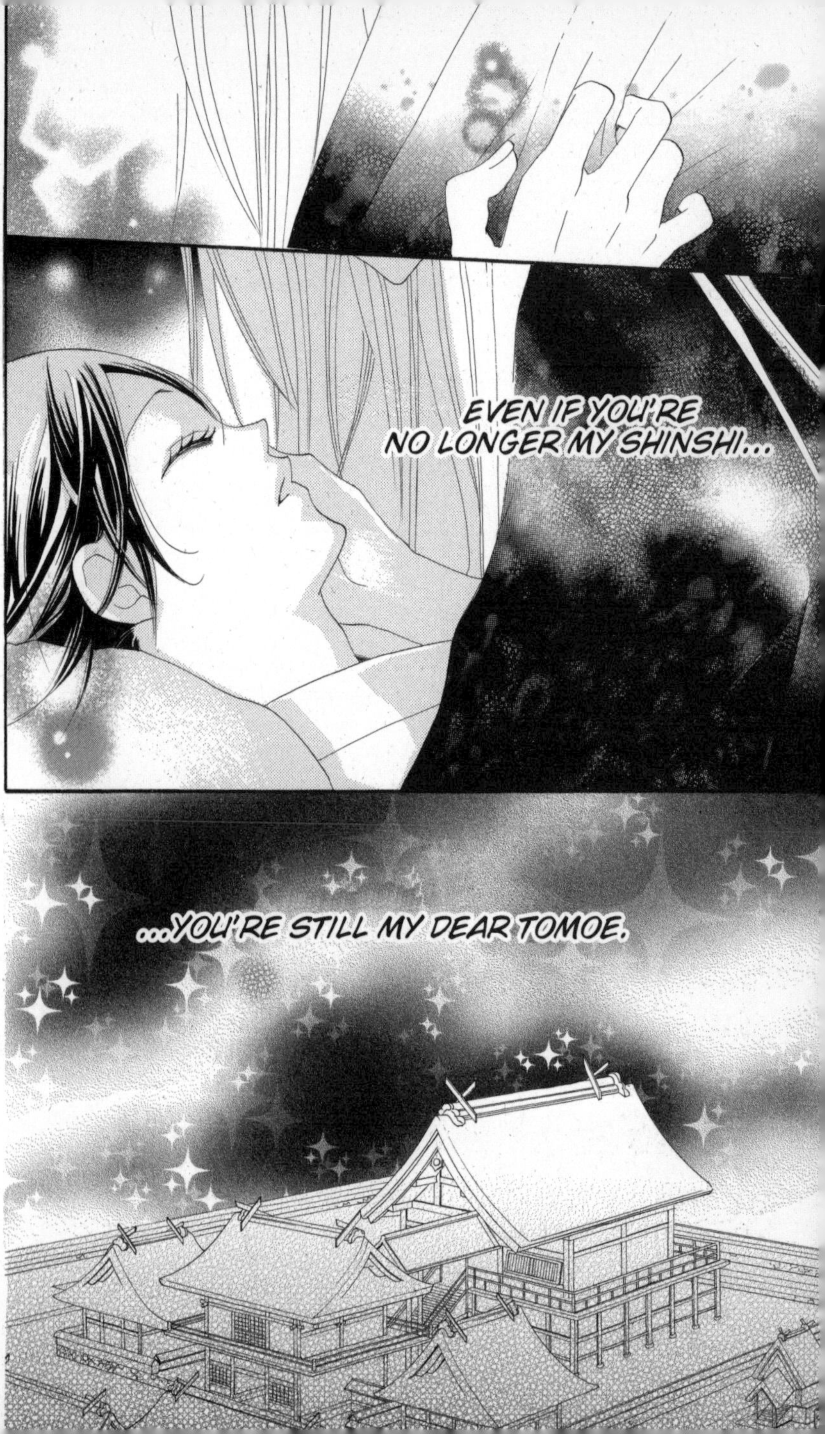
EVEN IF YOU'RE NO LONGER MY SHINSHI...
...YOU'RE STILL MY DEAR TOMOE.

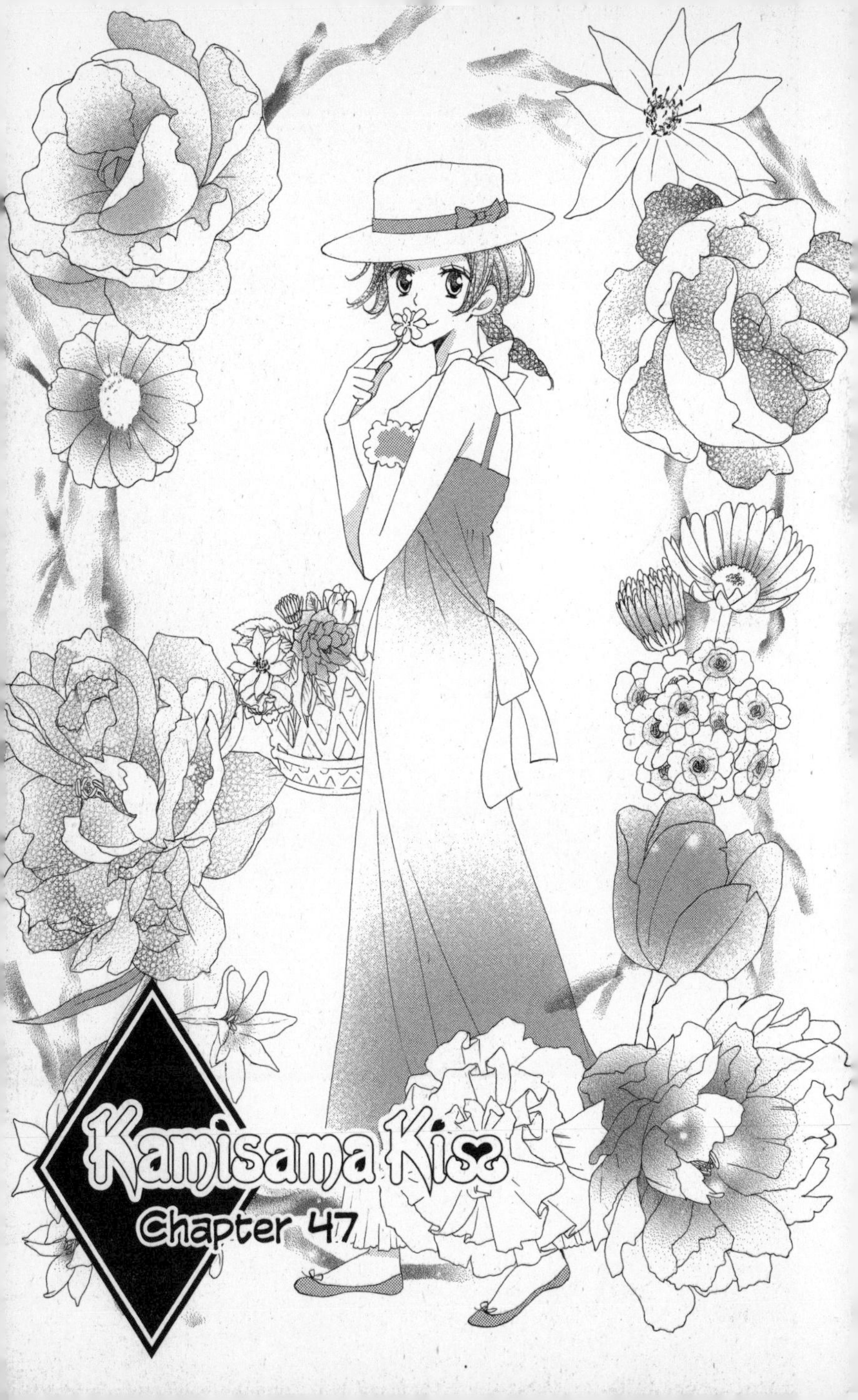
Kamisama Kiss
Chapter 47

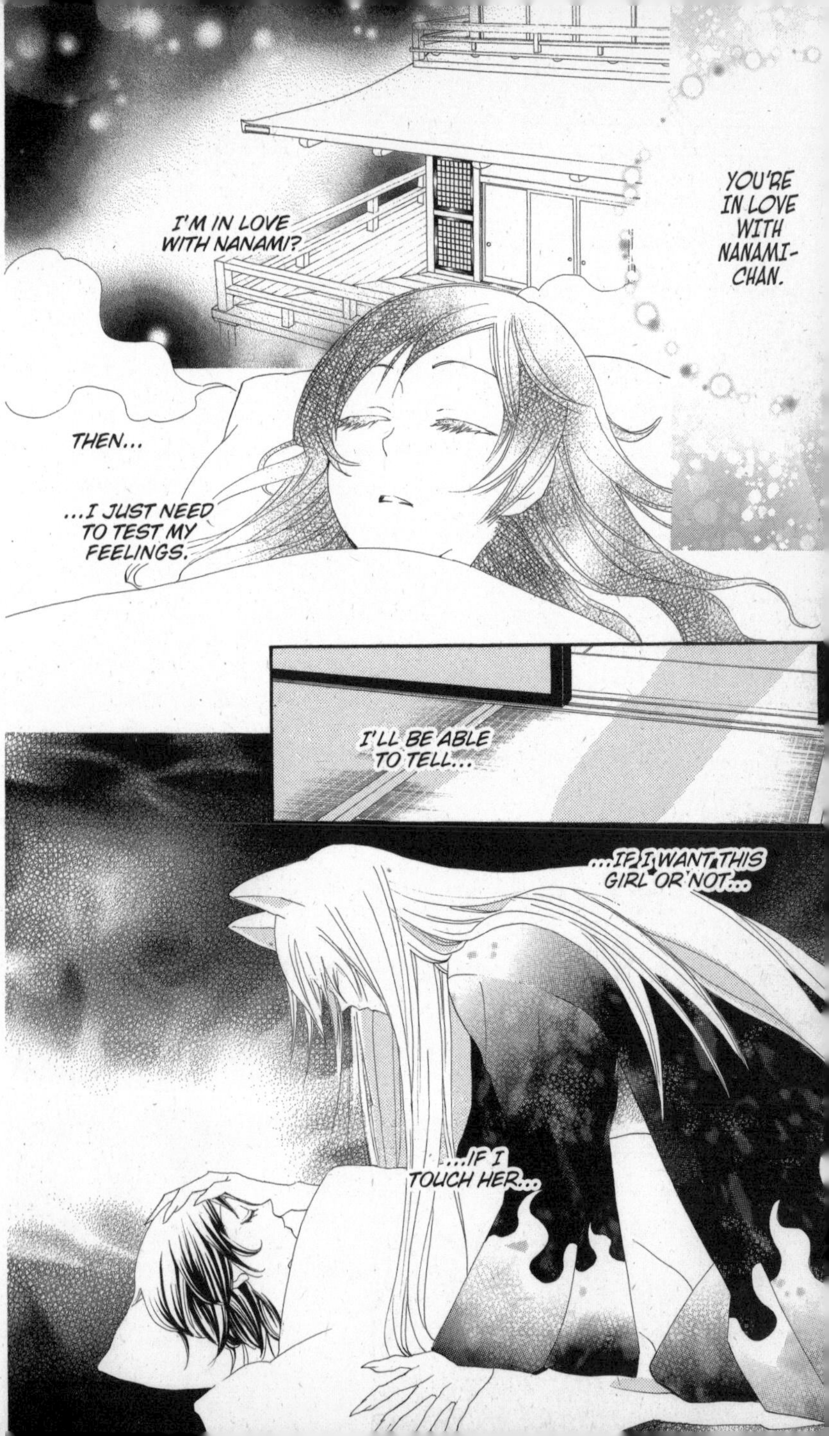
YOU'RE IN LOVE WITH NANAMI-CHAN.
I'M IN LOVE WITH NANAMI?
THEN...
...I JUST NEED TO TEST MY FEELINGS.
I'LL BE ABLE TO TELL...
...IF I WANT THIS GIRL OR NOT...
...IF I TOUCH HER...

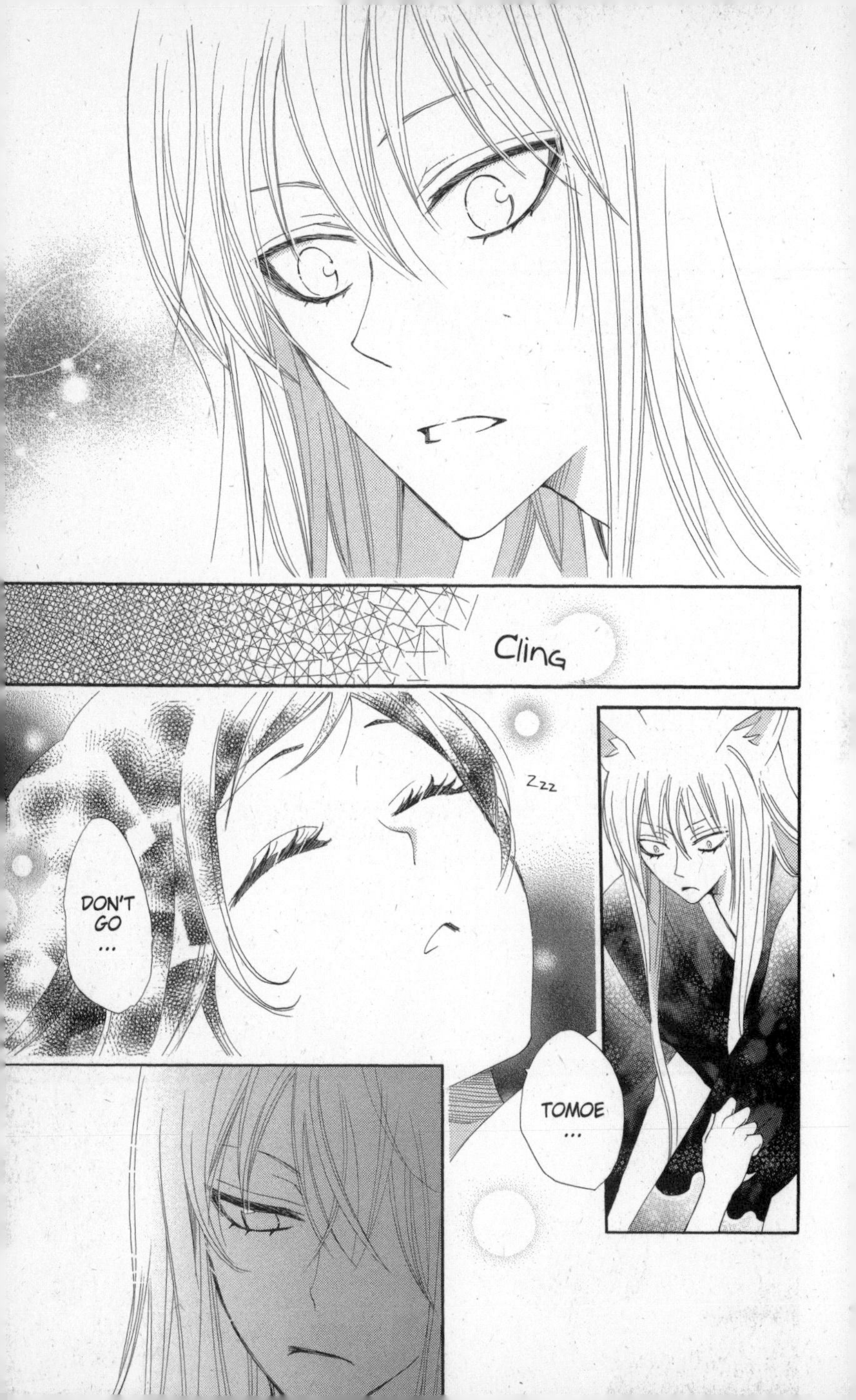
Cling
Zzz
DON'T GO ...
TOMOE ...

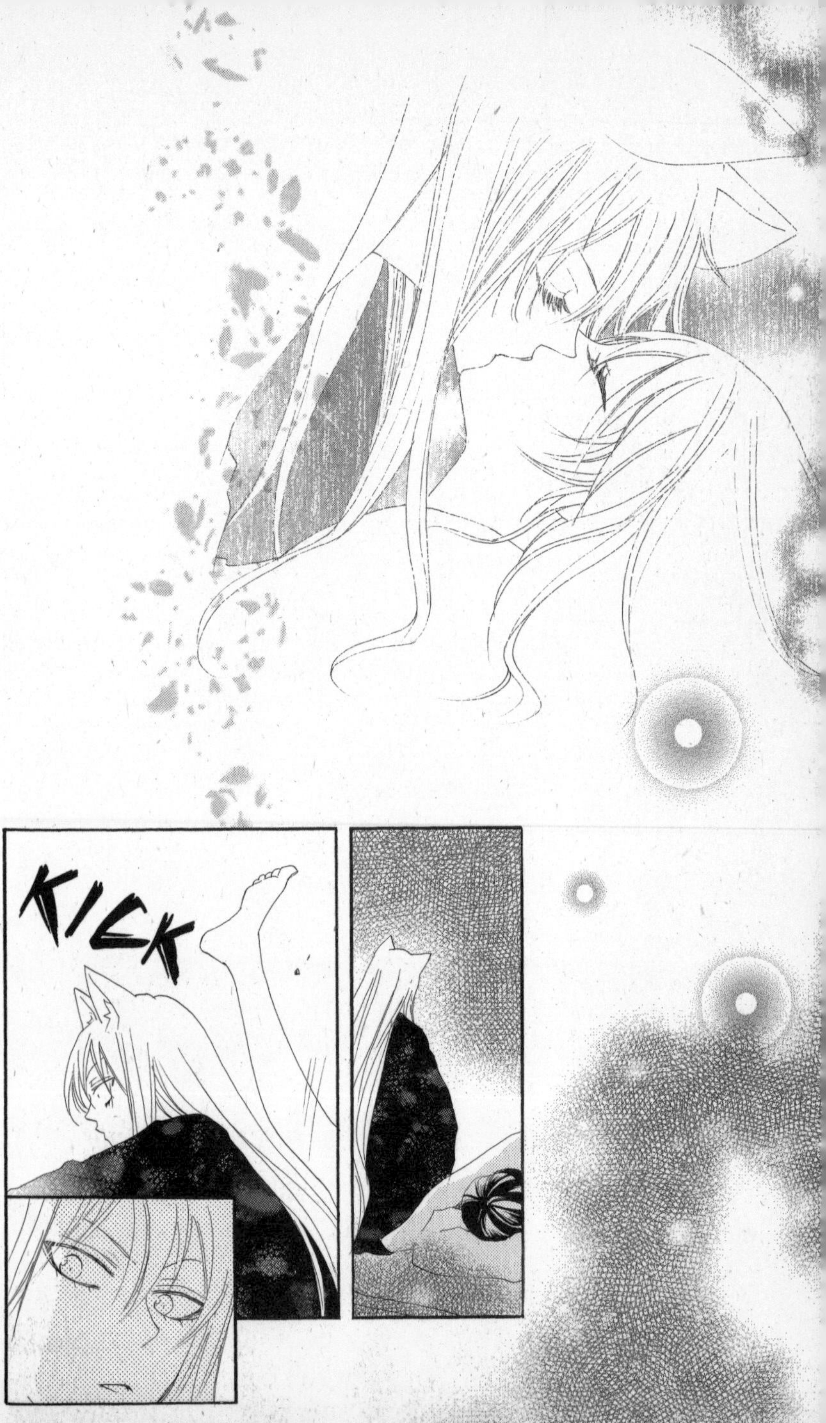
KICK

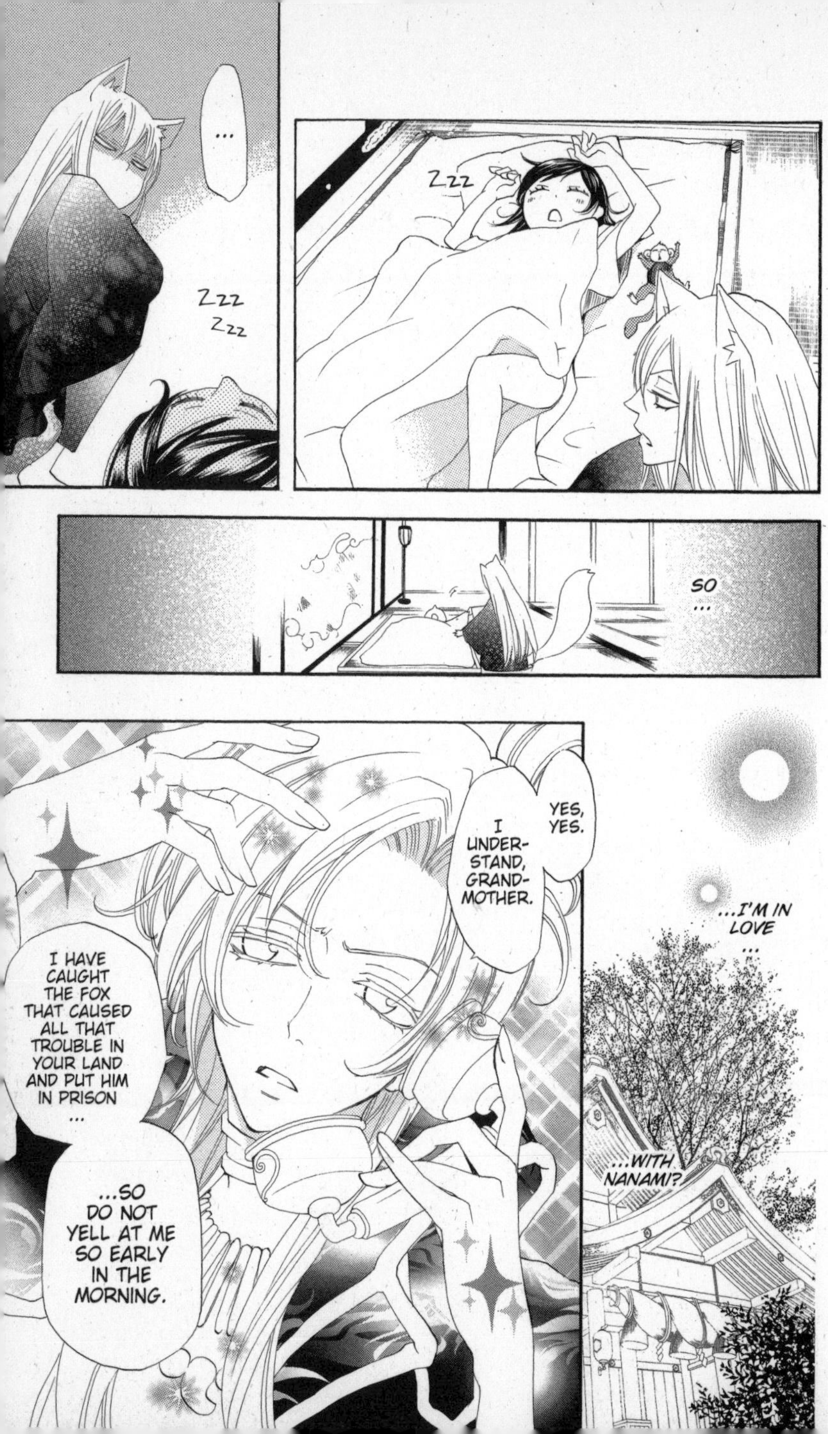
Zzz
...
Zzz
Zzz
SO ...
...I'M IN LOVE ...
...WITH NANAMI?
YES, YES.
I UNDERSTAND, GRANDMOTHER.
I HAVE CAUGHT THE FOX THAT CAUSED ALL THAT TROUBLE IN YOUR LAND AND PUT HIM IN PRISON ...
...SO DO NOT YELL AT ME SO EARLY IN THE MORNING.

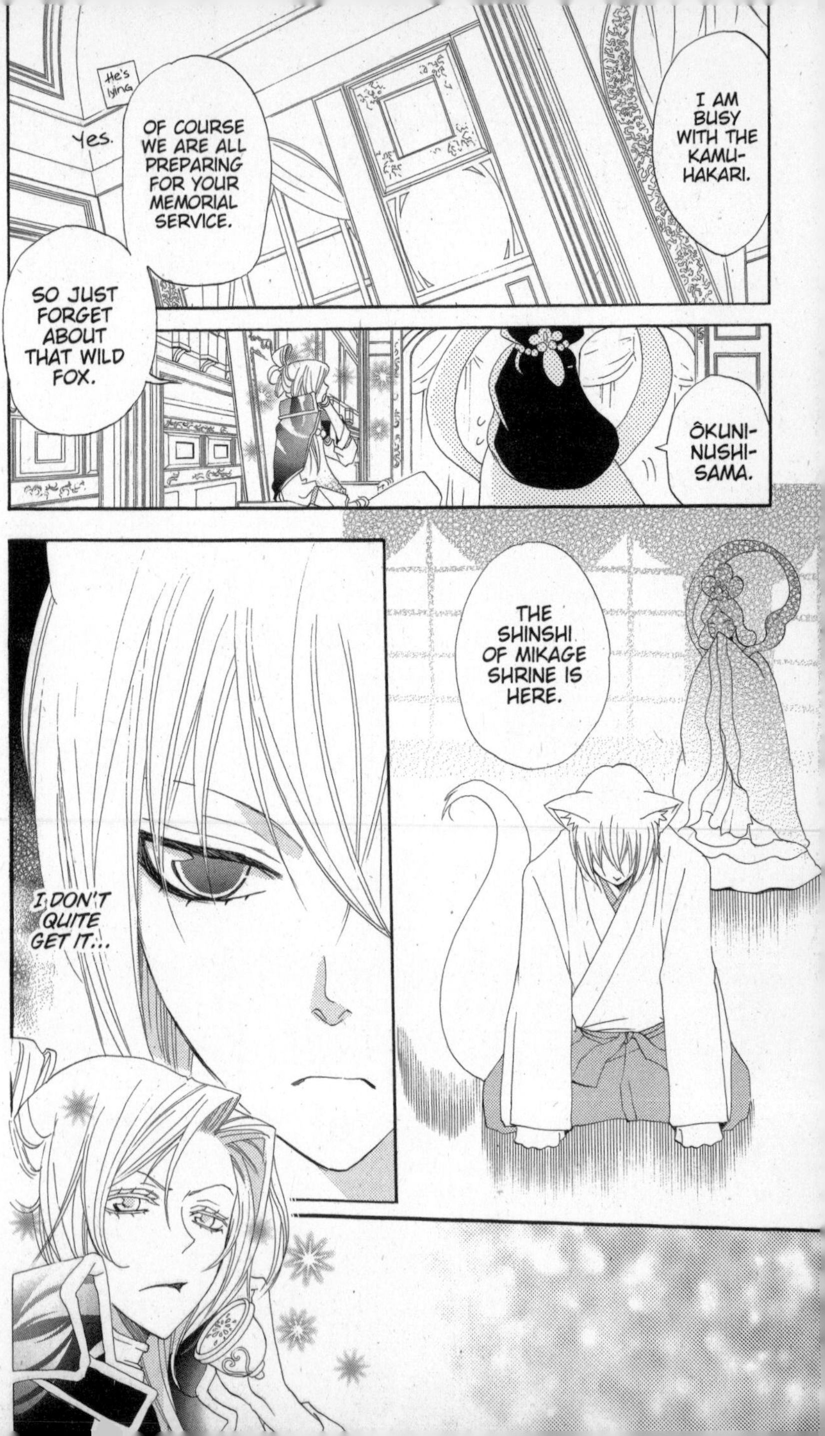
I AM BUSY WITH THE KAMU-HAKARI.
OF COURSE WE ARE ALL PREPARING FOR YOUR MEMORIAL SERVICE.
Yes.
He's lying
SO JUST FORGET ABOUT THAT WILD FOX.
ÔKUNI-NUSHI-SAMA.
THE SHINSHI OF MIKAGE SHRINE IS HERE.
I DON'T QUITE GET IT...

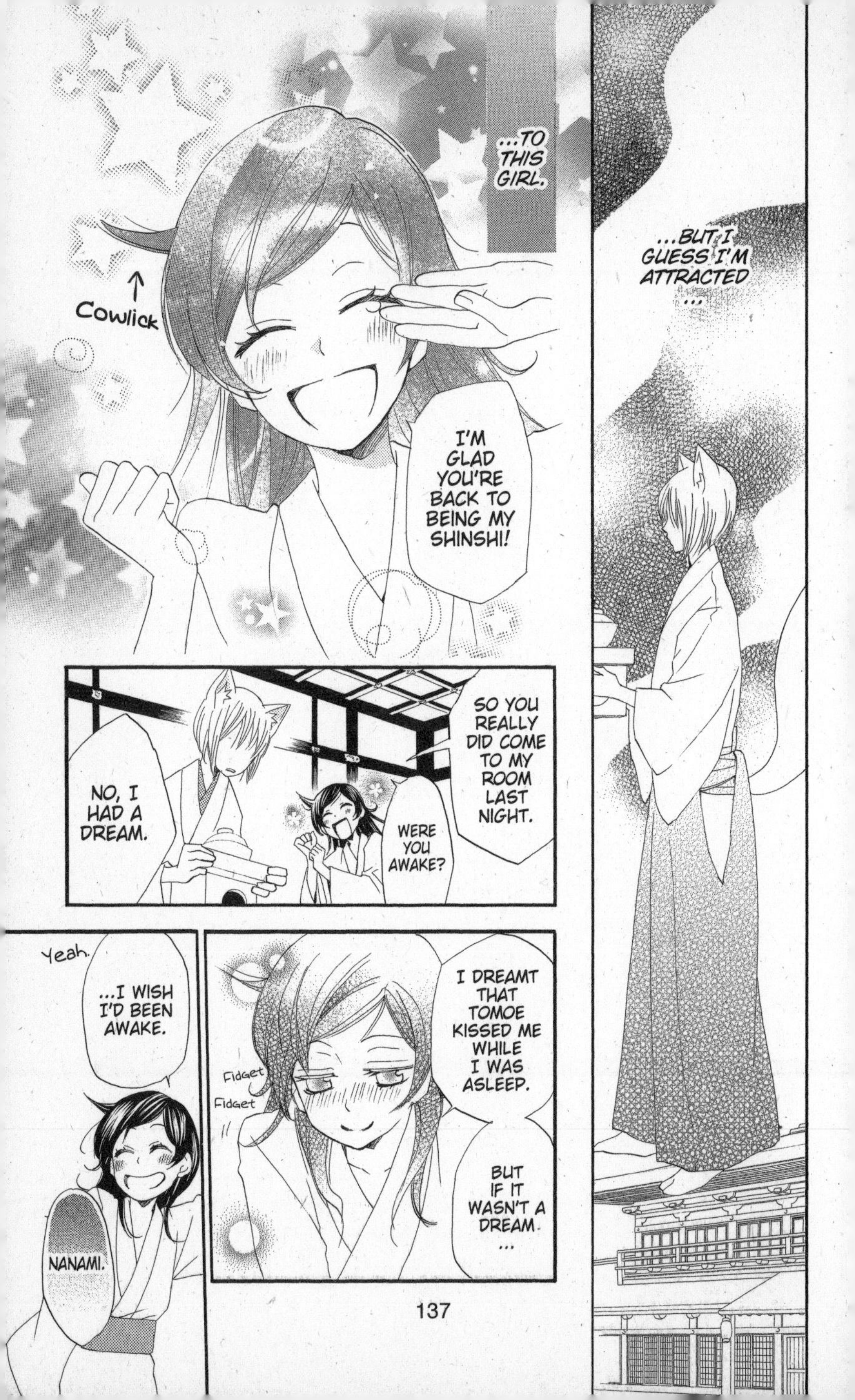
...BUT I GUESS I'M ATTRACTED ...
...TO THIS GIRL.
I'M GLAD YOU'RE BACK TO BEING MY SHINSHI!
Cowlick
SO YOU REALLY DID COME TO MY ROOM LAST NIGHT.
WERE YOU AWAKE?
NO, I HAD A DREAM.
I DREAMT THAT TOMOE KISSED ME WHILE I WAS ASLEEP.
Fidget
Fidget
BUT IF IT WASN'T A DREAM...
Yeah.
...I WISH I'D BEEN AWAKE.
NANAMI.

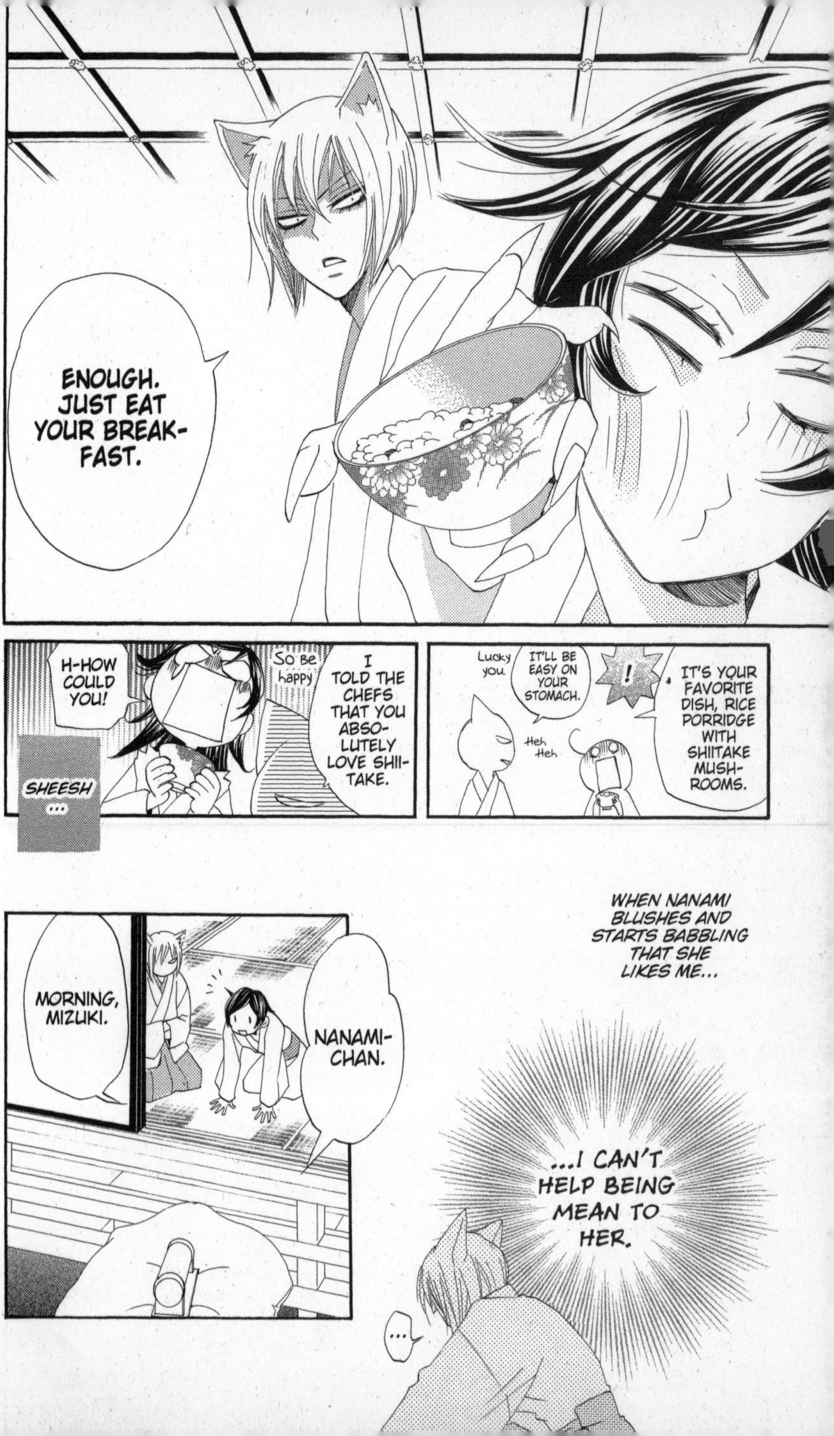
ENOUGH. JUST EAT YOUR BREAK-FAST.
IT'S YOUR FAVORITE DISH, RICE PORRIDGE WITH SHIITAKE MUSH-ROOMS.
!
IT'LL BE EASY ON YOUR STOMACH.
Lucky you.
Heh Heh
I TOLD THE CHEFS THAT YOU ABSO-LUTELY LOVE SHII-TAKE.
So be happy
H-HOW COULD YOU!
SHEESH...
WHEN NANAMI BLUSHES AND STARTS BABBLING THAT SHE LIKES ME...
...I CAN'T HELP BEING MEAN TO HER.
...
NANAMI-CHAN.
MORNING, MIZUKI.

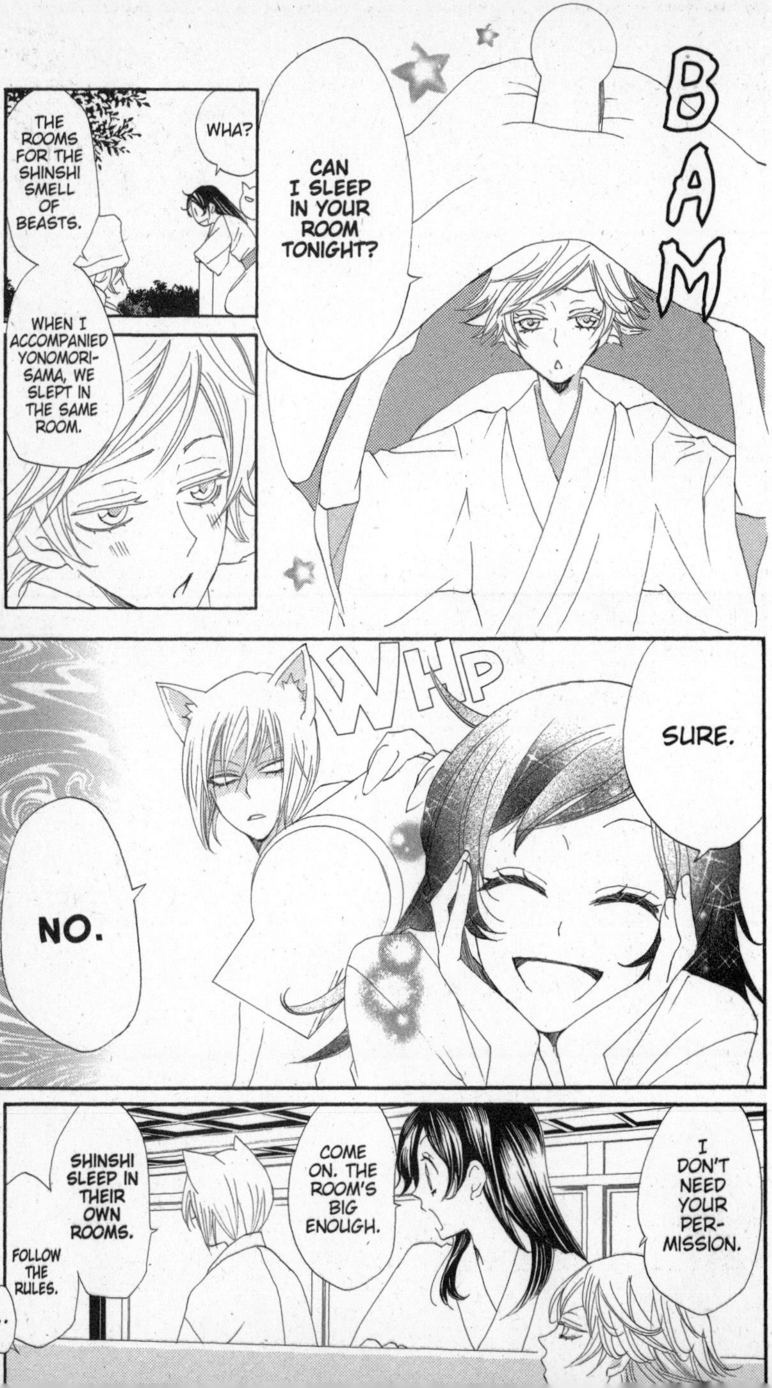
BAM
CAN I SLEEP IN YOUR ROOM TONIGHT?
WHA?
THE ROOMS FOR THE SHINSHI SMELL OF BEASTS.
WHEN I ACCOMPANIED YONOMORI-SAMA, WE SLEPT IN THE SAME ROOM.
SURE.
WHP
NO.
I DON'T NEED YOUR PER-MISSION.
COME ON. THE ROOM'S BIG ENOUGH.
SHINSHI SLEEP IN THEIR OWN ROOMS.
FOLLOW THE RULES.
...

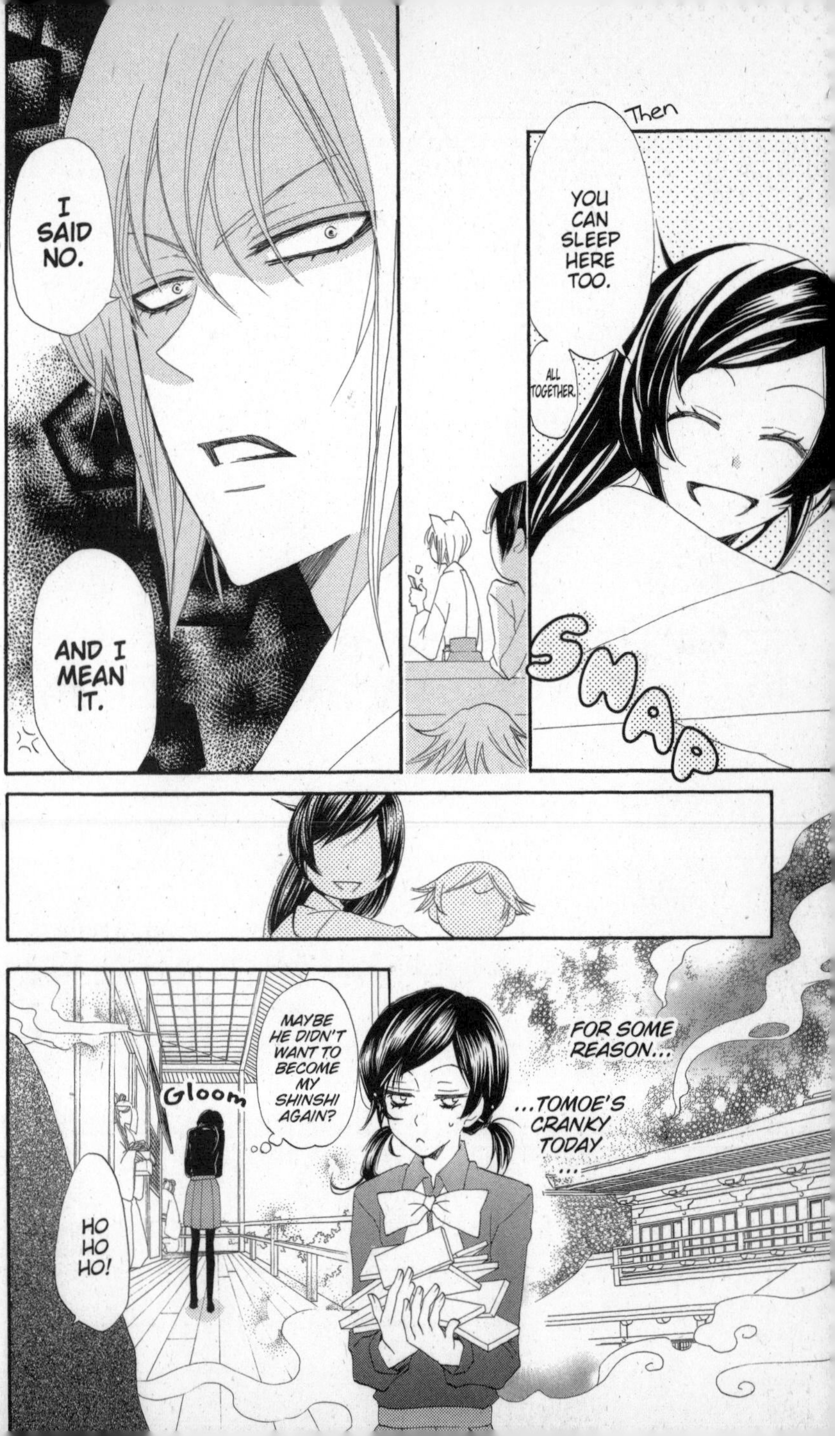
Then
YOU CAN SLEEP HERE TOO.
ALL TOGETHER.
SNAP
I SAID NO.
AND I MEAN IT.
FOR SOME REASON...
...TOMOE'S CRANKY TODAY...
MAYBE HE DIDN'T WANT TO BECOME MY SHINSHI AGAIN?
Gloom
HO HO HO!

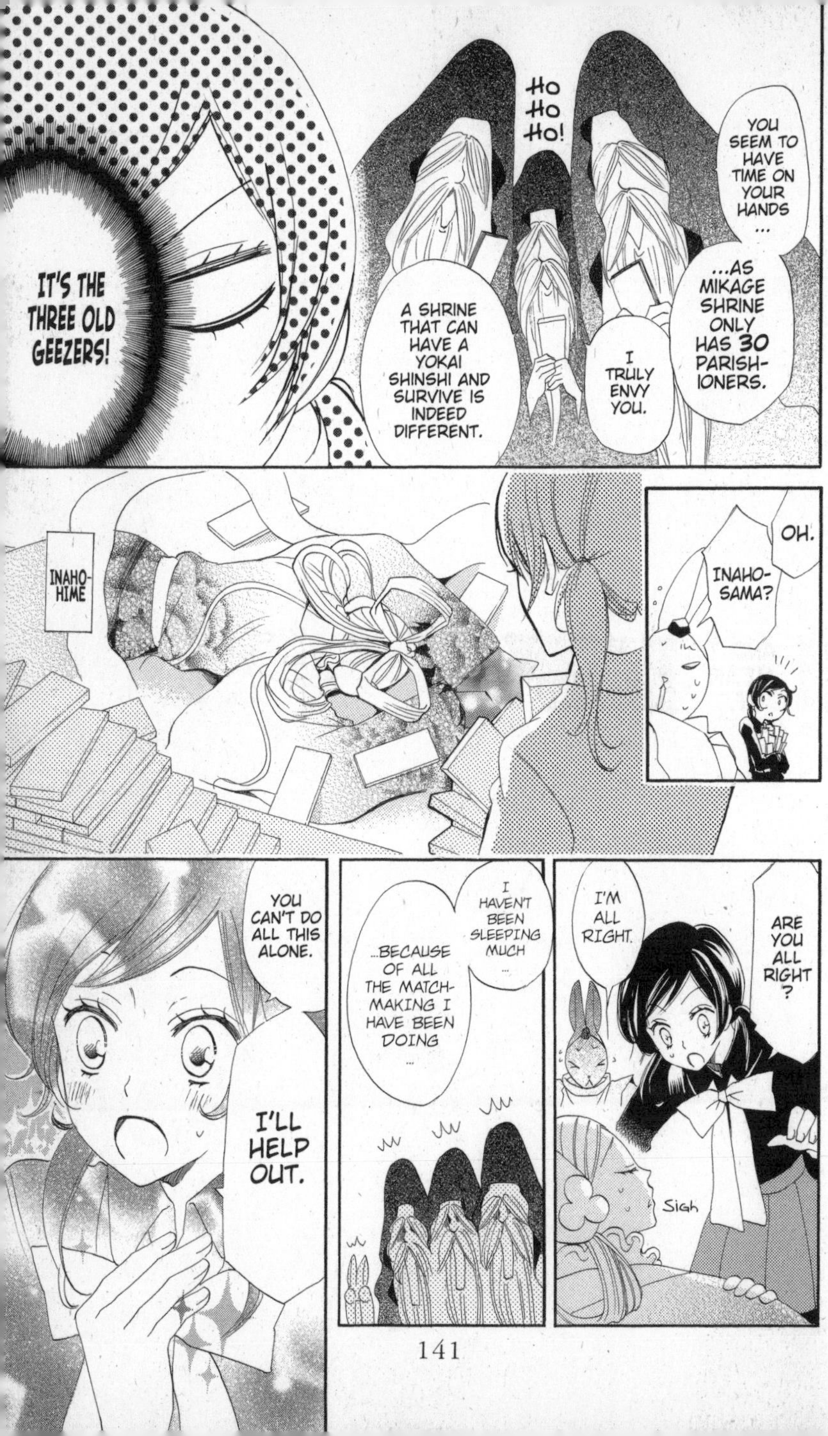
YOU SEEM TO HAVE TIME ON YOUR HANDS ...
...AS MIKAGE SHRINE ONLY HAS 30 PARISHIONERS.
HO HO HO!
I TRULY ENVY YOU.
A SHRINE THAT CAN HAVE A YOKAI SHINSHI AND SURVIVE IS INDEED DIFFERENT.
IT'S THE THREE OLD GEEZERS!
OH.
INAHO-SAMA?
INAHO-HIME
ARE YOU ALL RIGHT?
I'M ALL RIGHT.
Sigh
I HAVEN'T BEEN SLEEPING MUCH ...
...BECAUSE OF ALL THE MATCH-MAKING I HAVE BEEN DOING ...
YOU CAN'T DO ALL THIS ALONE.
I'LL HELP OUT.

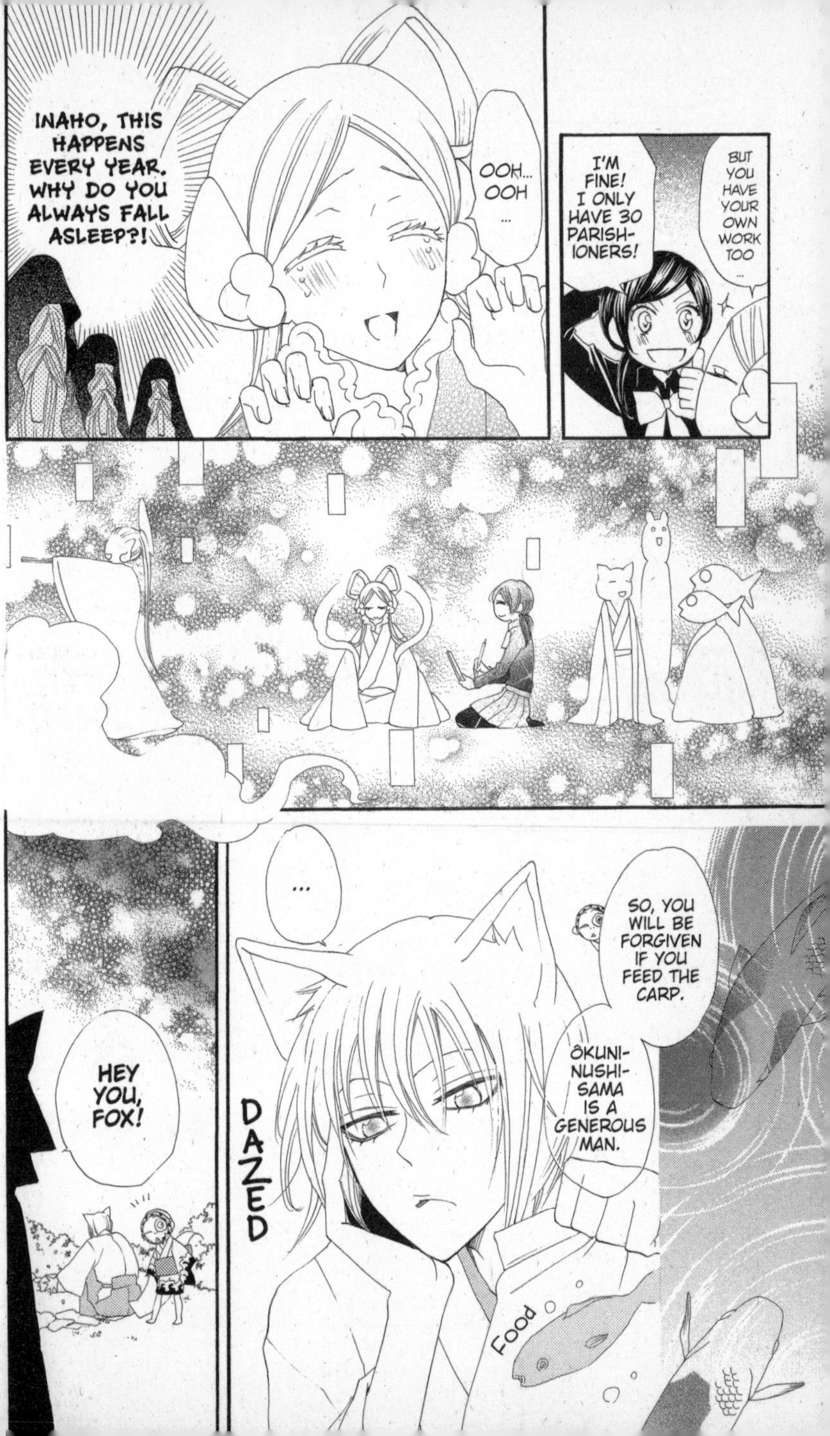
BUT YOU HAVE YOUR OWN WORK TOO ...
I'M FINE! I ONLY HAVE 30 PARISH-IONERS!
OOH... OOH ...
INAHO, THIS HAPPENS EVERY YEAR. WHY DO YOU ALWAYS FALL ASLEEP?!
SO, YOU WILL BE FORGIVEN IF YOU FEED THE CARP.
ÔKUNI-NUSHI-SAMA IS A GENEROUS MAN.
...
DAZED
Food
HEY YOU, FOX!

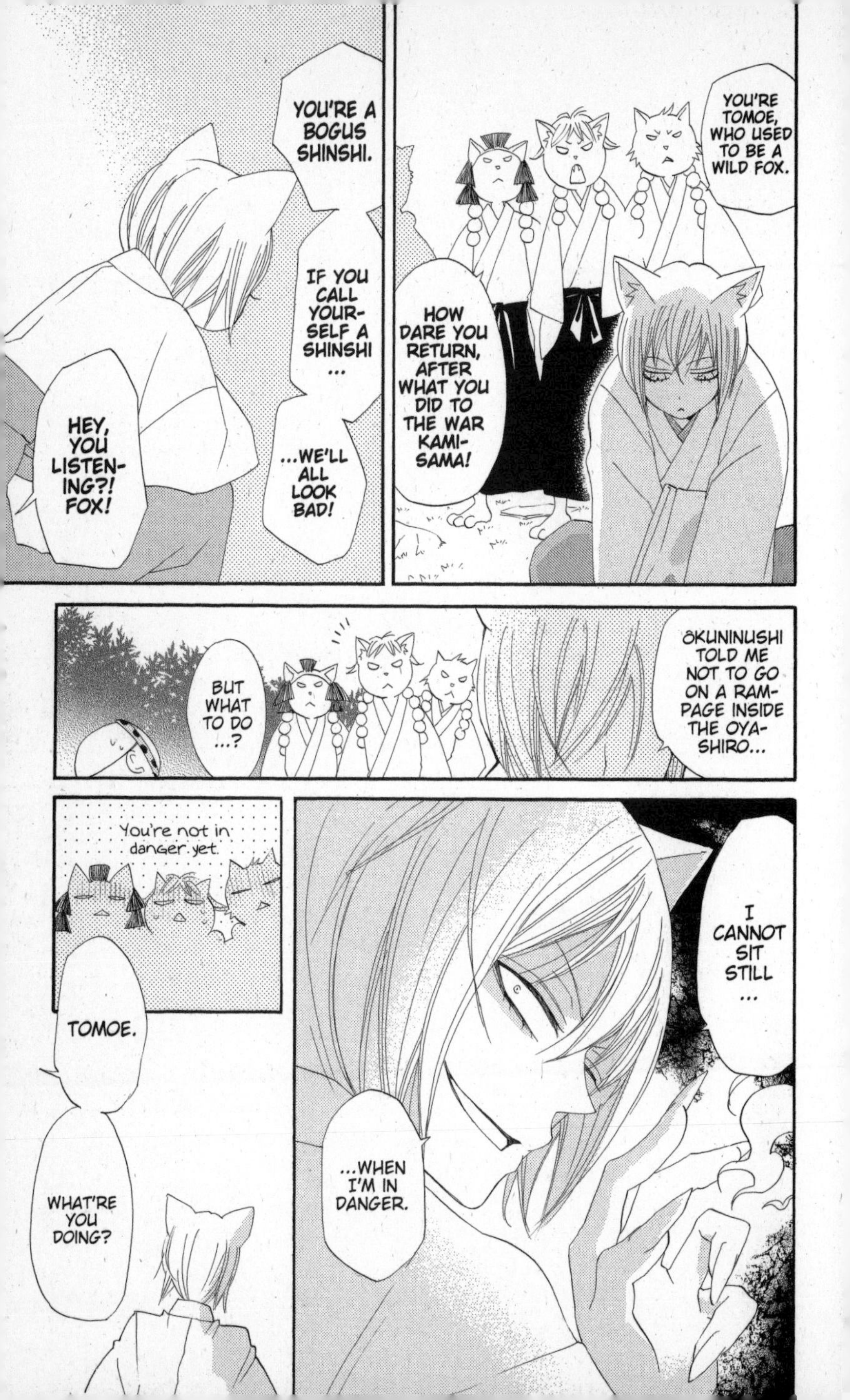
YOU'RE TOMOE, WHO USED TO BE A WILD FOX.
HOW DARE YOU RETURN, AFTER WHAT YOU DID TO THE WAR KAMI-SAMA!
YOU'RE A BOGUS SHINSHI.
IF YOU CALL YOURSELF A SHINSHI...
...WE'LL ALL LOOK BAD!
HEY, YOU LISTENING?! FOX!
OKUNINUSHI TOLD ME NOT TO GO ON A RAMPAGE INSIDE THE OYASHIRO...
BUT WHAT TO DO...?
I CANNOT SIT STILL...
...WHEN I'M IN DANGER.
You're not in danger yet.
TOMOE.
WHAT'RE YOU DOING?

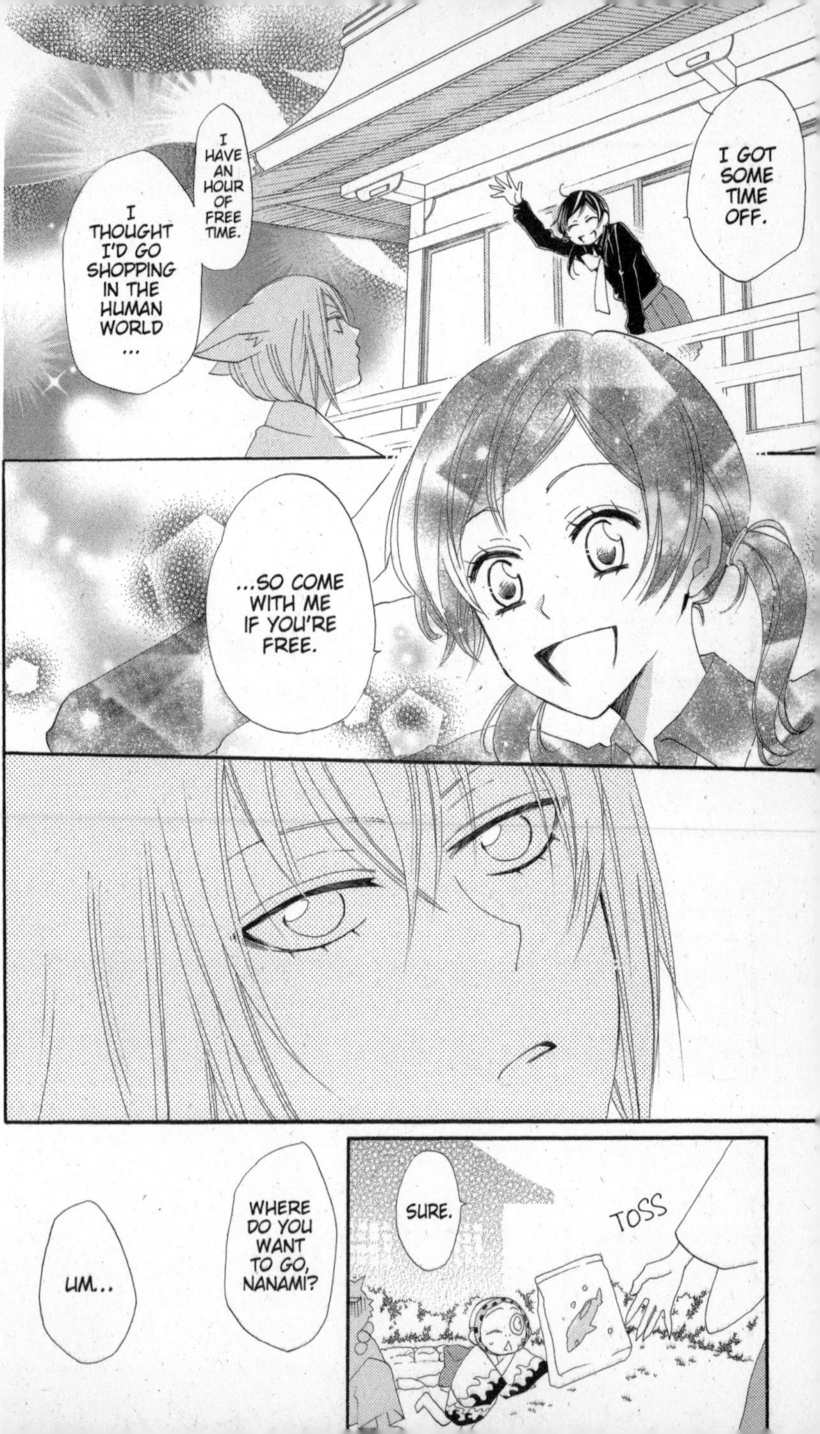
I GOT SOME TIME OFF.
I HAVE AN HOUR OF FREE TIME.
I THOUGHT I'D GO SHOPPING IN THE HUMAN WORLD ...
...SO COME WITH ME IF YOU'RE FREE.
SURE.
TOSS
WHERE DO YOU WANT TO GO, NANAMI?
UM...

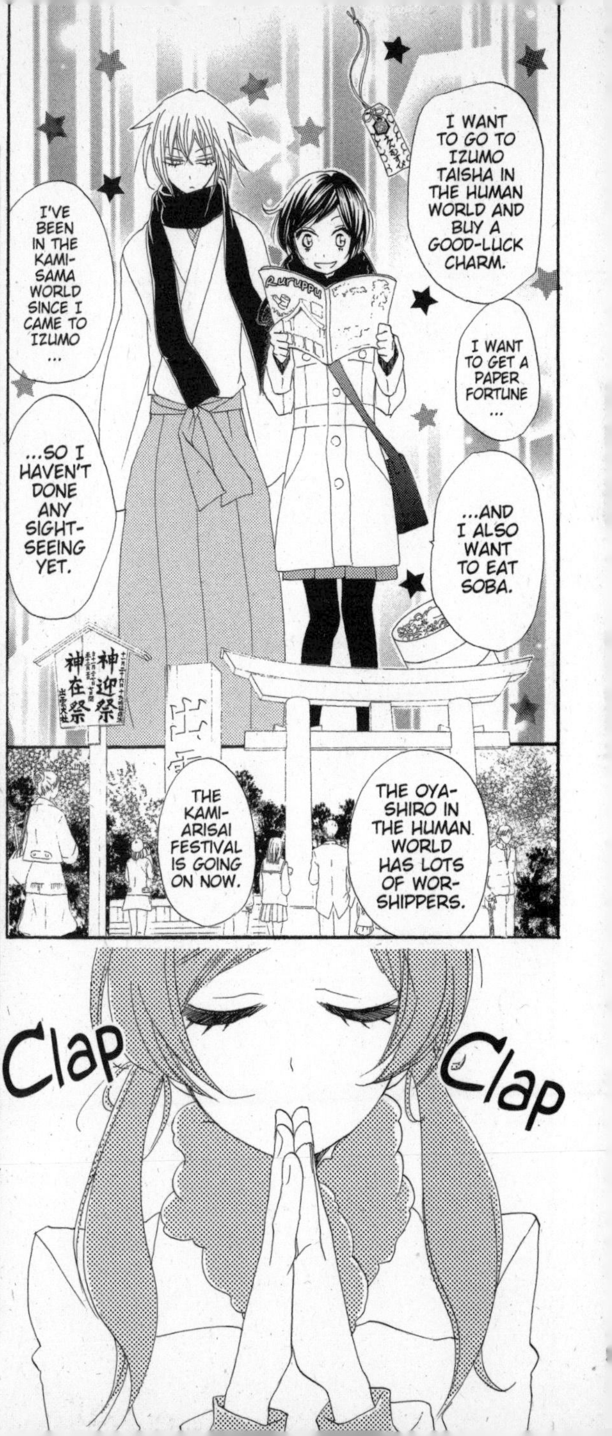
I WANT TO GO TO IZUMO TAISHA IN THE HUMAN WORLD AND BUY A GOOD-LUCK CHARM.
I'VE BEEN IN THE KAMI-SAMA WORLD SINCE I CAME TO IZUMO...
I WANT TO GET A PAPER FORTUNE...
...SO I HAVEN'T DONE ANY SIGHT-SEEING YET.
...AND I ALSO WANT TO EAT SOBA.
神迎祭
神在祭
THE OYA-SHIRO IN THE HUMAN WORLD HAS LOTS OF WOR-SHIPPERS.
THE KAMI-ARISAI FESTIVAL IS GOING ON NOW.
Clap
Clap

About the manga

Chapter 47

I wish I could've drawn more scenes where the two go sightseeing in Izumo, but because of how the story went, there weren't enough pages. Izumo was a wonderful place!

Chapter 48

Now that I think about it, the chapters in Volume 8 tell one story as a whole, like Volume 6 did. I think there were a couple one-shots in Volume 9. Which format do you prefer?

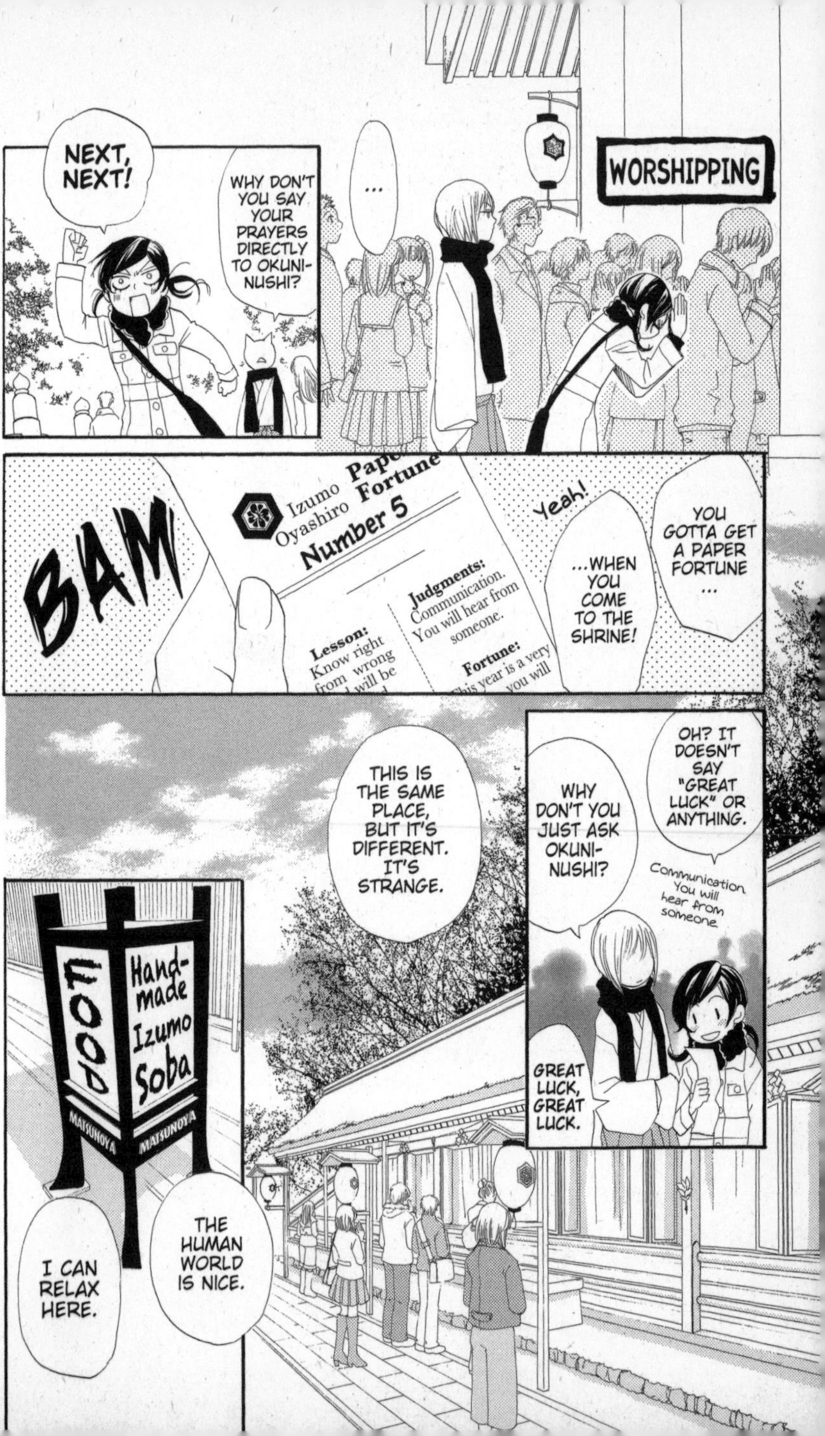
WORSHIPPING
...
WHY DON'T YOU SAY YOUR PRAYERS DIRECTLY TO OKUNI-NUSHI?
NEXT, NEXT!
YOU GOTTA GET A PAPER FORTUNE...
...WHEN YOU COME TO THE SHRINE!
Yeah!
Izumo Oyashiro
Fortune
Number 5
Judgments: Communication. You will hear from someone.
Fortune: This year is a very
you will
Lesson: Know right from wrong
will be
BAM
OH? IT DOESN'T SAY "GREAT LUCK" OR ANYTHING.
Communication. You will hear from someone.
WHY DON'T YOU JUST ASK OKUNI-NUSHI?
GREAT LUCK, GREAT LUCK.
THIS IS THE SAME PLACE, BUT IT'S DIFFERENT. IT'S STRANGE.
FOOD
Hand-made Izumo Soba
MATSUNOYA
MATSUNOYA
THE HUMAN WORLD IS NICE.
I CAN RELAX HERE.

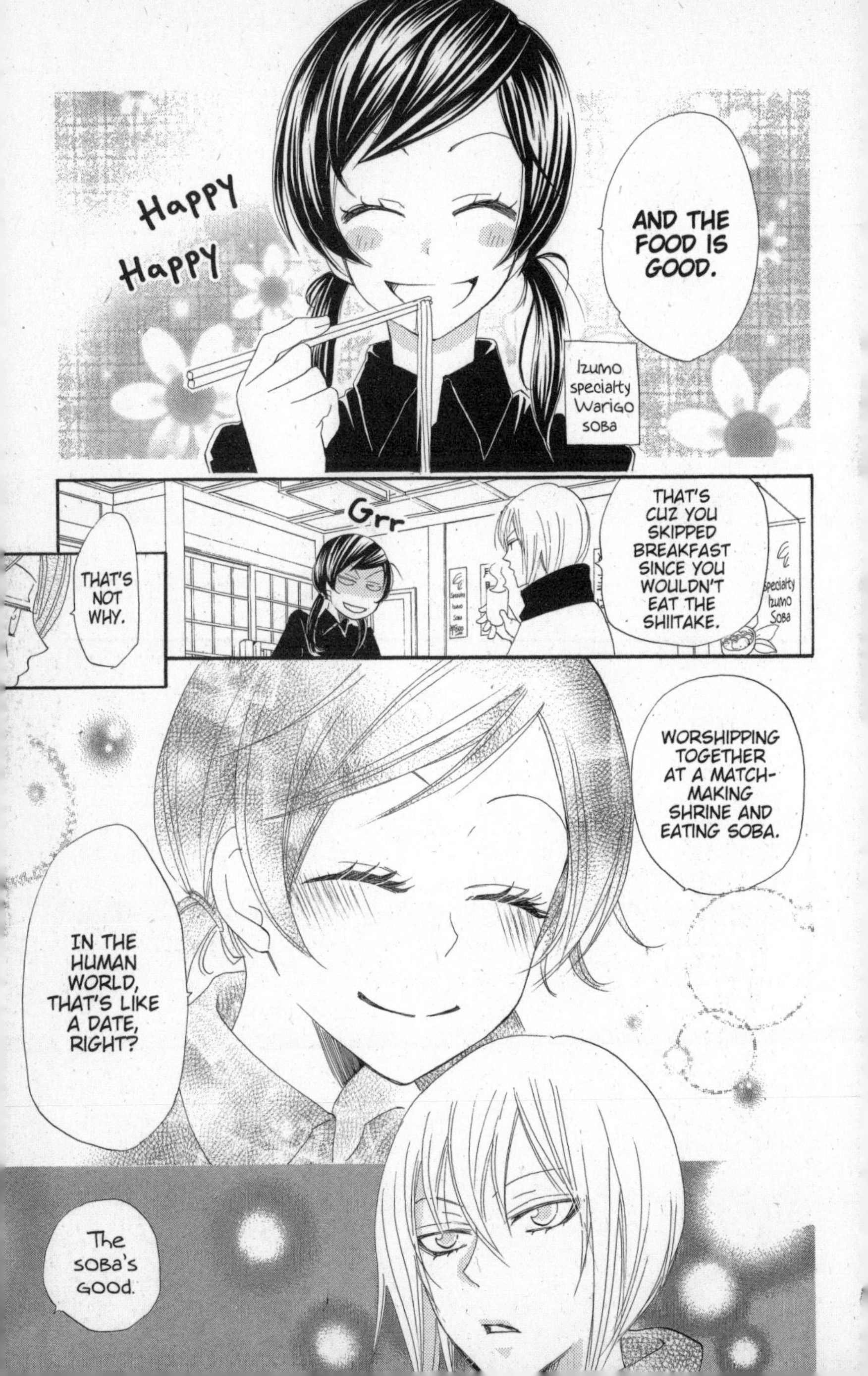
AND THE FOOD IS GOOD.
Happy Happy
Izumo specialty Warigo soba
THAT'S CUZ YOU SKIPPED BREAKFAST SINCE YOU WOULDN'T EAT THE SHIITAKE.
Specialty Izumo Soba
Grr
THAT'S NOT WHY.
WORSHIPPING TOGETHER AT A MATCH-MAKING SHRINE AND EATING SOBA.
IN THE HUMAN WORLD, THAT'S LIKE A DATE, RIGHT?
The soba's good.

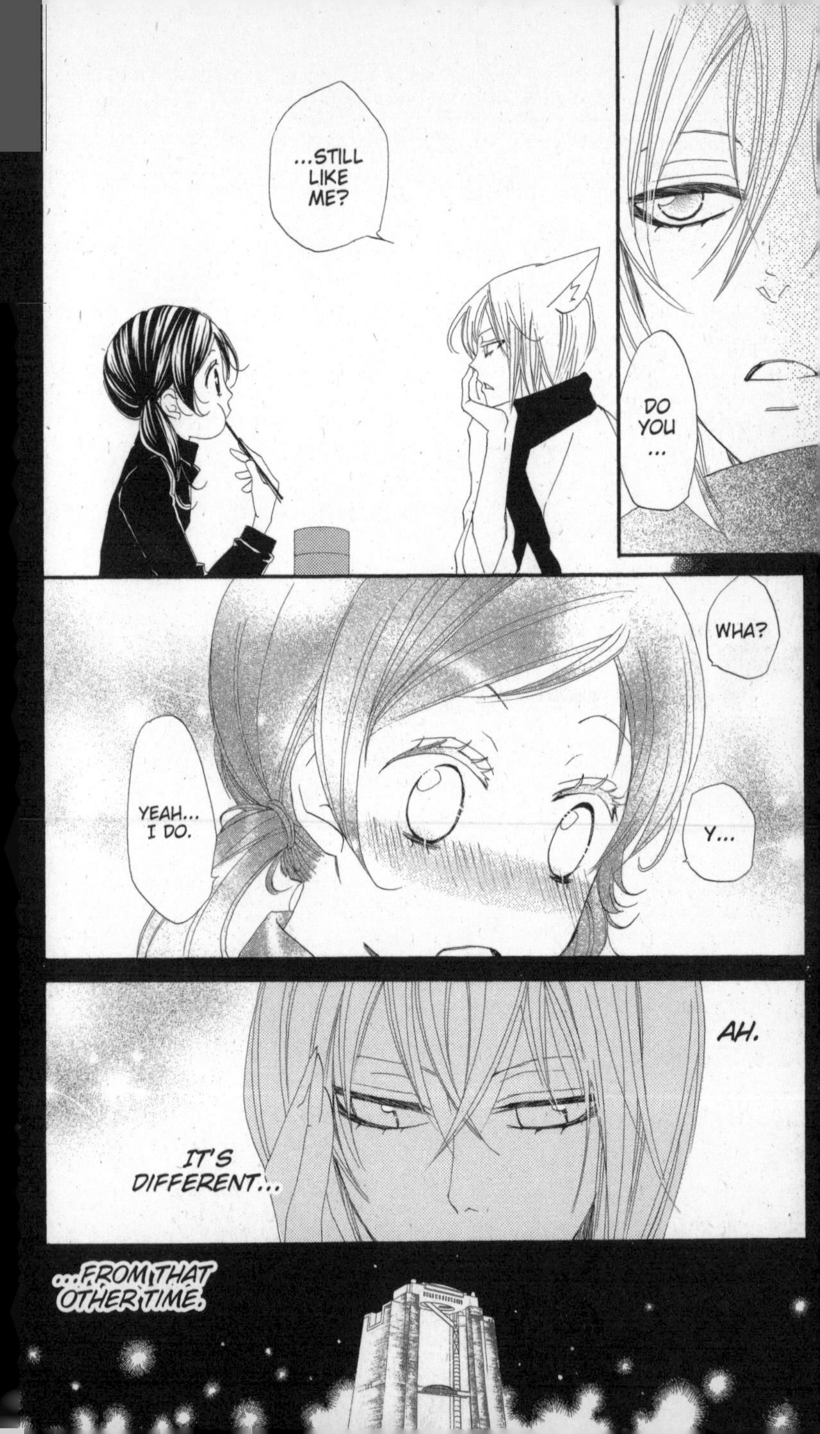
DO YOU...
...STILL LIKE ME?
WHA?
Y...
YEAH... I DO.
AH.
IT'S DIFFERENT...
...FROM THAT OTHER TIME.

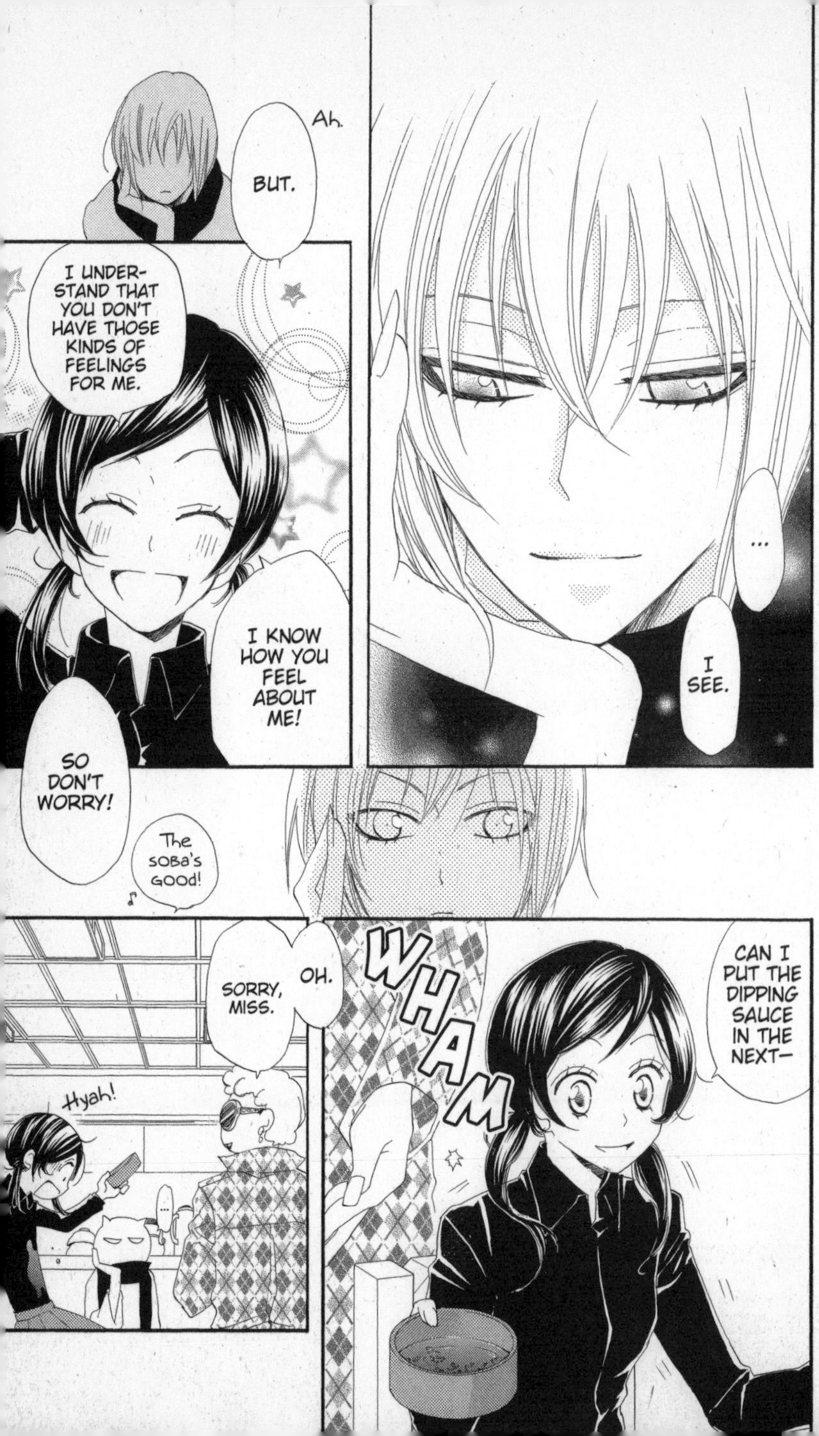
Ah.
BUT.
I UNDER-STAND THAT YOU DON'T HAVE THOSE KINDS OF FEELINGS FOR ME.
I KNOW HOW YOU FEEL ABOUT ME!
SO DON'T WORRY!
The soba's good!
...
I SEE.
CAN I PUT THE DIPPING SAUCE IN THE NEXT—
WHAM
OH.
SORRY, MISS.
Hyah!

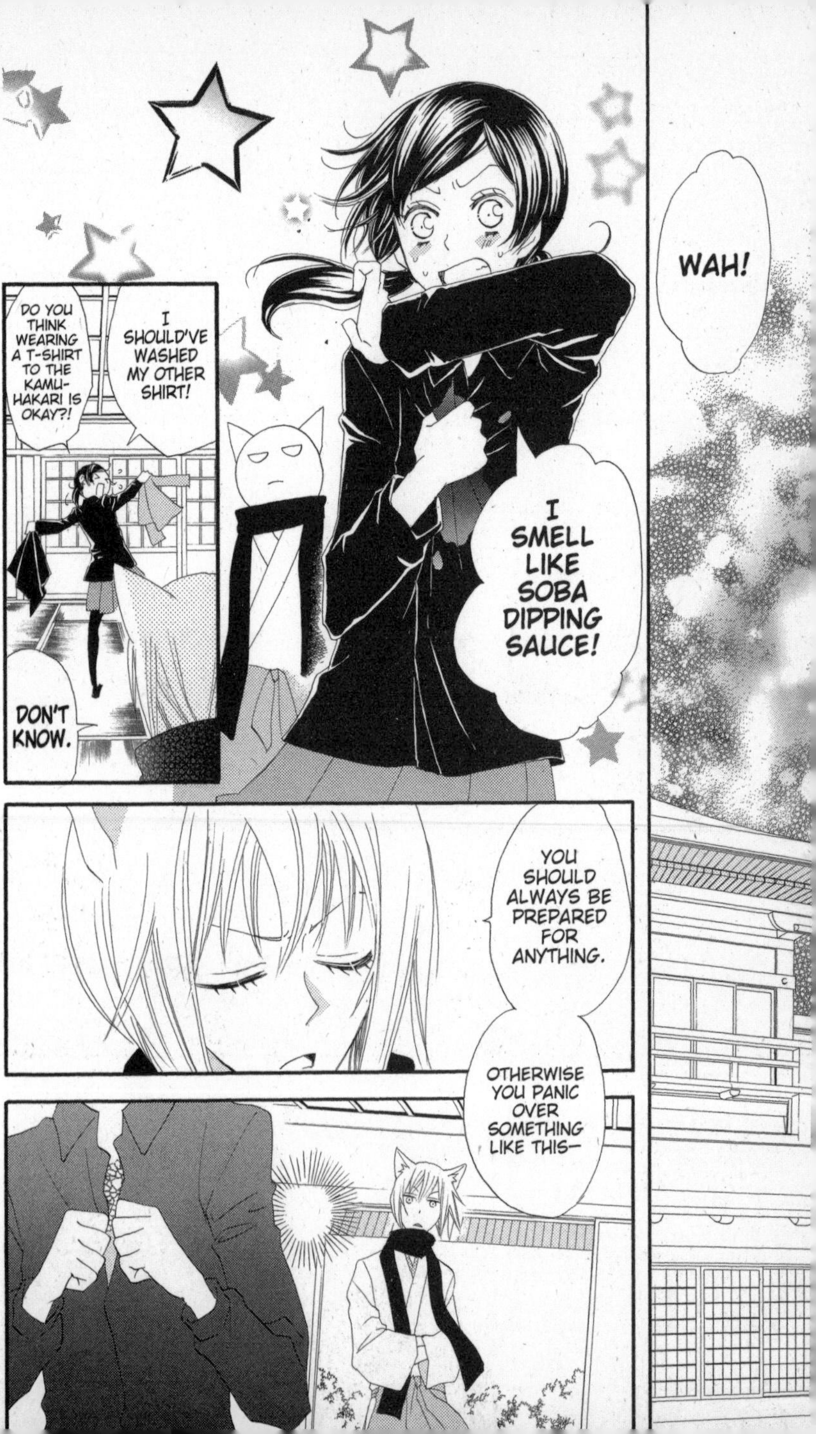
WAH!
I SMELL LIKE SOBA DIPPING SAUCE!
I SHOULD'VE WASHED MY OTHER SHIRT!
DO YOU THINK WEARING A T-SHIRT TO THE KAMU-HAKARI IS OKAY?!
DON'T KNOW.
YOU SHOULD ALWAYS BE PREPARED FOR ANYTHING.
OTHERWISE YOU PANIC OVER SOMETHING LIKE THIS—

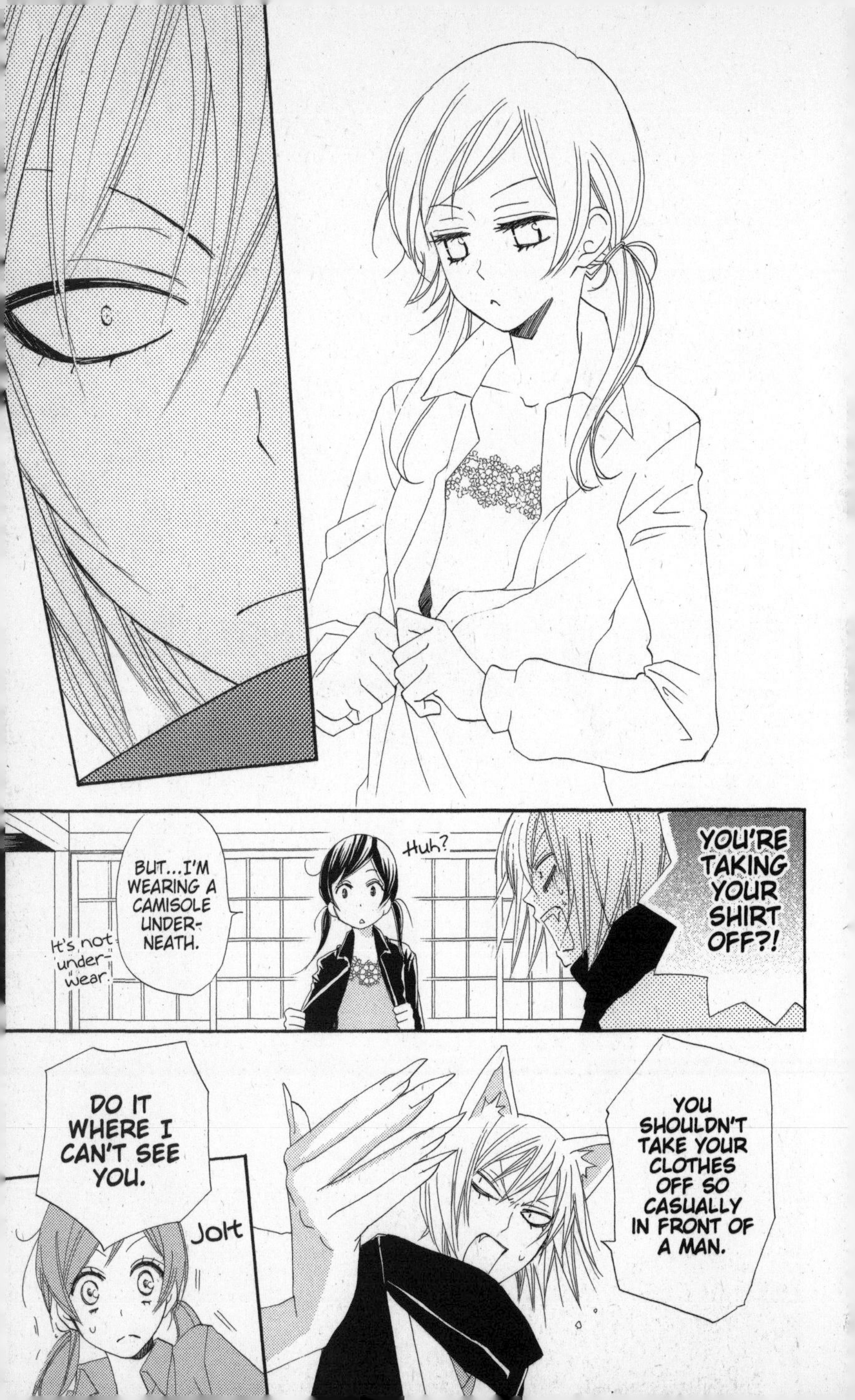
YOU'RE TAKING YOUR SHIRT OFF?!
Huh?
BUT...I'M WEARING A CAMISOLE UNDER-NEATH.
It's not under-wear.
YOU SHOULDN'T TAKE YOUR CLOTHES OFF SO CASUALLY IN FRONT OF A MAN.
DO IT WHERE I CAN'T SEE YOU.
Jolt

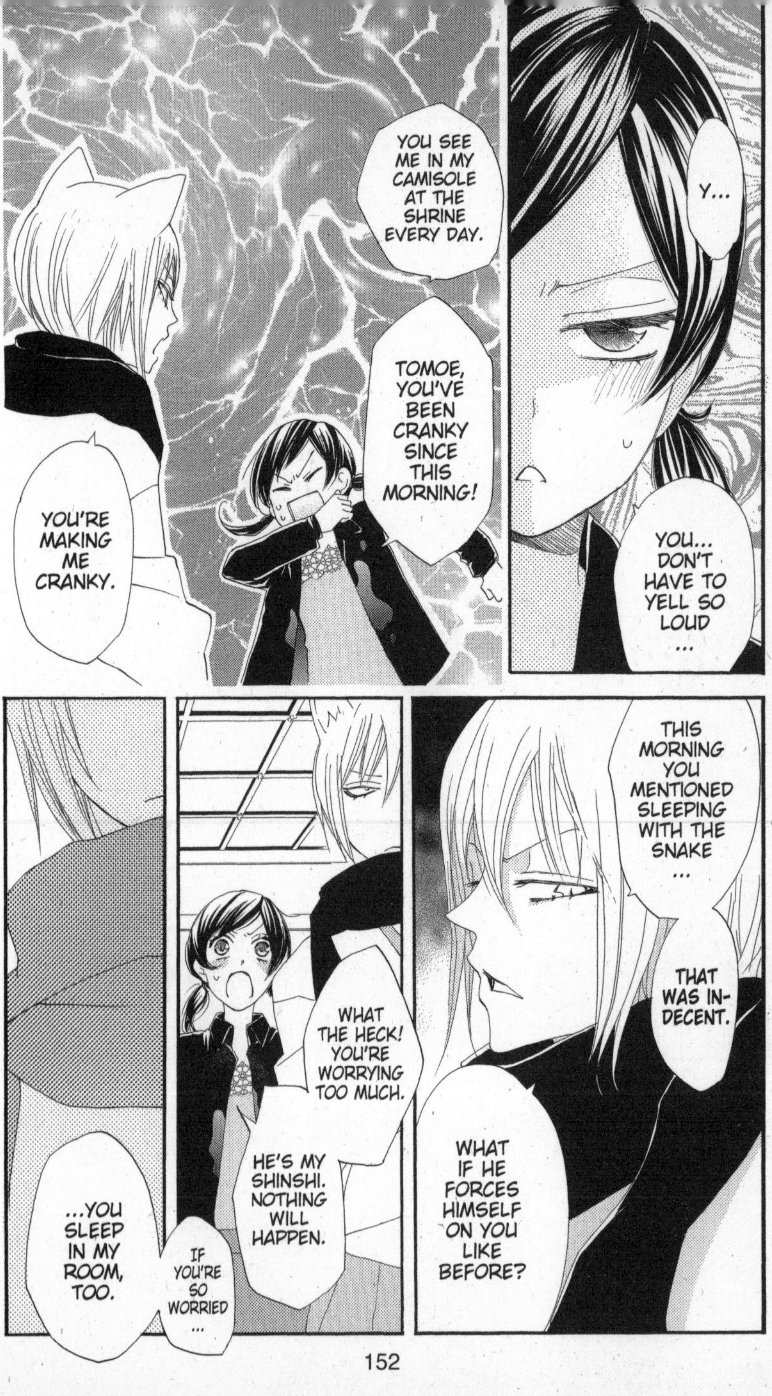
Y...
YOU... DON'T HAVE TO YELL SO LOUD ...
YOU SEE ME IN MY CAMISOLE AT THE SHRINE EVERY DAY.
TOMOE, YOU'VE BEEN CRANKY SINCE THIS MORNING!
YOU'RE MAKING ME CRANKY.
THIS MORNING YOU MENTIONED SLEEPING WITH THE SNAKE ...
THAT WAS IN-DECENT.
WHAT IF HE FORCES HIMSELF ON YOU LIKE BEFORE?
WHAT THE HECK! YOU'RE WORRYING TOO MUCH.
HE'S MY SHINSHI. NOTHING WILL HAPPEN.
IF YOU'RE SO WORRIED ...
...YOU SLEEP IN MY ROOM, TOO.

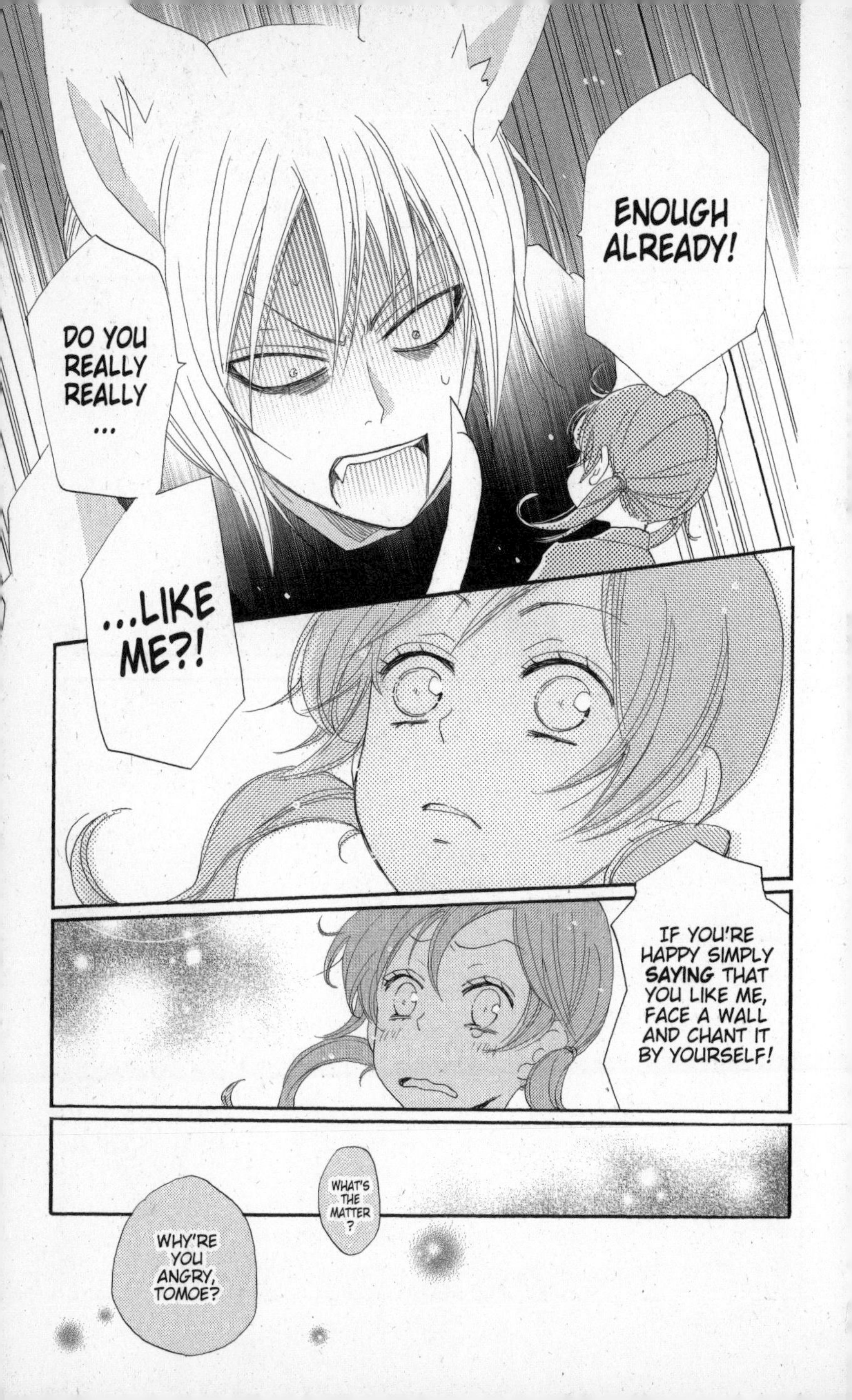
ENOUGH ALREADY!
DO YOU REALLY REALLY ...
...LIKE ME?!
IF YOU'RE HAPPY SIMPLY SAYING THAT YOU LIKE ME, FACE A WALL AND CHANT IT BY YOURSELF!
WHAT'S THE MATTER?
WHY'RE YOU ANGRY, TOMOE?

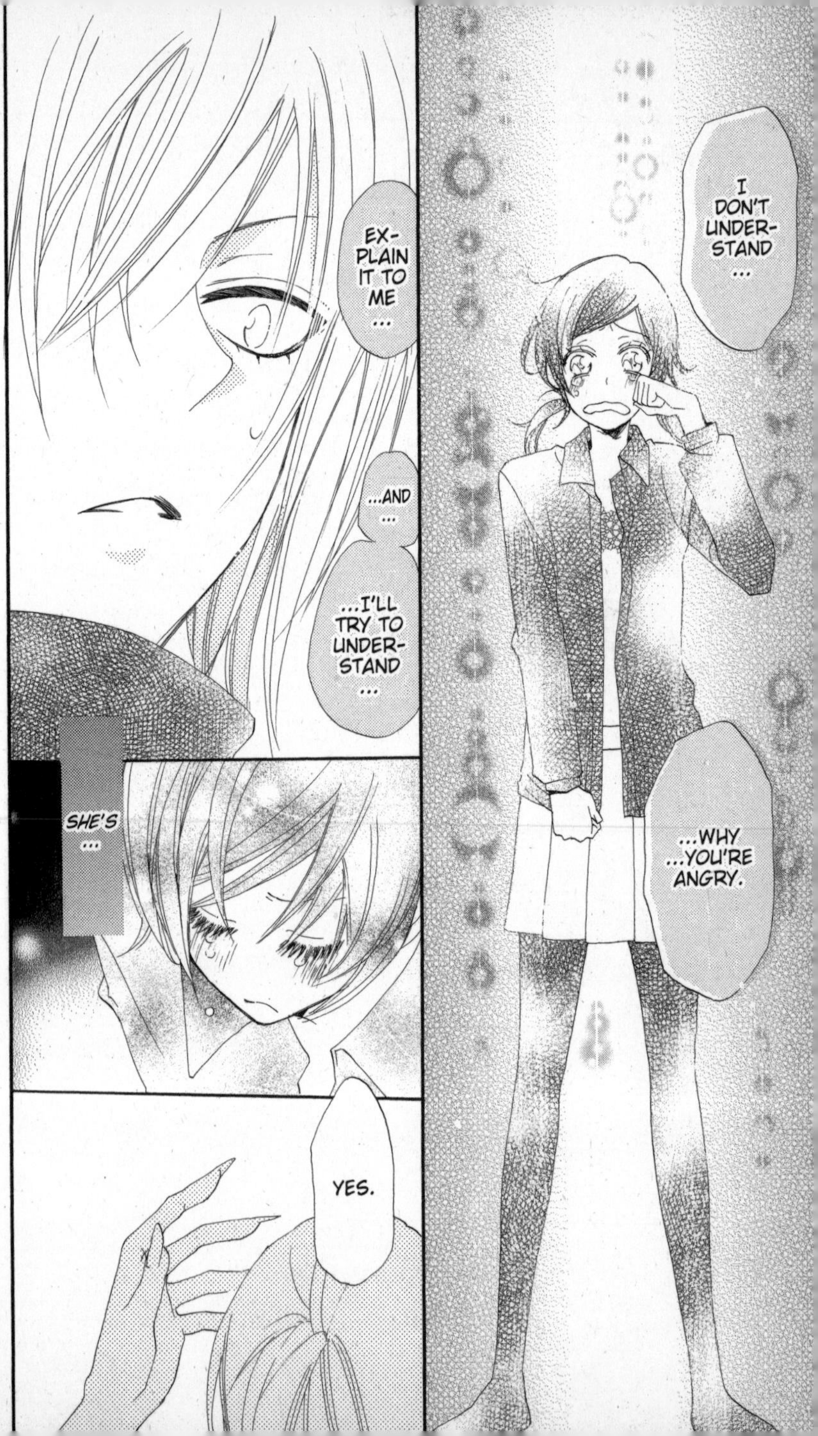
I DON'T UNDER-STAND ...
...WHY ...YOU'RE ANGRY.
EX-PLAIN IT TO ME ...
...AND ...
...I'LL TRY TO UNDER-STAND ...
SHE'S ...
YES.

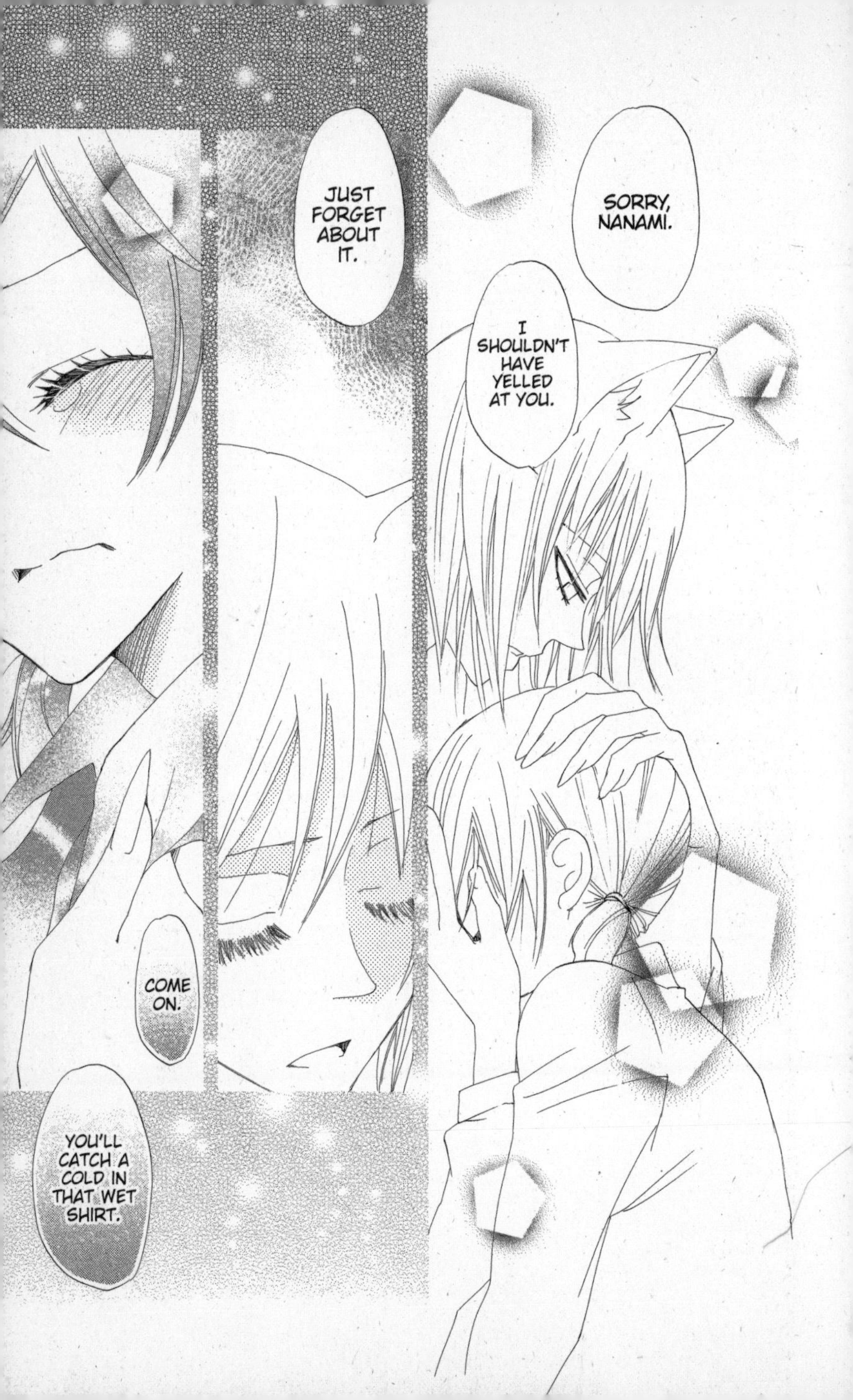
SORRY, NANAMI.
I SHOULDN'T HAVE YELLED AT YOU.
JUST FORGET ABOUT IT.
COME ON.
YOU'LL CATCH A COLD IN THAT WET SHIRT.

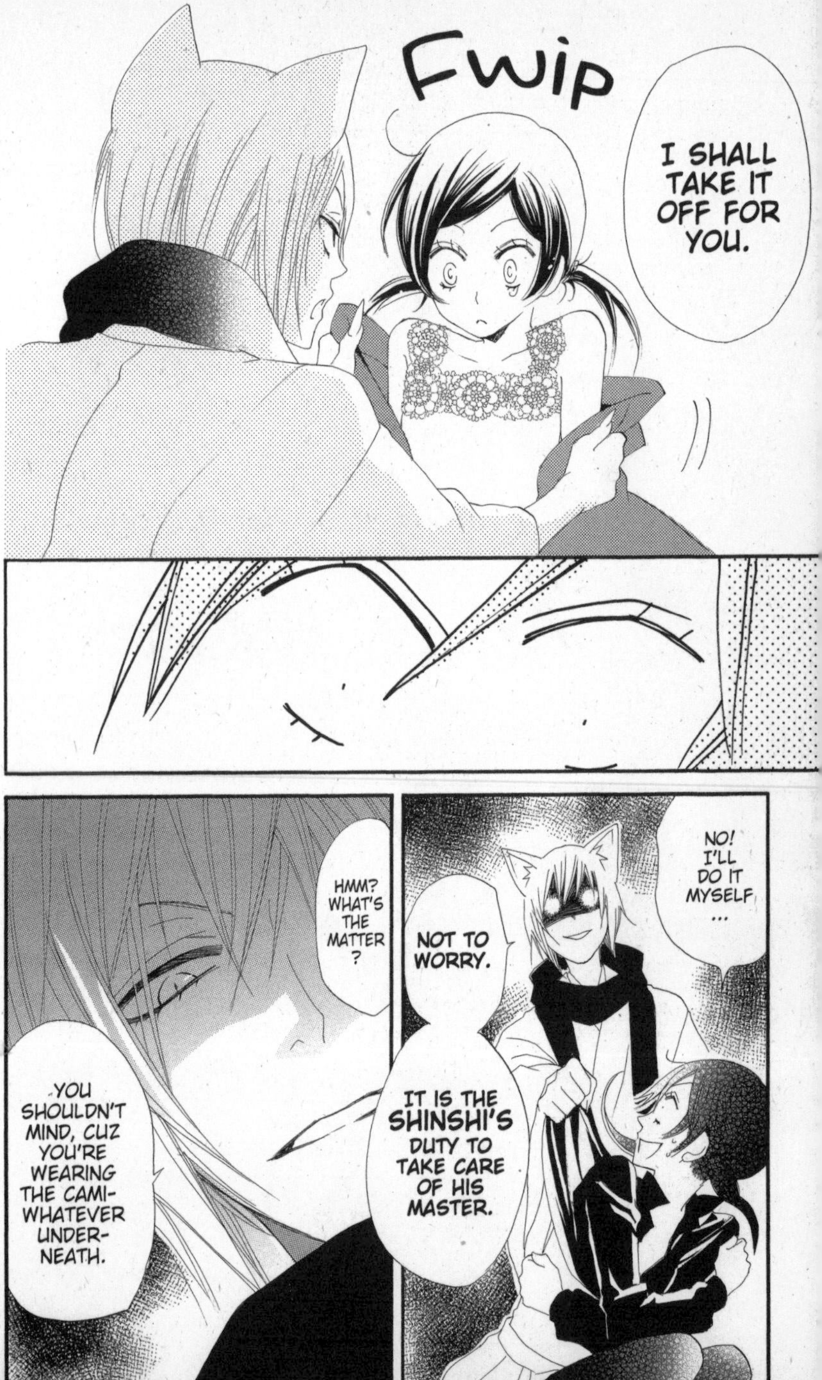
I SHALL TAKE IT OFF FOR YOU.
Fwip
NO! I'LL DO IT MYSELF ...
NOT TO WORRY.
IT IS THE SHINSHI'S DUTY TO TAKE CARE OF HIS MASTER.
HMM? WHAT'S THE MATTER ?
YOU SHOULDN'T MIND, CUZ YOU'RE WEARING THE CAMI-WHATEVER UNDER-NEATH.

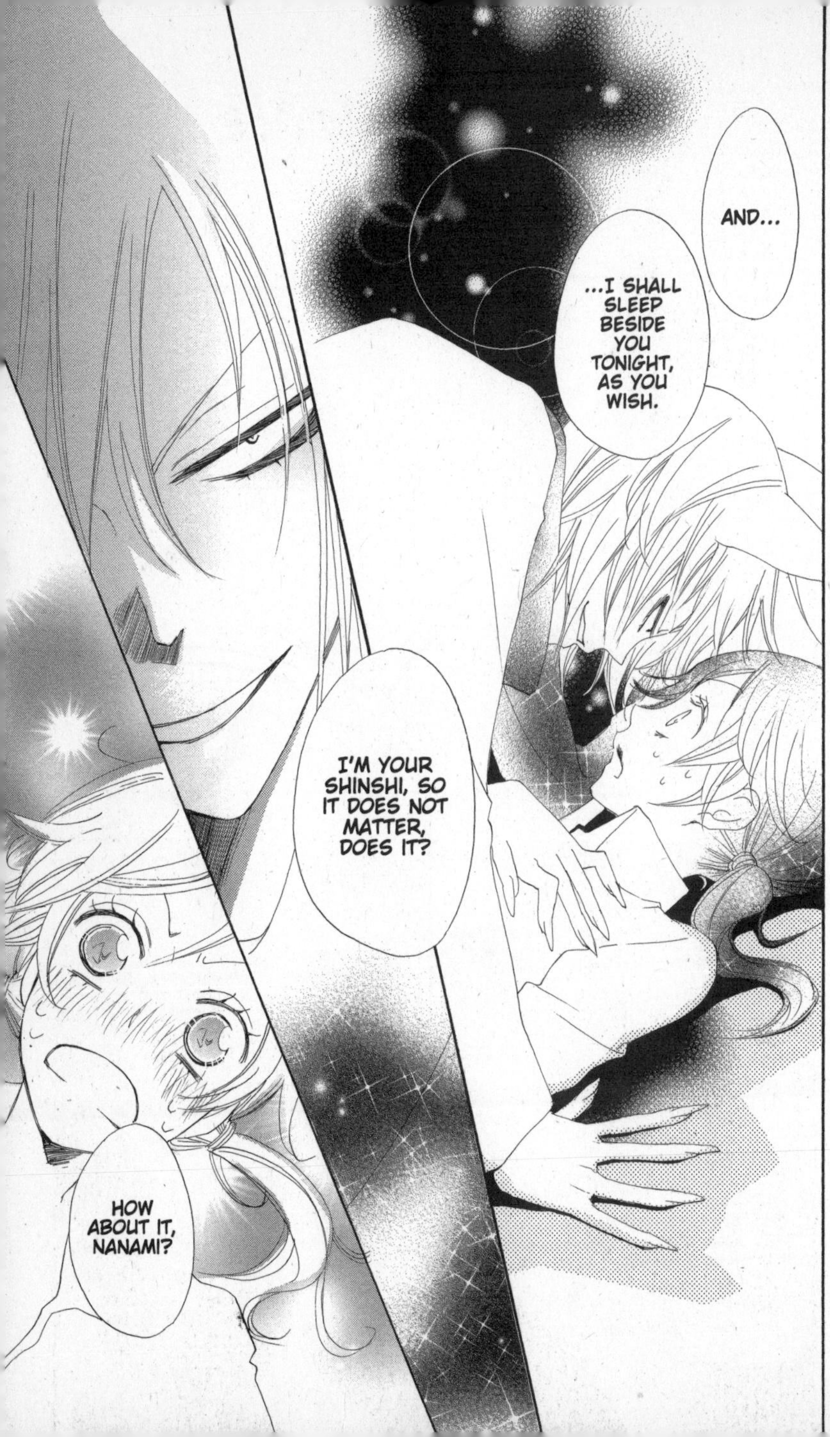
AND...
...I SHALL SLEEP BESIDE YOU TONIGHT, AS YOU WISH.
I'M YOUR SHINSHI, SO IT DOES NOT MATTER, DOES IT?
HOW ABOUT IT, NANAMI?

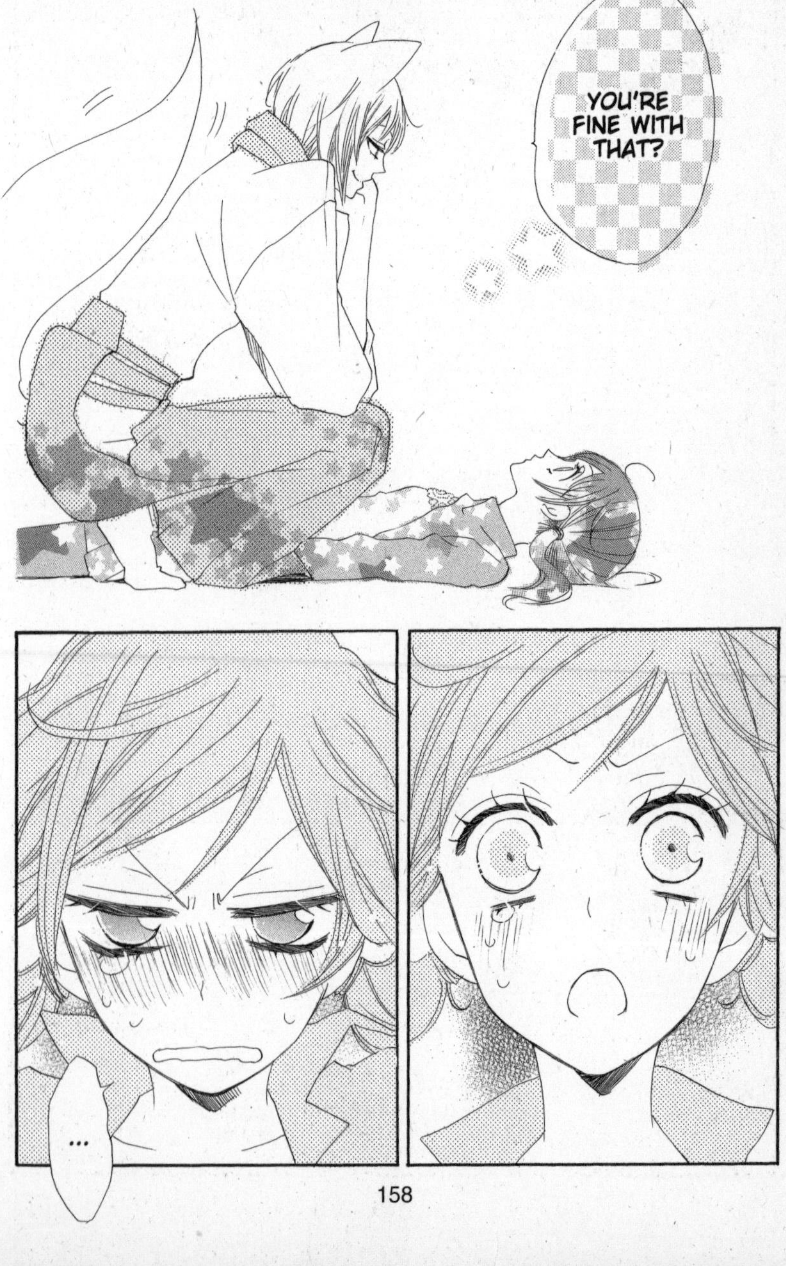
YOU'RE FINE WITH THAT?
...

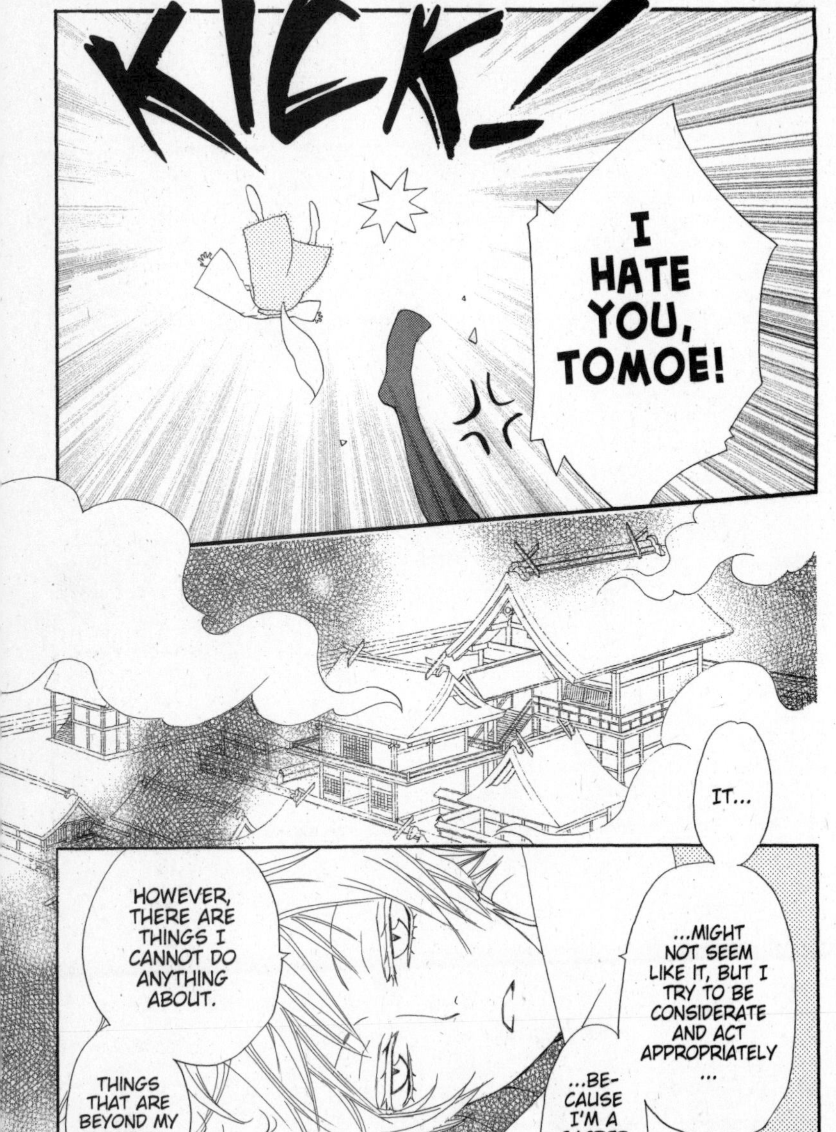
KICK!
I HATE YOU, TOMOE!
IT...
...MIGHT NOT SEEM LIKE IT, BUT I TRY TO BE CONSIDERATE AND ACT APPROPRIATELY ...
...BE- CAUSE I'M A SACRED SHINSHI.
HOWEVER, THERE ARE THINGS I CANNOT DO ANYTHING ABOUT.
THINGS THAT ARE BEYOND MY CONTROL.

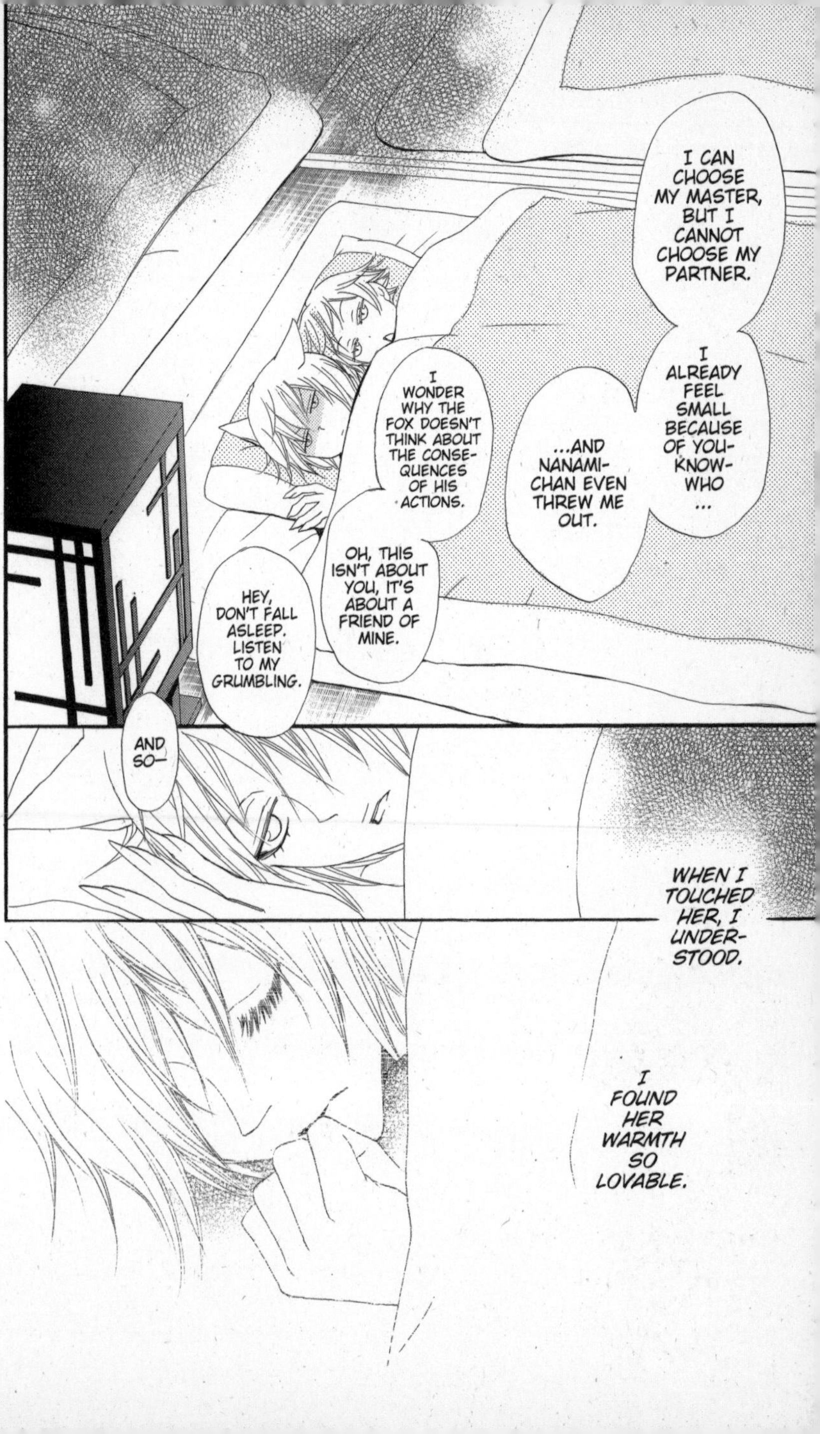
I CAN CHOOSE MY MASTER, BUT I CANNOT CHOOSE MY PARTNER.
I ALREADY FEEL SMALL BECAUSE OF YOU-KNOW-WHO ...
...AND NANAMI-CHAN EVEN THREW ME OUT.
I WONDER WHY THE FOX DOESN'T THINK ABOUT THE CONSE-QUENCES OF HIS ACTIONS.
OH, THIS ISN'T ABOUT YOU, IT'S ABOUT A FRIEND OF MINE.
HEY, DON'T FALL ASLEEP. LISTEN TO MY GRUMBLING.
AND SO—
WHEN I TOUCHED HER, I UNDER-STOOD.
I FOUND HER WARMTH SO LOVABLE.

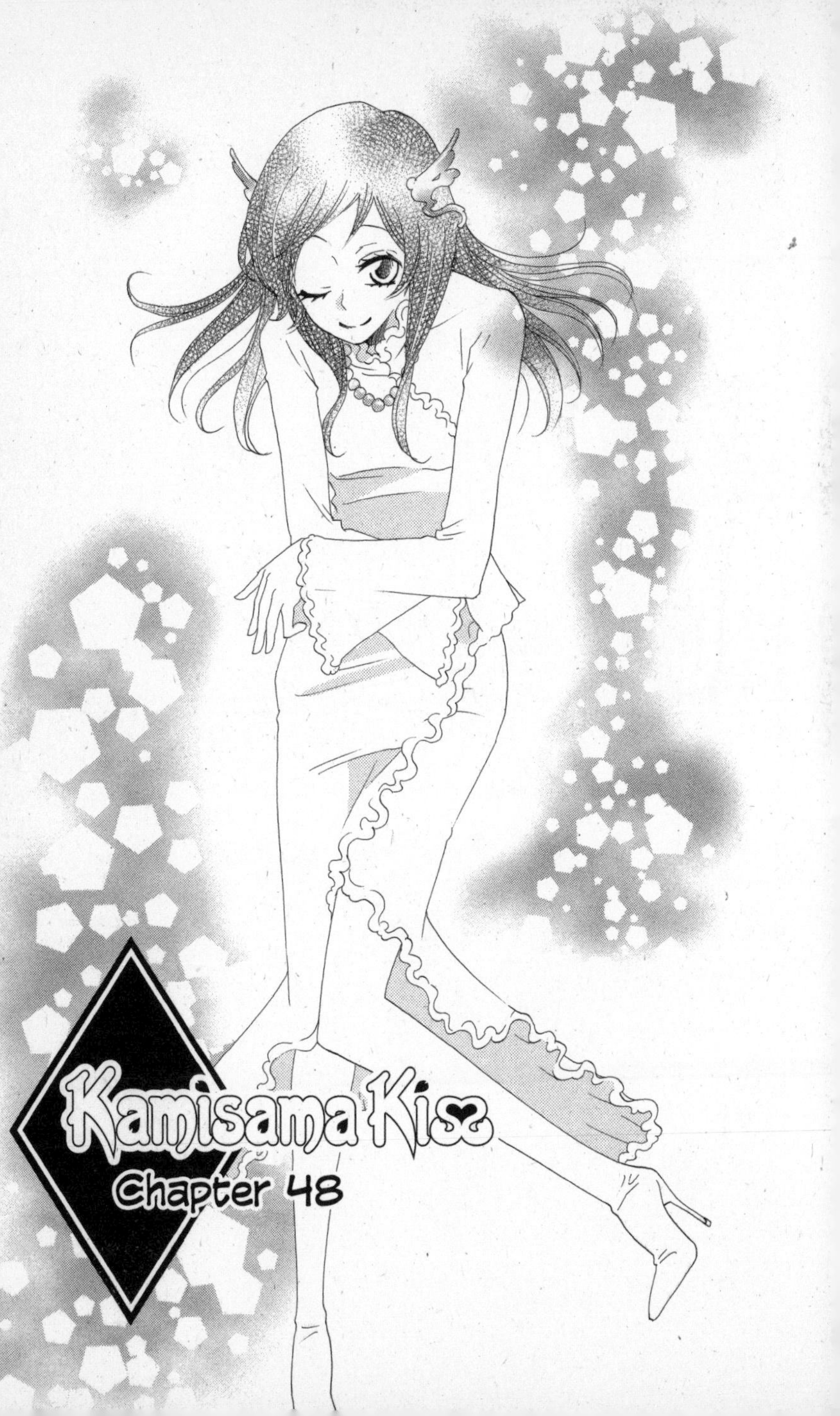
Kamisama Kiss
Chapter 48

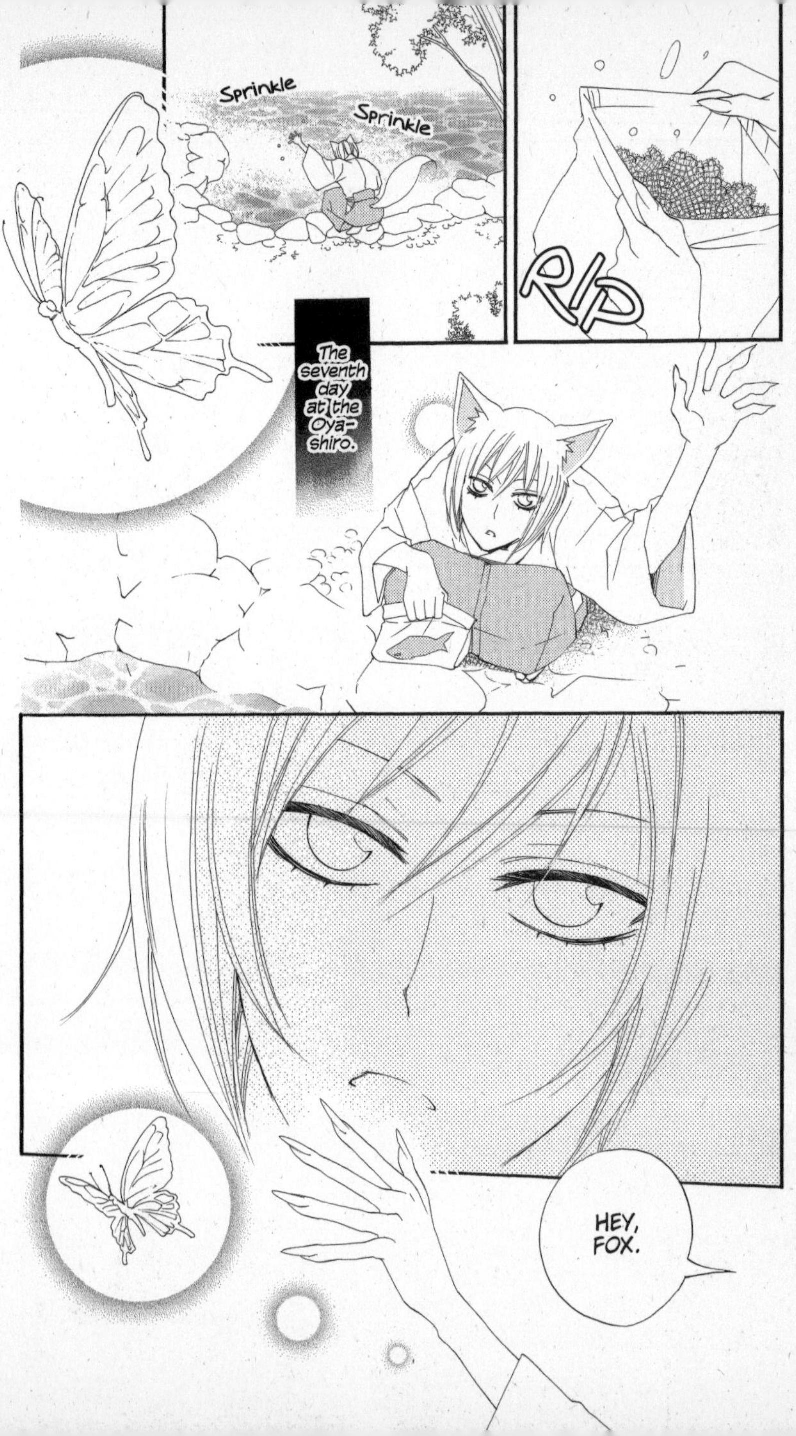
RIP
Sprinkle
Sprinkle
The seventh day at the Oya-shiro.
HEY, FOX.

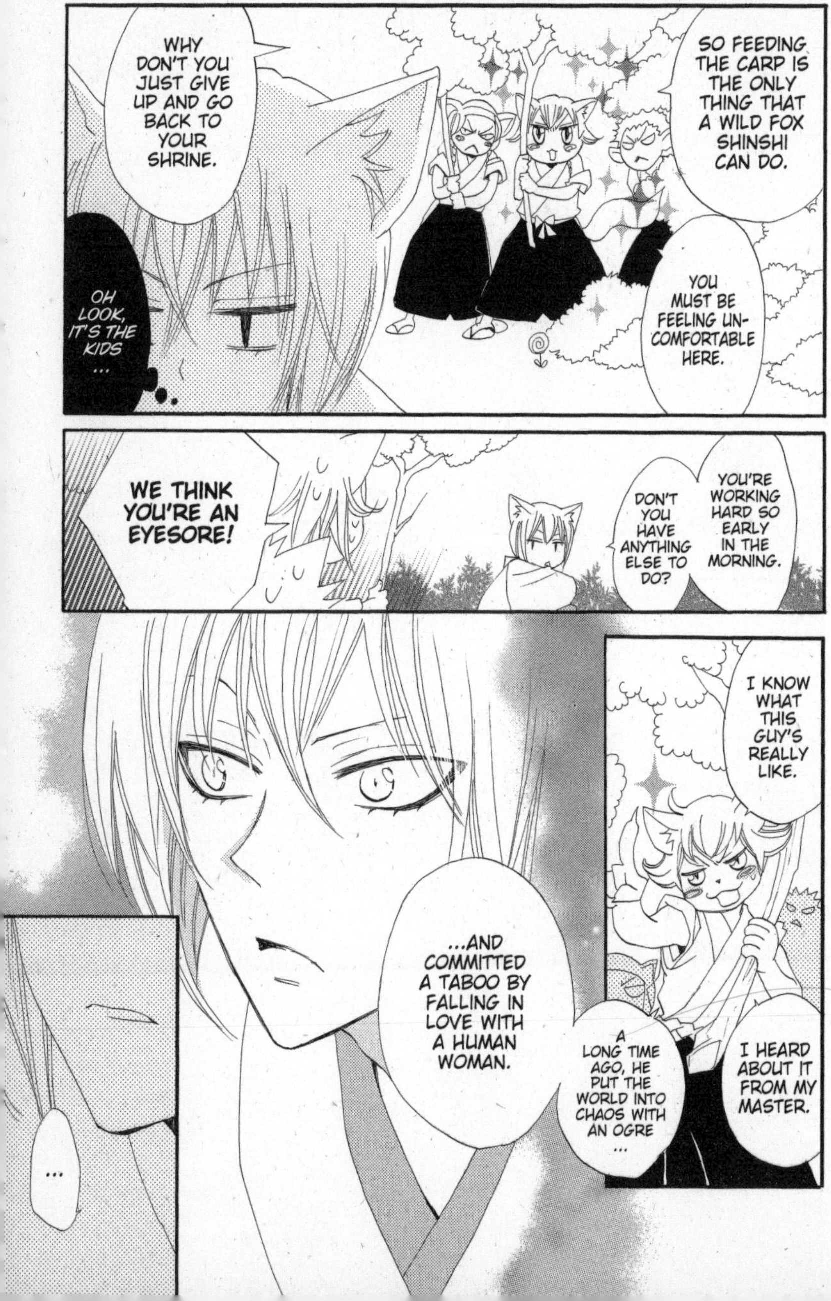
SO FEEDING THE CARP IS THE ONLY THING THAT A WILD FOX SHINSHI CAN DO.
YOU MUST BE FEELING UN-COMFORTABLE HERE.
WHY DON'T YOU JUST GIVE UP AND GO BACK TO YOUR SHRINE.
OH LOOK, IT'S THE KIDS ...
YOU'RE WORKING HARD SO EARLY IN THE MORNING.
DON'T YOU HAVE ANYTHING ELSE TO DO?
WE THINK YOU'RE AN EYESORE!
I KNOW WHAT THIS GUY'S REALLY LIKE.
I HEARD ABOUT IT FROM MY MASTER.
A LONG TIME AGO, HE PUT THE WORLD INTO CHAOS WITH AN OGRE ...
...AND COMMITTED A TABOO BY FALLING IN LOVE WITH A HUMAN WOMAN.
...

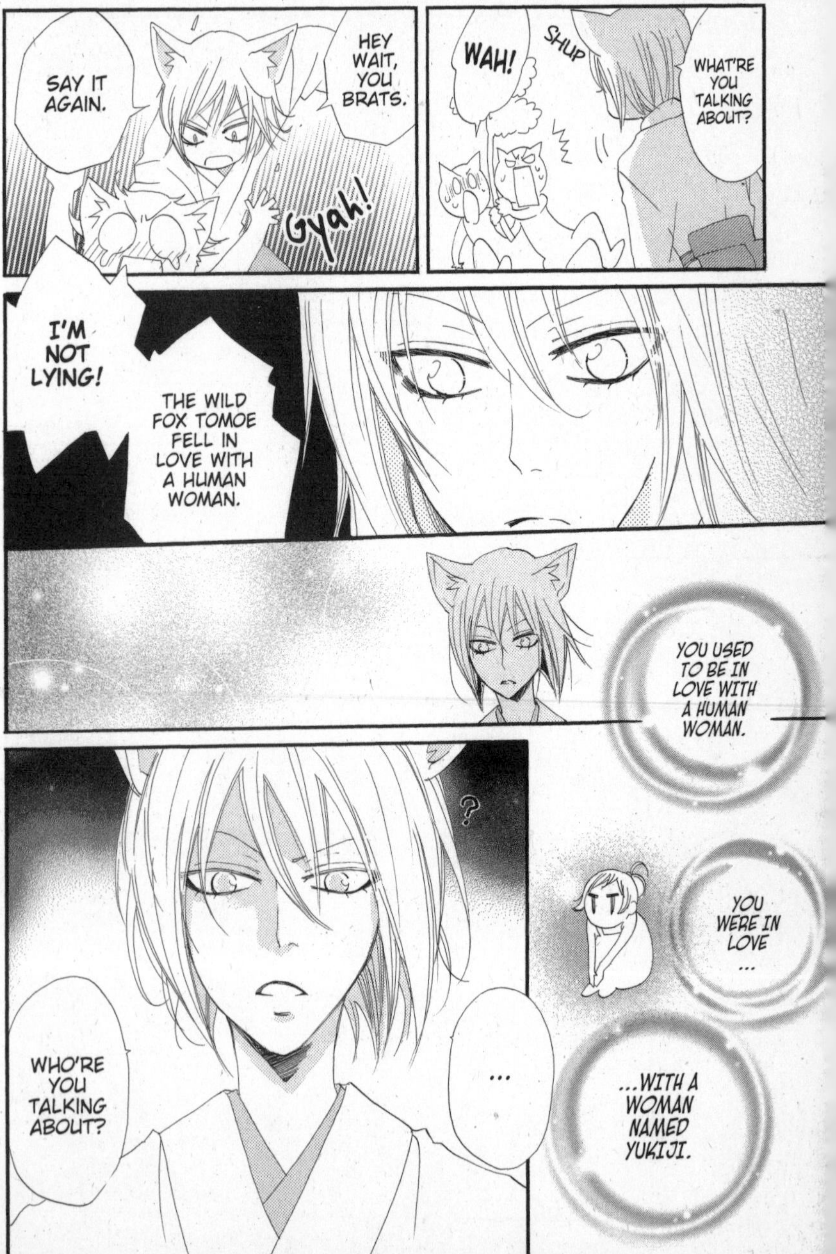
WHAT'RE YOU TALKING ABOUT?
SHUP
WAH!
HEY WAIT, YOU BRATS.
SAY IT AGAIN.
Gyah!
I'M NOT LYING!
THE WILD FOX TOMOE FELL IN LOVE WITH A HUMAN WOMAN.
YOU USED TO BE IN LOVE WITH A HUMAN WOMAN.
YOU WERE IN LOVE ...
...WITH A WOMAN NAMED YUKIJI.
...
WHO'RE YOU TALKING ABOUT?

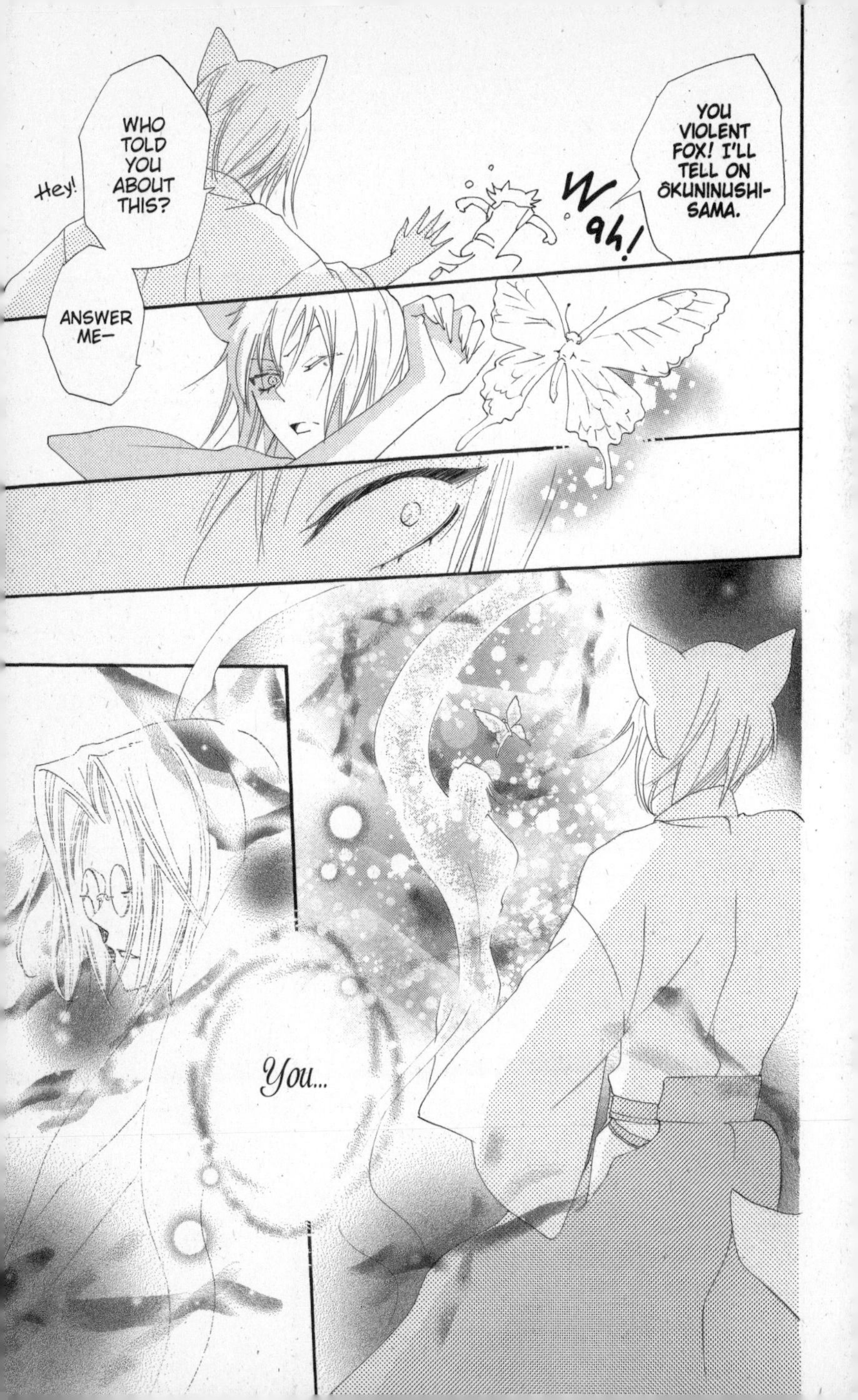
YOU VIOLENT FOX! I'LL TELL ON ŌKUNINUSHI-SAMA.
Wah!
Hey!
WHO TOLD YOU ABOUT THIS?
ANSWER ME—
You...

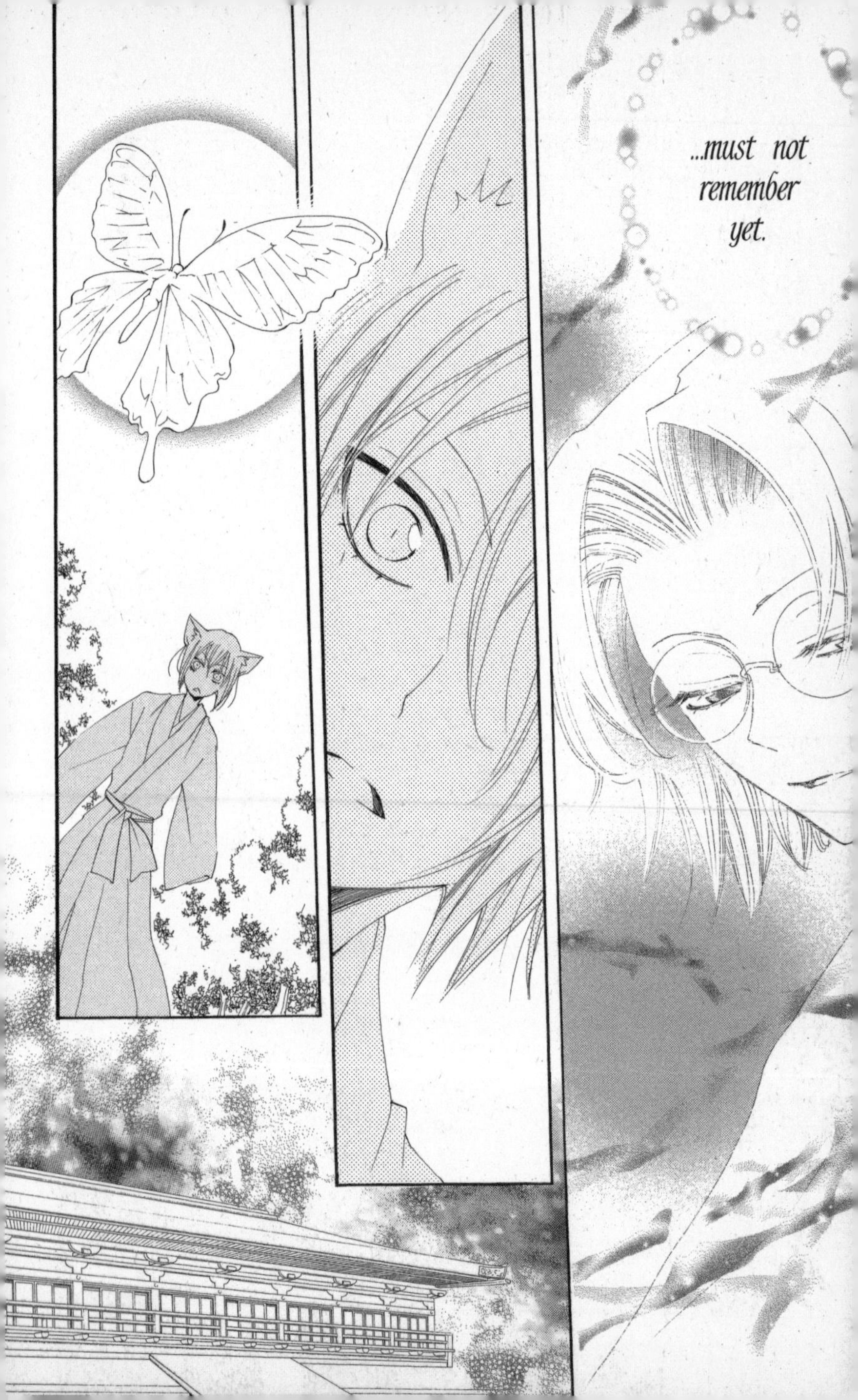
...must not remember yet.

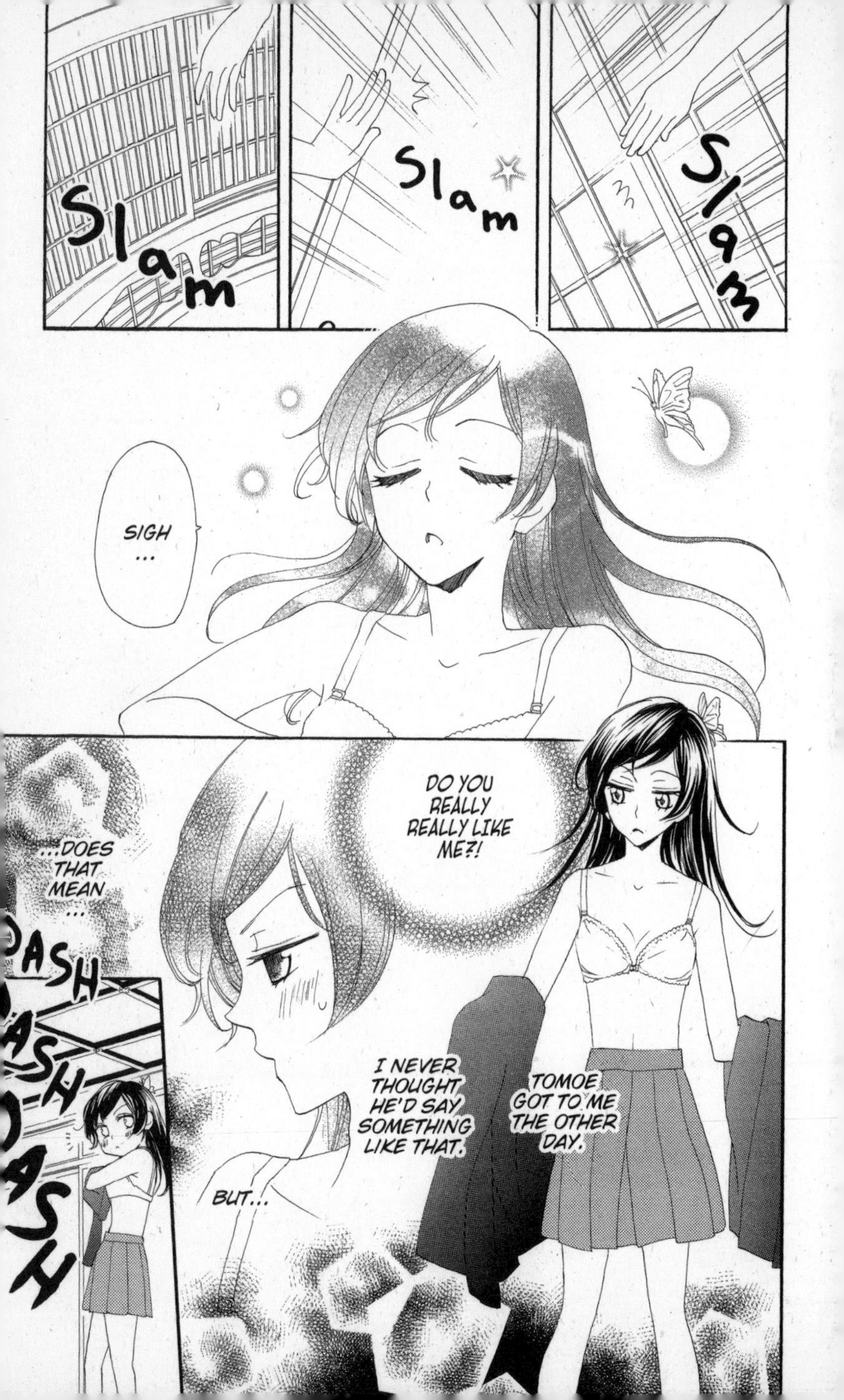
Slam
Slam
Slam
SIGH ...
DO YOU REALLY REALLY LIKE ME?!
...DOES THAT MEAN ...
TOMOE GOT TO ME THE OTHER DAY.
I NEVER THOUGHT HE'D SAY SOMETHING LIKE THAT.
BUT...

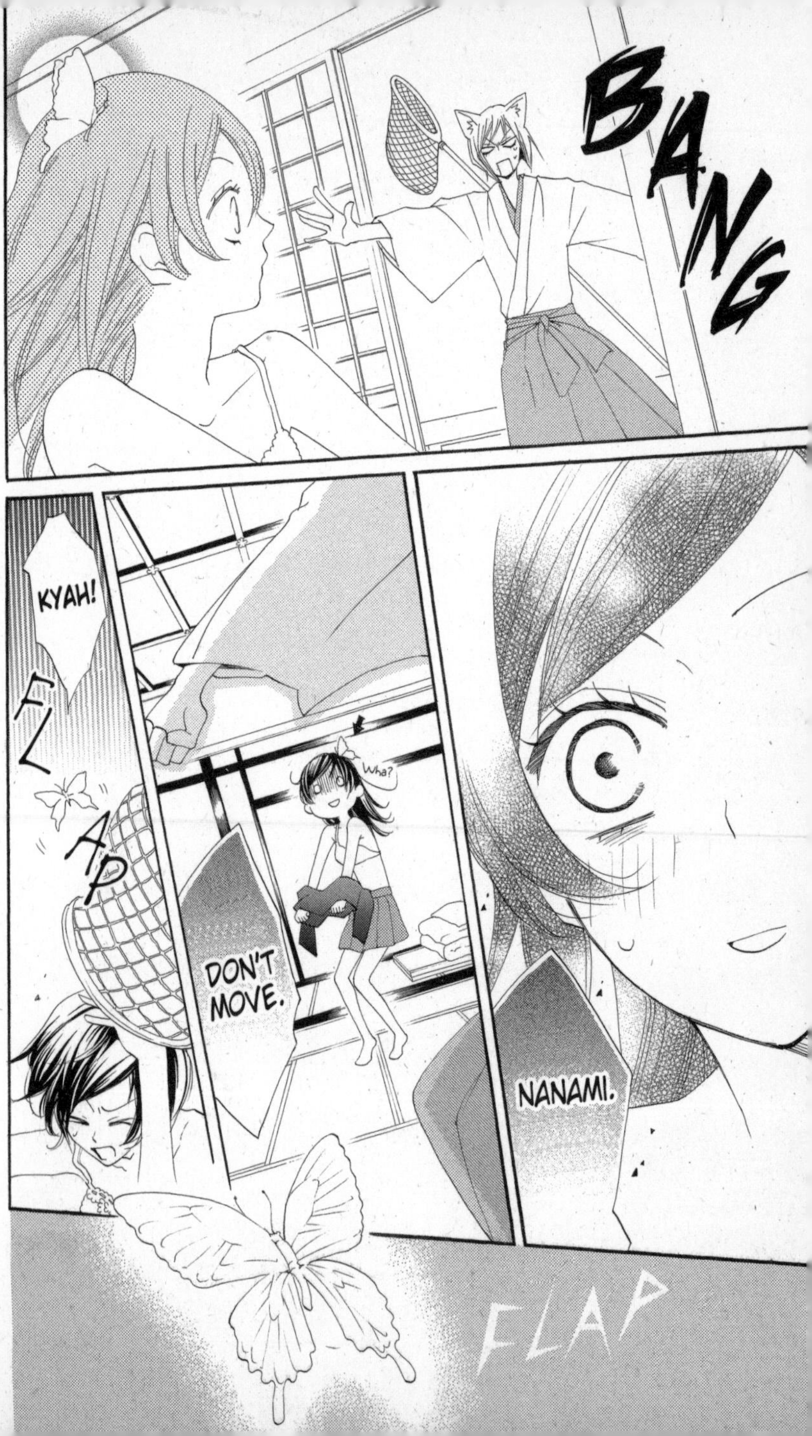
BANG
NANAMI.
Wha?
DON'T MOVE.
KYAH!
FLAP
FLAP

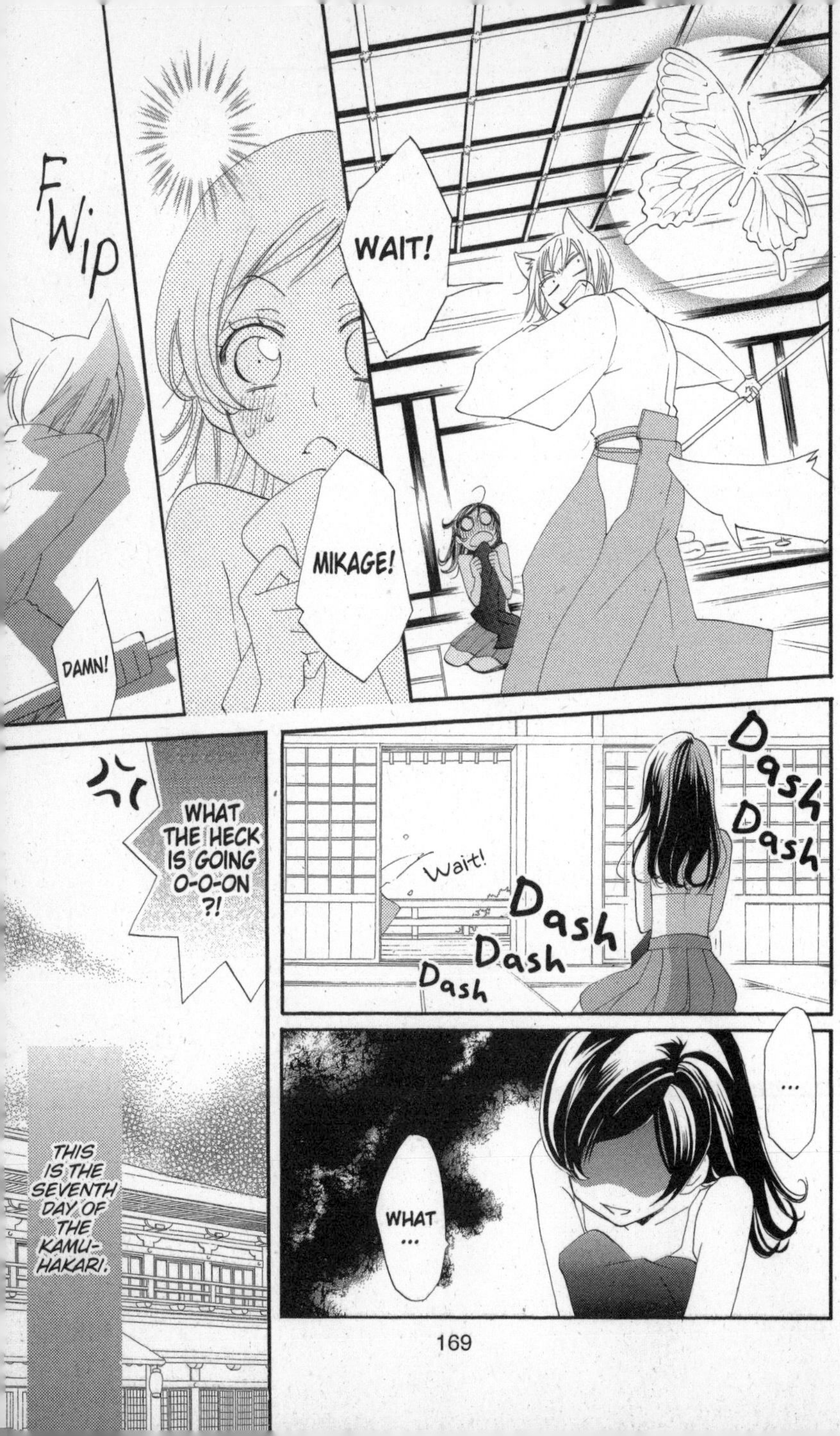
WAIT!
MIKAGE!
DAMN!
FWip
Dash
Dash
Dash
Dash
Dash
Wait!
...
WHAT ...
WHAT THE HECK IS GOING O-O-ON ?!
THIS IS THE SEVENTH DAY OF THE KAMU-HAKARI.

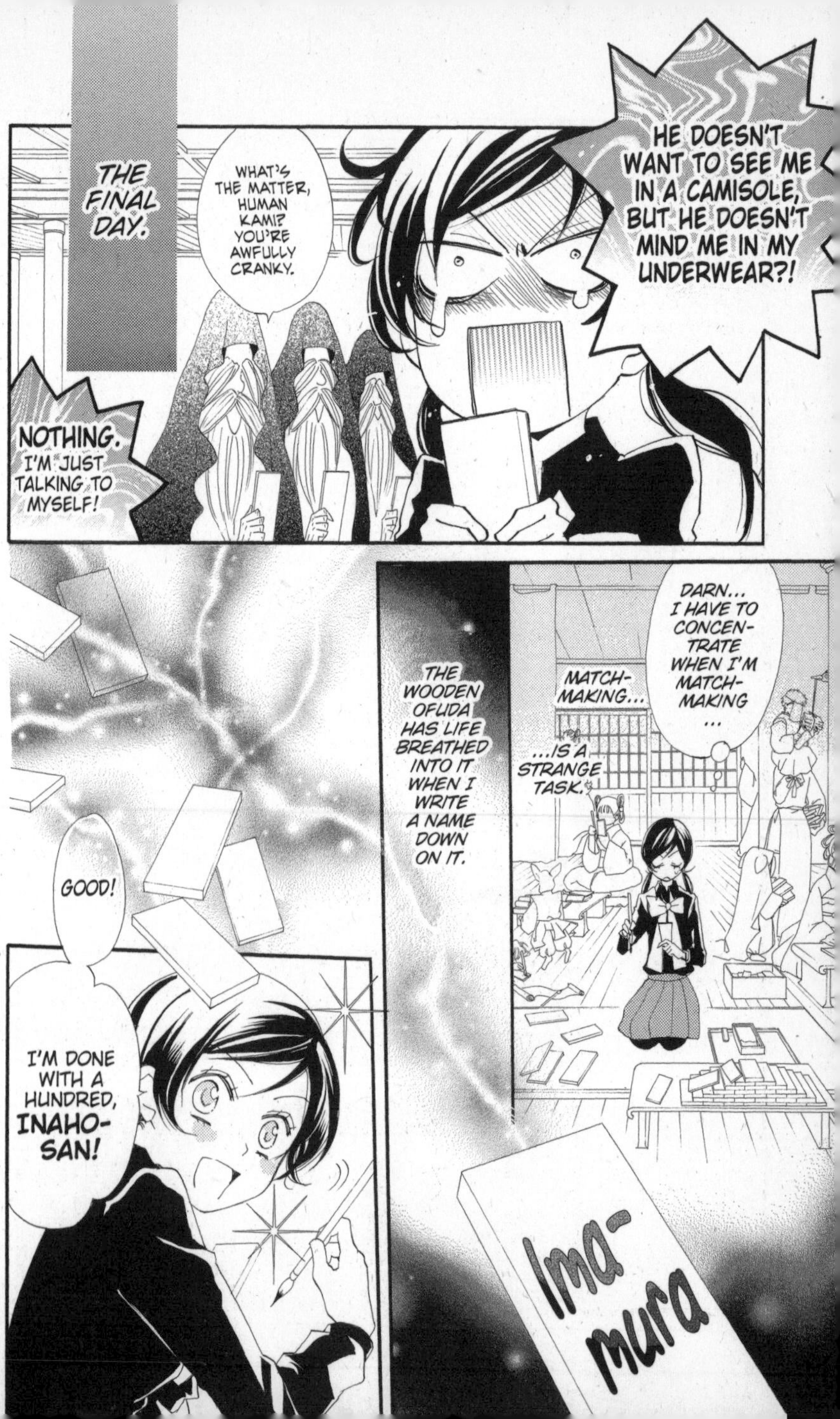
HE DOESN'T WANT TO SEE ME IN A CAMISOLE, BUT HE DOESN'T MIND ME IN MY UNDERWEAR?!
THE FINAL DAY.
WHAT'S THE MATTER, HUMAN KAMI? YOU'RE AWFULLY CRANKY.
NOTHING. I'M JUST TALKING TO MYSELF!
DARN... I HAVE TO CONCEN-TRATE WHEN I'M MATCH-MAKING ...
MATCH-MAKING...
...IS A STRANGE TASK.
THE WOODEN OFUDA HAS LIFE BREATHED INTO IT WHEN I WRITE A NAME DOWN ON IT.
Ima-mura
GOOD!
I'M DONE WITH A HUNDRED, INAHO-SAN!

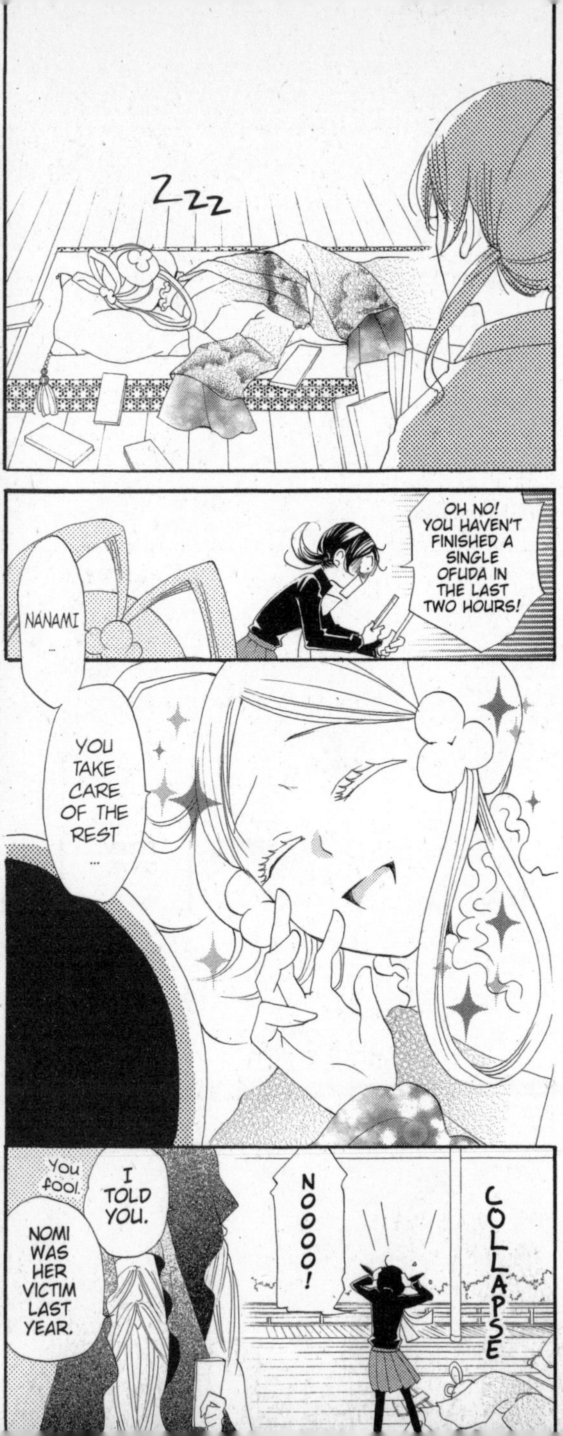
Zzz
OH NO! YOU HAVEN'T FINISHED A SINGLE OFUDA IN THE LAST TWO HOURS!
NANAMI...
YOU TAKE CARE OF THE REST...
COLLAPSE
NOOOO!
I TOLD YOU.
You fool.
NOMI WAS HER VICTIM LAST YEAR.

Thank you for reading this far!

If you have any comments, I'd be happy if you send letters to the following address...

Julietta Suzuki
c/o Shojo Beat
VIZ Media, LLC
P.O. Box 77010
San Francisco
CA 94107

Thank you! ☺

I pray from my heart that we'll be able to meet in the next volume as well.

✿

-Julietta Suzuki

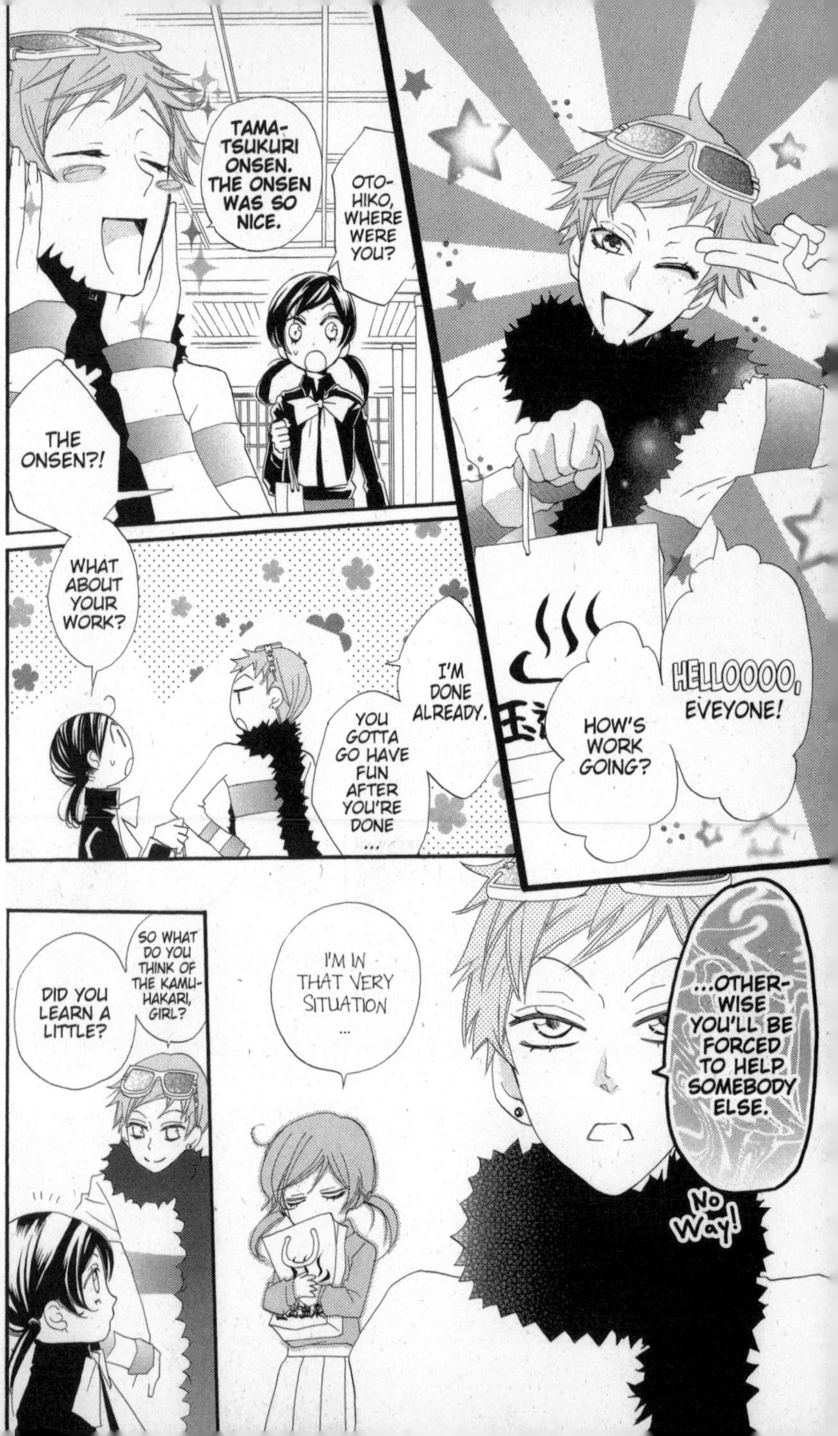
HELLOOOO, EVEYONE!
HOW'S WORK GOING?
OTO-HIKO, WHERE WERE YOU?
TAMA-TSUKURI ONSEN. THE ONSEN WAS SO NICE.
THE ONSEN?!
I'M DONE ALREADY.
YOU GOTTA GO HAVE FUN AFTER YOU'RE DONE...
WHAT ABOUT YOUR WORK?
...OTHER-WISE YOU'LL BE FORCED TO HELP SOMEBODY ELSE.
No Way!
I'M IN THAT VERY SITUATION...
SO WHAT DO YOU THINK OF THE KAMU-HAKARI, GIRL?
DID YOU LEARN A LITTLE?

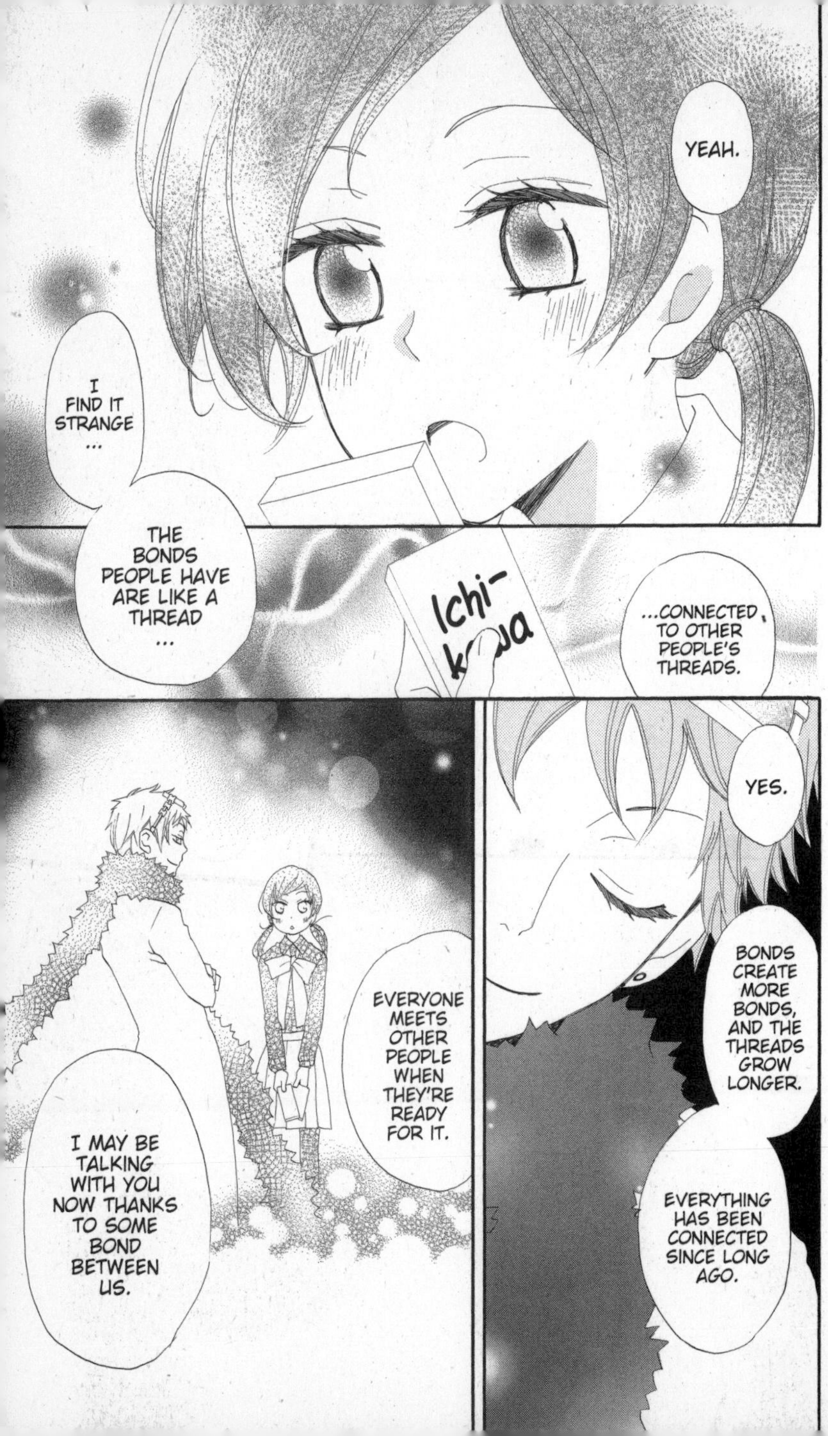
YEAH.
I FIND IT STRANGE ...
THE BONDS PEOPLE HAVE ARE LIKE A THREAD ...
...CONNECTED, TO OTHER PEOPLE'S THREADS.
Ichi-
YES.
BONDS CREATE MORE BONDS, AND THE THREADS GROW LONGER.
EVERYTHING HAS BEEN CONNECTED SINCE LONG AGO.
EVERYONE MEETS OTHER PEOPLE WHEN THEY'RE READY FOR IT.
I MAY BE TALKING WITH YOU NOW THANKS TO SOME BOND BETWEEN US.

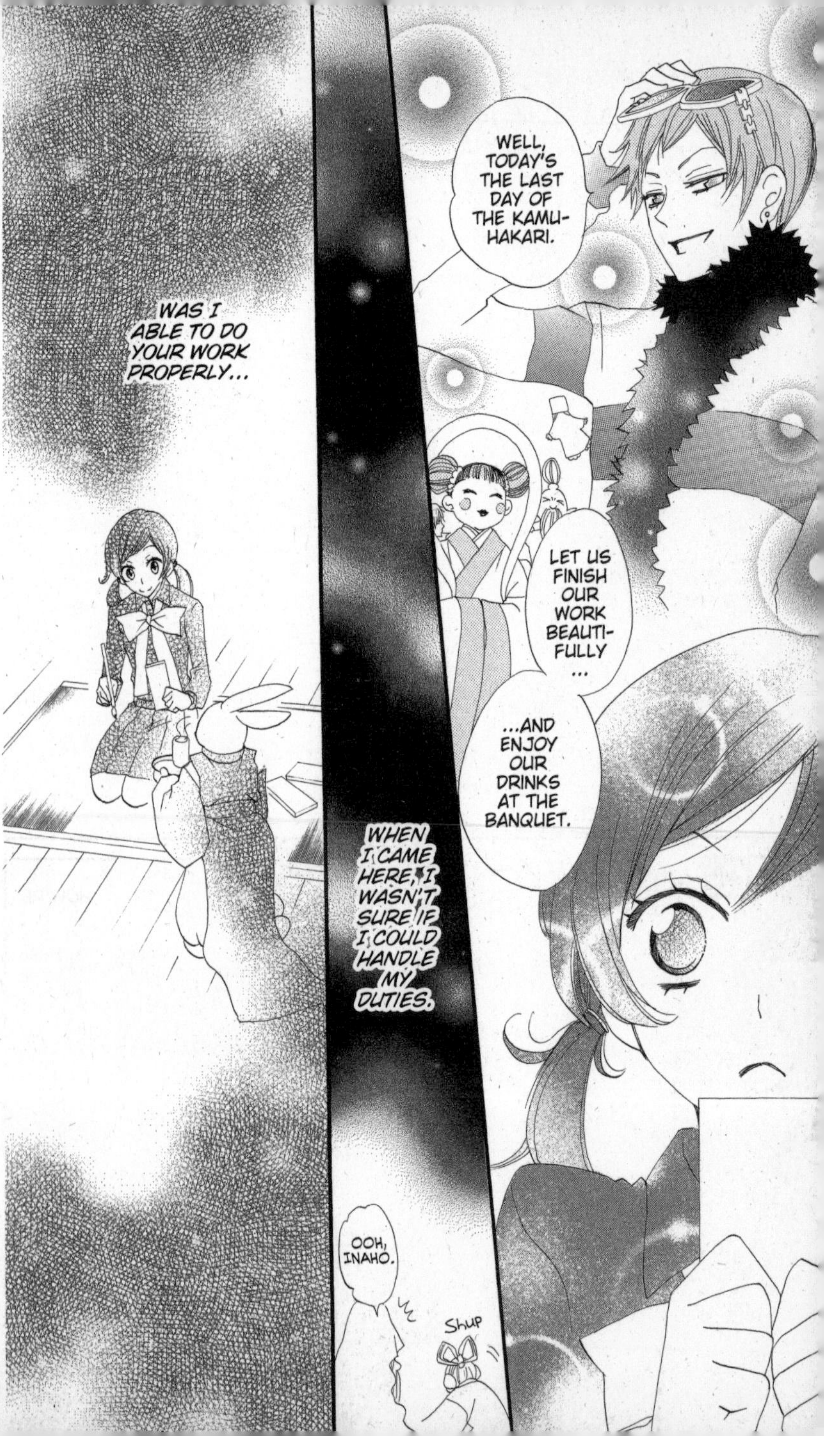
WELL, TODAY'S THE LAST DAY OF THE KAMU-HAKARI.
LET US FINISH OUR WORK BEAUTIFULLY ...
...AND ENJOY OUR DRINKS AT THE BANQUET.
WHEN I CAME HERE, I WASN'T SURE IF I COULD HANDLE MY DUTIES.
OOH, INAHO.
Shup
WAS I ABLE TO DO YOUR WORK PROPERLY...

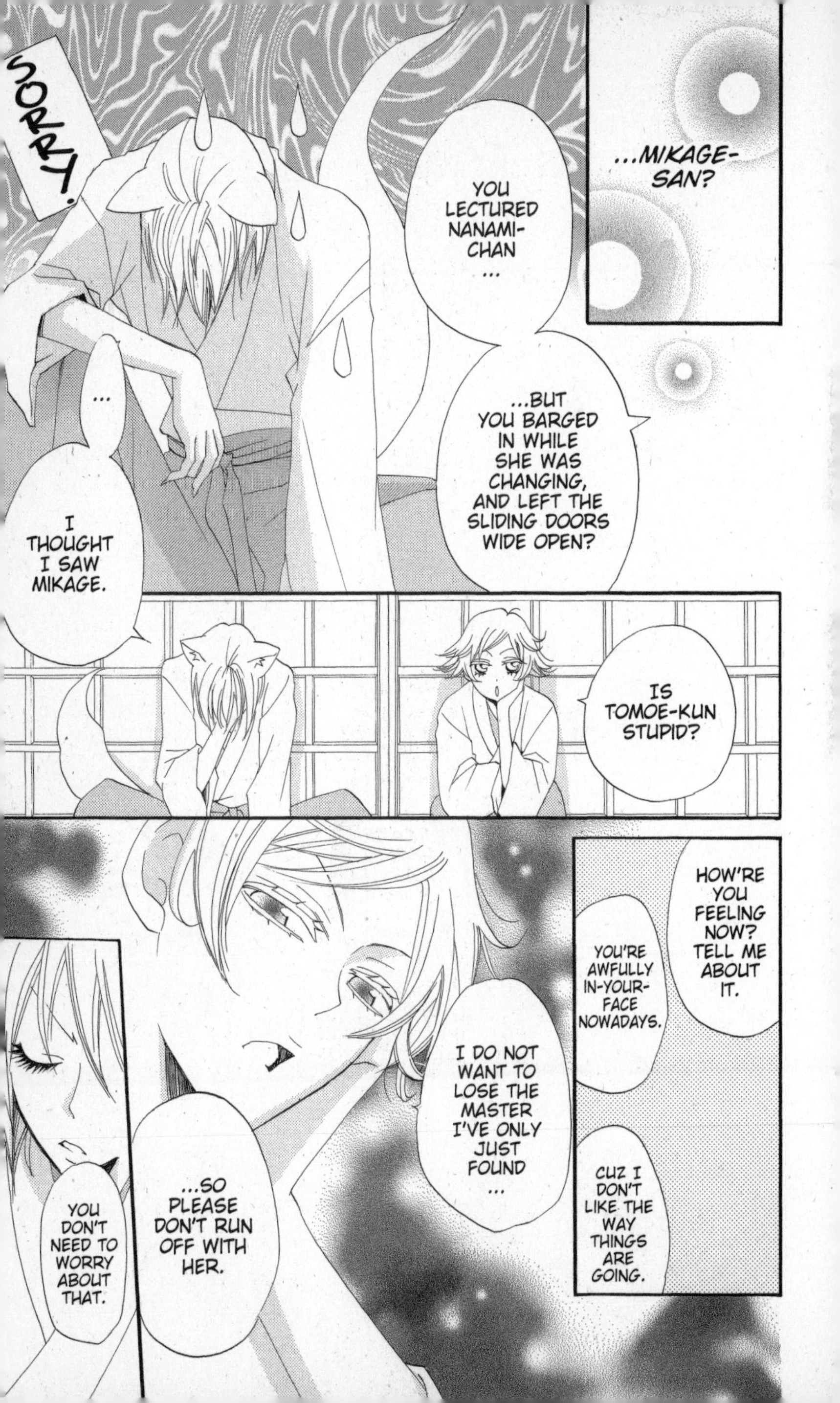
...MIKAGE-SAN?
SORRY!
YOU LECTURED NANAMI-CHAN...
...BUT YOU BARGED IN WHILE SHE WAS CHANGING, AND LEFT THE SLIDING DOORS WIDE OPEN?
...
I THOUGHT I SAW MIKAGE.
IS TOMOE-KUN STUPID?
HOW'RE YOU FEELING NOW? TELL ME ABOUT IT.
YOU'RE AWFULLY IN-YOUR-FACE NOWADAYS.
CUZ I DON'T LIKE THE WAY THINGS ARE GOING.
I DO NOT WANT TO LOSE THE MASTER I'VE ONLY JUST FOUND...
...SO PLEASE DON'T RUN OFF WITH HER.
YOU DON'T NEED TO WORRY ABOUT THAT.

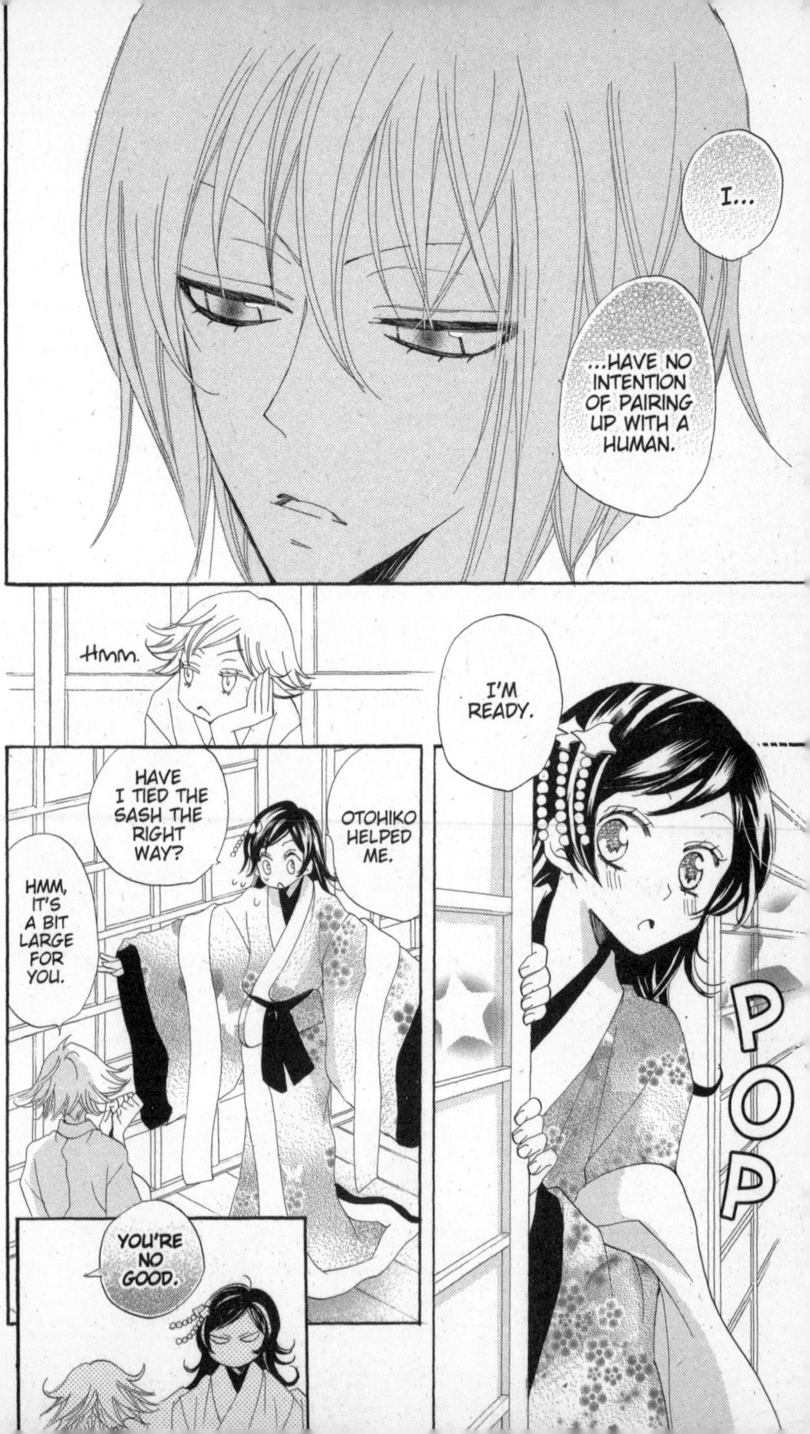
I...
...HAVE NO INTENTION OF PAIRING UP WITH A HUMAN.
I'M READY.
POP
Hmm.
OTOHIKO HELPED ME.
HAVE I TIED THE SASH THE RIGHT WAY?
HMM, IT'S A BIT LARGE FOR YOU.
YOU'RE NO GOOD.

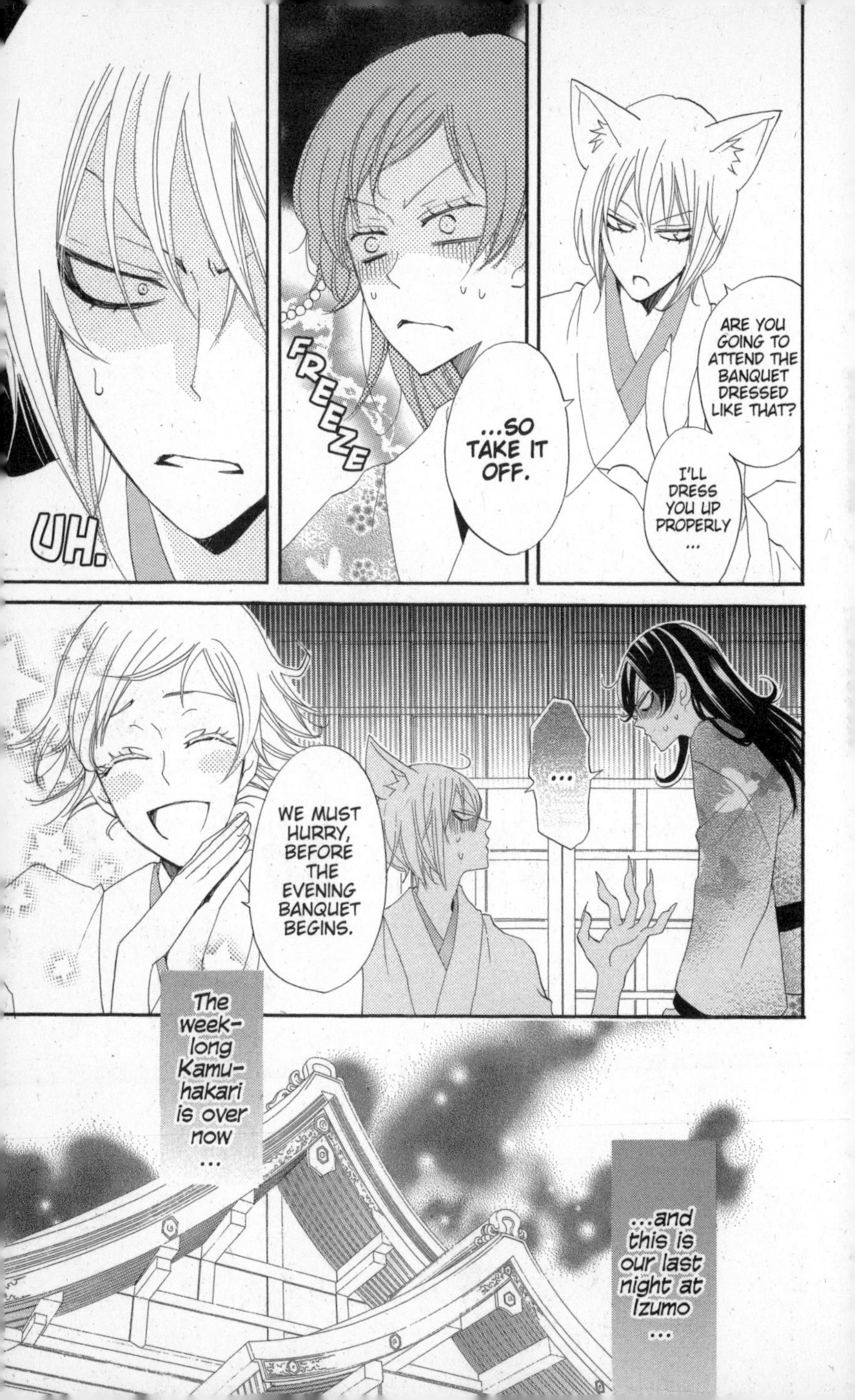
ARE YOU GOING TO ATTEND THE BANQUET DRESSED LIKE THAT?
I'LL DRESS YOU UP PROPERLY ...
...SO TAKE IT OFF.
FREEZE
UH.
...
WE MUST HURRY, BEFORE THE EVENING BANQUET BEGINS.
The week-long Kamuhakari is over now ...
...and this is our last night at Izumo ...

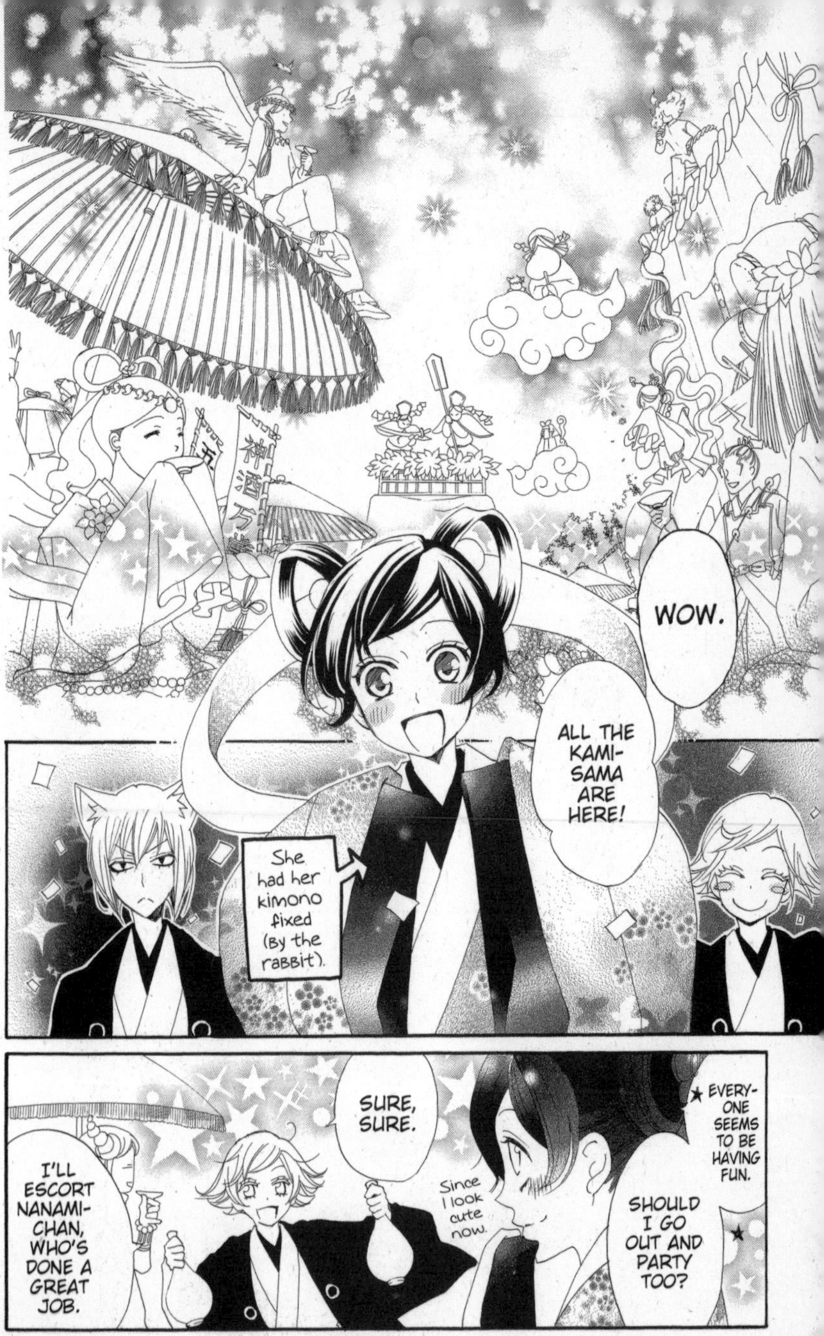
WOW.
ALL THE KAMI-SAMA ARE HERE!
She had her kimono fixed (By the rabbit).
EVERY-ONE SEEMS TO BE HAVING FUN.
SHOULD I GO OUT AND PARTY TOO?
Since I look cute now.
SURE, SURE.
I'LL ESCORT NANAMI-CHAN, WHO'S DONE A GREAT JOB.

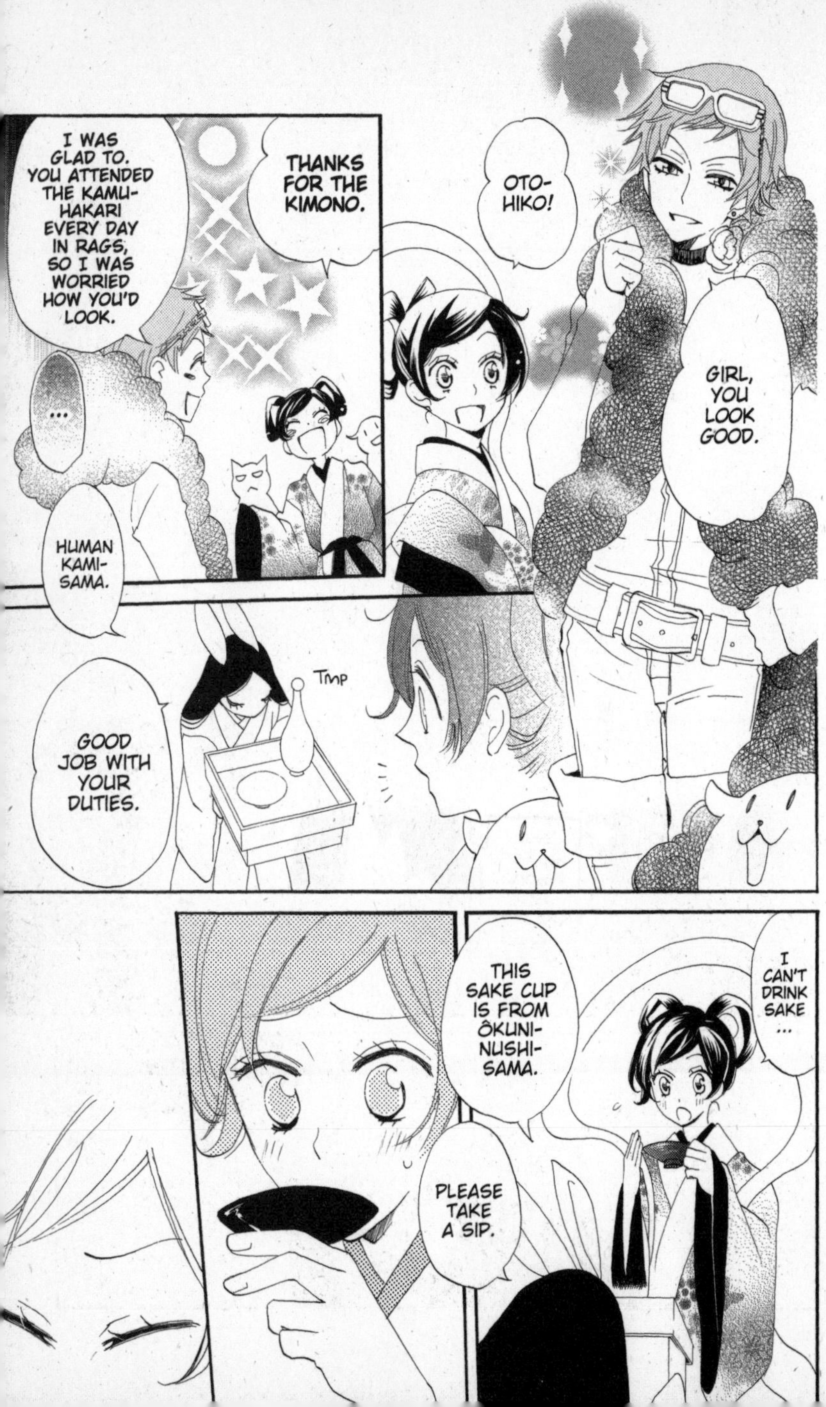
OTO-HIKO!
GIRL, YOU LOOK GOOD.
THANKS FOR THE KIMONO.
I WAS GLAD TO. YOU ATTENDED THE KAMU-HAKARI EVERY DAY IN RAGS, SO I WAS WORRIED HOW YOU'D LOOK.
...
HUMAN KAMI-SAMA.
Tmp
GOOD JOB WITH YOUR DUTIES.
I CAN'T DRINK SAKE ...
THIS SAKE CUP IS FROM ÔKUNI-NUSHI-SAMA.
PLEASE TAKE A SIP.

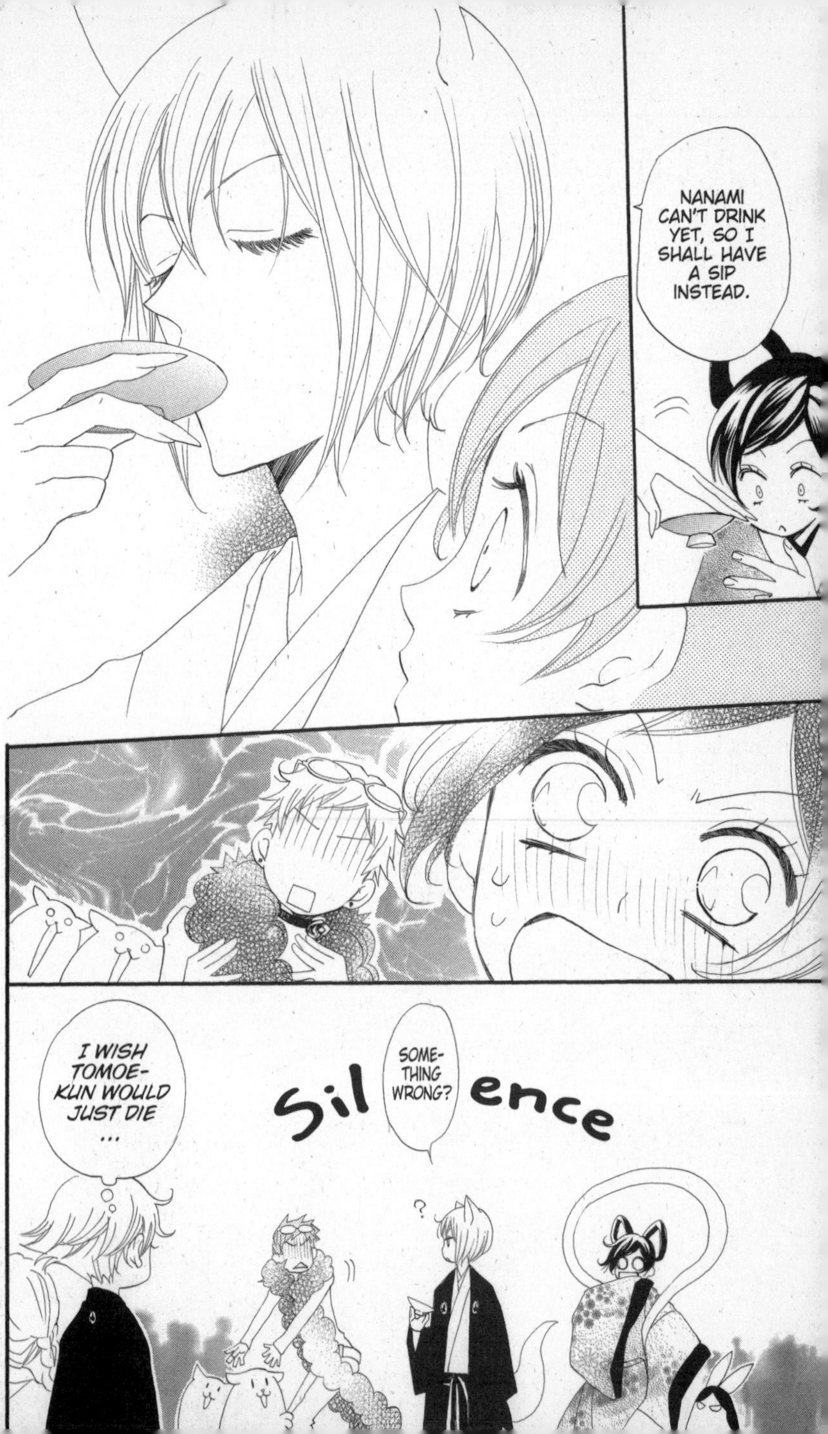
NANAMI CAN'T DRINK YET, SO I SHALL HAVE A SIP INSTEAD.
SOME-THING WRONG?
Sil ence
I WISH TOMOE-KUN WOULD JUST DIE ...

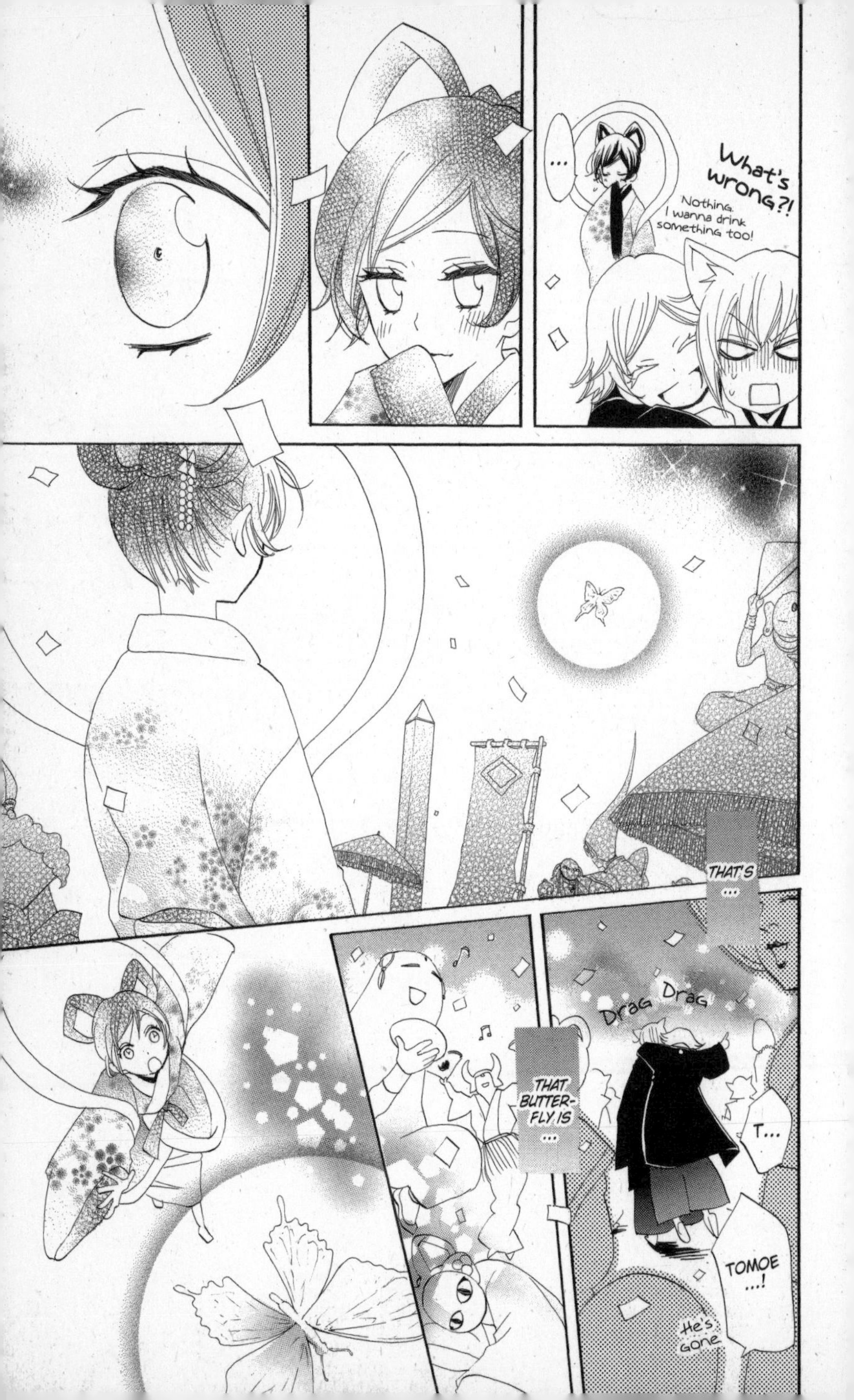
...
What's wrong?!
Nothing. I wanna drink something too!
THAT'S ...
Drag Drag
T...
TOMOE ...!
He's gone
THAT BUTTERFLY IS ...

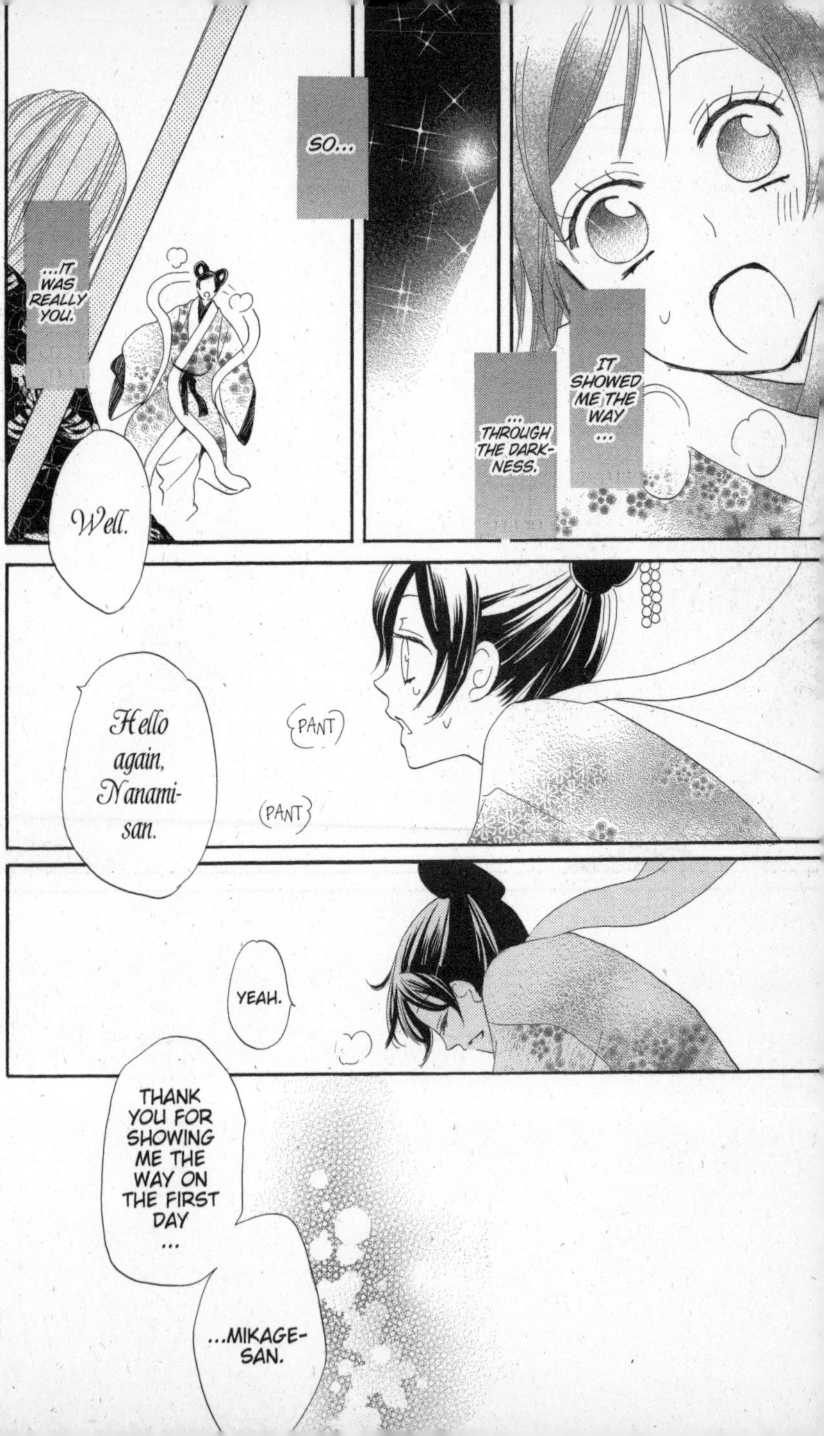
IT SHOWED ME THE WAY ...
... THROUGH THE DARK-NESS.
SO...
...IT WAS REALLY YOU.
Well.
PANT
PANT
Hello again, Nanami-san.
YEAH.
THANK YOU FOR SHOWING ME THE WAY ON THE FIRST DAY ...
...MIKAGE-SAN.

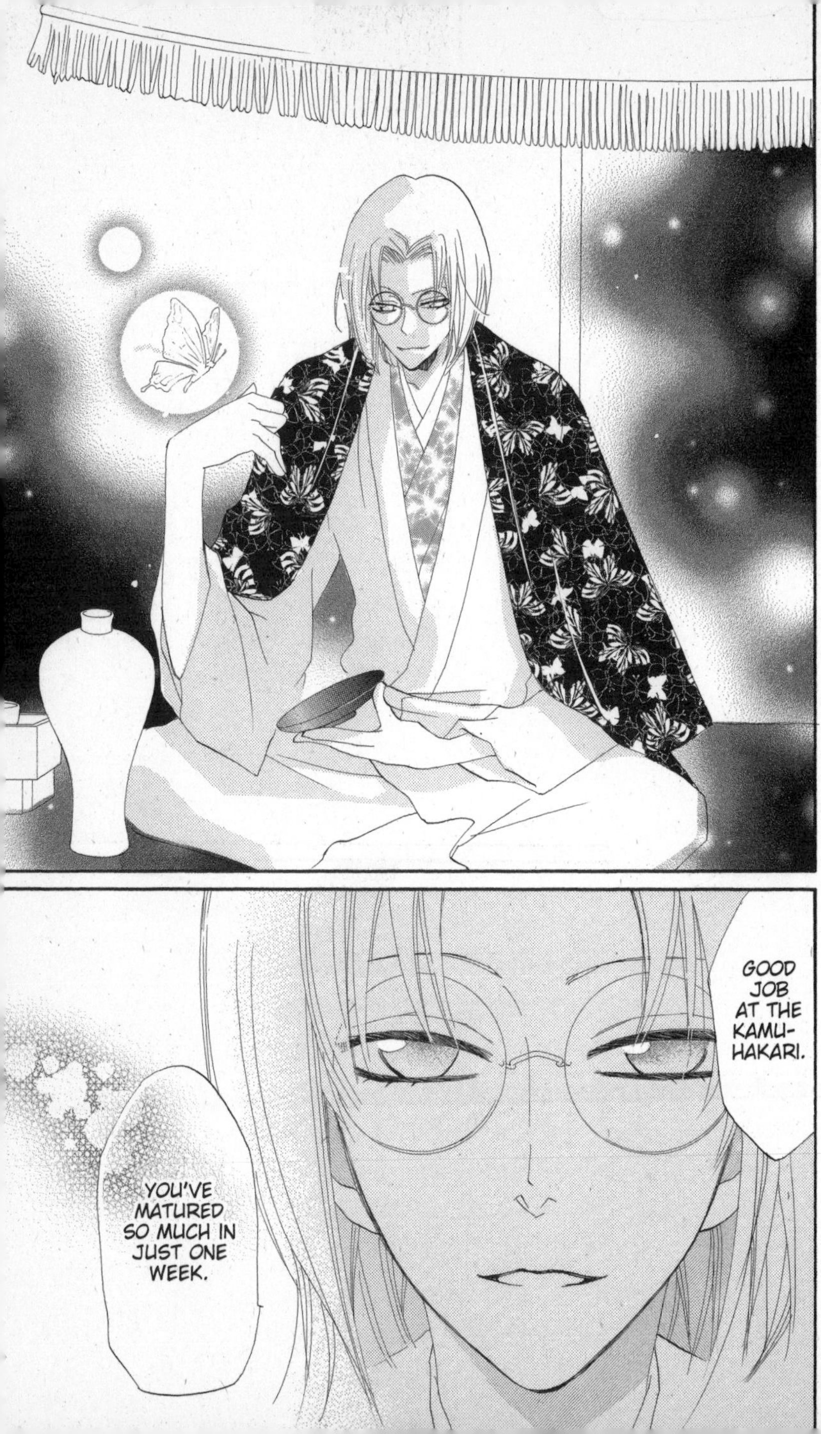
GOOD JOB AT THE KAMU-HAKARI.
YOU'VE MATURED SO MUCH IN JUST ONE WEEK.

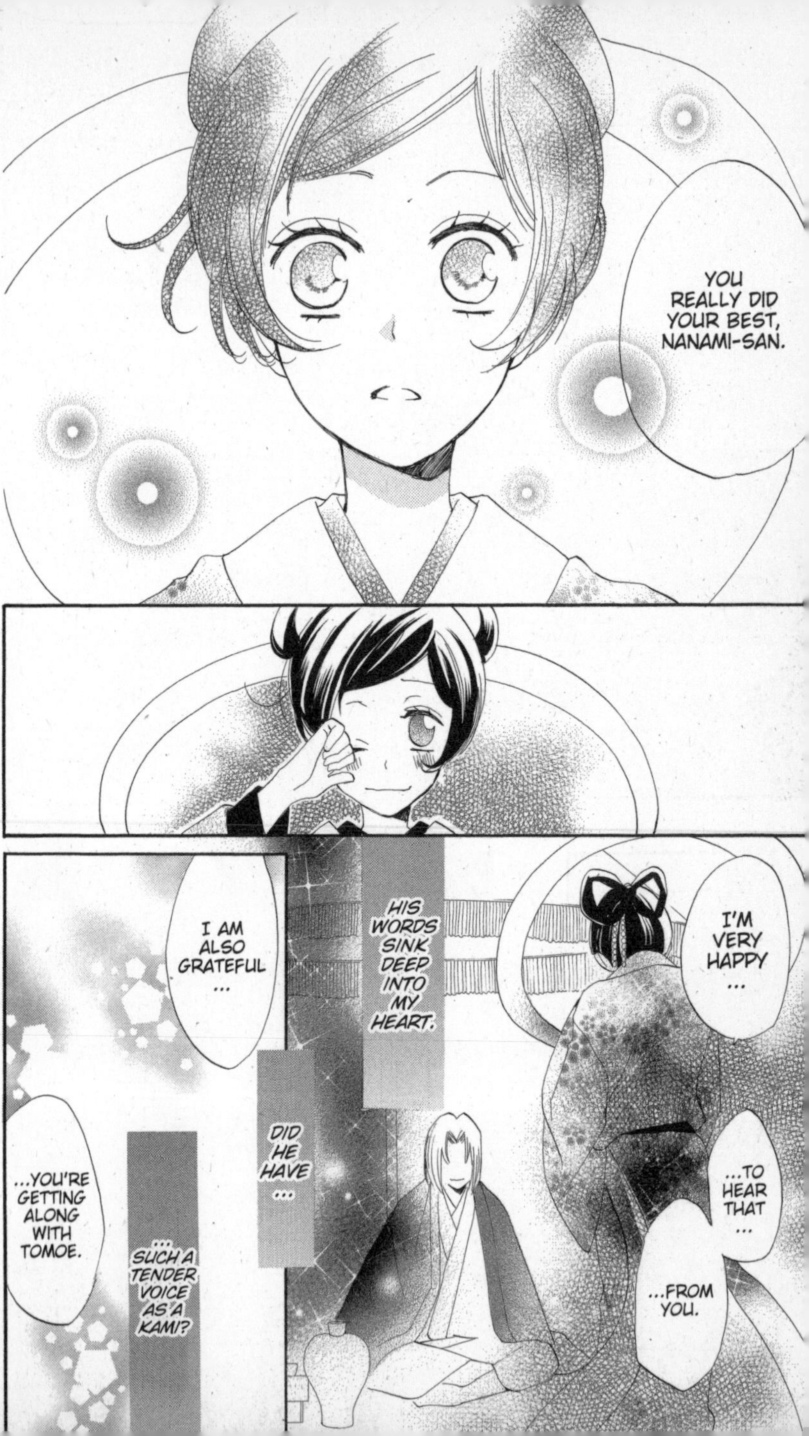
YOU REALLY DID YOUR BEST, NANAMI-SAN.
I'M VERY HAPPY ...
...TO HEAR THAT ...
...FROM YOU.
HIS WORDS SINK DEEP INTO MY HEART.
DID HE HAVE ...
... SUCH A TENDER VOICE AS A KAMI?
I AM ALSO GRATEFUL ...
...YOU'RE GETTING ALONG WITH TOMOE.

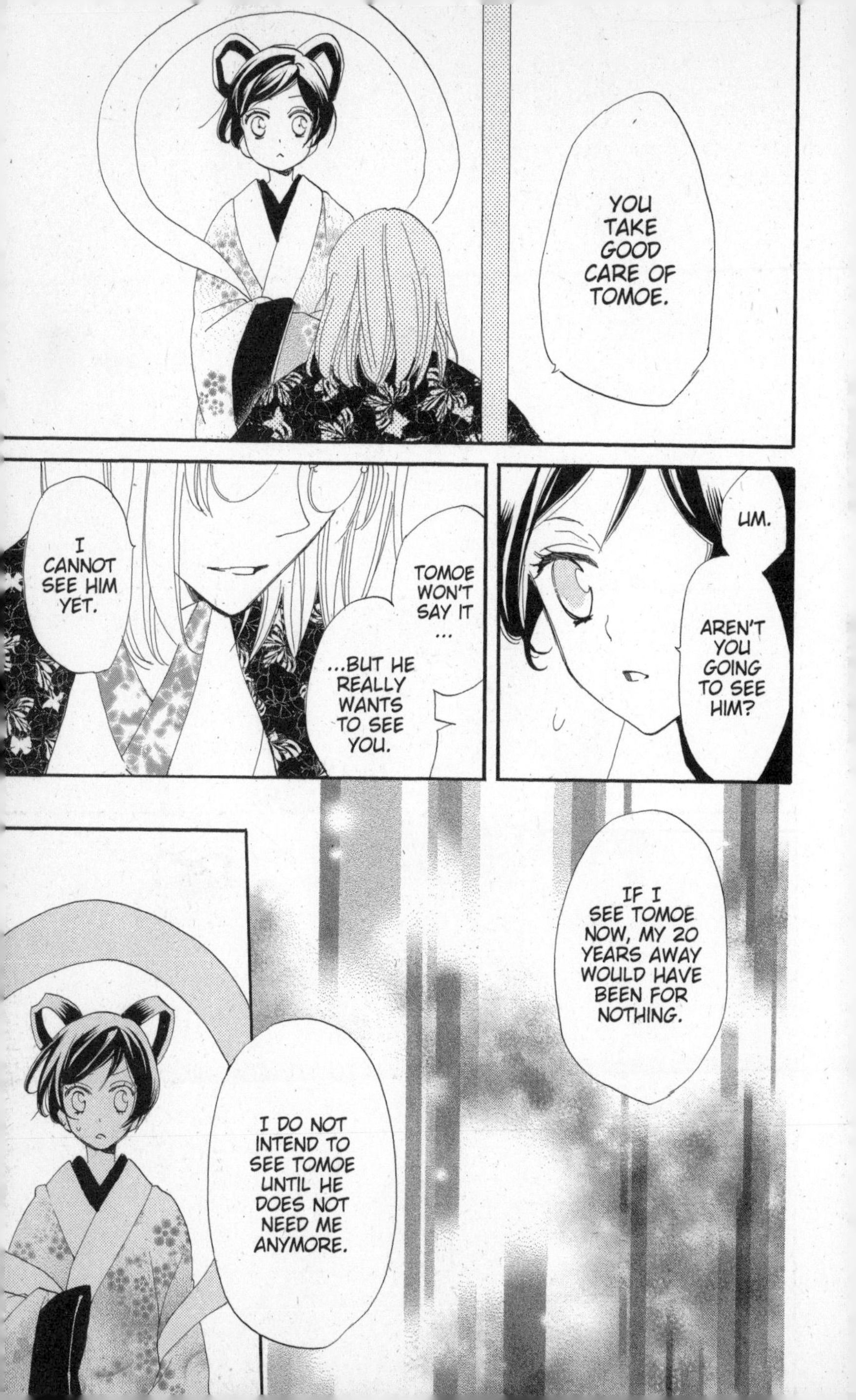
YOU TAKE GOOD CARE OF TOMOE.
UM.
AREN'T YOU GOING TO SEE HIM?
TOMOE WON'T SAY IT ...
...BUT HE REALLY WANTS TO SEE YOU.
I CANNOT SEE HIM YET.
IF I SEE TOMOE NOW, MY 20 YEARS AWAY WOULD HAVE BEEN FOR NOTHING.
I DO NOT INTEND TO SEE TOMOE UNTIL HE DOES NOT NEED ME ANYMORE.

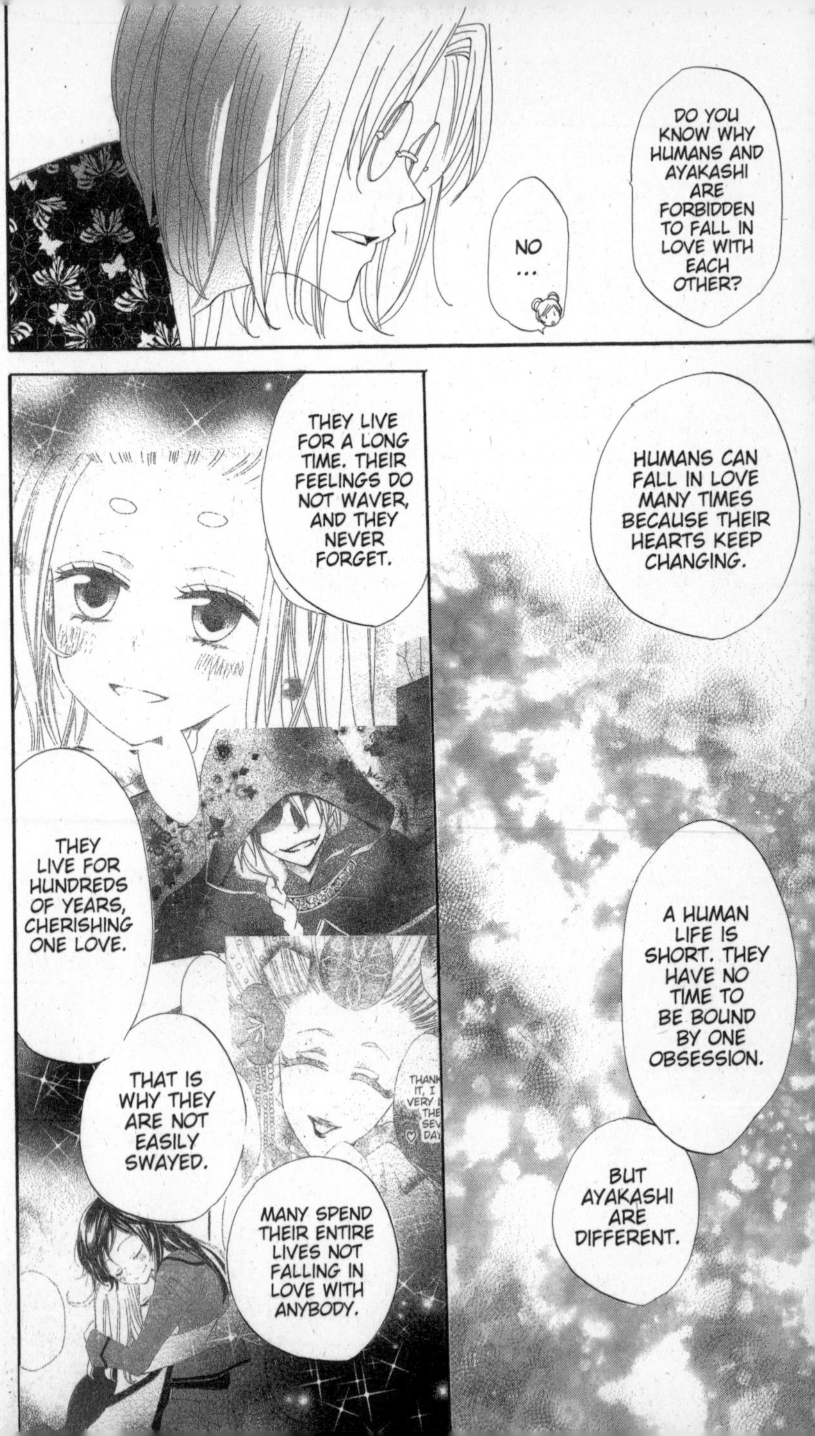
DO YOU KNOW WHY HUMANS AND AYAKASHI ARE FORBIDDEN TO FALL IN LOVE WITH EACH OTHER?
NO ...
HUMANS CAN FALL IN LOVE MANY TIMES BECAUSE THEIR HEARTS KEEP CHANGING.
A HUMAN LIFE IS SHORT. THEY HAVE NO TIME TO BE BOUND BY ONE OBSESSION.
BUT AYAKASHI ARE DIFFERENT.
THEY LIVE FOR A LONG TIME. THEIR FEELINGS DO NOT WAVER, AND THEY NEVER FORGET.
THEY LIVE FOR HUNDREDS OF YEARS, CHERISHING ONE LOVE.
THAT IS WHY THEY ARE NOT EASILY SWAYED.
MANY SPEND THEIR ENTIRE LIVES NOT FALLING IN LOVE WITH ANYBODY.

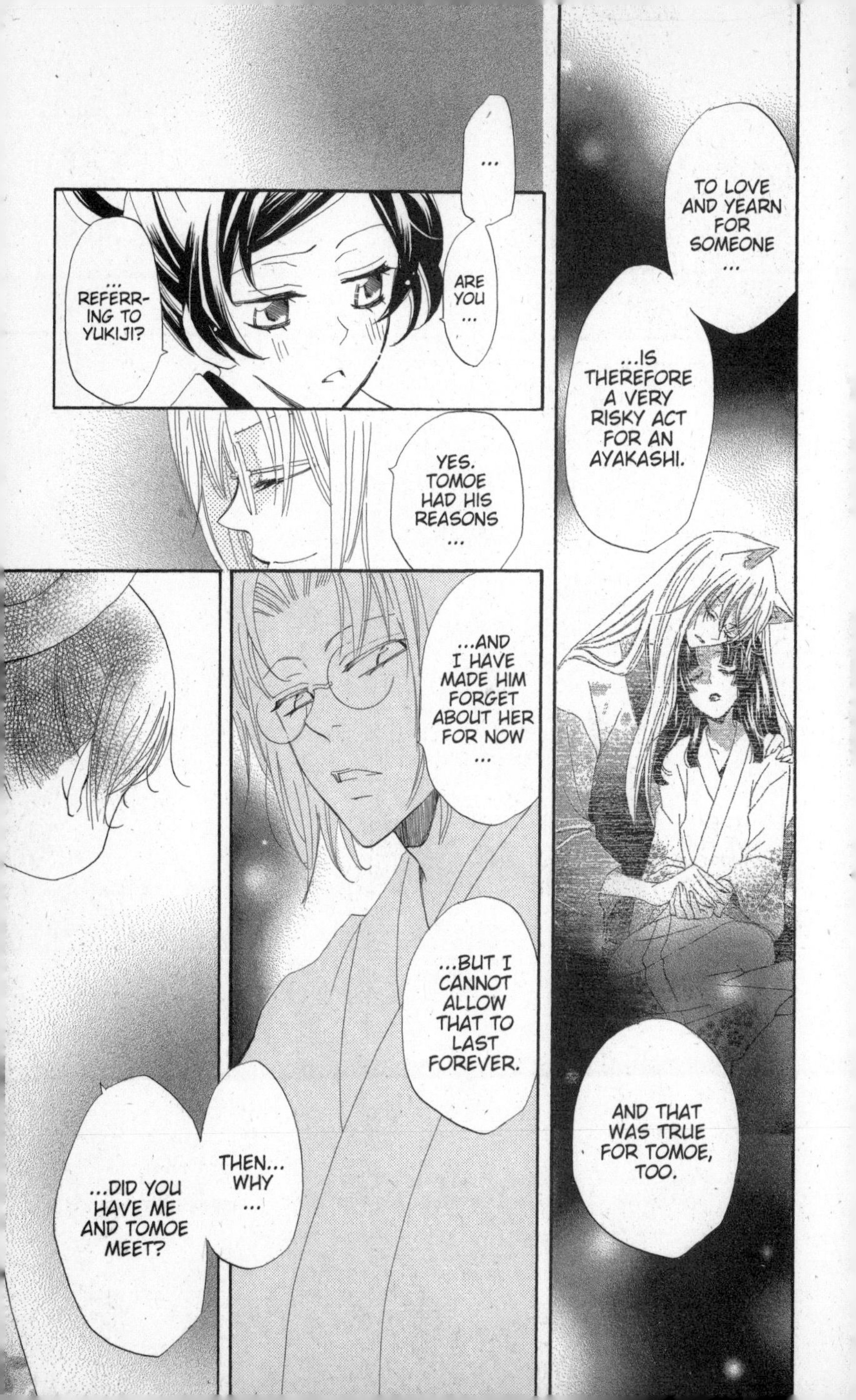

TO LOVE AND YEARN FOR SOMEONE ...
...IS THEREFORE A VERY RISKY ACT FOR AN AYAKASHI.
AND THAT WAS TRUE FOR TOMOE, TOO.
...
ARE YOU ...
... REFERRING TO YUKIJI?
YES. TOMOE HAD HIS REASONS ...
...AND I HAVE MADE HIM FORGET ABOUT HER FOR NOW ...
...BUT I CANNOT ALLOW THAT TO LAST FOREVER.
THEN... WHY ...
...DID YOU HAVE ME AND TOMOE MEET?

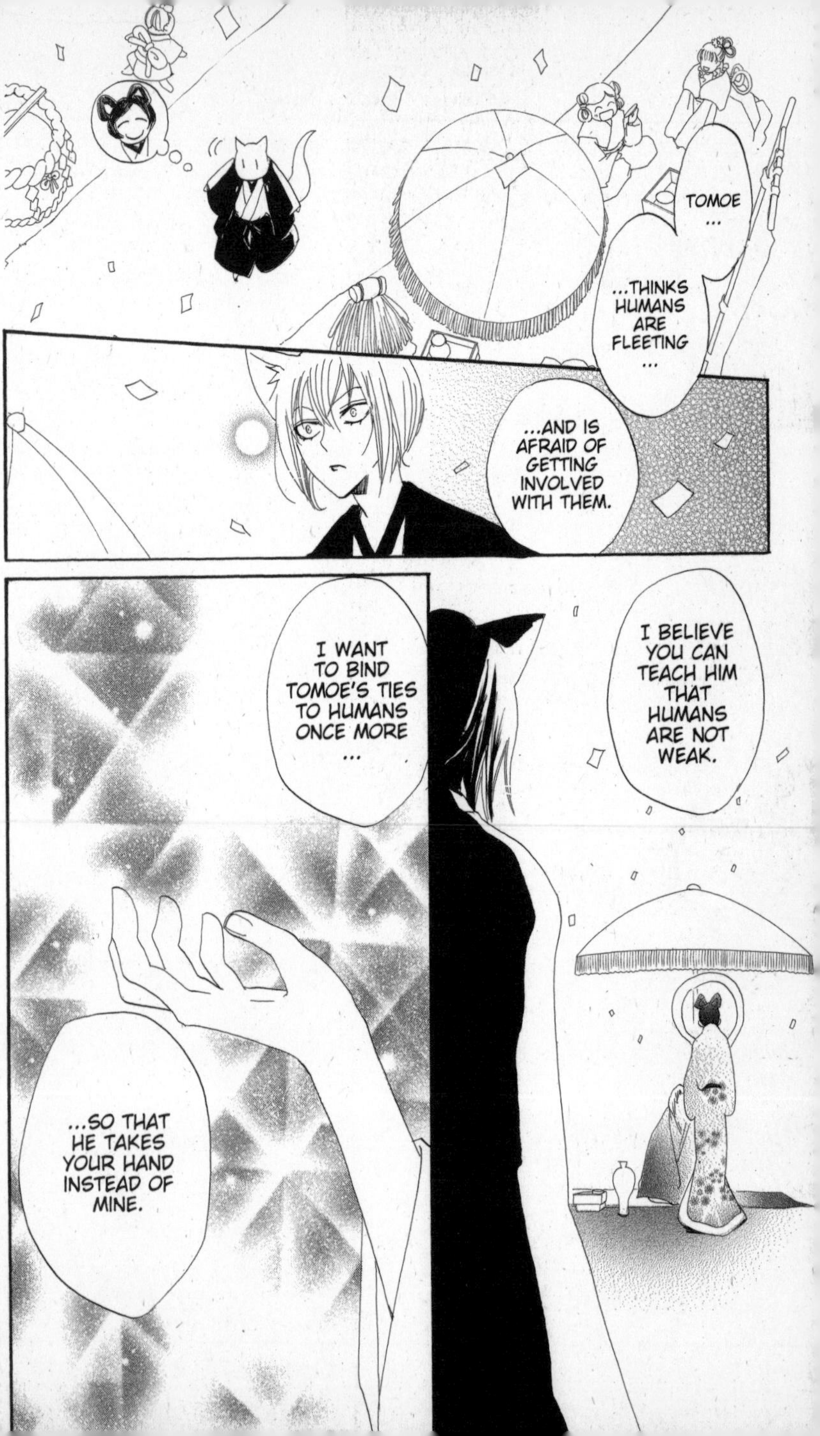
TOMOE ...
...THINKS HUMANS ARE FLEETING ...
...AND IS AFRAID OF GETTING INVOLVED WITH THEM.
I BELIEVE YOU CAN TEACH HIM THAT HUMANS ARE NOT WEAK.
I WANT TO BIND TOMOE'S TIES TO HUMANS ONCE MORE ...
...SO THAT HE TAKES YOUR HAND INSTEAD OF MINE.

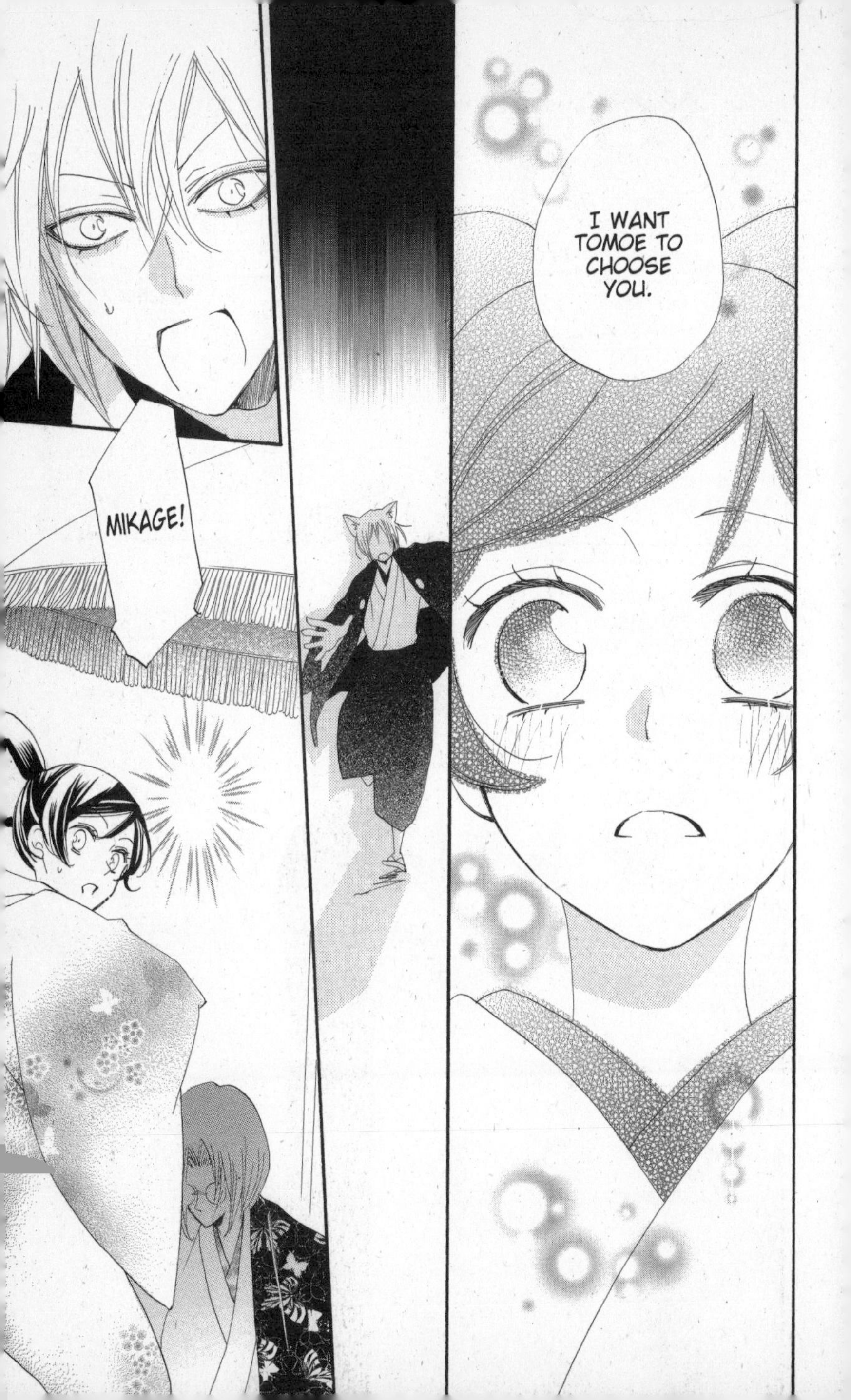
I WANT TOMOE TO CHOOSE YOU.
MIKAGE!

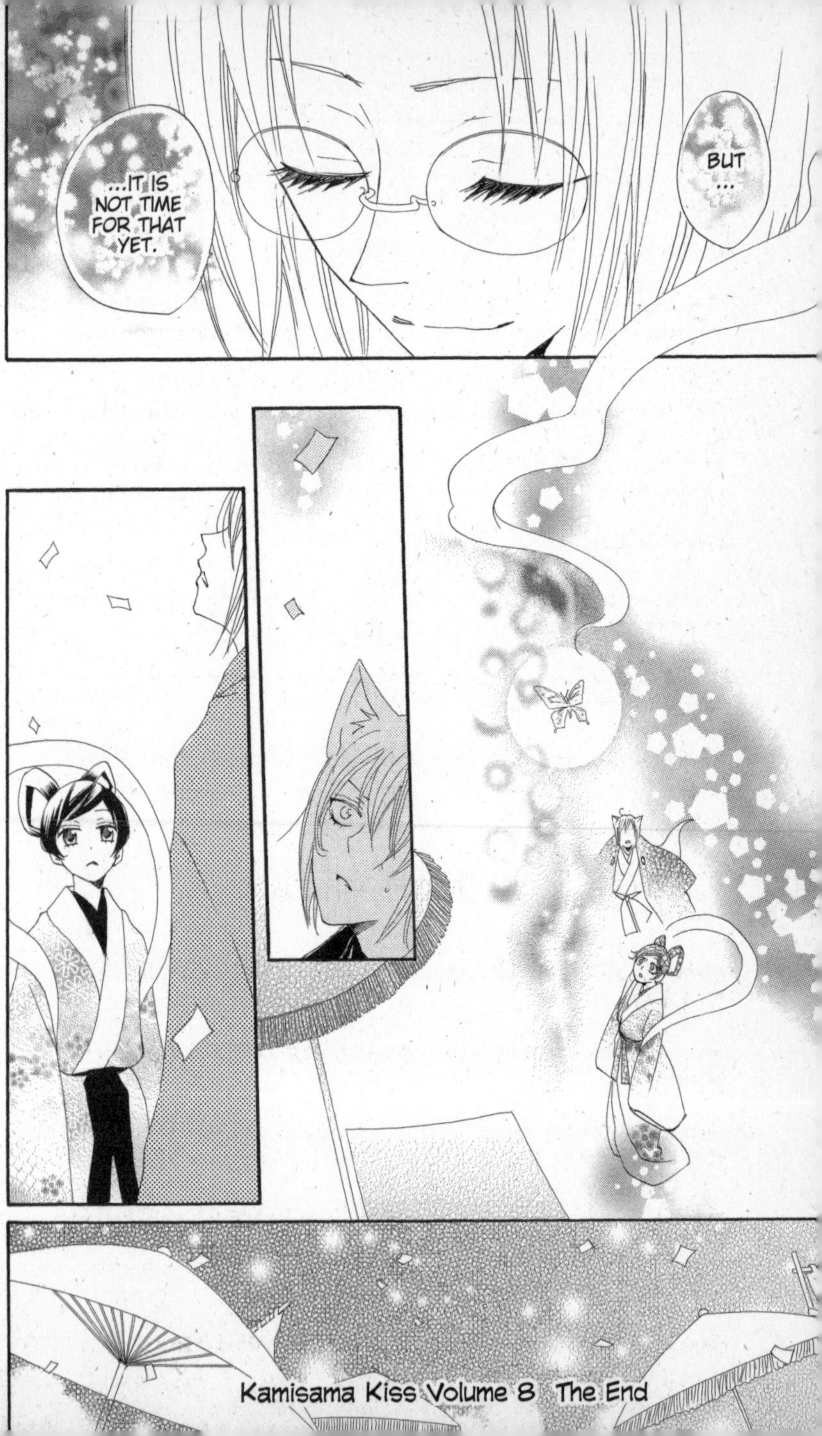
BUT ...
...IT IS NOT TIME FOR THAT YET.
Kamisama Kiss Volume 8 The End

The Otherworld

Ayakashi is an archaic term for yokai.

Kami are Shinto deities or spirits. The word can be used for a range of creatures, from nature spirits to strong and dangerous gods.

Kamuhakari is the weeklong convocation of kami at Izumo Oyashiro shrine, in October of the lunar calendar. Therefore in the lunar calendar, October is called Kamiarizuki (month-with-kami) in Izumo, and Kannazuki (month-without-kami) in other regions. Festivals are held at Izumo Oyashiro during the Kamuhakari.

Onibi-warashi are like will-o'-the-wisps.

Shikigami are spirits that are summoned and employed by *onmyoji* (Yin-Yang sorcerers).

Shinshi are birds, beasts, insects or fish that have a special relationship with a kami.

Tochigami (or *jinushigami*) are deities of a specific area of land.

Honorifics

-chan is a diminutive most often used with babies, children or teenage girls.

-dono roughly means "my lord," although not in the aristocratic sense.

-hime means princess, although a Japanese princess is not the same as a Western one and isn't necessarily the daughter of a king.

-kun is used by persons of superior rank to their juniors. It can sometimes have a familiar connotation.

-sama is used with people of much higher rank.

-san is a standard honorific similar to Mr., Mrs., Miss, or Ms.

Notes

Page 12, panel 1: Ofuda
A strip of paper or a small wooden tablet that acts as a spell.

Page 17, panel 7: 350 yen
About US $4.50.

Page 21, panel 2: Izanami
Japanese goddess of creation and death, and wife of creator god
Izanagi. She died giving birth to Kagu-tsuchi (a fire deity) and
now rules the land of the dead.

Page 21, sidebar: nabe, kotatsu
Nabe is a type of hot pot or stew. *Kotatsu* are low tables with
special heaters underneath. A thick tablecloth/blanket keeps in
the heat.

Page 145, panel 1: Paper fortune
Omikuji, or paper fortunes, are offered at many shrines, and it is
traditional to draw them at festivals.

Page 145, panel 2: Kamiarisai festival
The festival held by humans during the Kamuhakari.

Page 147, panel 1: Warigo soba
A style of soba served in Izumo. The noodles are served in three
stacked bowls, with condiments on the side including green
onions and seaweed.

Page 172, panel 2: Onsen
Hot springs.

Julietta Suzuki's debut manga *Hoshi ni Naru Hi* (The Day One Becomes a Star) appeared in the 2004 *Hana to Yume Plus*. Her other books include *Akuma to Dolce* (The Devil and Sweets) and *Karakuri Odette*. Born in December in Fukuoka Prefecture, she enjoys having movies play in the background while she works on her manga.

KAMISAMA KISS
VOL. 8
Shojo Beat Edition

STORY AND ART BY
Julietta Suzuki

English Translation & Adaptation / Tomo Kimura
Touch-up Art & Lettering / Joanna Estep
Design / Yukiko Whitley
Editor / Pancha Diaz

KAMISAMA HAJIMEMASHITA by Julietta Suzuki
© Julietta Suzuki 2010
All rights reserved.
First published in Japan in 2010 by HAKUSENSHA, Inc., Tokyo.
English language translation rights arranged with
HAKUSENSHA, Inc., Tokyo.

Printed in Canada

Published by VIZ Media, LLC
P.O. Box 77010
San Francisco, CA 94107

10 9 8 7 6 5 4 3 2 1
First printing, April 2012

www.viz.com   www.shojobeat.com

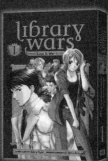

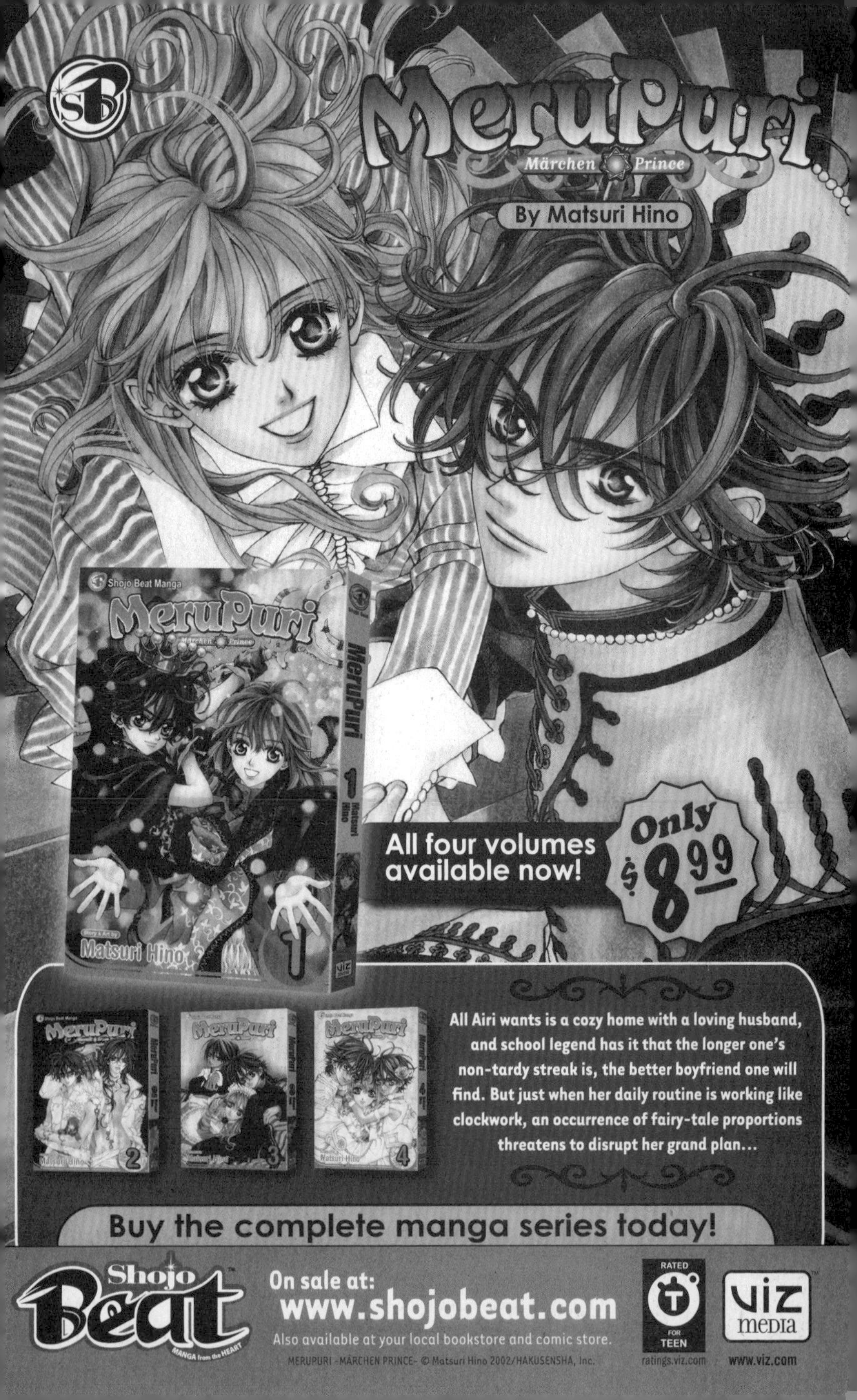
MeruPuri
Märchen Prince
By Matsuri Hino
Shojo Beat Manga
MeruPuri
Märchen Prince
Matsuri Hino
1
All four volumes available now!
Only $8.99
All Airi wants is a cozy home with a loving husband, and school legend has it that the longer one's non-tardy streak is, the better boyfriend one will find. But just when her daily routine is working like clockwork, an occurrence of fairy-tale proportions threatens to disrupt her grand plan...
Buy the complete manga series today!
Shojo Beat
MANGA from the HEART
On sale at:
www.shojobeat.com
Also available at your local bookstore and comic store.
MERUPURI -MÄRCHEN PRINCE- © Matsuri Hino 2002/HAKUSENSHA, Inc.
RATED T FOR TEEN
ratings.viz.com
VIZ media
www.viz.com

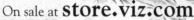

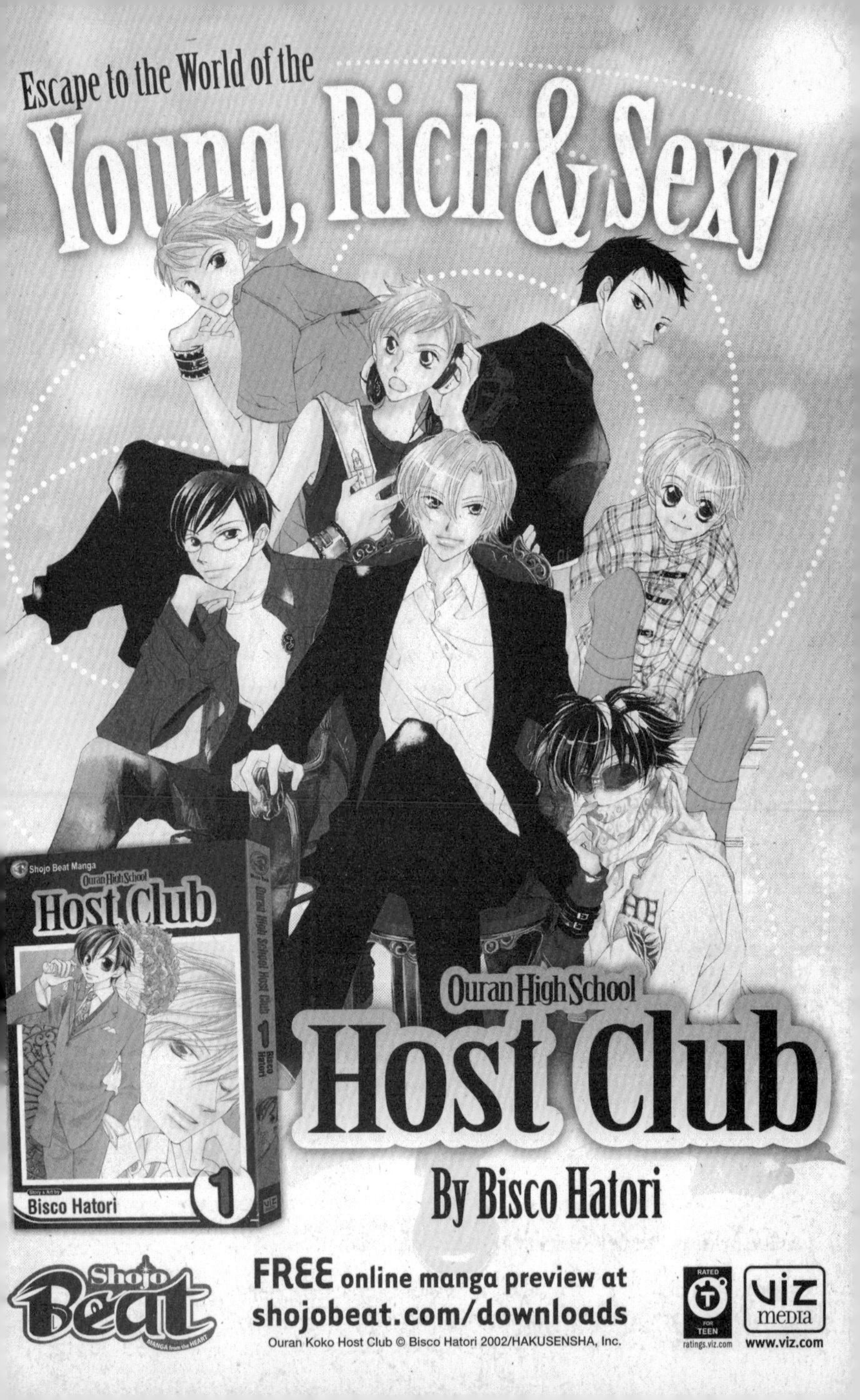
Escape to the World of the
Young, Rich & Sexy
Shojo Beat Manga
Ouran High School
Host Club
Bisco Hatori
1
Ouran High School
Host Club
By Bisco Hatori
Shojo Beat
FREE online manga preview at
shojobeat.com/downloads
Ouran Koko Host Club © Bisco Hatori 2002/HAKUSENSHA, Inc.
RATED
T
TEEN
ratings.viz.com
VIZ media
www.viz.com

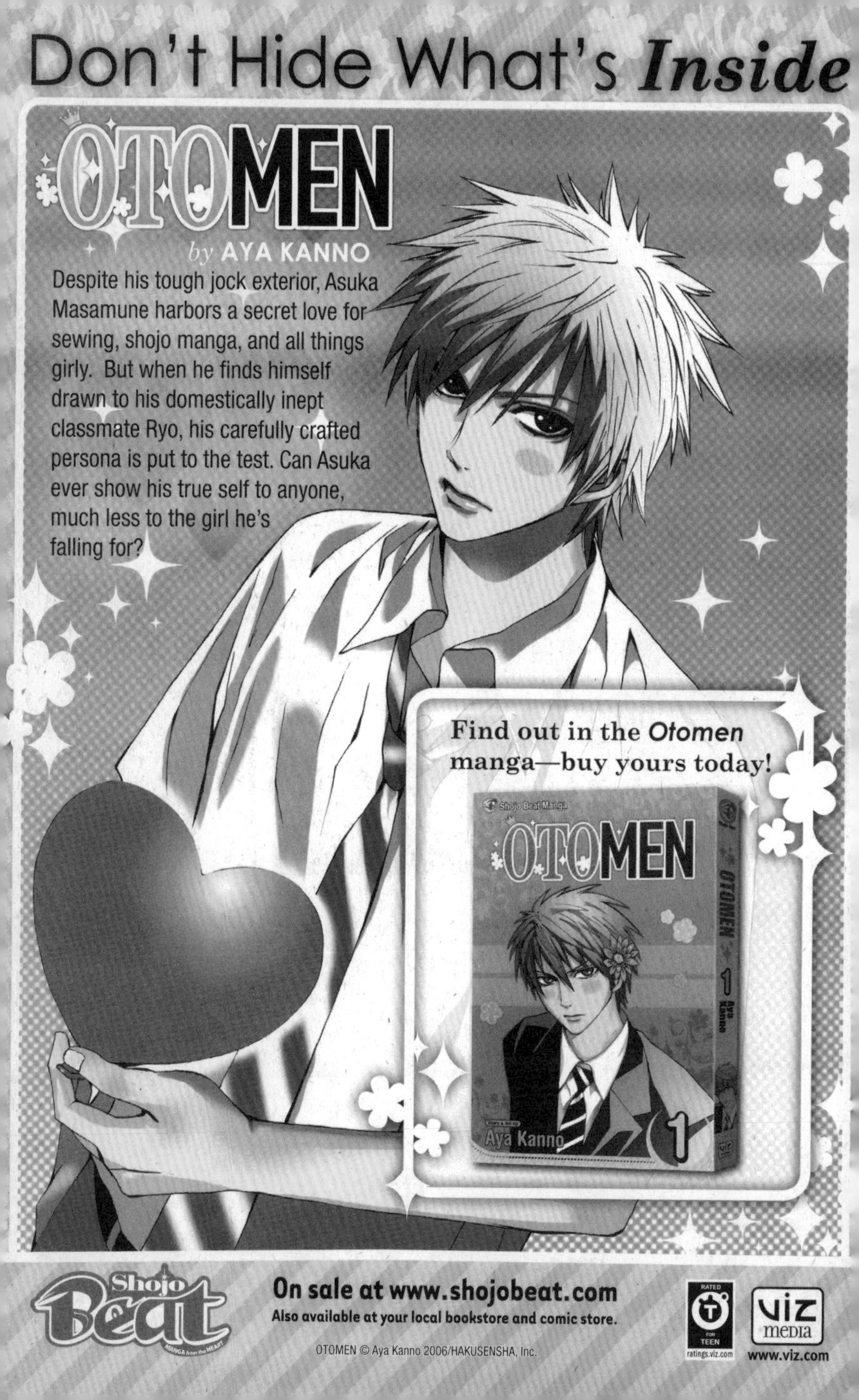
Don't Hide What's *Inside*
OTOMEN
by AYA KANNO
Despite his tough jock exterior, Asuka Masamune harbors a secret love for sewing, shojo manga, and all things girly. But when he finds himself drawn to his domestically inept classmate Ryo, his carefully crafted persona is put to the test. Can Asuka ever show his true self to anyone, much less to the girl he's falling for?
Find out in the *Otomen* manga—buy yours today!
Shojo Beat Manga
OTOMEN
1
Aya Kanno
Shojo Beat
MANGA from the HEART
On sale at www.shojobeat.com
Also available at your local bookstore and comic store.
OTOMEN © Aya Kanno 2006/HAKUSENSHA, Inc.
RATED T FOR TEEN
ratings.viz.com
VIZ media
www.viz.com

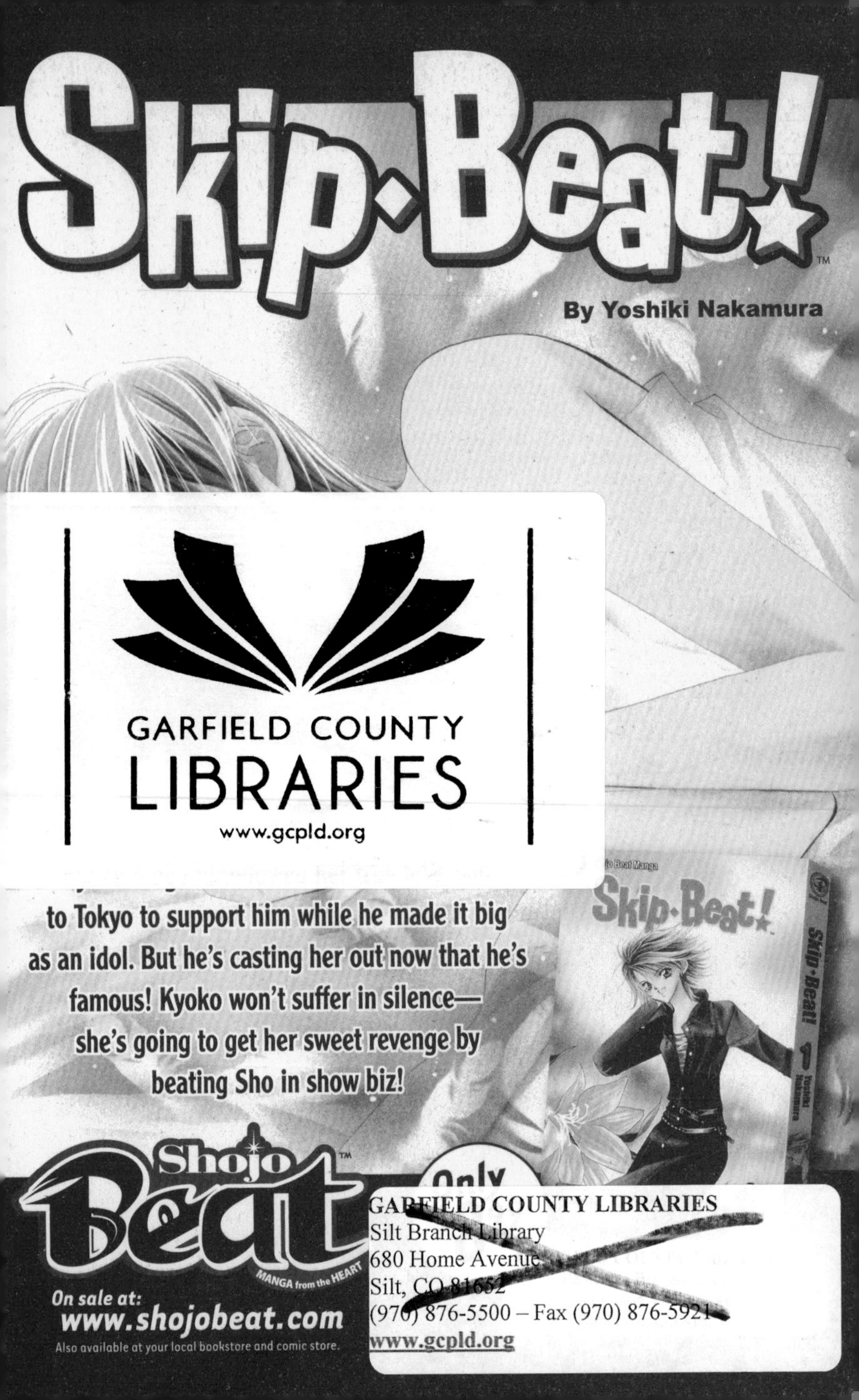

Skip·Beat!™
By Yoshiki Nakamura
to Tokyo to support him while he made it big
as an idol. But he's casting her out now that he's
famous! Kyoko won't suffer in silence—
she's going to get her sweet revenge by
beating Sho in show biz!
Shojo Beat Manga
Skip·Beat!
Skip·Beat!
Yoshiki Nakamura
Shojo Beat™
MANGA from the HEART
On sale at:
www.shojobeat.com
Also available at your local bookstore and comic store.